Directions in Modern Theatre and Drama

an expanded edition of
FORM AND IDEA IN MODERN THEATRE

72802

John Gassner

*Sterling Professor of Playwriting
and Dramatic Literature
Yale University*

PN 2189
G 25D

HOLT, RINEHART AND WINSTON, INC.

New York · Chicago · San Francisco · Toronto · London

March, 1966

23052–0915

Printed in the United States of America

PREFACE

Directions in Modern Theatre and Drama is an outgrowth of a number of significant tensions and developments since the 1870's, if not earlier, in Western theatre. It represents an effort to make some sense of the chaos of contrary winds of doctrine, inchoate experiments, and conflicts of a stylistic and formal character in a century notably unstable and distressingly confusing in artistic as well as social aims.

The development of playwriting and stage production since the nineteenth century has been characterized by efforts to put into effect various concepts or ideas of theatre. The leaders in these efforts—whether romanticists like Hugo, naturalists like Zola, or latter-day opponents of realism—have made theatrical history with strongly urged ideals and truculent formulations. Even the votaries of show business, indifferent though they may be to generalizations, have not been impervious to the programs of successive *avant gardes*. The pragmatists have usually appropriated (if also misapplied and vulgarized) the very aims they have professed to scorn.

Today, questions concerning the kind of theatre we have or ought to have crop up frequently, even in the press that covers Broadway presentations. The reviewers are apt to join the academicians in giving thought to the esthetics of the stage. This is especially the case whenever Broadway realism displays its threadbare tatters without colorful patches of entertainment or whenever an experiment in theatrical stylization proves particularly inviting or tantalizing. Thus, in one respect or another, matters of form and style have ceased to be exclusively esoteric considerations.

One would have to be singularly obtuse, however, to conclude from this that the stage, especially the American stage, is approaching well-defined objectives under the direction of leaders who manifest a clear understanding of its present situation. A clarification of that situation is still needed, and this cannot, I believe, be achieved without glancing at the paths hitherto followed by those who have sought to modernize dramatic art in conformity with some idea or ideal. The discussion therefore follows a largely historical sequence, although it is somewhat qualified by the supplements entitled Some Further Observations.

In my overview, the modern theatre appears as an enterprise strongly marked by instability, eclecticism, and a mélange of genres. Early in the nineteenth century, the theatre emancipated itself from conventionality with much romantic bravado only to accept, after a while, a new form of bondage in submitting to the ultrarealistic requirements of versimilitude and illusionism. A second revolt against the constraints of convention was therefore in the making by 1890 even while realism, the first major phase of modern dramatic art, was winning victories for the modern spirit. Departures from realism soon became numerous and produced new and overlapping phases of modernism. The theatre has swung from extreme to extreme around an indistinct core of opportunistic commercial enterprise. There has been no resting point for playwrights and devotees of the stage ever since realism reached its apogee about half a century ago. At best, it may be said that the multiplication of formal experiments since 1890 has resulted in an uneasy coexistence of poorly developed and haphazardly reconciled alternatives. A state of crisis has been chronic during the greater part of the century.

We cannot fail to realize that the future of our stage depends greatly upon the possibility of turning the present chaotic coexistence of realism and nonrealistic stylization into an active and secure partnership. A reconciliation of the polarities of realism and theatricalism is indeed inherent in the very nature of dramatic art; and so I bring the book to a climax in Chapter 4, the first part of which—The Plurality of Theatre—is an examination of the theatrical experience itself.

The book, however, does not end there. Chapter 5 is a diversified examination of directions proposed and debated, chiefly after World War II. This section constitutes indeed a small anthology of critical essays by other hands as well as my own. It includes some commentary on these essays, and concludes with a brief examination of the present situation, which is unlikely to undergo any radical transformation in the foreseeable future. This is the extent of the present undertaking, and it is hardly necessary for me to add that it is a tentative one, presented more as an inquiry than a manifesto, and more as an analysis of modern strivings and proposed solutions than as a conventional history of the theatre, a description of its memorable stage productions, and a criticism of its leading playwrights. The book has been put together with limited objectives in mind, and I shall be pleased if these are attained sufficiently to shed some light on areas of modern dramatic art where, more often than not, little armies of partisans have clashed by night.

With respect to reprinted material in the book, I am grateful to the editors of *Comparative Literature Studies* for my essay, "Varieties of Epic Theatre," the editors of *The Times Literary Supplement for* "The Cult of Dumbness," "Crisis in the Theatre," and "They Also Serve," Henry Adler and the editors of *The Listener* (London) for Henry Adler's "Bertolt Brecht's Contribution to Epic Drama," Edward Albee and the editors of *The New York Times* for Mr. Albee's Sunday Magazine Section essay "Which

Theatre Is the Absurd One?", Penquin Books, Ltd. for "The Elizabethan Stage and Acting" taken from *The Age of Shakespeare*
edited by Boris Ford, the Department of Drama of The University of Texas for my essay, "The Contemporary Situation," my
friend Arvid Paulson for his translation of Strindberg's Preface to
Miss Julie, and my friend Professor Marvin Rosenberg for his
essay, "A Metaphor for Dramatic Form."

I owe the genesis of this book to the invitation of Alabama
College in 1953 to deliver the biennial Dancy Lectures and to the
friendly interest of its then president, Dr. F. E. Lund, and his colleagues, especially Professor Walther Trumbauer, then chairman
of the Dancy Lecture Committee. For the book based upon the
Dancy Lectures and the present expanded edition, I am indebted
to friends at other institutions, and especially to my publisher-
friend Stanley Burnshaw's interest and criticism, and my wife
Mollie Gassner's customary and indispensable editorial assistance.

March 1965   *John Gassner*

CONTENTS

ILLUSTRATIONS

xvi

1

The Modernization of
Dramatic Art

THE REALISTIC PHASE

To discern causes is to turn vision into knowledge and motion into action.—GEORGE SANTAYANA, The Life of Reason

. . . naturalism has regenerated criticism and history by submitting man and his works to a precise analysis, taking into account circumstances, environment and organic cases. . . . I chose ridiculous and ordinary minor characters to show the banality of everyday life behind the grim anguish of my heroes. In staging the play [Thérèse Raquin] I tried to stress continually the ordinary occupations of my characters, in order that they might not seem to be "acting" but "living" before the audience.—ÉMILE ZOLA

If the actor must follow carefully the impressions of the audience, he must conceal the fact, must play as if he were at home, taking no heed of the emotions he excites, of approval or disapproval; the front of the stage must be a fourth wall, transparent for the public, opaque for the player.
—JEAN JULLIEN

Le classique se connaît à sa sincérité, le romantique a son insincérité laborieuse.
—CHARLES PÉGUY

". . . augmenter la réalité de l'oeuvre dramatique, progresser dans la vérité, dégager de plus en plus l'homme naturel et l'imposer au public."—ÉMILE ZOLA, Le Naturalisme au théâtre.

. . . la liberté dans l'art, la liberté de la société, voilà le double but . . . la liberté littéraire est fille de la liberté politique.—VICTOR HUGO,(Preface d' "Hernani," 1830.)

ONE DOES NOT UNDERTAKE TO DISCUSS FORM IN ANY ART WITHOUT qualms, and when the art under consideration is theatre there is the added complication that we are concerned with *two* arts, dramatic literature and stage production. Nor is stage production at all a simple matter, for it involves all the arts of the theatre— acting, music, the dance, scenic design, stage lighting, costume design, and architecture—that is, the kind of playhouse occupied by the actors and their audience and the kind of stage upon which the performance takes place. (See pp. 51-54.) All these arts, separately or in varying combinations, are involved in dramatic modernism, so that it becomes necessary to touch upon developments in different arts. Moreover, such terms as "form" and "idea" can become extremely troublesome when used in connection with these developments.

Without delving into the esthetic absolutes suggested by "form," it is necessary to resolve initial ambiguities by establish-

3

ing some arbitrary definitions. By "form" I mean the distinctive *structure* of a play and the distinctive *texture* of the writing—that is, the style in which it is written. I also use the term more loosely to signify an over-all type or style of theatre. Moreover, I relate the forms of modern drama to certain "ideas of theatre"—that is, to certain conceptions of theatrical art and certain expectations from it. By "idea" I do not mean subject matter, but the view of theatre apparent in the play or the production (or in both), and the special esthetic aim pursued in the work aside from the general one of interesting, entertaining, or stirring an audience. This idea, moreover, is to be thought of as more or less consciously held and deliberately served in playwriting and play production. It is held consciously by leaders of various types of theatre (for example Hugo, Ibsen, Zola, Antoine, Stanislavsky, and Shaw) and tacitly by less analytical persons as well as by the sedulous apes of fashion whose number is as great in the theatre as in any other art. Ideas, in the popular sense of subject-matter—namely, the ideas that constitute philosophy, sociology, topics of discourse, arguments, even propaganda—cannot, of course, be excluded from our purview. It is often difficult to distinguish between an artist's view of theatre and his view of life, society, politics, or religion. It is certain, for example, that Ibsen's idea of a realistic theatre and Zola's idea of a naturalistic one had affiliations with nineteenth-century social criticism and nineteenth-century enthusiasm for science, respectively. Nevertheless, I employ "idea" to mean something larger than a mere topic or opinion; I use the term to denote some specific way of conceiving the nature and use of theatre, which in turn determines or helps to determine dramatic form and the stage presentation.

As for the use of the term "modernity" in this discourse, a chronological approach is the best means of simplification. The generally accepted view that drama and theatre became distinctively "modern" during the last quarter of the nineteenth century is adopted here. The advent of modernity can be equated with the rise of realistic drama and stage production under the leadership of Ibsen, Zola, Shaw, Antoine, and Stanislavsky. The appearance of realistic technique and style was the first phase of modernism in drama. It is essential to realize that modern realism is not distinguishable in every instance and every respect from the art of theatre before 1875. Endeavors to make stage illusion stronger by using solid settings and abbreviating or removing the forestage made headway earlier in the century. And a trend toward realism that was foreshadowed by Elizabethan middle-class tragedy as well as by such eighteenth-century pieces as George Lillo's *The London Merchant* and Lessing's *Miss Sara Sampson* culminated in a variety of problem plays by Dumas *fils* and Émile Augier and in studies of middle-class Russian life by Alexander Ostrovsky. Indeed, the most durable examples of realism before the vogue of Ibsen came early: Nikolai Gogol's social satire *The Inspector-General* appeared in 1836, *Maria Magdalena*, Friedrich Hebbel's tragedy of middle-class values, in 1844, and Turgenev's "Chekhovian" drama of provincial stalemate, *A Month in the Country*, in 1849. Even the extremes of naturalism, without benefit of formulation by Zola, can be traced as far back as 1836, the year in which the short-lived genius Georg Büchner wrote his powerful play *Woyzeck*. Our chronological distinction is based on the fact that all such dramatic efforts before the last quarter of the century were sporadic.

Chronology, however, must be supplemented by the observation that realism by itself does not define dramatic modernism, because a second aspect, one of nonrealistic stylization, has been important in the modern theatre almost as long as realism has. Dramatic modernism consists of a succession and then an interweaving of strands that may be called Ibsenism and Wagnerianism, realism and symbolism, objective naturalism and both subjective and objective antinaturalism. (Subjective antinaturalism was manifested in expressionism; objective antinaturalism in epic theatre as formulated and presented by Erwin Piscator, Bertolt Brecht, and those who created "living newspapers," such as

Power and *One-third of a Nation,* during the climactic years of
the New Deal in the 1930's.) Even romanticism has been woven
into the fabric of modernism. Romantic drama, rejected as outmoded by pioneers of the 1870's and 1880's, came to be considered
"modern" again after Rostand wrote *Cyrano de Bergerac* in 1897.
And not only Rostand but Maxwell Anderson, whose popular
historical plays recall both Shakespeare and Schiller, and other
writers, such as Yeats and Paul Claudel, who combine romanticism with symbolism, belong to the modern theatre. Their work,
far from being dismissed as old-fashioned, has been acclaimed as
actually representing progress in the theatre. And although
claims on behalf of these playwrights can be questioned, one may
at least concede that their work, even when reminiscent, has been
less moth-eaten than many up-to-the-minute, quasi-journalistic
plays written in the realistic mode.[1] Whether judged by content
or by style, the post-1914 verse dramas of Yeats are certainly im-
measurably more remote from the mid-Victorian age than, let us
say, *Pollyanna,* vintage 1916, and *Abie's Irish Rose,* vintage
1922. Indeed, as I shall show, a seminal concept of modern
theatre was embodied in the very romantic movement that had to
end before the modern theatre could establish itself. In the process of nostalgically looking back to the Shakespearean stage, the
early-nineteenth-century exponents of romanticism were actually
looking forward.

It may be said, then, that in concerning ourselves with "modern" theatre we are dealing with a phenomenon the nature of
which will not be apparent until dramatic form and, especially,
the period's ruling views of theatre have been examined. We cannot know *what makes our theatre specifically modern* without
such an examination. Nor can we understand the contemporary

---

[1] I am not concerned here with distinctions between early-nineteenth-century romantic drama and the latter-day neo-romanticism, although the latter has been generally restrained in style and
tempered by psychological, social, or political realism. A comparison of *Cyrano de Bergerac* and *Hernani,* or Anderson's *Mary of
Scotland* and Schiller's *Maria Stuart,* would reveal this much.

theatre's seeming stalemate, or properly appraise the development of new forms as a means of breaking that stalemate.

The Idea of Freedom of Dramatic Form

The first ruling idea of modern theatre, and the one that is still dominant and most productive, although also conducive to some anarchy, is the idea of *freedom*. Its emergence was associated with the revolt of romanticism against the rigors of neoclassicism. Under the influence of romanticism, the theatre became an open rather than a closed, strictly conventionalized art. Romanticism sharply challenged the belief fostered by neoclassic critics that there are rules to which the theatre must adhere. Laws that had been especially insisted upon after 1650— rules concerning the importance of "decorum," the idea that tragedy may deal only with the fate of princes and nobles, and the primacy of the so-called unities of time, place, and action— were banished from the theatre. Romanticism introduced the principles of flexibility, adaptation of form to content, and intellectual and artistic independence which modernism, whether realistic or nonrealistic, has cherished, if not always kept inviolate.

These principles, first affirmed in the Germany of Lessing and Goethe after 1765, were reaffirmed in France between 1827 and 1830, especially by Victor Hugo. His romantic play *Hernani*, staged in 1830 amid rioting in the theatre, signalized the end of the domination of the theatre by arbitrary rules. And as the production of *Hernani* in 1830 occurred in Paris, then and for many years afterward the cultural capital of Europe, the event was of international importance.

The French theatre was the last stronghold of neoclassicism in Europe. Far from overthrowing the traditional style, the French Revolution and the Napoleonic regime had supported it.

Both the leaders of the Revolution and the supporters of the monarchy identified themselves with classicism: the former with the ideals of the Roman Republic, the latter with the glories of the Augustan age of Rome. The same observation may be made concerning the plastic arts, whose outstanding leader, Jacques Louis David, favored classic lines in his portraits, such as the celebrated one of Madame Recamier, and both classic form and subject matter in his historical paintings. The strong resistance to romanticism in painting is described in Élie Faure's treatment of David and his times;[2] among many passages on this subject is the following:

> For a quarter of a century, Antiquity has been before the minds of men. That way lies Virtue, and there also is Beauty. André Chenier [the period's most distinguished playwright as well as poet] dedicates hymns to David, in whose works Robespierre recognizes the physical expression of that which he himself represents in the moral world; and it is to David that the Convention intrusts the work of organizing Republican aesthetics on the model of the austerity, the pomp, and the stoicism of Rome. (p. 238)

The reaction against the decadent *ancien régime* of the Bourbons was moralistic as well as political, and republican probity was identified with Roman virtue. Cartesian rationalism, reinforced by ideals of Roman stoicism, erected barriers to romantic aims. This was especially the case in institutionalized art such as the theatre, which was partly subsidized by the state and partly dependent on the support of the moralistic middle classes before, during, and after the Napoleonic period.

Thus the dogma of the antique retained its hold on painter, playwright, and actor alike. Neoclassicism literally had a stranglehold on the theatre until the memorable evening of February 25, 1830, when Victor Hugo's youthful left-bank supporters, bearded, long-haired, dressed in the clothing of all ages but their own, and led by Théophile Gautier, wearing his rose-colored vest,

[2] *History of Art*, Vol. IV: *Modern Art* (New York: Dover Publications, 1924), pp. 236-253.

smothered the neoclassic opposition determined to hiss *Hernani* off the boards of the Théâtre Français.

Three years earlier, moreover, Victor Hugo, then twenty-six, had formulated a view of drama in which it was maintained that the theatre was free to present every subject and to employ any form or style. In the flamboyant introduction written in 1827 to his not particularly good play *Cromwell,* for which he had been unable to win a stage production, Hugo argued that life alone, life in its infinite variety, should be the playwright's model. In an age of "liberty," Hugo maintained,

> let us take the hammer to theories and poetic systems. Let us throw down the old plastering that conceals the façade of art. There are neither rules nor models; or, rather, there are no other rules than the general rules of nature, which soar above the whole field of art, and the special rules which result from the conditions appropriate to the subject of each composition.[3]

Hugo was arguing for his own brand of romantic drama, of course. For example, he made a strong plea for the place of the grotesque in art, since he made lavish use of this element himself in such plays as *The King Amuses Himself* and *Ruy Blas.* The element of the grotesque had come into favor with the rise of romantic literature, and its exploitation before and after Hugo's time is a familiar characteristic of romanticism. As late as the turn of the century Edmond Rostand was to get some of his best effects of pathos and irony from the length of Cyrano's nose. In the preface to *Cromwell,* however, Hugo recommended the use of grotesque characters and situations for the purpose of conveying "reality." He rejected as unnatural the absolute separation of comedy and tragedy that had been insisted upon by neoclassicism. He called for a combination of the sublime and the grotesque, which, he declared, should "meet in the drama as they

[3] Barrett H. Clark (ed.), *European Theories of the Drama* (Crown Publishers, 1947), pp. 374-379.

meet in life and creation.⟩ In support of this view Hugo cited the example of Shakespeare, calling attention to the confrontation of Romeo and the apothecary, Macbeth and the witches, Hamlet and the gravediggers, Lear and the Fool. In the name of nature and truth (which also led him to favor the use of local color), Hugo asserted a principle of freedom for dramatic art that is central to modern theatrical developments. When he proclaimed his defiance of "the customs officers of thought," he signalized a general loosening of critical bonds that had already been partly accomplished in Germany and England and that was long overdue in France. He did not, indeed, introduce the "idea of freedom" into the theory of drama; he had been anticipated, half a century before, by the German playwrights of the "storm and stress" school, who opposed neoclassicism by exalting "inner form" and by propounding the principle of unity in the individual atmosphere or, so to speak, in the soul of the play, in contrast to logical, external unity.[4] With support from Rousseauist enthusiasms and revolutionary political tendencies, the principle of a thoroughly free, rather than ruled and regimented, theatre was bound to prevail in Europe. Hugo's summary of principle, however, was historically the most important, and it became cardinal doctrine that has been constantly reaffirmed by the modern experimentalists.

Today the flexibility of dramatic and theatrical conventions is recognized everywhere. Although there has been no lack of censorship of a moral or political nature to curtail the freedom of dramatic expression, no esthetic principle has curtailed experimentation except when some reactionary regime, as in Hitler's Germany and Stalin's Russia, has assailed experimentation as a symptom of artistic decadence. The modern theatre has been the most experimental, and therefore the most varied, in history. From a view of the theatre as an institution that exists primarily for the preservation of some cultural norm (the mythos and ritualism of the city-state or *polis* in Athens, the sense of order and *bon sens* in

[4] See Siegfried Melchinger, *Dramaturgie des Sturms und Drangs* (Gotha, 1929), pp. 93-99.

the Paris of Louis XIV) we have arrived at the idea that theatre is the showplace of every conceivable display of ingenuity.

The sociological aspects of this conception of theatre need not detain us here after we have conceded that our theatre has reflected the instability of modern civilization. Nor need the question of content concern us greatly here. There can be no doubt that, despite the instances of moralistic or political censorship in the Victorian and post-Victorian periods, the modern stage has taken more liberties than at any time before in history. It has been truly the museum, forum, and marketplace of opinions, speculations, and aberrations. But although this freedom of content is obviously important, it has not been the major factor in the development of specifically modern modes of drama. That development has been a matter of form rather than content, except, of course, in so far as the struggle for form has been motivated by the need for a special means of expression. Content dictated dramatic structure, for instance, when English poets adopted choral drama for expressing an elegant religiosity, or when Marxist playwrights used "mass chants" and demonstrational devices in plays for the purpose of teaching the "class struggle." It is the effect of the idea of freedom on form that is of primary interest in the present inquiry. And justifiably, I believe, as it is not the "modernity" of the content that we can extract from a play that will distinguish the work from a Greek drama. There is no dearth of "modern" thinking about war and sex in *The Trojan Women* and *Hippolytus,* plays concerning whose distinctively classic form there can be no question. An even more obvious example is Robinson Jeffers' adaptation of *Medea,* which retains Euripides' subject without in the least constituting Greek choral drama. So close is the relationship of content to form that the difference between the two Medea plays is enormous; the story is the same but the life of the two works—which includes the meaning and the experience alike—is not at all the same.

Hugo's preface to *Cromwell* is a springboard for modern dramatic art because one of the manifestations of his idea of a free theatre was the rise of realism and naturalism, which effected a far more radical transformation of dramatic form than the wildest romantic drama, which was merely Shakespearean or pseudo-Shakespearean in structure and texture. Moreover, realism in playwriting and stage production was to be followed after 1880 by a variety of styles, such as symbolism, expressionism, theatricalism, constructivism, and surrealism, each accompanied by some program for a new dispensation.

These styles followed one another with increasing rapidity, and came to jostle each other not only in the small theatres playing to a cultural élite, but in all the marketplaces of commercial showmanship. Consequently, the modern stage became at once the battleground of multifarious, sometimes vituperative, factions and the parade grounds of a "live-and-let-live" eclecticism unmatched in any earlier period of theatre. Today, it is not unusual for Broadway to display in a single season a number of prosaically realistic plays, a romantic verse drama such as Anderson's *Anne of the Thousand Days* or Christopher Fry's *The Lady's Not for Burning,* a surrealistic effort such as Gertrude Stein's *Four Saints in Three Acts,* and numerous musical comedies of indefinable character. And the drama critics, as well as the playgoers, do not even blink at this profusion of styles until they reach surrealism, which is apt to disconcert them not because of its departure from realism, but because of its incomprehensibility. They would not dream of requiring playwrights and producers to adhere to any single dramatic convention. Demands for conformity in matters of dramatic form have been made only where totalitarian systems of government have prevailed, as in Germany and Russia. (In Germany, the National Socialist regime, between 1933 and 1945, declared all modernist art decadent. In Russia after 1935, the Stalinist dictatorship in the arts demanded conformity to an orthodox blending of elementary realistic technique with Socialist doctrine—a so-called "Socialist realism" in the arts.)

We are even likely to encounter an amalgamation of two or more different styles of composition in the very same play; the result, far from disturbing us, usually gains our approbation. Arthur Miller's *Death of a Salesman* contains scenes that belong to the most thoroughly realistic type of drama, but they alternate with recollected and hallucinated scenes that are more or less expressionistic in treatment. It is also to be noted that both the acting and the stage design of the 1948 Broadway production directed by Elia Kazan and designed by Jo Mielziner showed this alternation of styles. Miller's hero, Willy Loman, was characterized naturalistically. But Willy's remembered brother Ben was "stylized" by the actor who played the part. Ben's speech and stage movement were exaggerated, and an unnatural briskness and automatism characterized the performance; Brother Ben was Willy's unrealistic, indeed distorted, notion of a hard-driving, infallible, and invariably successful tycoon. The actor impersonating Ben was also eerily sudden and abrupt in making his entrances and exits; he gave the impression that he was a revenant in Willy's disturbed mind. Details of Willy's suburban home, such as the bedroom and the parlor, were rendered with an effect of cramped and unlovely realism; but the house itself was skeletonized and placed on a platform, and the stage space in front and at the sides of the structure was left scenically neutral. This space served as a backyard, as a restaurant, as a portion of a hotelroom, and, finally, without any scenery whatsoever, as the cemetery in which Willy is buried. The same setting, altered only by the lighting, was sometimes realistic, sometimes stylized and formal, but always fluid enough to let reality and dream intermingle.

In the modern theatre, indeed, there has been so much blending of effects that the question of which part of ·a play is "real" and which is "unreal" is sometimes meaningless. The question has hardly any meaning, for example, when asked about such plays as Strindberg's *There Are Crimes and Crimes* and Pirandello's three theatrical treatments of the subject of reality, *Right You Are (If You Think So!)*, *Six Characters in Search of an Author*, and *Tonight We Improvise*. Georg Kaiser's *From*

Morn to Midnight (once its cashier-hero runs away from the secure tedium of his job and home) presents reality and fantasy commingled in a new reality—that of the cashier's disorientation in a world already illusory enough without the superimposition of the character's fantasy. John Howard Lawson's *Processional* presents a picture that is both real and fantastically exaggerated into a sort of "jazz symphony" of society. "Which part is real and which is fantasy?" has little meaning, too, when asked about O'Neill's *The Hairy Ape:* first, because the play was intended by its author as a parable on the pathos of man's present stage in the evolutionary process that has separated him from the animal world but has not yet allowed him to attain complete humanity; and secondly, because even the most exaggerated of the scenes, the Fifth Avenue episode, is not presented as the dream of the protagonist.

To illustrate a mingling of genres and of angles of presentation, we can turn to an essentially simple play, Ferenc Molnar's *Liliom*. The present writer has encountered people in university departments of literature to whom *Liliom* is a difficult drama: it is considered "unclear" by them because the fantastic part is not differentiated from the "real" part (that is, the first four scenes) by being presented as the dying Liliom's dream or delirium. These critics of the play would have been put at ease only by a distinction between a character and his fantasy such as that which exists between the realistic and unrealistic scenes in *Beggar on Horseback* and *Lady in the Dark*, or between the "frame" in *The Emperor Jones* and the fleeing man's fantasies. Unfortunately for such critics, the posthumous portion of Liliom's career is not at all the dream of any character in the play.

A certain degree of sophistication concerning the nature of theatre has been required of us even by moderate ventures in dramatic modernism. We are expected to realize, in considering plays as different in numerous respects as *Liliom* and Brecht's *The Good Woman of Setzuan* and Giraudoux's *The Madwoman of Chaillot* (or, for that matter, *The Hairy Ape* and Wilder's *The Skin of Our Teeth*) that there is no meaningful difference between reality and fancy in a theatrical demonstration or imaginative construction. Everything in Molnar's play has *equal reality* as an element of the author's theatricalized argument, which may be stated as follows: "Liliom is the sort of individual who, if he were to go to the anteroom of heaven, would encounter just another police court. If he behaved in character after his death, he would steal a star out of the sky for his daughter; but if he were to meet her, he would be sure to lose his temper and strike her as he used to strike her mother despite his love for her—he would make the same mess of things he had made while alive." But, of course, this elementary retelling of the theme would only sentimentalize and weaken the impression of a work that is essentially a *jeu de théâtre* rather than a Sunday-school lesson.

A freedom that the stage had not enjoyed before except in Elizabethan times was bound to result in the mingling of formal elements which, even if not invariably gratifying, has helped to make modern drama and theatre stimulating. Even pastiche came into vogue, as did a mode of drama that was, if not pastiche, something close to it. There is a provocative mingling of the sacred and profane, for example, in *The Cocktail Party*, which in its mixture of the supernatural with British drawing-room comedy might give the impression of being the joint effort of Paul Claudel and Noel Coward. And there have been other alliances and misalliances in dramaturgy as striking as those which appear, for radically divergent purposes, in Eliot's *Murder in the Cathedral* and Brecht's *Caucasian Circle of Chalk*. The first-mentioned, and to us more familiar, work is composed of elements as varied as a chorus of Canterbury women, a Christmas Morning sermon, a fantasy of ghostly tempters, and a series of public addresses by Becket's murderers. Some of Brecht's and Piscator's "epic theatre" productions and our American "living newspapers" of the 1930's have had the qualities of a *collage*. Even the principle of esthetic unity has been challenged in the relentlessly iconoclastic modern theatre.

The idea of freedom in modern theatrical creation is an over-all principle, and the concept of a theatre shaped by the needs of expression rather than by the claims of tradition has been hospitable to both realistic and antirealistic art. It was this freedom of expression that sparked the naturalism of Zola, the critical realism of Ibsen, and the expressionism of Strindberg, during the last two decades of his life. Inevitably, then, the possibilities of dramatic art became enormous, and it is easy to understand why ours has been the most eclectic period in stage history. Eclecticism, of course, can be a vice as well as a virtue, and it has been accompanied by extreme instability in the modern theatre. Indeed, the theatre of our day may be condemned for its artistic flabbiness as much as it may be commended for its flexibility.

Modern experiments have become outmoded too rapidly, and we may well regret the quick obsolescence of such modernistic ventures as expressionism and surrealism. These required patient nursing if they were to prove their value as something more than expressions of eccentricity or calculated sensationalism. Only realism, both as a form of drama and style of performance, ever had the opportunity to develop its potentialities sufficiently.

Moreover, few modern playwrights have moved steadily toward consummation of their artistry by developing skill and depth in a single dramatic mode, as did Sophocles, who never abandoned the classic choral form, or Shakespeare, who never abandoned the free-flowing Elizabethan manner of playwriting. The course of a few authors is representative of the careers of many of their colleagues. Strindberg first earned an international reputation in 1887-1888 as a naturalist with such plays as *The Father* and *Miss Julie,* then embarked upon the perilous course of an expressionist playwright a decade later in such plays as *To Damascus, The Dream Play,* and *The Ghost Sonata.* In between, he wrote more or less symbolist plays and historical dramas. He also returned to extreme naturalism, in 1902, with his appallingly sordid drama of domestic hatred *The Dance of Death.* It may be said of Strindberg, as of many of his twentieth-century successors, that he never lighted upon a single mode which could a tissue of conventions, including the convention of naturalness. But in the theatrical world, as in the literary, we find romanticism paving the way for realism as well as for the later neoromantic and antirealistic styles that followed on the heels of triumphant realism. The idea of a "free theatre" inevitably became the concept of a theatre that was to reflect reality: having been liberated from subservience to neoclassic convention, the stage was to be free to follow "nature" or "truth," and indeed was considered to have an obligation to do so. Hugo implied an allegiance to this conception in his preface to *Cromwell* when he rejected the neoclassic ideals of "the graces," "good taste," "selectivity," and "ennoblement," and instead wanted art to "set about doing as nature does, mingling in its creations . . . darkness and light, the grotesque and the sublime . . . the body and the soul, the beast and the intellect." [5] He wanted the stage, in short, to reflect reality.

The romantic movement in the French theatre dribbled out within a decade of its beginnings. Hugo's victory in the theatre in 1830, when his adherents routed the conservatives in the so-called "battle of *Hernani*," was followed by the vogue of Eugène Scribe's formula for the speciously realistic "well-made play." The theatre was pre-empted by a species of intrigue-drama from which neither such French writers of problem plays as Dumas *fils* and Émile Augier nor even Ibsen, as late as the time of writing *A Doll's House*, could quite win divorcement. But the movement toward realism seems in retrospect to have been inevitable as nineteenth-century Europe became increasingly industralized and as its outlook grew more materialistic, scientific, and sociological.

All that was necessary by 1850 was for dramatic realism to become crystallized as a form of drama and a style of play production—that is, as a style of acting, décor, and *mise en scène* or staging. This is what occurred after 1875, and two ruling concepts made this possible—the idea of illusionism (that the theatre must provide the illusion of reality on the stage) and the idea of en-

[5] "Preface to *Cromwell*," in Clark, *European Theories of the Drama*, p. 369.

satisfy his need for self-expression. O'Casey abandoned realistic dramaturgy after having given the century two of its dramatic masterpieces, *Juno and the Paycock* and *The Plough and the Stars*. He turned to expressionist drama with *The Silver Tassie*, tried his hand at choral poetic drama with *Within the Gates*, and made experiments in dramatic form in every succeeding work. O'Neill provides still another example of fluctuation. He gave the American stage many of its most powerful realistic plays, such as *Beyond the Horizon, Anna Christie*, and *Desire Under the Elms*, although he enriched his realism with the symbolist use of such elements as the sea, "dat ole davil sea" that stands for malign fate in *Anna Christie*. Never satisfied with realism, however, O'Neill resorted to expressionistic fantasy and distortion in such plays as *The Emperor Jones* and *The Hairy Ape*, and to other kinds of stylization, including the use of masks, in his later work.

We can observe the same fluctuations even in the still incomplete careers of our best-known recent playwrights. Arthur Miller wrote *Death of a Salesman* after having succeeded with the tightly knit, thoroughly realistic social drama *All My Sons;* Tennessee Williams followed the poetic naturalism of his *Streetcar Named Desire* with his extravagantly symbolical *Camino Real*.

The Idea of Environment

So much for the "new freedom" so memorably promulgated by Hugo. We must note, however, that experimentation first became canalized in a single direction—that of realism, or, as it was generally called on the European continent, naturalism. (See pp. 66-70.)

Freeing the theatre from all convention, propounded at first for the practical purpose of freeing it from neoclassic regulations, is a romantic ideal that cannot possibly be realized. All theatre is vironment. The first idea is an old one which developed in the Italian court theatres of the Renaissance. The second, that of the stage as an environment, was relatively new in the theatre. Without it, we could not have had the dramatic realism that has modernized the stage. First of all, nothing in the second half of the nineteenth century could have strengthened the illusion of reality more than the use of the box set and the replacement of painted scenery by solid objects and workable doors and windows. Secondly, nothing at that time could have contributed more to a theatre concerned with contemporary issues than a presentation of environment as a conditioning element and as a reality to be reckoned with, opposed, or changed by the individual.

If we return to the preface to *Cromwell,* we observe that when Hugo claimed a place for the grotesque in the theatre he opened the floodgates to every kind of tabooed material, including the most sordid. Ultimately, freedom for the drama came to include the freedom to present pictures of seedy characters, low life, gross appetites, disease, and all the conditions of living associated with poverty and even degeneracy. The credo of naturalism which developed in France during the 1870's justified the representation of these conditions and the inclusion of tabooed material on the ground that the theatre should show the truth. But however much the playwright's exploitation of the grotesque affected the content of modern drama, it did not have any relation to the development of dramatic form. It was the concept of environment, or, more specifically, the idea of the stage as an environment, rather than as simply or mainly a platform for acting, that effected fundamental changes in dramatic art.

Hugo referred to local color as something more than pretty nature painting: "People are beginning to understand in our day that exact localization is one of the first elements of reality." [6] He added that "the place where this or that catastrophe took place

[6] Clark, *European Theories of the Drama,* p. 376.

becomes a terrible and inseparable witness thereof." But he actually lagged some three quarters of a century behind the concept of environment as evolved by the French encyclopedists and *philosophes* of the eighteenth century. Montesquieu, in writing his influential study *The Spirit of the Laws,* gave environment a greater role than that of serving as a setting for men's action. In Montesquieu's opinion, environment was not merely a background but a *condition* of human activity, a condition to which the very forms of government tend to conform. As long ago as 1758, moreover, the *philosophe* Denis Diderot had already acknowledged the importance of social position, its obligations and circumstances, as a factor in human life that should be allowed to play a role in the drama. Thus the idea of environment, given ever-greater prominence in the nineteenth century by sociologists and revolutionists as well as by such advanced critics as Hippolyte Taine, inevitably became a decisive factor. In the theatre, the stage setting, which had been treated as magnificently irrelevant to the actor's performance or only operatically valuable in baroque and rococo theatres, was now regarded as essential to the meaning of the play.

The growing use of the concept of environment is well illustrated by the numerous comments of the leaders of our nineteenth-century modernism. That pioneer play producer the Duke of Saxe-Meiningen, standing at the threshold of modern theatre, saw a function in the objects on the stage, declaring that it was "always an advantage to have an actor touch a piece of furniture or some other near-by object naturally. That enhances the impression of reality." Antoine, writing in 1903, was emphatic in sharing this view, declaring that "we must not be afraid of an abundance of little objects, of a wide variety of small props. . . . These are the imponderables which give a sense of intimacy and lend authentic character to the environment the director seeks to re-create." The cluttered setting implied in this comment is enough to drive a lover of simplified design such as Craig to desperation. But not Antoine, who went on to say: "Among so many objects . . . the performers' acting becomes . . . more human, more intense, and more alive in attitudes and gestures."

Antoine also counted on ceilings in relief and visible beams to provide "the impression of solidity and weight which was unknown in the make-believe painting of the old stage sets," and he believed it to be important "to fashion complete doorframes and window frames." An interior on the proscenium stage should be designed with "its four sides, its four walls" in mind (as in the world outside the theatre), "without worrying about the fourth wall, which will later disappear so as to enable the audience to see what is going on." And Antoine went so far as to declare that he found it indispensable to *first create the setting and the environment,* "without worrying at all about events that were to occur on the stage." For him it was "the environment that determines the movements of the characters, not the movements of the characters that determine the environment." And he could not even claim novelty for his views, since his patron Emile Zola had announced as early as 1873 that modern drama would delve into "the twofold life of the character and its environment." [7]

Such statements introduced a point of view encountered with increasing frequency after the founding of Antoine's epoch-making Théâtre Libre in 1887. We find in them a sturdy allegiance to reality as the middle-class civilization of the late nineteenth century conceived it to be. It was, distinctly, a reality of human beings feeling and acting in places and with objects about which there could be no mistake: the characters were specifically located and specifically occupied with material realities in a material world.

We may contrast this view—although it could be humanistic as well as materialistic—with the classic opinions of the leaders of antirealistic design or stylization. For example, there is Adolphe Appia's remark, in 1904, that

the human body does not seek to produce the illusion of reality *since it is in itself reality!* What it demands of the *décor* is simply to set in relief this reality . . . we must free

---

[7] Preface to *Thérèse Raquin.*

staging of everything that is in contradistinction with the actor's presence. . . . Scenic illusion is the living presence of the actor.

And we may take note of Gordon Craig's desire, expressed in 1911, to cover the actor's face with a mask "in order that this expression—the visualized expression of the Poetic spirit—shall be everlasting," as well as Craig's longing for acting wholly free from human "egotism" and for performances possessing "the fire of the gods and demons, without the smoke and steam of mortality." [8]

Environment came to be presented as a source of conflict in many modern plays. It was already present as the very matrix of middle-class tragedy in Hebbel's early play *Maria Magdalena*, written in 1844. In *A Doll's House*, the milieu was the dramatic factor; a provincially limited society has kept Nora ignorant of the world outside her home and is thus partly responsible for her leaving her husband. In *Ghosts*, environment imposed conformities upon Mrs. Alving that had kept her tethered to an unfaithful husband, and the unfortunate results of her compliance are demonstrated with consummate pathos and irony in the denouement. In Henry Becque's *La Parisienne*, the amorality of Parisian society is the paramount consideration; the comic action consists entirely of the married heroine's assumption that her extramarital relations are entirely correct, harm no one, and actually enhance her husband's position. Becque's Clotilde considers herself not only a devoted wife but a right-thinking woman. "You even pass for a free thinker," she reproves her lover Lafont, "and no doubt would get along famously with a mistress who had no religion at all."

In some modern plays, environment even assumes the role of a diffuse or concentrated antagonist. In Hauptmann's *The Weavers*, the economic situation of the cottage weavers of Silesia is the central fact, and the depression of their wages caused by the

[8] All of the quotations in this paragraph are from *Directing the Play*, ed. Toby Cole and Helen Krich Chinoy (Bobbs-Merrill Co., 1953), pp. 71-135.

introduction of machinery is the precipitating force in their conflict with an employer who is himself a victim of economic forces
unleashed by the Industrial Revolution. Chekhov noted the corrosive effect of provincial life in several of his plays. Environment
is so important a factor in *The Three Sisters* that Fate is identified
with stagnation in a provincial town. And, not surprisingly, it
was Ibsen who set the modernists an almost classic example when
he pitted the reformer Dr. Stockmann against an entire Norwegian
town in *An Enemy of the People:* Dr. Stockmann wants to expose
the contaminated condition of the waters of a bathing resort; the
town, which derives considerable income from those who come to
the resort in search of health, suppresses the idealist.

Details of setting thus became decisive and playwrights began to count upon stage settings to convey the conditions of life
that were the subject of a play and that sometimes played the role
of destiny. Without a sordid environment, for example, Gorki's
famous play about derelicts and social outcasts *The Lower Depths*
would lose its meaning and force, as would O'Casey's *The Plough
and the Stars,* which requires us to "experience" life in a Dublin
slum if we are to comprehend the author's viewpoint.

as a char.

That a ruling idea rather than the availability of technical
means was decisive in the rise of modern realism is proved by the
fact that the ability to create illusion had been demonstrated
again and again in Renaissance and Baroque stage design. The
tendency of illusionism was toward realistic scenery and, as the
settings were built and painted behind the proscenium arch, they
could have suggested an environment. But the modern concept
of environment as a dynamic element of human experience had
not yet developed. Environment had little, if any, significance to
most playwrights before the last quarter of the nineteenth century—that is, before the application to playwriting of the naturalistic idea of environment as a determinative factor. And the
actor, who had no responsibility for the content and philosophy

of a play, was even less likely to succeed by himself in developing the implications of Renaissance-born illusionism. Feeling most at home on a platform, not yet willing to isolate himself psychologically from the public, the prerealistic actor treated the stage setting as mere *background* by playing in front of the scenery and by playing to the audience.   not with

The maintenance of the pre-illusionistic acting tradition of direct communication with the spectator made it impossible to establish a true sense of environment. In this respect the actor collaborated with the prerealistic playwright, who kept his characters in communication with the spectator by employing soliloquies and asides as the easiest way to convey information and express sentiment. In turn, the Renaissance and post-Renaissance stage designer exercised great talent in inventing spectacles in which he used tricks of architectural perspective that would have been ridiculous if the actors had actually played inside the set, instead of at some distance in front of it. And his spectacles, of course, would have been utterly incongruous if they had been associated with productions resembling modern realistic drama. They were used instead for court masques, pastorals, and opera that grew grander and grander. The astounding settings of the Bibiena family of baroque designers in Italy and Austria were not intended as décor for any dramatic genre represented by *Ghosts* and *All My Sons*.

As a means of achieving architectural perspective, the floor was raked, or tilted, up toward the back; acting on such a plane could not have been conducive to either comfort or naturalness in performance. The perspective of the series of flats or side-wings also diminished rapidly; the shallower the stage, the more rapid the reduction of size. Actors playing inside such settings might have found their eyes on a level with a second-story window or balcony painted on a flat, and the resulting illusion of giantism might well have startled an audience. And indeed, the stage became increasingly shallow after the eighteenth century. In the heyday of baroque perspective scenery the stage space was at least as deep as the auditorium, if not one and a half times as deep; it eventually became equivalent to not much more than one half of the auditorium. Lee Simonson writes in *The Stage Is Set* (p. 266) that "once the average stage became so shallow that an actor moving twelve or fifteen paces up stage had the sky at his elbow, the entire structure on which the illusions of scene-painting were based collapsed." In order to make scene shifting easy it also became necessary to paint furniture and stage properties on the canvas flats; it is hardly necessary to point out that such painted two-dimensional scenery was unsuitable for the creation of an environment for the performer, and that it also made impossible the creation of an *illusion of environment* for the spectator.

Finally, it is not to be forgotten that prerealistic scenery was usually changed during the action in the presence of the audience, rather than behind the proscenium curtain as was done after the advent of realism. Indeed, the mechanical changing of scenery was often an important part of the "show," so that illusionistic scenery served the purposes of spectacle rather than drama. The result was artifice rather than realism, theatrical jugglery rather than the establishment of environment. In Paris in the early eighteenth century there was actually a show at the Salle des Machines in the Tuileries that consisted entirely of displays of scene-changing by stage machinery.

Obviously, in these conventions there is reflected a conception of theatre radically different from that of the age of Stanislavsky. And this conception was also sustained by the prerealistic conventions of acting based on the principle—a thoroughly theatrical one—that the actor's first prerogative is to exhibit himself and display his skill. Nor is there any reason to suppose that the audience felt it imperative for him to lose himself in his role. Like his predecessors, the old mimes and virtuosi of the *commedia dell' arte,* he stood out as a *performer* rather than as a character. At his best, in the tempestuous acting of a Rachel Felix or an Edmund Kean, the actor developed character, but by giving primacy to "temperament" and the "passions" he *theatrical-ized* it and thus managed to display his virtuosity and uniqueness. Typically, the actor was a star rather than a member of an ensemble. It was especially difficult for the pioneering modernists to destroy the prerealistic "star system" that was prevalent everywhere except in the Duke of Saxe-Meiningen's company, the Meininger, before Antoine founded his Théâtre Libre in 1887.

In brief, the prerealistic theatrical orientation, carried over from the pre-Renaissance platform stage, thrust the actor forward to win far more admiration than conviction, even when he ran the gamut of the emotions discoverable in his role. And to forego admiration was the hardest demand that realism and naturalism ever made of the old-fashioned actor or actor-manager like Sir Henry Irving, who resisted dramatic realism long after he began to play in "solid" realistic settings. Not surprisingly, Irving usually turned even these into *coups de théâtre*. He accomplished this not only by giving the scenery spectacular qualities but by subordinating every element in the production to his personality. Thus arose the contradiction that still appears in many quasi-realistic productions. The scenery provides an environment (in the physical sense), but the actor nullifies its value by thrusting into the limelight the glamorized personality of star actress or matinee idol. The actor, who is presumably in a realistic environment (in the box set consisting of three "walls" formed by lashing together a number of flats), manages to turn the set into the semblance of a platform for himself. And more often than not, the result is a tremendous box-office success. It would be a mistake, of course, to assume that the average audience cares a straw whether the rules of realism are observed or violated.

The style of acting introduced by realism not only called for natural behavior and speech, but for the observance of what came to be called the "fourth-wall" convention—the assumption that the open space framed by the proscenium arch is the fourth wall of a room. Consequently, the actor is not supposed to see the audience; the playgoers are simply not supposed to exist. The actor can turn his back to the spectators whenever the action requires such a position. Furniture can be placed right at the footlights. In fourth-wall staging every effort is made to disguise the fact that the stage is a platform for players and to create the illusion that it is a true environment, separate from and independent of the auditorium. (See pp. 54-64.) Common sense has dictated discretion in the practice of realists, of course. It was considered sufficient to suggest the new convention instead of following it to the letter. For example, the actor can call attention to the fourth wall by turning his back now and then for a moment only. The important point has become, indeed, not what the actor does, but what he refrains from doing—what he does to avoid violating the illusion of reality by blandly playing and reciting to the public.

Historians may assure us that the aim of reproducing actuality on the stage was associated with the practicality of the middle class, whose rise was a major factor in nineteenth-century civilization. Supposedly, a good bourgeois soul was made to feel as secure by "solid" settings and practical windows and doors (with real door knobs in productions of Tom Robertson's plays in the 1860's) as by the designation of prayers for business success in a Gideon Bible. But there are also simpler explanations for the naive realism in the work of the pioneering stage companies. Their leaders were motivated partly by the desire to counter the extreme artificiality of the commercial theatres and partly by the enthusiasm of discovery. Thus, the discovery of realism led Antoine to hang chunks of real meat in a butcher-shop scene, and the desire for perfection of detail caused the Moscow Art Theatre to take two years for the production of *Hamlet* and to rehearse a dramatization of *Crime and Punishment* 150 times.

The Moscow Art Theatre, especially, was dominated at first by the passion for detail and the fourth-wall fanaticism that characterized naturalism. There was a museum quality about the décor of the first production, Alexis Tolstoy's historical drama *Tzar Fyodor Ivanovich,* for which the actual costumes of the periods were used. According to one writer's reminiscence, "During the presentation of Chekhov's *The Cherry Orchard* the spectators can detect the genuine aroma of fresh ripe cherries. A real wind blows the curtains . . . beating of hoofs on a wooden bridge." [9] And the elaborate preparations for *The Lower Depths* (such as Mme Chekhov's odd effort to "live" herself into the part of Natasha by getting a common prostitute to room with her) are recounted in detail by Stanislavsky's associate Vladimir Nemirovich-Danchenko in *My Life in the Russian Theatre.*

It is a mistake, of course, for either friends or foes to underestimate the importance of the element of imagination for the training of the actor in the ultimately evolved Stanislavsky "system." (No system, indeed, but a flexible method for the personal work of actor and teacher.) Michael Chekhov, whose notes were used by the New York Group Theatre in their training program, tried hard to prevent misinterpretations of his master's method. In these notes, made in 1922 while he was a member of the Second Moscow Art Theatre Studio, he reminded himself that "to portray life without an element of fantasy is to make a photographic copy, not to recreate it." The actor was to work just as hard to develop his imagination as his powers of concentration, and imagination was to be defined as "the union and combination of diverse elements into a whole which does not correspond to reality." At the same time, however, Chekhov made plain his advocacy of Stanislavskian realism in acting by observing that "the materials of imagination are always taken from life. . . . Imagination consists in associating known objects, uniting, separating, modifying, recombining them. . . . He [the actor] must learn to draw on life, study, seek out the most diverse aspects of it, create for himself conditions in which he will be exposed to manifold expressions of it—and not wait until life by chance thrusts some striking scene under his nose." [10]

Stanislavsky, after discarding his early emphasis on *external*

[9] Alexander Chramoff, "Moscow Art Theatre," *The Liberator* (February 1923), pp. 15-20.
[10] A. M. Chekhov, "Stanislavsky's Method," *New Theatre* (November, 1935), pp. 6-7.

realism, began to evolve a realism of performance that is essentially an *inner realism* of character creation. Stanislavsky expected this to be developed through methods of training that would enable the actor to react as he would if he were actually the character rather than the player. Stanislavskian training, which involves the use of sensory and emotional stimuli by the actor, is a separate subject that cannot be considered here in detail. Its basis is not simply the idea of environment, but rather that idea of "truth," of fidelity to life, which is the over-all principle of realism. But this training for performance, which has proved useful even for poetic drama and fantasy as a means of creating the illusion of reality, was generically associated with the entire movement which made the fourth-wall convention desirable, if not indeed imperative. If it was considered important to maintain the illusion of a "real" environment, such illusion could be valuable only if the acting also conveyed reality. (See pp. 54-64.)

It is to be noted, too, that the pioneers of the realistic theatre laid great stress on ensemble playing, and that an ensemble creates a sort of environment for the main characters. Under the star system the leading actor had inevitably been a showman surrounded by secondary stock characters upon whom he shed his luster. (It was customary, for instance, for nineteenth-century stars to travel as far west as San Francisco by themselves, or with one or two associates, to make quickly rehearsed guest appearances with local companies that they had never seen before.) Ensemble acting was not considered important for bravura showmanship, whereas in good ensembles the actor who played the chief role was genuinely a part of his human environment. The development of good ensemble playing had other advantages, of course; mainly, it ensured a unity of acting in the stage production that could be favored even by artists who were not particularly devoted to realism and naturalism. Thus the management of stage crowds by the celebrated Duke of Saxe-Meiningen, an important part of his effort to integrate all details of a production, had a tremendous influence, even though his Meiningen Company performed Shakespearean and Romantic drama from 1874 to 1890. But realism at Antoine's Théâtre Libre and Stanislavsky's Art Theatre benefited especially from the stage-struck princeling's passion for ensemble. To coordinate performances is to create an environment even when there is virtually no scenery on the stage; people *are* environment.

Realism and the Illusion of Reality

So much for the effect on the stage of the idea of environment. The effect on dramatic form, which has already been introduced in general terms, is even more important. Before the end of the nineteenth century it was understood that only behind the imaginary fourth wall could the theatre consistently present the *lambeau d'existence,* the fragment of life, demanded by Zola, or the *tranche de vie,* the slice of life, required by Zola's disciple and Antoine's staunch supporter Jean Jullien (see pp. 66-70). Playwrights were soon expected to observe the fourth-wall convention as strictly as actors and stage producers; and once this doctrine had come into vogue, various changes in dramatic structure and texture ensued.

In the first place, soliloquies and asides became obsolete in the realistic theatre. Playwrights did not at first follow the logic of the fourth-wall convention to its conclusion. Even Ibsen used soliloquies in his early realistic work; there are at least four in *A Doll's House.* And Tolstoy employed soliloquies as late as 1886 in his otherwise intensely naturalistic peasant tragedy *The Power of Darkness.* It soon became apparent, however, that soliloquies and asides were not only generally unrealistic but actually breached the fourth wall. "Asides" can have a theatrical justification only when addressed to the audience, which the realistic actor was expected to ignore as nonexistent; and soliloquies are a means by which a stage character explains himself to the public. Only when the soliloquy was psychologically motivated— that is, when it was presented as a credible manifestation of the disturbed mental state of a character—could the author escape the charge of violating realism.

After 1840, moreover, the increasing use of the solid box set caused changes of scenery to be difficult, slow, and expensive. Romanticism, in defying the neoclassic principle of the unity of place, brought back the vogue of the multi-scened play. The romanticists returned to Elizabethan play structure. A loosely organized play was, therefore, in vogue in the early part of the last century, and even late romantic plays such as Ibsen's *Brand* and *Peer Gynt*, written in the 1860's, are diffuse. The use of solid settings, however, made a return to unity of place desirable. A major reason for the butchering of Shakespearean plays by such actor-managers as Sir Henry Irving and Sir Herbert Beerbohm-Tree during the last quarter of the century was the vogue of the realistic setting. In order to escape the necessity of shifting scenery frequently and thus slowing up the production, the actor-managers transposed scenes, eliminated some, and fused others. This meretricious practice came to an end only when producers adopted suggestive scenery, used unit sets, or returned, as did William Poel, after founding the Elizabethan Stage Society in 1894, to methods of staging resembling those of the Elizabethan theatre.

In the writing of the new-fashioned realistic plays after 1875 there was, indeed, virtually a return to neoclassic structure. There arose the tightly knit play for which a single setting, or at most two or three changes of scene, would be needed. Realistic plays became masterpieces of compression. Strindberg pared down the action to psychological crises; Ibsen telescoped the crises of a life story by exposing them only in some grand climax of reckoning and revelation. The main structural feature of Ibsen's plays during the middle period of his career and afterward is the presence of *retroactive* action.

This method is actually classic; it was used constantly in the drama of the fifth century B.C., where it effects great economy in playwriting. In *Oedipus the King*, for example, the story starts many years after Oedipus killed his father and married the widowed queen Jocasta. A plague has broken out in Thebes and the hunt has begun for the unknown individual who, according to the Delphic oracle, has brought this curse upon the city. The Greek play starts close to the climactic point at which Oedipus will discover that he himself is the man whose presence pollutes Thebes. The action moves rapidly to the king's discovery that the man he actually slew long ago was his father, and that the woman to whom he has been married for many years is none other than his mother. The audience is shown only the last stages of the unraveling of the unfortunate hero's destiny.

Compactness distinguishes the structure of *A Doll's House, Ghosts,* and many other realistic plays written after 1880. *A Doll's House* begins when a bank clerk, who is about to be dismissed by Nora's husband, threatens to expose her forgery of a signature on a promissory note; past action is here projected into the present. *Ghosts* begins when Mrs. Alving is about to open an orphan asylum in memory of her late husband. The play deals with a series of closely related events, primarily revelations, which demonstrate Mrs. Alving's tragic folly in having obeyed the dictates of convention many years before. This, in brief, is the retrospective method of playwriting, which gave the modern theatre the taut dramatic form usually identified with realism. One might say, then, that the freedom of dramatic art advocated by Victor Hugo first led to a tightening, rather than a relaxation, of dramatic form. The neoclassic unities of time, place, and action which Hugo and other romanticists routed from the theatre around 1830 came to be more or less restored half a century later as a result of the ascendancy of realistic drama.

Whether the result has been advantageous or disadvantageous is the crux of many a discussion about the state of con-temporary drama. There is always danger that the compressed realistic play will become dismally dull. Mediocre playwrights have succumbed to that danger ever since Ibsen's time. Never-theless, the gain in dramatic tension is apparent in many plays by Ibsen, Strindberg, and certain of their successors. If most prod-ucts of the realistic dramatic method fall considerably below the dramatic excellence of *Macbeth* or *Hamlet,* there are surely other reasons for failure than taut realistic construction; lack of sus-tained poetic and tragic power is very often to blame. In their own ways *Macbeth* and *Hamlet* are also tightly knit plays, and many of the works of Shakespeare's contemporaries, who lacked his poetic power and his ability to create absorbing characters, fall to pieces precisely because they are haphazardly assembled.

We may agree with William Archer, even without sharing his smugness about realism,[11] that realistic dramaturgy resulted in better rather than worse playwriting on the whole. The tight dramaturgy associated with the fourth-wall convention certainly did not inhibit playwriting as much as has been alleged. It could not suppress the imagination and poetic sensibility of writers who possessed them to begin with, even if realism *per se* did not encourage the development of the creative imagination. The en-vironment in *A Streetcar Named Desire,* for instance, was real-ized by Tennessee Williams atmospherically as well as realisti-cally, and his observance of the rules of realistic credibility did not interfere at all with his penchant for poetic dialogue. He simply motivated "poetry" in the dismal surroundings and the sordid plot. A febrile and overcompensating poetic dialogue was "natural" to his Blanche Du Bois, daughter of the Southern gen-try, ex-teacher, and pretender to vanished glories. Nor did the observance of the fourth-wall convention prevent Elia Kazan, the director of the Broadway stage production, from using tawdry, naturalistic exterior and interior scenes imaginatively without a

[11] *The Old Drama and the New* (London, 1922).

change of setting. Present-day stage directors and scene designers have no difficulty in showing several levels of a house or several rooms of an apartment simultaneously, or in getting the action of a multi-scened play to flow freely from place to place in almost Elizabethan fashion.

Modern realism, however, has other important characteristics in addition to compressed play structure. Compression cannot serve as the sole criterion of realism, for the neoclassic drama exhibits an even greater degree of condensation. Tight construction, besides, has been frequently violated throughout the modern period. It has been violated, although not wantonly, in such modern realistic chronicles as Gerhart Hauptmann's *Florian Geyer* (1894), Arnold Bennett and Edward Knoblock's *Milestones* (1912), Noel Coward's *Cavalcade* (1931), and Robert Sherwood's *Abe Lincoln in Illinois* (1938); in some naturalistic "slice-of-life" sequences, such as Arthur Schnitzler's *Anatol* and *Reigen* (*La Ronde*); and in some notable group dramas such as Hauptmann's *The Weavers* and O'Casey's *The Plough and the Stars*. The severe limitation of action frequently attributed to Ibsen's example and influence (most recently by Walter F. Kerr in his vigorous book *How Not to Write A Play*, published in 1955) is not in itself either a virtue or a defect. It is a virtue only in so far as the condensation of action provides an intensified field of observation and thought. The limitation of action in realistic drama can represent a legitimate fusion of form and content.

"Tight" realistic dramaturgy has differed from artificially taut melodrama as well as from the drama of plot intrigue and calculated suspense that Scribe and his followers made known as the *pièce bien faite*, the well-made play. The naturalist program, in particular, was severely critical of that kind of tightness. Realists, from Ibsen, writing in his middle period in the 1880's, to Galsworthy, in the first quarter of our century, avoided it. Shaw excoriated plot contrivance when he wrote dramatic criticism in the 1890's, and alert critics have been wary of it wherever they have detected it. Realistic drama attained a high degree of concentration by organic means, not by means of tricks and devices. Whenever condensation has not been inherent in the character drama or in the substance of the argument, the good realistic playwright has not felt constrained to adhere to rules of neat packaging. O'Casey, for instance, provided a tight structure in the family drama *Juno and the Paycock* and a loose one in *The Plough and the Stars,* the national drama of the Easter Rebellion; and, so appropriate is the structure in each play, it would be difficult to determine which is more "correct" or "dramatic."

In realistic theatre, it is true, there has not been the structural variety that characterizes the best examples of condensation in other types of drama. The limited action of the characters in Greek plays was supplemented by the action of the chorus and enriched by the poetic ambience of both the choral and nonchoral passages of drama written, as it happens, by three of the world's great dramatic poets. Greek dramatic form bears no resemblance to the dramatic form represented by the trim little play set in a living room or bedroom that abounds indeed in the realistic theatre but which should not be wholly identified with realism. A tragedy by Racine is not concentrated in the same way as *Ghosts* or Strindberg's *Miss Julie; Phèdre,* to take a familiar example, benefits from dramatic extension by the poetry or rhetoric of Racine's *tirades,* the amplitude of his dialogue, the semiritualistic formalism of his Alexandrines, and the propulsion of passion that carries us clear out of the workaday world. The talented realist has indeed been prompted to look for means of dramatic extension and enrichment. Whether or not he has found them, he has not identified his ideal of realism with condensed dramatic structure *per se.*

Realism began early to encourage other developments. Many modern plays have a collective rather than an individual hero. Hauptmann's weavers, Gorki's derelicts in *The Lower Depths,* and O'Casey's Dublin slum dwellers in *The Plough and the Stars* are group protagonists. No matter how vividly the individuals of the group may be distinguished from one another, they are most important to the meaning of these plays as members of a group. By way of contrast, it might be noted that in *Henry IV* we are concerned with the actions of Falstaff and Prince Hal as individuals; in *King Lear,* with the destiny of Lear as a unique character whose fate is merely paralleled by that of the Earl of Gloucester. In *The Weavers,* on the contrary, it is the collective action of the Silesian workers that matters most. Until the rise of the modern theatre, the hero of an action was almost invariably an individual.

The difference between the individual hero and the group protagonist becomes, in a profound sense, a difference in dramatic form. First, there is a sharp change of focus when the drama concentrates on the group, rather than on the individual, as the initiator or the object of an action. When this occurs the stage becomes a moving camera closing in now on one person, now on another, and then moving back to include the entire group as protagonist or participant. A play, such as *The Plough and the Stars,* that has a group protagonist may be metaphorically called a symphony in contrast to the concerto-like play in which an individual hero is merely supported by other characters.

It is also true, however, that when the camera pulls back, the single actor dwindles in size. When the group is the hero, the individual thus loses stature. When stature is so lost, the creation of standard tragedy becomes difficult, if not impossible. If we consider a collective drama a tragedy, then it may be necessary to redefine the latter term. Such dramas, unlike classic tragedies, are not concerned with the representation of the catastrophic career of a character who stands measurably above his fellow men and falls down to destruction impressively.

This need to establish a new definition does not trouble the present writer; if a literary term such as "tragedy" does not fit new works, it should be extended or other, more suitable, terms should be invented. It is the specific work, not the descriptive term, that matters. The Greeks displayed more common sense in this connection than have some modern scholars and critics. They did not withhold the designation "tragedy" from such works as Sophocles' *Philoctetes,* a tragicomedy, and Euripides' *Helen,* a romance, even though these plays do not end in disaster for the protagonist. Nor does it seem to have occurred to the classical world to call into question Euripides' great drama *The Trojan Women* because it concerns the collective fate of the women of conquered Troy.

Nevertheless, we cannot deny that modern authors employing a mass-hero have tended to reduce the dimensions of individual characters. (One may cite Hauptmann's *The Weavers* and *Florian Geyer,* Ernst Toller's *Man and the Masses,* and even Gorki's *The Lower Depths* among the plays in which this is evident.) And the granting of primacy to environment has reduced the stature of the individual even in other plays in which there is no collective hero. One of the most conspicuous shortcomings of modern playwriting has been the insignificance of the individual. Even when characters have been drawn in the round, they have often lacked the capacity for independent action that would have made them representative of humanity's greatest potentialities. Many characters have represented men rather than Man. In consequence, modern realistic drama has proliferated in the valleys instead of ascending to the heights of experience.

Like the scarcity of great poetry, the scarcity of high tragedy in modern drama is a serious limitation. A strong deterrent to the development of tragic art has been the treatment of environment as a prime determinant of human conduct and destiny. As dramatic characters have lost distinction, moreover, their capacity for expressing themselves in distinguished language has dwindled proportionately. Prose is the suitable language for such characters. In earlier ages, of course, the greatest playwrights were also the greatest poets. Since 1875, in the main, poets have been one breed of men and playwrights another.

The state of modern realistic playwriting would be depressing indeed but for a number of compensations. There have been gains in the plausibility and intimacy of dramatic composition. Also, a sympathetic interest in the common man has brought into the theatre the often vigorous and colorful prose of common speech. And as Shaw's plays have shown, the discussions given a place in the theatre by modern realists can rise to eloquence when a talented author's partisanship reaches white heat.

The deluge of commonplace writing in the thousands of plays that have appeared since the 1870's should not cause us to underrate the powerful prose, often verging on poetry or constituting a sort of prose poetry, that some modern realists have brought to the theatre. It is well to bear in mind that in the past there have been large quantities of miserable writing in verse drama, too. Marlowe, Shakespeare, and Ben Jonson were surrounded by a host of mediocre playwrights, and there is no reason to believe that the forgotten playwrights who competed with Aeschylus, Sophocles, and Euripides in fifth-century Athens were distinguished dramatists. Racine had genius, but other writers of neoclassic French tragedy after 1650 are now virtually forgotten. An age and an art form are properly judged by their best products, not by their worst.

The disappearance of rhetorical devices, inessential and not infrequently injurious to the drama, also brought a general improvement in playwriting. Under the restraints imposed by the fourth-wall convention, characters are not allowed to address the public in fustian. Nor are they supposed to speak for effect unless they are naturally eloquent, as are Synge's and O'Casey's Irishmen, or unless they are "motivated," as when they try to convince or stir up other characters in such modern plays as *An Enemy of the People, Saint Joan,* and *Abe Lincoln in Illinois.* Elizabethan drama provides striking examples of the opposite type of dramatic utterance—speech that is not realistically motivated. The writers of the Elizabethan and Jacobean ages favored rhetorical virtuosity either with or without dramatic motivation, and they also had acquired the habit of figurative writing from the overuse of analogy in philosophy and pseudo science.[12] George Chapman, in his dedication of *The Revenge of Bussy D'Ambois*, maintained that "elegant and sententious excitation to virtue and deflection from her contrary" are "the soul, limbs, and limits of an authentical tragedy." Ben Jonson, referring to his own tragedy *Sejanus*, called for "gravity and height of elocution." Realism emphasized the scrupulous construction of a play, by means of character-determined and otherwise plausible action, as strictly a dramatic and unitary work rather than as elocutionary pyrotechnics or a parade of haphazardly assembled episodes.

Ibsen was the first modern playwright to demonstrate that powerful dialogue could be written in the realistic mode. Henry James characterized Ibsen's art pointedly when he wrote that Ibsen "arrives for all his meagerness at intensity." Describing Ibsen's "rare mastery of form" in *John Gabriel Borkman*, James wrote, "Well in the very front of the scene, lunges with extraordinary length of arm the Ego against the Ego, and rocks in a rigour of passion the soul against the soul." [13] James, writing about *Little Eyolf*, a distinctly minor work, showed a great realistic writer's awareness of environment when he referred to Ibsen's "confined but completely constituted world, in which, in every case, the tissue of relations between the parts and the whole is of a closeness so fascinating." [14] In Ibsen's cramped world, compressed action struck sparks of intense dialogue precisely because in that world so little was left to do and so much was left to say.

[12] See David Klein's *Literary Criticism from the Elizabethan Dramatists* (New York: 1910); Clemen's *Shakespeares Bilder* (Bonn: 1936), pp. 278-285, 306 ff.; and Hardin Craig's *The Enchanted Glass* (New York: Oxford University Press, 1936, Chap. 3), and *Wit and Rhetoric in the Renaissance* (New York: 1937).
[13] See Henry James's review of *John Gabriel Borkman* in *The Scenic Art*, ed. Allan Wade (New Brunswick: Rutgers University Press, 1948), p. 293.
[14] *Ibid.*, p. 289.

Ibsen first showed the possibilities of his method of creating a drama of climactic disclosures and realizations in *A Doll's House*. Toward the end of the play, Nora makes her husband, Torvald, sit down across a table from her in order to "talk things over." Why has the threat of scandal wrecked their marriage? The exchange of views which follows is memorable. When he asks her, "Have you not been happy here?" she replies, "No; only merry." And she explains ". . . our house has been nothing but a play-room. Here I have been your doll-wife, just as at home I used to be papa's doll-child. And the children in their turn have been my dolls. I thought it fun when you played with me, just as the children did when I played with them. That has been our marriage, Torvald." And she leaves Torvald with a terse Euripidean line. Torvald hopes that they will come together again when, as she has put it, "the miracle of miracles" will happen. He asks, "We must so change that—?" She answers that they must so change *"That communion with us shall be a marriage"* (italics added).

Much can be said about the variety and range possible to realistic dialogue. But here it is necessary to note only that memorable dialogue, as contrasted with merely fine writing, is mainly the attribute of a special kind of realism associated with character probing and with provocative drama of ideas. If we do not sufficiently recognize this fact, it is because we tend to identify realism with any sort of play in which prose is spoken and in which the situations represent the commonplaces of everyday living.

That kind of playwriting, practiced by second-rate writers before and after Ibsen, is, indeed, realism, but it is not modern realism in any meaningful sense. Shaw used the term "discussion" to define the new dramaturgic element that distinguishes modern realism. This "new" element can be associated with arresting details of exposition (such as the medical details in *Ghosts* and in José Echegaray's *The Son of Don Juan*) to enforce the making of a value-judgment. But it should not be forgotten that realism was valued by its proponents, not for any absolute merits alleged to be possessed by realistic dramaturgy, but for its usefulness in providing insight into men's minds.

"Formerly," Shaw wrote in *The Quintessence of Ibsenism*,[15] "you had in what was called a well-made play an exposition in the first act, a situation in the second, and unravelling in the third." He was describing plotty plays of intrigue such as those written by Scribe and Sardou and still being written today. "Now," Shaw explained, "you have exposition, situation, and discussion."

For Shaw the modern drama actually began when Nora compelled her husband to sit down and discuss their marriage. Ordinary plays of intrigue, melodramas and crime dramas—the "commonplaces of the Newgate Calendar," to use Shaw's apt phrase— are not distinctly *modern,* even though many are written in our day. "Up to a certain point in the last act," Shaw wrote, "*A Doll's House* is a play that might be turned into a very ordinary French drama by the excision of a few lines and the substitution of a sentimental happy ending for the famous last scene." But when Nora and Torvald sat down to examine their relationship, the dramatic form of the so-called well-built play began to be altered by this extension of complication into analysis. Shaw referred to it as the "addition of a new movement, as musicians would say, to the dramatic form." [16]

In Ibsen's next drama, *Ghosts,* and in still later plays, the element of analysis or evaluation arrogated to itself more and more of the body of a play. As Shaw put it, "the discussion has expanded far beyond the limits of the last ten minutes of an otherwise 'well-made' play." Accordingly, he added, "we now have plays, including some of my own, which begin with discussion and end with action, and others in which the discussion in-

---

[15] Originally read to the Fabian Society in 1890, published in 1891, and revised and expanded in 1913. In *Major Critical Essays* (London: Constable & Co., 1932), p. 135.
[16] *Ibid.,* p. 138.

terpenetrates the action from the beginning to the end." [17] And Shaw himself went even further in writing such pieces as *Getting Married* and the *Don Juan in Hell* interlude, in which the discussion embodies the sole action or dramatic movement of the play.

Shaw's analysis can be accepted as substantially correct. If it is possible to suspect him of writing more about his own methods than Ibsen's, this suspicion need not prevent us from recognizing the importance of the element of discussion as a feature of modern realism. It is necessary only to understand "discussion" figuratively as well as literally. "Discussion" should be equated with the manifestation of a critical spirit that helps to shape the modern realistic play and to give it a significance well above that of merely pictorial realism. It is also important to realize, of course, that Shaw's polemical intentions in *The Quintessence of Ibsenism* made him play down Ibsen's exceptional ability to create absorbing characters. The younger Dumas had dealt with social problems before Ibsen and had congratulated himself for doing his "duty as a man" as well as his part "as a poet." Not only did Ibsen "out-think" and "out-challenge" Dumas *fils*, however, but he "out-created" him. The Scandinavian masterbuilder gave life to characters who have outlasted all the creations of the writers of problem plays. Indeed, a new character-realizing rather than conventionally histrionic, "show-stopping" kind of acting was called into being for the kind of realism Ibsen led his contemporaries in introducing into the theatre. Ibsen, moreover, managed to get along as a dramatist without the crutch of intrigue which Scribe and his followers considered indispensable, and in so doing set modern authors a valuable example. Even *A Doll's House* is actually free from intrigue, in spite of Krogstad's effort to blackmail Nora, which is used only to help teach Nora that her doll's house has cardboard walls. (*The Pillars of Society*, written two years before *A Doll's House*, was Ibsen's last intrigue-drama.) It is not in one way only, but in many respects, that Ibsen, whom Archer called "the creator of men and women, the

[17] *Ibid.*, p. 136.

searcher of hearts, the weaver of strange webs of destiny," [18] proved the power of the drama of ideas. And it has since been demonstrated repeatedly that social situations, in particular, can provide engrossing drama when they are presented largely through discussion or argument. The best part of Miller's *All My Sons,* for instance, is not the establishing of Joe Keller's guilt which constitutes the plot, but the "discussion," by means of both argument and dramatic action, of the fallacy of exclusive family loyalty. Miller's play, we may add incidentally, also proves that undistinguished lines can have emotional power in the context of strong dramatic situations—a power that seems continually to surprise literary critics but would not at all have surprised Aristotle, who recognized the primacy of action.

Inevitably, however, one turns to Shaw himself for a lesson in how magnificent, as sheer writing, discussion-dramaturgy can be. The reader of English can get at Shaw's writing directly rather than in translation, and, after all, Shaw was one of the masters of English prose. He made discussion incandescent and exciting throughout his work, being more resolved than even William Blake not to "cease from mental fight." He had great comic genius, of course, but he did not need his native eloquence for comedy; he needed it for trying to build a Fabian Jerusalem in England's no longer entirely green and pleasant land. Hence the great passages: Father Keegan's "three-in-one" speech on the country of his dreams "where the State is the Church and the Church the people," the tent and trial scenes in *Saint Joan,* Don Juan's apologia in *Man and Superman,* and Undershaft's credo in *Major Barbara.* Shaw's writing was not hobbled as Galsworthy's was by the self-imposed "naturalistic" requirement of copying the speech of floundering characters. A typical and extremely frustrating Galsworthian conversation is the following, between the Parson and the escaped convict in *Escape:*

[18] In the preface to Vol. I of the standard translation of Ibsen's plays.

MATT: Wonder what Christ would have done.

PARSON: That, Captain Denant, is the hardest question in the world. Nobody ever knows. The more you read those writings, the more you realize that He was incalculable. You see—He was a genius! It makes it hard for us to try to follow him.

Someone once asked, "What is the prose for God?" The best rejoinder comes from the London critic Kenneth Tynan: " 'What is the prose for God?' cries one pundit, quoting from Granville-Barker and forgetting that the answer to the question is on almost every page of the Bible." Mr. Tynan goes on to say what every sensible man in the theatre must think, "Nobody wants to banish the luxury of language from the theatre: what needs banishing is the notion that it is incompatible with prose, the most flexible weapon the stage has ever had, and still shining new." [19] There is no prose for God when Galsworthy's characters are speaking,[20] but there is prose for God in the utterance of Shaw's characters.

That psychological conflicts can also be conveyed with great force through discussion and argument was demonstrated in the province of psychological drama by Strindberg and his successors. Strindberg's gripping treatment of female vampirism in *The Creditor* consists almost entirely of discussion. And nothing is more forceful in his sex-duel tragedy *The Father* than the verbal skirmishes between the Captain and his wife when they strip their souls bare. It is in the culminating argument toward the close of the second act that both the dramatic conflict and the dialogue rise simultaneously to a shattering climax: here the action is thought and the thought is action. To what heights the mere statement of the issue rises, how completely the conflict be-

[19] "Prose and the Playwright," *The Atlantic Monthly* (December 1954).
[20] All the more regrettable in view of Galsworthy's attractive writing in *The Apple Tree* and *The Indian Summer of a Forsyte* when he did not feel that he had to be "natural," like his characters, rather than "natural" like himself.

tween husband and wife becomes a flame of language, may be observed in the Captain's last words in that discussion. Speaking of the dissatisfaction they both came to feel in marriage when he had allowed Laura to sap his strength, the Captain says:

> . . . like the rest of mankind, we lived our lives unconscious as children, full of imaginations, ideals, and illusions,—and then we awoke. That would have been well enough. But we awoke with our feet on the pillow, and he who waked us was himself a sleepwalker. When women grow old and cease to be women, they get beards on their chins; I wonder what men get when they grow old and cease to be men. Those who crowed were no longer cocks, but capons, and the pullets answered their call,[21] so that when we thought the sun was about to rise we found ourselves in the bright moonlight amid ruins, just as in the good old times. . . . It had only been a little morning slumber with wild dreams, and that was not an awakening.

In contradiction, then, to glib generalizations to the effect that modern realism has caused the quality of dramatic dialogue to deteriorate, it can be maintained that dialogue has actually been strengthened by being made inviolably functional. Verse may have been largely banished from the theatre, but dialogue far from taking a secondary part, has become if anything more truly dialogue, whether or not it is extractable for quotation as "literature." Dialogue itself became drama again in the realistic theatre, as it is in the best work of Sophocles, Shakespeare, and Racine, instead of being confounded with embellishment.

It is above all necessary to realize that this question of dialogue, which has led us to Shaw's conception of "discussion" as

---

[21] Elizabeth Sprigge's translation, *Six Plays by Strindberg* (Doubleday Anchor Books, 1954), p. 42, here reads: "In this false dawn, the birds that crowed weren't cocks, they were capons, and the hens that answered their call were sexless, too."

the new element, has to do with an important change in dramatic form. The change from prerealistic playwriting consisted principally of a concentration upon the issues in which characters are involved, whether these be sociological, as in *A Doll's House,* or psychological, as in *The Father.* Modern realistic form became distinguishable from every kind of pre-Ibsenite dramaturgy employed by writers who proclaimed their allegiance to "reality."

Thus the form changed in response to the "idea," even while the idea itself was in flux. Whether playwrights held that human behavior was determined by environment and considered themselves rigorous naturalists, or merely maintained that environment affected conduct, they tended to adopt methods of presentation that produced a change in dramatic form. Drama as an acted-out adventure or intrigue came to be displaced by drama shaped and expressed as experience. Regardless of whether a play created under the banner of revolutionary realism resembles Shavian discussion, Ibsenite disclosure and demonstration, or "Chekhovian" stasis, the dramatic form was, so to speak, organic. The play invariably manifested characteristics of informality, spontaneity, unexpectedness, or disregard for mere theatrical effect. "Plot," if at all conspicuous in the work, was always the servant, never the master, of psychological or social reality. The new dramatic form represented, to a greater or lesser degree (usually to a lesser degree in popular pseudo- and semi-Ibsenite drama such as Sudermann's *Magda*) the liberation of dramatic action from the dominance of plot. Action was brought more or less into conformity with the norms of experience. Life is usually independent of intrigue, suspense, and the other trumperies of dramatic contrivance that strike us as so ridiculous in the dialogue of Victorian melodrama. And naively or not, sincere realists and naturalists of the second half of the nineteenth century had set out to imitate "real life."

Mimesis, fortified after 1875 by a thoroughly realistic technique and attuned to modern sensibility, whether mechanistic, skeptical, reformist, or revolutionary, became the dominant principle. The aim was to make dramatic art as *untheatrical* as possible. No one with any experience in the theatre, of course,

expected it to be entirely untheatrical; but for purposes of propaganda or in the zeal of advocacy the fact that the theatre was,
after all, *the medium of the playwright and the actor* was
conveniently dismissed. Thus, to call something "theatrical" in
playwriting or acting was tantamount to denouncing it as meretricious, just as it was enough to call a play one didn't like "contrived." The embattled realists who fought for a new order in
playwriting and play production were fed up with empty showmanship. The question for them was not how much a drama
was like "theatre," but how much it was like life. Dramatic art
that had only the stage for its frame of reference had disgraced
itself so greatly with jejune plays and "ham acting" that it could
not command the respect of forward-looking men who had good
reason to regard with envy the towering achievements of the
nineteenth-century novel. Experience of reality was action enough
for them, and such experience embraced the entire social
and intellectual activity of the modern world. Modern dramatic
realism was exploratory and critical, analytical and rebellious.

If realism carried mimesis to greater lengths than had earlier forms of theatre, this was not because the realistic stage performed greater miracles of scenic illusion than had the stage of
the Bibiena family. Mimesis had a different function for the
pioneering realists who had in view neither plot nor spectacle,
regardless of the degree of illusionism or verisimilitude in a production. Verisimilitude, for them, was a means for furthering a
meaningful experience, just as plot was regarded as merely the
means for sustaining an action of social or psychological character. We may remark indeed that the example of the realists was
followed in some respects by postrealistic playwrights. Modernism as advocated by Ibsen and Shaw has this in common with the
symbolist drama advocated by Maeterlinck and Andreyev:[22] it is

[22] Maeterlinck, *Le Tragique quotidien* (1896), in *The Treasure
of the Humble,* reprinted in Clark's *European Theories of the
Drama,* pp. 412-413. Also, Maeterlinck's preface to Vol. I of his
collected works (Brussels, 1901), of which there is an extract in
Clark, pp. 414-416.

not primarily plot drama. It has this in common with imaginative work such as, let us say, *The Madwoman of Chaillot*: it favors the play of mind, for which Ibsen, Strindberg, and Shaw had, indeed, a special aptitude. Nor is the critical or analytical mode of realism as remote as has sometimes been thought from that ultra-intellectual technique which constitutes Brechtian "epic realism"; for, after all, what is *Ghosts* but an intensely ironic demonstration, though in a non-epic context, that the wages of Victorian virtue may be death? And did not that pillar of Victorian society Mrs. Humphry Ward, Dr. Thomas Arnold's novelist granddaughter, call *Ghosts* "a piece of moral vivisection . . . fit only for an audience of doctors and prostitutes." [23]

Maeterlinck wrote a tightly drawn, completely self-contained drama when he composed his symbolist mood-piece *Pelléas et Mélisande*. Even Ibsen's realistic masterpieces are not much tighter or more self-contained than this play; the difference is one of tone, texture, and dynamics. Giraudoux' *The Madwoman of Chaillot* is a *jeu d'esprit*, but no more so than many a play by Shaw. Also if Maeterlinck's symbolist plays are mood-pieces, so are the plays of Chekhov, who is considered a supreme realist or naturalist. Nor is the present writer convinced that Brecht's *Mother Courage*, a celebrated "epic drama," is basically or radically different from O'Casey's *The Plough and the Stars*, an exemplary realistic or naturalistic drama. The former has formal features that the latter does not have. The difference in effect, however, is not as great as one might expect after reading Brecht's theoretical writings. However, the difference could be great in stage production if, for example, Brecht's Theatre Ensemble in East Berlin played *Mother Courage* and the Abbey Theatre in Dublin played *The Plough and the Stars* in their respective and distinctly divergent styles. But, then, the difference might be quite as marked if the Brecht group performed *The Plough and the Stars* and the Abbey played *Mother Courage*!

There is little doubt that realism was not only the first phase

[23] Elizabeth Robins, *Both Sides of the Curtain* (London: William Heineman, 1940), p. 198.

of modern theatre, but the decisive one. However, protests and rebellion against realistic and naturalistic theatre became frequent and strong after 1890. And the protests have had particular cogency in recent decades for the good reason that the meaning of realism, as exemplified in the work of Ibsen, Strindberg, Shaw, and a few other playwrights, became attenuated in general practice. Realism became primarily descriptive rather than exploratory and critical, or it was critical in a manner that was at best unimaginative or obtrusively propagandistic. The point was reached where continued adherence to the canons of realism in playwriting and production was justifiably regarded as an impediment to creativity.

This brief account of the first phase of modernism might end here. Realism was once a subject of paramount interest, but it is no longer that. Among critics it has evoked more boredom than interest, and its possibilities have been met with indifference rather than elation. In 1921, Ludwig Lewisohn had no reservations in focusing his *Modern Drama* on advances toward realism in playwriting, whereas the latter-day critic Eric Bentley, in his book *The Playwright as Thinker* (1946), rightly placed stress upon the departures from strictly realistic writing after 1890. Realism has been the prominent interest in recent criticism only when the critics' interest was decisively sociological.

We cannot, however, leave the subject at the point of an absolute impasse or surrender. We may or may not regard the sociological reasons for recovering or refreshing our interest in realism as extraneous to dramatic art. But in neither case should we accept the limits set for realism in the nineteenth century by the founding fathers. There were several such limits.

One limit was set by their acceptance of the "picture-frame" development of the stage and the development of the playhouse along opera-house lines. We can realize today that the realists were unnecessarily content with the combination of a court the-

PREREALISTIC OPERATIC ILLUSIONISM   *Among the numerous designs by members of the Bibiena family, this celebrated one by Ferdinando Galli di Bibiena (1657-1743) is an example of baroque illusionism on the extravagant scale that made illusionism operatic and "theatrical," as indeed illusionism often was in the seventeenth and eighteenth centuries. The illusionist theatre of Ibsenite realism was, on the contrary, generally characterized by modesty of scale and comparative austerity. It should be borne in mind, of course, that the astounding designs of the baroque scenic artists were not necessarily executed with perfection and that they were rarely as effective on the stage as they are in pictures. The effects achieved by painted scenery supplemented by built-up constructions could be eye-filling without in the least providing modern realism; they provided only* illusion.

POSTREALISTIC DYNAMISM   *The New York Theatre Guild's 1924 production of Ernst Toller's expressionistic social drama* Man and the Masses (Masse-Mensch) *was directed and designed by Lee Simonson after the 1921 Jürgen Fehling production at the Volksbühne in Berlin. This rather abstractly rendered mob scene, representing a popular uprising in Germany after 1918, was staged without illusionistic scenery, on a steep ramp made up of steps set against a black curtain. Here the antagonists, the exponent of violence known as "The Nameless One" and the representative of humanitarianism or liberalism called "The Woman," were placed at the extreme ends of the diagonal formed by the mob. This placement of the incendiary at the top, while "The Woman" stood below, symbolized their relative strength at the moment when "The Nameless One" was successfully inciting the mob to violence.* Photograph: Brugière.

STYLIZED REALISM   *A scene from* Bus Stop *by William Inge, produced on Broadway in 1955, illustrates the expressive use of realism, achieved not merely through that simplification of the interior for which the term "selective realism" has been in vogue but through the simultaneous, hence somewhat stylized, presentation of both interior and exterior. Part of the ceiling was omitted in order to show an exterior part of the building at the left and the tree at the right.* A Robert Whitehead–Roger L. Stevens Production directed by Harold Clurman and designed by Boris Aronson. Photograph: Zinn-Arthur. Courtesy of Barry Hyams for the producers.

ENVIRONMENT AND SYMBOL   *Jo Mielziner's permanent setting for the William A. Brady Broadway production of Elmer Rice's* Street Scene, *1929, illustrates the symbolic possibilities of an ostensibly naturalistic setting. (See also Mordecai Gorelik's analysis on pages 214-215.) The dual functioning of this scenic construction as both environment and symbol would indicate that the blending of a degree of realism with a degree of theatricalism is natural in the creative process. The point at which environment exerts its full power is the point at which the factual may become symbolic as well.* Photograph: Vandamm.

atre and a peephole stage that was evolved after the Italian Renaissance. They were too conservative in restricting their innovations to scenic modifications, to elimination of apron stages, the reduction of ornateness in the auditorium, and the abolition of boxes. Although at first they derived advantages from adopting camera-like illusionism, these began to succumb soon to the law of diminishing returns. It is questionable today whether realism would not have developed more vitally in the first place if producers had not clung so closely to old-fashioned theatre architecture. It is also a question, and a more important one, whether realists of the present and the future could not, and should not, utilize other forms of architecture. This subject will be considered further below (see pp. 51-54).

Related questions are whether the pioneering realists did not take too narrow a view of environment, and especially whether the visual realization of environment is as necessary to dramatic realism as its nineteenth-century proponents thought. Realism can have considerably more freedom in respect to physical environment than was once believed. This topic is considered below under the heading "Environment—Illusion or Realism?" (see pp. 54-65).

A third inquiry concerns the relation between realism and naturalism. Although the subject is familiar and the present writer, for one, can add nothing to our present knowledge, it is nevertheless reviewed in an extended note (pp. 66-70) with the intention of removing some possible confusions (more likely to occur in America than abroad) and determining to what extent the problems of realism can be considered cognate with those of naturalism.

Finally, we may inquire to what degree drama and verse actually had to undergo separation for the sake of realistic theatre and follow separate destinies. This is the subject of the comments entitled "Verse and Verse-Realism" (see pp. 70-76).

SOME FURTHER OBSERVATIONS

Stage Architecture and the Play

Some present-day proponents of central staging or arena theatre are oddly unwilling to acknowledge that there is a relationship between the architecture of the playhouse, or even the architecture of the stage, and the play. They maintain that every sort of play is suitable for central staging. I suspect that this view arises in part from a disinclination to limit the repertoire and thus deprive local audiences of interesting plays. Nor is a discrepancy between the style of a play and the style of its production likely to be detected by the public when the community affords no opportunity for making reliable comparisons. And, of course, discrepancies between the style of the play and the style of the stage production have been frequent even in the most highly professionalized theatre. Sometimes, indeed, the discrepancies have been deliberately cultivated in modern stage practice.

It is nevertheless a mistake to disregard the relationship between architecture and the drama. Our "peephole" stage is obviously not ideal for Shakespearean drama, which needs a platform stage. And it is actually no less incongruous to perform realistic drama in these theatres. Except for some concessions to modern ideas of functional simplicity, most professional playhouses are simply opera houses in which the public is incongruously offered intimate realistic drama requiring psychological acting which probably eludes half the audience, by whom the actors' facial play cannot be seen clearly. Incongruously, too, these playhouses are post-Renaissance and pseudo-Renaissance court theatres now occupied by plebeian playgoers.

Open-air theatres for productions of "pageant drama" or "symphonic drama" (I have in mind such theatres as those on Roanoke Island, N.C., and at Williamsburg, Va.) are admirably suited to the plays they accommodate, since they were built with a special purpose in mind. Arena theatres have been designed for intimacy, a generally laudable objective. But they have not been built in response to the requirements of a particular mode of playwriting any more than they have grown out of a modern cultural matrix.

In the absence of the necessary relation between play and playhouse, curious things can happen. There is the case of Tennessee Williams' *Summer and Smoke*. Not written especially for central staging, the work was nevertheless brought into final shape at Margo Jones's arena theatre in Dallas, where it proved immensely successful and aroused great expectations for a successful translation to Broadway. But the Broadway production in the fall of 1948 at a typical Broadway playhouse, the Music Box, was a failure, although the play, again staged by Margo Jones, had an excellent cast which performed at the top of its bent as well as scenery by Jo Mielziner which drew plaudits from all the newspaper reviewers. Somehow this particular play was, or had become in the course of revision, an ideal arena-theatre play. Brooks Atkinson, while praising the New York production, felt obliged to concede that he had seen the play go better (this, with a less professional cast) in Margo Jones's Dallas theatre. Then, as if to clinch the point, several years later *Summer and Smoke* was produced again, this time in a Greenwich Village arena theatre, Circle-in-the-Square, where it brought stardom to Geraldine Page and great repute to José Quintero, the director. A circle, as in Dallas, or a three-sided stage, as in Greenwich Village, "contained" this novelistic play with its heroine's history of failure and deprivation, whereas the Broadway production forced the action toward the wings and failed to center the heroine on the stage except in the prologue and the epilogue. Centralized staging, in brief, corresponded with the essential character or form of Williams' play.

When the same kind of staging at Circle-in-the-Square was given Truman Capote's Broadway failure *The Grass Harp*, however, it proved to be less effective. It failed to improve the play, which suffered from a tendency toward stalemate after its early sensational show of activity with the flight of three rebellious characters to a tree-house in the woods. It was *development*, not containment, that this particular play needed: when the tree-house scenes were played, there was evident discordance between the temporarily forward-thrusting action and the three-sided rectangular stage. The action of the main characters occupied only a corner of the rectangle, with the rest of the space remaining fundamentally functionless. The main characters, looking down the length of the rectangle, the shape of which called for movement on their part, were constrained by the plot not to move forward, for the play suffered from a deficiency of developing action. (The denouement consisted of the characters' return to the home of the tyrannical woman against whom they had rebelled.) Yet the natural thrust of the long narrow space was a forward one. The rest of the space was used by characters who came on to oppose the occupants of the tree-house, and since the role of the former was altogether negative (and not very interestingly so), the greater part of the rectangular stage was psychologically empty and dramatically useless.

When we add to these illustrations the many others that could be cited, especially the late nineteenth-century efforts to frame stage pictures for Shakespeare, it is evident that we should not neglect the question of the correspondence between stage architecture and the play.

Yet it is precisely this correspondence that has been ignored, because of ignorance, indifference, or expediency, whenever the commercial theatres have produced plays notable for antinaturalistic stylization. The expedients usually resorted to—the addition of a little forestage or apron, the building of a false proscenium behind the permanent proscenium arch, the placing of a few actors in the boxes or the orchestra—are sometimes downright pitiful. Only rarely have special theatres been built for nonrepresentational stage productions—theatres, like Copeau's Théâtre du Vieux-Colombier, which abolish the distinction between the stage and the auditorium, thus eliminating the convention of the fourth wall.

Luckily for dramatic representationalism, the prerealistic picture-frame stage that was developed from the late fifteenth century to the middle of the nineteenth century offered possibilities for the pictorial reproduction of domestic scenes. After 1850, moreover, once the box setting came into vogue, the picture-frame stage, with a "picture" made up of the scenery placed behind the "frame" (the proscenium arch), became a *peephole stage*, with the entire action enclosed in the box. In the second half of the nineteenth century, realists and naturalists found at least one architectural change to be decidedly helpful to representational, truly environmental, theatre; the abbreviated post-Renaissance platform, the narrow stage in front of the proscenium arch known as the "apron," was removed.

Environment—Illusion or Idea?

Because some architectural or scenic effects will be found in every production, it is important to distinguish between mere illusionism and the modern concept of environment. A setting, in itself, is not an environment, nor is a scene an environment, in any true dramatic sense, unless it encloses the characters and the stage action. Moreover, illusion can be created for the works of nineteenth-century realists and their twentieth-century successors only when the acting area is treated as both geographically and psychologically distinct from the area occupied by the audience.

The alternative is to treat the stage and the auditorium as a single environment, and this alternative was adopted by both romanticists and realists of our century. In Reinhardt's staging of *The Miracle,* for instance, the auditorium of the playhouse was treated as a portion of a Gothic cathedral and the stage as the transept and apse. The object was to create more perfect illusion, although it is questionable whether this arrangement induced empathy or resistance in an experienced playgoer, who, like Hamlet, knew that he was being played upon. And in productions of *Waiting for Lefty* in the 1930's, to cite another example, the stage and the auditorium were fused into single environment by treating the theatre audience as an audience of taxicab drivers who were being addressed by union delegates (the actors) on the question of whether or not to call a strike against the taxicab companies. Again, it is questionable whether the regular playgoer felt at all like a taxicab driver.

The creators of modern realism, from Antoine to Stanislavsky, however, would probably have rejected both these examples as stunts and as examples of self-conscious make-believe. The playgoer was being required to make a pretense, and a theatre of transparent pretense is precisely what the nineteenth-century pioneers had set out to destroy in the service of their idea of theatre as a theatre of "truth." The argument could run as follows: It is one thing to ask the actor to play at make-believe; it is his *métier,* and he performs his job seriously and efficiently. It is another thing to require the *spectator* to play at make-believe—that is *not* his métier.

The realist sought to create an environment solely for the

character on the stage, an environment in which he could simulate reality while the audience observed him and achieved various degrees of identification with him. (The identification, I venture to say, was never absolute.) And this was particularly important for the development of critical realism by Ibsen and his successors, whether or not these dramatists were aware that their realism was one of thought (of so-called ideas) rather than of verisimilitude. Only an actual gulf between the stage and the auditorium can sustain the illusion of a distinctive environment. Only a spectator who is physically separated from the stage can function as a detached observer and can partake of the illusion that the stage is an environment. And only the actor who can ignore the audience can consistently treat his stage as an environment rather than a platform on which to play to the audience. Consequently, the consistent realists felt the need to abide by the fourth-wall convention. Without the assumption that a wall separated actors from audience, the theatre could never have become thoroughly illusionistic or, more important, realistic, in the sense of establishing the illusion of a specific, nontheatrical location for the action.

Never, to my knowledge, did the pioneers in realism question the premise stated above, although it does not follow that all of them were aware of the fourth-wall convention or that those who were aware of it understood all of its implications. The more we work in the theatre, however, or reflect upon its workings, the more certain we are to arrive at the conclusion that the decisive question concerns the effect on the actor's performance.

We may present the problem in the form of questions and answers:

Does the actor need a thoroughly simulated environment in order to perform effectively? Experience in the theatre dictates an answer in the negative. The good actor can *imagine* whatever environment is needed for his playing. He does so, in fact, whenever he rehearses without scenery. Just as he does not need a cup and saucer and hot water in order to pretend that he is drinking tea, he does not need an exactly reproduced living room in order to conduct himself as though he were in a parlor.

In that case, why should a simulated environment be considered necessary to his giving a convincing performance? If the actor or actress had the genius of a Garrick or a Duse, a simulated environment would probably not be at all necessary. But Garricks and Duses are few and far between. Moreover, even they would be playing with other, less talented, actors. The question is on a par with the old one of feeling or not feeling one's part—the question of how much real emotion the actor should experience while performing, raised as long ago as 1770 by Diderot in *Le Paradoxe sur le comédien.*

The great Garrick supposedly did not immerse himself wholly in his role: he was likely to jest in the wings after having made a noble exit from the stage. Does this mean that he had not identified himself with the character he was playing, and that he would not do so again a few minutes later? Not at all, says Lee Strasberg, probably the greatest American teacher of acting in our time. We may conclude simply that Garrick "was not strained or forced, that he possessed the muscular relaxation Stanislavsky considers so necessary for acting, that his concentration was excellent when it had to be. He could stop and start easily at will." [1]

We also know that a century later Constant Coquelin, the very first of the Cyranos of the stage, maintained in *L'Art et le comédien* that the actor must "remain master of himself throughout the most impassioned and violent action . . . in a word remain unmoved himself, the more surely to move others . . ." Asked during the long run of *Cyrano de Bergerac* what he thought of, Coquelin replied candidly, "*Souvent je pense à autre chose.*"

Even J. T. Grein, founder of that little outpost of realism the Independent Theatre in London, admitted that "overwhelming sincerity" in playing a part may "kill the projection," and his recollection of the conduct of the Flemish actor Victor Driessens in Antwerp is worth repeating:

[1] *Theatre Arts* (May 1950), pp. 39-42.

He was one of those who commanded tears; his voice was moving; his personality monumental. . . . His peculiarity was rarely to be word-perfect. The prompter in front of him knew this, and from his box watched him like a lynx and always managed to give him the right cue. . . . Now once, in the midst of a terrific scene of Victor Hugo's "Bellringer of Notre Dame," the prompter did not catch the speaker's eye. And would you believe, Driessens, in the most dramatic moment, instead of halting, flung at the prompter a furious "*Verdomme*—what is the word?", caught it, went on, brought the house down. He had not a second's anxiety, he said afterwards; all he wanted to do was to get even with the prompter.[2]

However, neither Coquelin's "I often think of something else" nor Driessens' blast at the prompter proves that every actor can perform without identifying himself with the character he is playing. Coquelin could move in and out of a familiar part with an agility not at the command of a less self-assured actor. The story merely proves that Driessens was so extraordinary an actor that he could get back into his role more rapidly than an ordinary performer.

The realistic setting, which can be selective rather than naturalistically literal, fixes the environment for all the actors. It objectively determines the physical movement and helps to make it natural. Above all, the stage space, when transformed into environment (or when the rehearsing actor expects it to be so transformed), serves as a psychological frame of reference for the performer. This was virtually an article of faith among stage directors of Antoine's persuasion after 1887.

If they could have their way, some scrupulous realists would even turn the offstage areas, the wings of the stage, into an "environment." According to report, the talented director Benno Schneider, in staging the depression-drama *But for the Grace of God* for the Theatre Guild, had one member of the cast flying an

[2] *The New World of the Theatre* (London: Hopkinson, 1924), pp. 150-151.

imaginary pigeon in the wings during rehearsals. The actor was playing the role of a tubercular youth who spent the greater part of the day flying pigeons on the roof.

The point of the procedure is not, of course, in any passion for literal realism or "actualism" on the part of Mr. Schneider, who, as director of the remarkable Artef group of players during the 1930's, had given New York some provocatively stylized productions; the point is simply that he believed that the actor would have more reality onstage if he had more reality offstage. And it happens that the tubercular youth's offstage environment "on the roof" was an important part of his onstage environment in the slum-tenement apartment beneath it. His home was charged with economic pressures and personal tensions that drove other characters to desperation and a younger brother to crime. The roof environment and the pigeon-flying represented the detachment of the ailing elder brother, who was unable to assist his impoverished family. For hours before entering the action of one of the scenes of the play, he had been looking into the sky and watching the flight of birds; Benno Schneider believed that it was important to make the offstage life of this character an onstage reality.

Granted that one can go too far in this direction, it is nevertheless true that environment can be an action or the equivalent of action, and that anything a character does at any time and anywhere may be supposed to contribute to present and onstage reality. It is also true that actors' inadequacies in performance are often attributable to lack of concentration on the reality of their parts, which involves action in an environment. In discussing the performance of scenes with student actors, for example, I found it necessary to ask them where they (as characters) had come from and what they had been doing before appearing on the stage and speaking their lines. It was necessary to remind them that their life as characters was only fractionally stated in the lines written for delivery by them. What was their life or action between pauses, for example? The answer was only roughly given by the stage business assigned to them in the author's script. How had they lived, functioned, and felt, and in what circumstances had a personal tension arisen, before the scene in which they were performing?

Realism, one may add, can often seem picayune until we refer to the effect on the actor. An elementary, perhaps rather naive, example was described by Seymour Peck in an article about the acting of Arthur Kennedy in Arthur Miller's *The Crucible*. In this play Mr. Kennedy, who had hitherto been playing boys' roles, as in *All My Sons* and *Death of a Salesman*, had to play a mature Puritan farmer. Jed Harris, who directed *The Crucible*, asked Kennedy to dye his blond hair to a dark brown. Mr. Harris is quoted as saying, "I was looking for something that would make him aware of himself in a way he hadn't been before. Dyeing the hair changes people. Take a mousy woman with mouse-colored hair, she dyes it blonde, she may change, expand, she may act like a blonde, she may assume some of the coquetry of a blonde." [3]

Regardless of the conclusions stated above, we must observe one fact: the actor himself can establish environment for the spectator. A sense of place at the Globe was conveyed, at least to some degree, by the level (upper or lower) upon which the action was performed, and the illusion of place was no doubt furthered by the use of some stage properties such as seats, thrones, heraldic banners, and other hangings. But a sense of environment, in the final analysis, could be convincingly conveyed only by the actor—by the way he related himself to stage areas, properties, other actors, and the audience.[4] We can observe the same thing today in the arena theatres. Especially

[3] "Growth and Growing Pains of an Actor," New York *Times Magazine* (Feb. 15, 1953), p. 34.
[4] Shakespeare's plays afford the actor many opportunities to use a variety of means, ranging from an elementary statement concerning the locus of the action to the complex and intensely dramatic means to be found in the first act of *Hamlet* and the second act of *Macbeth*.

in complete theatre-in-the-round, the actor performs on a floor without surrounding walls and with only vague boundaries of environment—conventionally, the area around which the seats of the spectators are arranged. Theoretically, then, theatre-in-the-round should not communicate a sense of environment at all. Yet this sense can be established by the fact that the actors' action occupies a certain space on the floor in the midst of the audience, *provided* that the actors perform as though they were living and acting in a specific, enclosed area. The audience encloses it physically, and the actor creates the enclosure psychologically, by the way he treats the space surrounding the acting area as nontransparent and by his ignoring the audience. The fact that the furniture is usually scaled down a good deal, in order to avoid obstructing the audience's view of the action, makes no difference; the public doesn't come to the theatre to measure the height of the tables, chairs, and couches.

The illusion of environment may be disturbed by the fact that one section of the audience can see another section on the opposite side of the threatre-in-the-round. Therefore, an effort was made in the arena theatre in use at Fordham University around 1950 to place a scrim around the acting area; with proper lighting it was possible for spectators at one side to observe the performance without also seeing the spectators behind the actors. So strong, however, is the power of illusion when the actor does not go out of his way to violate it that most arena theatres have not adopted the scrim. We may count on the actors' treatment of the acting space, combined with the playgoer's will, to produce an illusion. It is to be noted, besides, that "fourth-wall playwriting" has prevailed even during the vogue of theatre-in-the-round staging, and such playwriting has been well sustained without fourth-wall settings. As for nonrealistic presentational playwriting, as in a Shakespearean drama, I have not noticed that it harmonizes better with theatre-in-the-round (although theoretically it should) than with the picture-frame theatre. The reason may be that contemporary performances are usually oriented toward fourth-wall playing, both in proscenium and arena theatres.

It may be noted, finally, that no matter how detailed the realism of environment may have become in the last decades of the nineteenth century, it was bound to be somewhat ineffectual in large theatres because the details were blurred for the playgoers seated in the balconies and in the back rows of the orchestra. This detailed realism was also doomed to be overshadowed by the pictorial naturalism of motion pictures. There could be no doubt about this after 1915, the year in which D. W. Griffith released *The Birth of a Nation*—a motion picture that was to gross about $18,000,000 within the next few years. Showmanship had been straining toward illusionism for nearly a century and a half,[5] and had acquired a realistic direction after 1860 from Tom Robertson, the Duke of Saxe-Meiningen, Antoine, and others. But after 1915 it was patently hopeless for the theatre to expect to equal the capacity of the screen for conveying realistic detail —indeed, not merely visual detail, but emotional accent as well. "Every little series of pictures, continuing from four to fifteen seconds, symbolizes a sentiment, a passion, or an emotion," wrote the New York *Times* critic Henry MacMahon in his review of *The Birth of a Nation;* and there were "more than five thousand pictures" in that film! Obviously, the theatre could not expect to change its setting every "four to fifteen seconds" and still be theatre.[6] Audiences that came to expect this kind of pictorialism were bound to be lost to the so-called legitimate stage even before the high cost of Broadway stage production and the price of theatre seats became factors in the economics of entertainment.

It was apparent, then, at the beginning of the new century that realism of environment on the stage could not be mere pic-

[5] This has been true ever since Garrick had employed the Alsatian scene designer P. J. de Loutherbourg at the Drury Lane in 1771; the latter moderated eighteenth-century conventional stage practices with naturalistic pictorialism, although he used little practicable scenery.

[6] See A. Nicholas Vardac, *Stage to Screen* (Harvard University Press, 1949), pp. 223-225.

torialism. Eventually even a Belasco was to find his match in a Cecil B. De Mille, and the film's canned scenery would soon overshadow the theatre's settings. The point is, of course, that the value of modern dramatic realism was not dependent upon pictorialism, but upon convincing representations of meaningful experience; and environment, too, was fundamentally far less a matter of verisimilitude in details than of *significant* representation.

As for motion pictures, it is obvious that pictorialism could be used to subvert realism as well as to serve it, and that, characteristically, the pictorialism of the mass communication media (films in 1915 and television today) has been naturalistic-romantic rather than realistic. Genuine realism strove, and still must strive, not to *deceive* the playgoer, but to make him perceive.

The environment, as realized illusionistically on the stage, serves the audience as well as the actor. The visual illusion enables the average playgoer to observe the relationship between the individual and his milieu more or less directly. But, of course, the *illusion* of environment which began to be introduced into Western theatre during the Renaissance is less important than awareness of the *effect of environment*. It isn't a floor plan or a combination of flats and levels that makes the difference between, let us say, Ibsen's *Ghosts* and Goethe's *Faust,* but the awareness of milieu as destiny. Mrs. Alving's story is conceivable only under conditions that are primarily environmental or, broadly speaking, social. The *raison d'être* of the play arises from this fact, and a stage production that failed to communicate awareness of it would endanger the author's argument.

The modern idea of environment is a dynamic concept, and it expresses an awareness of kinetic relations between the individual and his society. Environment need not, therefore, be confined to or be dependent upon technical realism. On the contrary, environment has become a factor in modern nonrealistic drama too.

THEATRICAL NATURALISM *In the last scene of the Elia Kazan 1947 production of Tennessee Williams'* A Streetcar Named Desire, *the blending of exterior and interior views and the distribution of the play's grimly naturalistic action over five areas constitutes an imaginative,* theatrical *employment of realism. Design by Jo Mielziner.* Photograph: Graphic House. Courtesy of Tennessee Williams and the producer, Irene Selznick.

THEATRICAL PICTORIALISM   *Horace Armistead's sketch for the storm scene of the 1955 production of* The Tempest, *directed by Denis Carey, at the American Shakespeare Festival Theatre, Stratford, Conn., illustrates the encompassing of pictorial illusionism by formal and theatrical means. Although it never concealed its theatricality, a production like this one contrasts sharply with the space-stage presentation of Appia and of Craig, which continues to be resisted in its pristine form as too austere for the commercial theatre.* Courtesy of Philip Bloom for the American Shakespeare Festival.

Environment has a dramatic reality, intensely immediate as well as suggestive, in *Riders to the Sea* and *The Playboy of the Western World,* plays presented by Synge to the reading public with strong protests against the realistic school of playwriting. Environment is a dynamic factor in many expressionist works, such as Kaiser's *From Morn to Midnight,* Toller's *Man and the Masses* (*Masse-Mensch*), and George S. Kaufman and Marc Connelly's *Beggar on Horseback.* It is of paramount significance in the epic theatre of Erwin Piscator and Bertolt Brecht, both of whom have consistently deplored naturalism; that is, it is significant as a factor in the dramatic action and the thesis of the play.

Shaw and Realism

First, a clarification. Throughout the present work I refer to Shaw as an outstanding representative of the realistic theatre. I do not believe that Shaw can be pigeonholed as easily as Galsworthy, and I am not in the least disposed to deny the presence of extravaganza, fantastication, and bravura writing in Shaw's plays. But Shaw belongs to realism as a critic by virtue of his having made himself Ibsen's champion in England. And as a playwright as well as critic he belongs to realism because he exemplifies the realistic belief that the theatre is a place for the examination of facts and issues rather than a place for the service of "beauty" and the worship of "universals." Shaw's use of discursive prose is a further reason for classifying him as a realist, as is his fundamental adherence to the fourth-wall convention even in the long speeches of *Getting Married,* the Don Juan episode of *Man and Superman* and the tent scene of *Saint Joan.* His detailed, often rounded characterizations, too, would distinguish his work from that of devotees of antinaturalism. As Eric Bentley has reminded us, the same thing may be said of Shaw that Shaw said of Dickens: that he combined "a mirror-like exactness of character-drawing with the wildest extravagances of humorous expression and grotesque situation." Shaw had no use for the usual "cup-and-saucer" type of British realism except when he could transfigure it with his intellect, as he did in *Candida,* and he rapidly made himself the master of a brilliant dialectical method of instructing the mind while delighting it. It was to implement this kind of realism that Shaw rejoiced in extensive rhetoric, called for "the exciting or impressive declamation I had learned from old-timers like Ristori, Salvini, and Barry Sullivan," and did not hesitate to employ fantasia, in the fourth act of *Man and Superman* and the epilogue of *Saint Joan,* not to mention the whole of *Back to Methuselah.*

The form of discursive drama that became most distinct in Shaw's playwriting is, indeed, intrinsic in the Hegelianism that became so widespread and influential in Europe, both in its idealistic and materialistic aspects. Its implications for drama were perhaps best understood before the advent of Ibsen and Shaw by the poet and dramatist Friedrich Hebbel, who was a devout Hegelian and is best remembered in English-speaking countries for the middle-class tragedy *Maria Magdalena* (1844). "The drama," Hebbel wrote in his diary, "is not to tell us new stories, but to show new relations." He went on to say that modern drama, if it is ever to arise, would have to transcend Shakespearean playwriting and be different from it in the respect "that the conflict of dramatic reasoning is to be not *only within the characters but is to be transferred to the idea itself.*" Not only *"the relations of men to moral concepts,"* but *"the validity of those very concepts,"* is to be debated.[1] A better anticipation and description of ultra-Shavian drama would be hard to find. Of course, there is also more to Shaw's good plays than this element of discussion, and, to be sure, Shaw realized that there was something more than "discussion" in Ibsen's plays when he published his exegesis *The Quintessence of Ibsenism* in 1891 and amplified it for a new edition in 1913. But one thing is certain: Shaw

[1] The italics are mine. I quote from an out-of-print Boni and Liveright Modern Library volume, *A Modern Book of Criticism* (1919), edited by Ludwig Lewisohn.

could have easily agreed with Matisse's statement that in art "l'exactitude n'est pas la vérité," as well as with Picasso's that "art is a lie that makes us realize the truth," without feeling that this made him less of a realist.

The issue of intellectual content versus mere verisimilitude can be similarly joined in the case of Ibsen, who had no reason to consider himself less of a realist when he wrote atmospheric drama and employed some symbolism, as in *The Master Builder* and *John Gabriel Borkman,* than when he wrote *A Doll's House* and *Ghosts.* Nor are we likely to make the mistake of saying that Ibsen is not a realist in any of these plays because he does not allow the action of a play to run on freely. Ibsen is all the more an adherent of critical realism because he has *arranged* events. The coincidences in *Ghosts,* for example—the fire in the orphan asylum erected in honor of Alving, and the discovery of the illness of Alving's son, are related to the revelation that Mrs. Alving's conformity to convention in returning to her husband had been a disastrous error of judgment. Arthur Miller, speaking at Harvard in 1953, referred to Ibsen as one who "squeezed out" the "hidden connections" of events "to the mores, habits, and social institutions of the time—so that a *tension,* a contradiction, immediately appeared." Hebbel's call for the presentation of "relations" was vigorously met by Ibsen, and this readiness to make dramatic associations and dissociations that had been ignored by most playwrights defines Ibsen's realism. Miller, speaking as a younger writer, conceded that there was reason to mistrust the machine-like precision of Ibsen's plots, but declared that Ibsen nevertheless had significance for him in "his remorselessness, his hard logic, the clean edges of his work."

Naturalism

Naturalism can be defined broadly or narrowly. In the preceding text I employed this rather ambiguous term as though it were generally interchangeable with "realism." This has, indeed, been the case on the European continent, as Europeans will say "Naturalismus" or "naturalisme" when we would say "realism."

As an intensive term, however, naturalism signifies not only a strict, often extreme, mode of realism, but a rather narrow dogma introduced into dramatic theory by Émile Zola in 1873, in his familiar and perhaps overrated preface to *Thérèse Raquin*, the unsuccessful play that he had fashioned out of his own naturalistic novel. Zola formulated a creed that was consonant with nineteenth-century idolatry of mechanistic science as the key to all truth. He especially reflected the advances made in physiology by Claude Bernard (1813-1878), the founder of experimental medicine, with whose researches, as recorded in *An Introduction to the Study of Experimental Medicine* (1865), Zola was extremely impressed.

Zola's program for the theatre called upon writers to concentrate on data arrived at objectively, and to adopt the hypothesis that man is primarily an animal whose emotions can be submitted to the same laboratory tests as "sugar and vitriol," to use Taine's expression. The strictly naturalistic view was mechanistic, physiological, and deterministic. The individual was to be exhibited as the product, puppet, and victim of the inexorable forces of heredity, instinct, and environment, for man was to be regarded as a wholly natural object subject to natural processes. Since the naturalists could consistently consider moral issues only as manifestations of the "laws" of physiology and psychology, they were more inimical to Victorian moralism than were Ibsen and Shaw, who were strong believers in the moral will.[1] Naturalists subordinated morality to the order of nature.

The strict application of these standards of naturalism to playwriting resulted in the presentation of environments and of more or less animal (that is, instinctive) behavior on the stage.

---

[1] That is, the naturalist would have done so, had he been consistent, had he been heeded, and had naturalism persisted.

Pictures of degradation, disease, and sexual license abounded in advanced theatrical circles after 1880. (As usual, there was a time lag in the theatre; naturalism had established itself in European fiction about two decades earlier.) Among plays reflecting the naturalist dogma are Gerhart Hauptmann's *Before Sunrise* (1889), *The Beaver Coat* (1893), and *Rose Bernd* (1903); Strindberg's *The Dance of Death* (1901); and Schnitzler's *Reigen* (1897), best known here by the title of the French motion picture made from it, *La Ronde*. Naturalism became a *cause célèbre*, and its progress was punctuated by conflicts with censorship.

Naturalists required of the actor the utmost authenticity in speech, appearance, and movement, even encouraging him to turn his back to the audience when the action called for it, thus giving the proscenium arch the character of a fourth wall. They also called for the utmost naturalness in playwriting, discouraging plot maneuvering even more than Ibsen did, and favoring the employment of dialect. They advocated dialect not for poetic effect, but for the sake of realism of the phonograph, supplementary to their ideal realism in scenery, which constituted a realism of the camera. Dialect in a play by Hauptmann or Galsworthy was, indeed, likely to be unlovely and jangling.

Zola's passion for naturalism in 1873 also made him a quixotic advocate of "naturalness." He seemed bent on liberating the drama from dramatic structure, although his *Thérèse Raquin,* a play of murder and revenge, was anything but uncontrived. He declared somewhat grandiosely, "The word *art* displeases me: it contains I do not know what ideas of necessary arrangements. . . . To make art, is it not to mistake something which is outside man and outside nature?" Zola was successful, perhaps, in helping to rid the stage of romantic "heroic drama" and its "paraphernalia of armor, secret doors, poisoned wines and the rest," which were to find a refuge ultimately in the Hollywood factories of historical romance. But Zola came up against the refractoriness of the dramatic medium, which requires that a story must be greatly condensed and arranged. And the natural opposition of the artist to a consistent naturalism was stated, or rather thundered, by Nietzsche in *Twilight of the Idols* when he deplored the results of nonselection, "a mass of daubs, at best a piece of mosaic," and protested that "nature is no model. . . . This lying in the dust before trivial facts is unworthy of the thorough artist." Zola's call for thoroughly "unarranged" drama was heeded only to a limited extent. The realistic plays of Ibsen and Strindberg and Shaw were certainly not "unarranged," and Chekhov's only seemed so. The realists' use of the materials of social reality was interpretative, whereas Zola's "scientific" program for naturalism demanded absolute objectivity and clinical detachment.

Naturalism, however, did not cause any changes in dramatic form that were not implicit in realism as practiced by courageous playwrights. If the naturalistic theatre encouraged the use of dialect on the stage, so did the poetic-nationalistic Irish movement. In demanding that the drama consist of "slice of life" scenes, Zola and his followers also discouraged plottiness and theatrical contrivance; but so did realists, such as Ibsen and Shaw, who opposed drama of intrigue without embracing a Naturalist program. Of the preference for naturalness erected (and somewhat distorted) into an article of naturalistic faith by Zolaism, the kindest thing to be said is that it was, on the negative side, a renunciation of easy and banal means of winning public interest; and, on the positive side, that it expressed one of the oldest ideals of art—namely, the Horatian one of the art of concealing art. Perhaps Randall Jarrell has expressed it best in contemporary terms when, in writing of Robert Frost's poetic power, but mentioning also Thomas Hardy's, he referred to "the tremendous strength . . . of things merely put down and left to speak for themselves." [2] But, as in the case of all theories of art, the worse practice of the theory prevailed far more frequently than the better.

For my argument, then, the term "naturalism" has no partic-

[2] *Poetry and the Age* (Vintage Books ed., 1955), p. 28.

ular meaning not already embodied in the term "realism." I would note only two historically important points: the first is that the naturalists led by Zola, most of whom had a flair for publicity, were particularly effective in championing dramatic realism and encouraging its extension. They supported the plays of Ibsen, Strindberg, and Tolstoy, and they were the first to rally to the support of Antoine's historic Théâtre Libre, although Antoine himself tried to disclaim exclusive adherence to naturalism. A second fact to bear in mind is that doctrinaire naturalists soon alienated the public with the grossness of their plays and the tawdriness of their stage productions. Naturalism was responsible to a considerable extent for the antirealistic reaction represented by Maeterlinck's "symbolist" plays and Rostand's flamboyantly romantic pieces before the nineteenth century came to a close. Deterministic views and fascination with raw animalism, however, received too much support from the social conflicts and wars of the twentieth century to permit them to wither away quietly. And it may also be argued that by minimizing the role of reason in human life, naturalism prepared the ground for the excesses of expressionists and surrealists.

Verse and Verse-Realism

On reflection it would appear that the verse-prose polarity had little validity during the formative period of modern realism and has even less today. We know that Ibsen deliberately abandoned verse dialogue after having written *Brand* and *Peer Gynt*, two of the greatest verse dramas composed after the death of Racine. They were completed in 1866 and 1867, respectively, and not until 1881, when he created *Ghosts,* did the "father of modern drama" write a prose work of comparable stature. Not until then did he compose comparably penetrating drama of ideas or drama of critical realism, too.

Ibsen, it is true, believed that the use of prose was essential to realistic drama, and other pioneers agreed with him. But his theory is confounded by his own practice. He was able to attain heights of realistic theatre "theatrically," and to write poetically both in prose and verse. He could have returned to verse in his last play, *When We Dead Awaken*. The feebleness of that work is due to weak playwriting, not to the use of verse. *When We Dead Awaken* was preceded by ten other plays in prose, and probably only *A Doll's House* would have lost force as realistic drama if it had been written in verse. Nor can one be certain of the necessity of making even that single exception when one considers how well T. S. Eliot's parlor conversation is conducted in verse during the first act of *The Cocktail Party*. Verse would have harmonized well enough with the dramatic intensities of *Ghosts* and *Hedda Gabler* and with the symbol-charged conflicts of *An Enemy of the People*, *The Wild Duck*, *Rosmersholm*, *The Master Builder*, *Little Eyolf*, and *John Gabriel Borkman*. Considerable expository and disquisitory dullness might have been spared us if the dialogue had been fined down and submitted to a governing verse rhythm.

The age in which Ibsen and his successors made their mark was distinctly an age of prose—of journalism and of the prose-epic or novel. The Romantic poetry of the nineteenth century tended to be too luxuriant for drama; it was certainly more descriptive and reflective than dramatic. The neo-Romantic poetry of the latter part of the century was principally escape poetry. It was either pseudomedieval, and thus decidedly more suitable for Rossetti-tinted blessed damozels than for unvarnished Noras and Hedda Gablers; or it was allusively private, "symbolist" poetry. In the modern period, besides, most writers for the stage have graduated from fields in which prose is the medium —fiction, journalism, law, sociology, or even science. Chekhov called literature his mistress and medicine his lawful wife. Even if we refuse to take Chekhov's statement at face value, it is still true that this master of the short story came to the theatre as a prose writer, as did Gogol, Turgenev, Tolstoy, Gorki, Shaw, Galsworthy, Maugham, Molnar, Pirandello, Saroyan, and many other playwrights.

Finally, it is probable that the impulse to write verse drama was lessened by the vogue of prose-poetry, which started when the boundaries between verse and poetry began to be blurred by Romantic writers such as Novalis, Poe, and De Quincey. Reasons for composing verse drama became less than compelling when playwrights could employ cadenced prose as evocative, imaginative, or atmospheric as Synge's, O'Casey's, and Chekhov's. So exquisite a poet as García Lorca turned from the writing of verse tragedies such as *Yerma* and *Blood Wedding* to prose drama for his last play, *The House of Bernarda Alba*. Even Eliot (who nevertheless cast his final vote for verse) was moved to express amazement at the power of prose drama: "There are great prose dramatists—such as Ibsen and Chekhov—who have at times done things of which I would not otherwise have supposed prose to be capable . . ." Eliot concluded that "no play should be written in verse for which prose is *dramatically* adequate."[1]

Nevertheless, the vogue of prose dialogue proved to be a pitfall for ordinary writers, who lacked the power to transcend the commonplace and who did not realize that even dramatic prose is already well above the level of the fumbling language of ordinary conversation. And notably, too, the rage for familiar characters and situations deprived the drama of that "fascination of the abomination," the stock in trade alike of gothic romanticism and popular melodrama, that had motivated both eloquence and magniloquence for more than three-quarters of a century before *Ghosts*.

A countermovement did arise in the 1890's with the atmospheric prose of Maeterlinck and the pyrotechnical verse of Rostand. But the trend, whether toward prose-poetry, of which O'Casey and Giraudoux became the masters in our time, or toward verse drama, for which Claudel, Hofmannsthal, Yeats, García Lorca, and Eliot maintained an uninterrupted apostolate,

[1] *Poetry and Drama* (London: Faber and Faber, 1951), p. 12.

has been associated with realism only intermittently. The prose-poets tended to disavow realism from the start, as did Maeterlinck and Synge, or to abandon it, as did Strindberg, Masefield, and O'Casey. It remains to be remarked only that, despite such defections, dramatic realists have continued to use prose-poetry; examples can be found in the work of such reputable contemporaries as Carl Zuckmayer, Charles Vildrac, Albert Camus, Paul Vincent Carroll, Clifford Odets, Tennessee Williams and Arthur Miller. And Eliot's terse fragment *Sweeney Agonistes,* portions of *The Cocktail Party* and *The Confidential Clerk,* Fry's *Venus Observed* (if it is not too tenuous for realism), and some scenes in *Winterset* suggest that verse is not essentially in conflict with dramatic realism. The "language of power" lends itself naturally to rhythmic utterance.

There still exists the danger of turgidity that was great in nineteenth-century verse-making, as Maxwell Anderson's lapses in several verse plays made evident. Yet how can we possibly ignore the fact that much of the greatest verse ever written— that of Homer, Sophocles, Dante, and Racine, for instance—was notably simple and direct, even when characterized by regularity of meter? Besides, there is a long "tradition of conversational language in poetry," as Eliot has reminded us, so that the "tone of common speech" can be applied to "the topics of common intercourse." [2] It was unnecessary for realists to forego the use of verse in order to further their cause, although it is perhaps only now, long after the period of struggle for realism, that we can realize the extent of the loss and conclude that it was not necessary. And the loss certainly need not have been entailed because of the resolve of the realists, as foreshadowed by Hugo's preface to *Cromwell,* to show the seamy side of life. If they had no beautiful world to exhibit, they could nevertheless have been the first to realize, with Hugo, that poetry is not dependent

[2] From *The Use of Poetry and the Use of Criticism* (London: Faber and Faber, 1933).

on beauty in its object; and verse, of course, is even less so. Again we are indebted to Eliot for a terse statement on a subject within his competence when he states that "the essential advantage for a poet is not to have a beautiful world with which to deal: it is to be able to see beneath both beauty and ugliness; to see the boredom, and the horror, and the glory." [3]

Nor is the loss of verse to realistic drama irrecoverable, even at this time, though I know only of unproduced verse plays (by the American poet Ettore Rella) which are realistic from beginning to end, as neither *The Cocktail Party* nor *Winterset* is. Not even the realists' concern with "this time, this place," their very necessary concern with environment, need be an impediment. Some excellent verse does not convey the sense of an action taking place at a particular time in a particular place, but some very good verse (Homer's, Chaucer's, Villon's, Dante's, Wordsworth's, and Frost's) does. There can only be agreement among poets today that in using verse they need not forego the advantages of prose. Finally, it must be conceded that in English literature, if perhaps still not in French literature, there are no great requirements of regularity and there is much freedom within the flexible boundaries of form.

It may be argued, with seeming logic, that if verse can be free enough to adopt "the tone of common speech" and to talk of "the topics of common intercourse" there is no need for versification at all. If we are asked whether prose won't do just as well, we are forced to concede that prose has often served well enough. And I refer to straightforward, "plain" prose, not to that "half-formed poetry" which is "prose-poetry" and which does not invariably possess the virtues that are attributed to it. In prose-poetry the writer may succumb to prolixity and thus graze the periphery instead of striking at the heart of the matter, for there are excesses native to emotion and imagination that must be controlled if art is to have an effect of finality. But if prose has served the drama well enough, we have not yet found the answer to the question of why verse is desirable. One answer,

[3] *Ibid.*, p. 106.

already proposed, is that good versification can discipline prose. It can also discipline prose-poetry, which sometimes needs the bit and the bridle even more. Also, poetry "is language in depth, language at its most intense; which makes it peculiarly fitted for drama, which is life at its most intense." [4] Verse, as Eliot and others have noted, can prove helpful in keeping the actor and the audience attuned to the harmonies of true poetry when they appear, as they should, in the climaxes.

Verse, even when it looks like "sliced-up prose," can also provide dramatic punctuation, causing the eye—and, what is far more important, the ear—to rest on the word that should be dramatically emphatic. In the play *Venus Observed,* in the lines

I'd like it,
Father, if Mrs. Dill would have an apple,

the word "father" is much more heavily pointed, seeming to say "Father, are you attending?" than it would be if the lines were typed or printed as prose.[5] And, as the same commentator, A. L. Pattison, points out, prominence can also be given to words by means of the assonances and alliterations that are native to verse. We may note particularly the significance of "stranger" and "unexpected," the words used by the celestial psychiatrist Sir Harcourt-Reilly in the lines

But let me tell you, that to approach the stranger
Is to invite the unexpected. . . .

in the first act of *The Cocktail Party.* We note "stranger" because it stands at the end of the first line, and "unexpected" because of the alliterative echo of "approach." If the emphasis had been different, the dramatic meaning would have been different. Nor is it certain that these two significant and poetic

[4] A. L. Pattison, "Which Is the Opposite of Prose?", *Drama* (Summer 1954), p. 30.
[5] *Ibid.,* p. 31.

lines would have come with the same force of order and music[6] had not verse, however prosaic, been used in the play.

Whether for the tragic sense or for the comic spirit, for the storm of passion or for the thrust of satire (for which versification can often sharpen the point), verse, we must conclude, could have been used to good purpose by dramatic realism. And there is no reason why it cannot be so used now or at some favorable time in the future.

[6] We may hear the musical effect of the *r* in "approach" and "stranger," of the *t*'s, and, the modulation of the vowels.

The Second Transition

FROM REALISM TO EXPRESSIONISM

The intelligible . . . lies at the periphery of experience, the surd at its core; and intelligence is but one centrifugal ray darting from the slime to the stars. . . .
. . . the core is an irresponsible, ungoverned, irrecoverable dream.
—GEORGE SANTAYANA

. . . what I have called a story, Mr. Archer calls a plot . . . the resultant play must on my method be a growth out of the stimulated imagination of the actual writer, and not a manufactured article constructed by an artisan according to plans and specifications supplied by an inventor.—BERNARD SHAW

[The Hairy Ape]: The bell rings for the Stokers to go on duty . . . they all stand up, come to attention, then go out in a lockstep file . . . it is only symbolic of the regimentation of men who are the slaves of machinery. In a larger sense, it applies to all of us, because we are all more or less slaves of convention, or of discipline, or of a rigid formula of some sort. The whole play is expressionistic. The coal shoveling . . . for instance. Stokers do not really shovel coal that way. But it is done . . . to contribute to the rhythm—a powerful factor in making any-thing expressive.—EUGENE O'NEILL

Tragic art, passionate art, the drowner of dykes, the con-founder of understanding, moves us by setting us to reverie, by alluring us almost to the inten-sity of trance.—WM. BUTLER YEATS

[To Jürgen Fehling, director of Masse Mensch]: Certain critics have deplored the fact that your production . . . weakens its contrasting elements of reality and dream by wrapping the picture of "reality" in the same visionary atmosphere as that which rightly surrounds the "dream pictures." [But] you have carried out my meaning. Pictures of "reality" are not realism, are not local color; the protagonists (except for Sonia [The Woman]) are not individual characters. . . .
—ERNST TOLLER

. . . the play in which there is no argument and no case no longer counts as serious drama.
—BERNARD SHAW

Imitation is one instinct of our nature . . . [It] is implanted in man from childhood, one difference between him and other animals being that he is the most imitative of living creatures, and through imitation learns his earliest lessons, and no less universal is the pleasure of experience.—ARISTOTLE

Realism as Modern Classicism

REALISM, CRYSTALLIZED IN EUROPE BETWEEN 1875 AND 1890, RAP-
idly became the classic form of modern drama and theatre there.
From it stemmed developments ranging from naturalism to poetic realism. In reaction against it arose those other dramatic
styles, comprising the *second phase* of modernism, that have
borne such names as symbolism, expressionism, and surrealism,
all indicative of their antirealistic nature. Moreover, as so often
happens when a reaction sets in against something that exerts a
strong hold, the very departures from realism have each incorporated one or more of its principles or elements. In one way
or another, indeed, opponents of realistic art have tended to
justify their endeavors, no matter how bizarre, on the grounds
that only their way of writing or staging a play expresses reality.
The one principle to which certain antirealists subscribed more
or less generally, sometimes even extravagantly, is the same one
that sparked the realistic movement—namely, the concept of
theatre as a means of revealing "truth."

79

Even in 1890 it might have been apparent to a student of civilization that realism would retain its hold upon the Western theatre. Excesses of illusionist detail or of verisimilitude might disappear from the stage, it was clear, but the objective presentation of social circumstances and psychological tension would not. It is surely not difficult to understand why Ibsenism, unlike the romanticism envisioned by Hugo and realized later in the Wagnerian art-synthesis,[1] was bound to prevail in the modern theatre long after realistic playwriting and stagecraft had lost their novelty. The concern with facts was not likely to diminish after the time of Ibsen and Zola. The sociological interest could only be intensified in an age of social crises and conflicts. The generally positivist doctrine of the world after 1875 also lent support to the social problem play and the psychological drama. The creators of realistic theatre felt rooted in the modern world, whereas the proponents of the new modes of theatrical stylization beginning with the eighteen-nineties were apt to make a cult of their sense of alienation. With the exception of a few revolutionary Central European expressionists and epic realists after 1918, the antirealists tended to cultivate a private world. One may concede, of course, that expressionists, dadaists, and surrealists reflected the confusion and disintegration of society as many more placid playwrights and showmen did not. One might say, for instance, that after 1914 Cocteau was a better barometer of the social weather than Galsworthy, just as Ibsen had been better than Pinero after 1875. But for all that, theatrical estheticism was not a social force in the direct and constructive manner in which realism was a social force following the appearance of *A Doll's House* in 1879.

[1] Wagner's most completely realized "composite art works," the music-dramas *Tristan and Isolde* and *Die Meistersinger,* were completed in 1865 and 1868 respectively; his *Ring of the Nibelungs* tetralogy, in the years 1869 to 1876. Ibsen's *A Doll's House* appeared in 1879; *Ghosts,* in 1881. The first theatre consistently devoted to realistic stage production, André Antoine's Théâtre Libre, opened in 1887; its equivalent in Germany, Die Freie Bühne, in 1889.

The realists *felt at home* in the very world they intended to reform. They were confident that they could know virtually everything that needed to be known about man, society, and life, and they appeared to believe that all they needed—all that humanity ever needed—was the will to discover the truth and to put rational policies into operation. This was explicit doctrine in the work of Shaw. Doctrinaire naturalists, of course, were confident that they could unlock all mysteries with their little key of mechanistic science. Neither realists nor naturalists felt ineffectual. Nor did either their friends or their enemies consider them ineffectual.

Fierce battles were fought over Ibsenism. Advocates of critical realism took up arms as though they were serving the cause of enlightenment and the emancipation of the human race. And their Victorian opponents held their ground as stubbornly as if they were repelling the forces of hell; they thought of themselves as defenders of civilization rather than of an insignificant world of make-believe. Among critics, for example, the most obdurate of the American conservatives, William Winter, complained in *The Wallet of Time* (1913) that not only had the Ibsenites "altogether mistaken the province of the Theatre in choosing it as the fit medium for the expression of sociological views," but that these views "would disrupt society." Ibsen's plays were "intolerable," according to Winter, because "in the expressive phrase of Wordsworth, they 'murder to dissect.'" A "reformer who calls you to crawl with him into a sewer, merely to see and breathe its feculence, is a pest," Winter protested. He could only conclude that Ibsen had a "disordered brain" and suffered from "mental astigmatism."

A new Ibsen production or the opening of a new theatre dedicated to realism was likely to be considered an event of major importance, an event to which even governments and political parties were far from indifferent. The production of Hauptmann's *The Weavers* in 1892 resulted in the removal of the Kaiser's coat of arms from the Deutsches Theater, the foremost theatre of Berlin, and the premiere was the occasion of a demonstration by the German Social Democratic Party, led by the veteran socialist August Bebel. Police were stationed around the Moscow Art Theatre in order to prevent a revolutionary outburst when Gorki's *The Lower Depths* opened in 1902. An outgrowth of the Irish nationalist movement after 1899, the Abbey Theatre of Dublin served as an outpost of the Irish intelligentsia during the first quarter of our century. As late as 1925, O'Casey's realistic drama of the Easter Rebellion in *The Plough and the Stars* could still arouse political demonstrations. And censorship battles raged over realism everywhere. Ibsen was compelled to supply a tame ending, one in which Nora returned to her husband, before *A Doll's House* could get its first production in a German theatre. America first saw the play, under the title of *Thora*, in a bowdlerized version in which husband and wife were conventionally reconciled. We can learn much from the review of this production in the Louisville *Courier-Journal* of December 8, 1883.[2] The reviewer was satisfied with the play until the discussion scene of the last act, which Shaw later singled out for praise as the truly modern feature of the work. The act, this reviewer wrote, "begins dramatically, but ends turgidly."

The change in the dénouement, made by someone responsible for the production in which the celebrated actress Helena Modjeska went on tour, is described as follows:

> Thoroughly disillusioned as to his [Helmer's] character, she [Nora-Thora] withdraws, dons a street dress, and announces her intention of leaving her husband for ever. He expostulates, argues, and pleads in vain, but finally, through the medium of the children, some indefinite talk about "religion," there is a reunion and a falling curtain on a happy family tableau.

The anonymous American critic's comment is instructive: he is obviously too intelligent to be convinced by this reconciliation

[2] Reprinted in *The American Theatre as Seen by Its Critics*, ed. Montrose J. Moses and John Mason Brown (Norton, 1934).

and too Victorian to be able to approve of Nora's leaving her home. "The principal inconsistence," he writes, "is at this point. . . . In the original drama, Thora carries out the logical situation by leaving her husband. Probably after all, the most consistent ending would be in her death."

There can be no doubt that the establishment of realism in the theatre involved moral and intellectual conflicts. The battle over realism was not a mere quarrel between rival groups of entertainers. It would be difficult to find a single problem of the age or a single idea associated with modern thought that did not enter the theatre. If the stage became so important in the opinion of the public and drew into its orbit intellectual leaders who encouraged the pioneering dramatic companies, the reason is that the theatre became, for better or worse, a sort of forum. Perhaps even Shaw did not express the essence of critical, "modern," realism as well as did Ludwig Lewisohn when he reminded us in *The Creative Life* that there are actions in life that require "assumptions into which are packed whole histories, mythologies, philosophies." An idea underlying an action could be "of far more startling import, of far more searing terror, than the individual action itself." Plays dealing with such ideas (Lewisohn called them "ideas of actions") were the extra-artistic justification of dramatic modernism. But such plays could also possess artistic justification: "plays in which the ideas of actions are brought to the bar of dramatic justice make the mere rattle of action seem as tame and senseless as the movements of little animals." One was not to be deluded by the practical showmen who found such plays "talky"; the plays in which "ideas of actions" are exhibited and judged were significant (and here the extra-artistic and artistic judgments blended, as they did in other intellectual endorsements of realistic drama) because "by these ideas we live and die." [3]

It is true that the realistic drama and the type of stage pro-

[3] Barrett H. Clark, *European Theories of the Drama* (Crown Publishers, 1947), p. 511. These claims for realism were made, it is

duction in which the fourth-wall convention is observed are not perfectly adapted to the forensic development of a subject and the making of direct appeals to the audience. The play structure is too confining; the style of stage production is too self-limiting. Both the play and the performance favor the objective representation of character and action. Nevertheless, representationalism did not make impossible the thrust of argument and the exemplary (or even case-history) exhibition of issues that related the stage to society; and critical realism actually favored the presentation of arguments and the examination of issues. It is not wrong to attribute an almost forensic form as well as forensic tone to realistic plays otherwise as different as John Galsworthy's *Justice* and Sidney Kingsley's *Dead End,* Shaw's *Major Barbara* and Miller's *All My Sons,* Henry Becque's *The Vultures* and Lillian Hellman's *The Little Foxes.* The action of *All My Sons,* for example, is drawn as tight as a noose around the offending character's throat while his petty *laisser-faire* philosophy is exposed. His story may be defined as a case history of antisocial individualism. The other plays (along with many others since the writing of *A Doll's House* and *Ghosts*) also move steadily toward their objectives of exposing a situation or indicting a social philosophy or a convention. Even so seemingly casual a work as *The Cherry Orchard* is a relentless demonstration of social fact. It is even more evident that such a play as *Death of a Salesman* constitutes forensic drama: it is both a modification and an extension of dramatic realism. The play is not only a case history of success worship and self-delusion in a materialistic society; it has many of the formal features of a demonstration —much debate, much retrospective exposition and analysis, and a final, pointed summation in the cemetery scene. What values a man shall live by is the question that is examined. For *Death of a Salesman* to become a dramatic demonstration pure and simple, only a more candid use of the stage as a platform would be re-

---

worth noting, in 1924, in the very midst of the swirl of non-realistic art movements abroad and the continued resistance of Broadway to "talky plays."

quired. In this work, as in more conventionally realistic plays, the nuances of characterization and the tangled threads of human motivation constitute the dramatic texture. But it is an explicit issue or argument that gives these works their particular direction or flow of action. And in the drama, indeed, the *movement* is the *form* to an even greater degree than is the formal structure.

It is to be noted, of course, that the "classical" elements of realism are not solely those of an expository or argumentative character. We can speak with some accuracy of the presence of musical form in the work of Chekhov and Shaw; the former wrote social fugues, as it were, and the latter, comedies of ideas in sonata form or in the form of a theme and variations.[4] In each, the musical form is a model of lucidity; the movement proceeds with logic and clarity. There are also many distinguished works of dramatic realism which simply represent a situation instead of pressing an argument; Elmer Rice's *Street Scene* may serve as an example. Or a realistic play may be a "slice of life," and not necessarily a "naturalistic" one like *Street Scene*. Two familiar examples would be the 1955 Broadway dramatization of *The Diary of Anne Frank* and Carson McCullers' *The Member of the Wedding*. The dramatic structure, as in the last-mentioned play, may be fluid instead of forced, but the form will still be found to be more or less classically stable. Unless the playwright has botched his job, the work will have clear outlines, point-by-point development, instantly recognizable norms of character, and action set in a clearly indicated environment. It would seem that the realistic theatre has been preserved in our century not merely out of inertia, but as a result of the unwillingness of the age to abandon a mirror in which it sees reflections of whatever

[4] An example of the "theme and variations" type of play is Shaw's *Getting Married*. Edmund Wilson has written stimulatingly on the musical character of Shaw's plays in *The Triple Thinkers* (Harcourt, Brace, 1938).

sanity it still retains. The mirror may be somewhat cracked and flyblown, but there are recognizable images in it.

In criticism, whether it is as favorable to modern drama as Ludwig Lewisohn's *Modern Drama*, published in 1920, or as unfavorable as Joseph Wood Krutch's *"Modernism" in Modern Drama* (1953), dramatic realism has been considered to be the polar opposite of classicism. Usually, too, this contrast is so presented by contemporary critics as to suggest that the modern realistic theatre has lacked nobility or has failed to endow man with tragic stature.[5] Nevertheless, it is possible to contend, as I do here, that realism has the essential character of a modern classicism. Its world is one of objectivity, reason, order, and responsibility—the responsibility of the individual to his fellow man and the responsibility of the artist to his society.

I would not be so extravagant as to maintain that realistic drama since *A Doll's House,* or even the best work in that mode, is "classical" according to any definition dominant in the age of Pericles, Elizabeth I, or Louis XIV. Nor would I argue that there has been absolute accord between the humanistic views of those ages and the views expressed by Ibsen and his successors. But I would suggest that the existence of differences is not decisive, since there were also differences—and rather marked ones—between the classicism of Greece and that of Louis XIV's France. Finally, we must realize that the aspects of modern realism we have been most apt to consider unclassical—the clinical examination of men's motivations, the readiness to define as neurosis that which earlier ages explained as fate or will, all the belittlement of the individual that psychiatry and sociology have insinuated into dramatic art—are not intrinsic to dramatic form. There can be little doubt that the weakening of humanism was essentially a moral and not a dramaturgic manifestation, a matter of value judgments and not of realistic style and dramaturgy. Moreover, it is obvious that the realistic drama and humanism have agreed very well, since among the realistic writers will be

[5] *The Modern Temper,* by Joseph Wood Krutch (Harcourt, Brace, 1929).

found distinguished advocates of the worth and responsibility of the individual such as Ibsen, Tolstoy, Chekhov, Shaw, and O'Casey.

Above all, we must insist upon the difference between the idea of a realistic theatre and the vulgarized, pseudonaturalistic version of that idea—namely, the idea of a theatre as merely the show place for illusionism. When antirealists belabor illusionism, they are actually flogging a dead horse—and one that had never had much life in it anyway, so far as Ibsen, Strindberg, Chekhov, and Shaw were concerned. No one despised mere verisimilitude as much as they did, as Shaw's contempt for Pinero's pseudo-Ibsenism alone would indicate. To what, indeed, could present-day critics of illusionism subscribe with more enthusiasm than to Strindberg's complaint, in the foreword to his naturalistic masterpiece *Miss Julie*, that the theatre has been "an elementary school for the young, for the semi-educated, and for women who still have a primitive capacity for deceiving themselves and letting themselves be deceived." [6] Mere illusionism had no future, for it could never have become anything more than stage trickery. The melodramas of the late nineteenth century became veritable orgies of sensationalism of the *Ben Hur* variety; and, in time, they were quite naturally succeeded by the lavish motion-picture spectacles typified by Cecil B. De Mille's productions. The illusionism of David Belasco's spectacular stage productions in the early years of our century also made no contribution to realistic modernism. If illusionism were mistaken for realism, it could be maintained that realistic theatre art was the culmination of a long story of decline rather than of progress, a decline that started as soon as the European theatre began to discard the platform stage of Shakespeare and Lope de Vega.

Verisimilitude in playwriting, even in combination with middle-class moralism and democratic interest in the common man, did not make any significant contribution to a vital modern

[6] *Six Plays by Strindberg* (Doubleday Anchor Books, 1955), p. 61.

theatre. The middle-class drama of the late eighteenth century, Diderot's genre of *drame bourgeois,* easily sank into complacency and sentimentality. The result could be a moralizing play like George Lillo's eighteenth-century melodrama *The London Merchant,* to which employers are said to have sent their apprentices so that they might take its story to heart as a warning against wayward behavior. Even the more or less critical problem plays of the pre-Ibsen theatre, for example Émile Augier's *The Marriage of Olympia,* stood only at the foothills of modern drama. In that play, written as late as 1855, the author was primarily concerned with the fact that "women with a past" were worming themselves into good society. Classicism should not be confused with the defense of convention, but with the preservation of the values of civilization.

It was one of the failings of the pseudomodern Victorian playwrights, whether in England or France, that they treated respectable society as though its standards lay at the very heart of the principles of Western civilization, instead of being simply manifestations of its superficial materialism and complacency. Classicism in art is not the amber that preserves a period's commonplaceness, but instead its most meaningful human experience and its most perturbing dilemmas and discoveries—those of an Antigone or an Oedipus. The pre-Ibsenite writers of problem plays were not concerned with these realities any more than were their pseudo-Ibsenite successors after 1880, such as Sir Arthur Wing Pinero and Henry Arthur Jones in England. At best, playwrights of this breed were concerned with a morality that was barely, if at all, distinguishable from middle-class prepossessions or interests.

In commenting on Pinero's *The Second Mrs. Tanqueray,* once heralded in England and America as an extremely advanced, realistic work, Shaw pointed out how adroitly the author contrived to avoid the challenge of realistic inquiry and left Victorian convention intact by making a woman with a past fail in honorable wedlock. In order to do so, Pinero went out of his way to provide a transparently contrived circumstance: the second

Mrs. Tanqueray turns out to be the discarded mistress of a man who becomes her stepdaughter's fiancé. Pinero, then, used realistic detail as little more than a façade behind which to conceal the rigid dictate of Victorian moralism according to which a fallen woman must remain fallen. Victorian playgoers could assume that Pinero's contrivance was "reality," whereas Pinero had actually gone out of his way to spare his public any realistic analysis of the problem. The method is comparable to that used in producing the Hollywood motion picture in which every visual detail is so accurate as to cause the unwary spectator to assume that the film's premises are also accurate. Shaw, writing in 1895, correctly described Pinero's kind of playwriting (in *The Notorious Mrs. Ebbsmith*) as "the barest art of theatrical sensation." Shaw added that in this case Pinero had "no idea beyond that of doing something daring and bringing down the house by running away from the consequences."

Dramatic realism had classical qualities not because it came as an end phase of stage illusionism and *drame bourgeois*, but because it crystallized a responsible view of theatre. In all classical art the work stands in some fundamental relation to its age. This is as true of the farces of Aristophanes as of the tragedies of Sophocles, of the "low" and "high" comedies of Molière as of the tragedies of Racine. As Francis Fergusson says in *The Idea of a Theatre*, the classical stage is indeed an institution "formed at the center of the life and awareness of the community." But it does not follow that the classical writer feels invariably obliged to endorse the life of his times, since it may deteriorate as Athenian life deteriorated after the death of Pericles and during the career of Euripides. Nor is the playwright committed to the glorification of commonplaces or to the sedulous support of the values of the unimaginative, the smug, or the self-interested. The true classicist is devoted to ideal values, not to adulterated ones. Also, if the age grows in self-criticism, as the modern period has done, the spirit of an age may be more deeply expressed by playwrights who defy convention than by those who accept or simply ignore it.

The tragedians of Athens expressed the Periclean humanism of the democratic *polis* or city-state; Shakespeare, the individualistic and enterprising humanism of the Renaissance; Molière and Racine, the cult of reason and order that prevailed in the times of Louis XIV. Modern realism is an expression of modern liberal humanism, not merely in echoing modern ideas, but in representing those ideas concretely in characterization, environmental reality, and dramatic action.

There is also a sort of classicism in the suitability of means to ends and in the proper use of the theatrical medium. We cannot deny that the living actor is the true medium of theatre art, this despite the artistry evidenced in stage production or scenic design. If the actor's means are inadequate to the end of character creation, excellence in all other aspects of the production is of little value except in opera, where the musical rather than the dramatic element is the paramount consideration. Realism has not proved to be the dead end in acting it has been in scenery. It could not be surpassed, and therefore made obsolete, by the illusion-making motion-picture camera.

The very nature of some notable principles of antirealistic theatrical art, such as those of Appia and Copeau, made convincing performance in acting essential. ("Scenic illusion," declared Appia, "is the living presence of the actor." [7]) When Appia and Copeau fought naturalism by stripping the stage bare, molding the actor in light, and treating acting as mobile sculpture, they only made inner realism more necessary. By disengaging the actor from the décor they made him the center of attention. *More* reality, rather than less, was bound to be required of the performer on a so-called plastic or space stage. No longer in a naturalistic setting or related to the décor of a shallow stage like a figure in relief, the actor had to achieve some

[7] "Comment reformer notre mise en scène," *La Revue*, June 1, 1904. Translated in *Directing the Play*, ed. Toby Cole and Helen Krich Chinoy (Bobbs-Merrill, 1953), pp. 111-119.

roundedness of characterization if he was not to look like an animated dummy. On the non-naturalistic ramps and levels of "space" and "plastic" stages, the usual alternative to being a thoroughly realized human being was to be a dancer-actor of choreographic theatre in the Tairov style, a phantasmagoric figure in an expressionist nightmare, or an actor-athlete performing acrobatic feats in Meyerhold's theatrical experiments.

William McCollom was surely correct in his statement, which is applicable to all normal productions outside a circus and away from an erector-set construction on stage, that "in acting regarded as sculpture . . . the continuity is determined not so much by the laws of composition as by the mind of the character-actor." [8] The search for psychological realism has had to go on, if only because the actor has to play a part convincingly even when the production is a stylized one. Brecht understood this fact, as shown by his not abolishing *all* realism in acting in his epic-theatre productions even while proposing degrees of alienation, or disengagement, from the character the actor is playing. The succinct statement of William McCollom is appropriate here as a warning to fanatical stylizers:

> The actor's art should be, in the best sense, naturalistic, the director's should not. The director must give expression to symbolic, abstract, and plastic values, but for the actor such values are secondary. . . . *The actor must be subjective, the director objective.*[9]

The actor must certainly create a life for the character he is playing, for otherwise he will merely articulate the lines written for him by the playwright. This is not enough, since even Shakespeare did not put into words all the thoughts and feelings that many characters must express on the stage. Also, what will the

[8] "Reflections on the Art of Acting," *National Theatre Conference Bulletin* (March 1950), pp. 31-42.
[9] *Ibid.*

actor do with himself between speeches when he must remain on the stage? McCollom once asked a professor of English what he thought Juliet was doing while the Nurse rambled on about her aches and pains instead of giving Juliet the news she had been waiting for. "Since Juliet was not speaking at this point in the play, the professor had no idea what she was thinking about." The actress, of course, would have to know; and as Shakespeare does not tell her in dialogue, she has to create an inner life for herself.

Nor is it always sufficient for the actor to project the emotional and mental life of his own part; it is often necessary for him to enter into the life of some other character in the play as well, so that he knows—and lets the audience know that he knows—what the other is feeling and thinking. He needs a *realistic imagination* and a realistic capacity for empathy. If he learns to make himself at home in his own character's skin, he may also learn how to look beneath the surface of other characters. Nina Gourfinkel, writing about Stanislavsky, reminds us that

> psychological depth of acting came to Stanislavski by way of Ibsen, Hauptmann, and Tchekov, who offer little opportunity for external characterization. Here interpretation "must be based on the inner life of the characters and pruned of all pseudo-scenic elements." [10]

By "pseudo-scenic elements" it is assumed that Stanislavsky meant posture, various physical indices of a character, and make-up. Stanislavsky came to minimize their importance, so that in playing Lövborg in *Hedda Gabler* he dispensed with strongly distinguishing features such as he had used earlier in playing Dr. Stockmann in *An Enemy of the People*. For Stockmann he had invented characteristic features such as shortsightedness, hesitating speech, and a tripping way of walking. Of Stanislavsky's Lövborg a critic is said to have remarked, "His make-up seemed

[10] Nina Gourfinkel, "L'Acteur selon Stanislavski," in *World Theatre*, Vol. LV, No. 1 (1955), pp. 15-16.

to come from inside." [11] Contrast Brecht's statements: "The actor on the stage will not identify completely with the character. . . . He is not Lear, Harpagon, Schweik—he shows them." [12]

Involved in these problems of acting, above all, is the *centrality of man* that constitutes the ultimate classicism of the theatre's great periods. It is granted that dramatic realism has given priority to men of average rather than exceptional stature. However, was the individual treated more fully by the postrealistic schools of dramatists if we except such self-elected neo-romanticists as Rostand and D'Annunzio? The contrary was generally true. In comparison to rival modes of theatre, dramatic realism gave man a distinct habitation and relatedness to his milieu: a set of coordinates, so to speak, by which he could be located in time and space. Realism gave him the recognizable features of a functioning human being. It endowed him with "existence," if not "essence," whereas in antirealistic drama he is likely to have essence without existence.[13] In extreme instances man has become a shriek and a gesture in an expressionist storm, an interchangeable part of an abstraction or a social machine, or a protean character in a Pirandellian universe, whereas in the realistic theatre he has been, at worst, only a dullard. As elevated by romanticists, he has been in danger of being elevated out of the modern world. Symbolist playwrights have treated him as a sensorium in a fairyland or as a shadow in a landscape of nuances, if not, indeed, in a forest of symbols. (It is remarkable how unsymbolic are the human characters of the great classic drama of Athens, England, and France, how securely they belong to an objective world from which the playwright did not appear to be particularly alienated.) The differences between the realistic and stylized antirealistic modes of

[11] *Ibid.*
[12] *Ibid.*, p. 17.
[13] Compare *The Weavers,* for instance, with Andreyev's symbolist drama *King Hunger;* the latter deals with hunger, whereas the former deals with hungry men.

PIONEER SYMBOLISM *The ghost scenes (Scene 1, above, and 4, below) of the first act of* Hamlet *were conceived thus by Gordon Craig. The first scene uses vertical masses as a characteristic expression of Craig's symbolist idea of theatre; the second illustrates, in addition, the use of the screens and curtains upon which Craig relied for simplification of the stage picture. Despite Craig's scant success in putting his ideas to work, the theatre was stimulated by his general principles. He reduced the presentation of environment to a few significant details endowed with poetic or symbolic value—a pillar, a door, a block of masonry, and so on. Although his sketches did not require any fundamental violation of the fourth-wall convention, he did "spiritualize away" the realists' kind of environment. The symbolists, as Gorelik says, showed "how the soul of environment is separated from its body . . . by using a part as a symbol of the whole."*

Craig did not confine his symbolist ministrations to poetic drama; he also designed Ibsen's Rosmersholm, *for example, in 1906. Peter Brook (writing in the British periodical* Drama, *Winter 1954) conceded that "the ideas of Craig are not applicable to much of the world's theatre" —an important admission on the part of the most imaginative contemporary British director. Brook also declared that Craig overestimated the power of the spotlight and was mistaken in regarding it as a painter's brush capable of producing endless variations: "The beams of a lamp are straight, unbending and tinted only by the tones of gelatine that hang in front of them. In range and subtlety, in shade and colour they can never equal the painter's brush." It is especially true that Craig expected too much dramatic statement from scenery alone.*

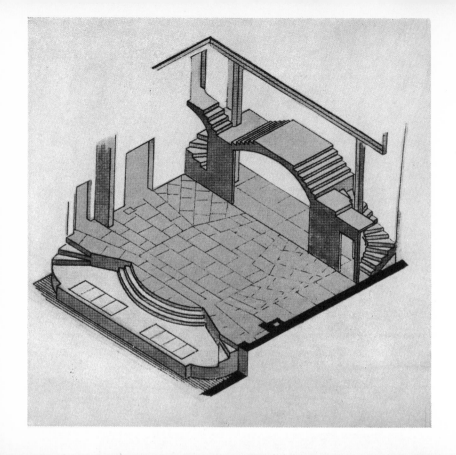

FORMALISM—A STAGE FOR ACTION *Louis Jouvet designed the stripped permanent stage—un* tréteau nu—*shown in this model for Jacques Copeau's small Parisian playhouse the Théâtre du Vieux-Colombier, founded in 1913 and modified in 1922.*

On Copeau's functional stage the action could take place more or less "presentationally," for, in contrast to a picture-frame stage, there was no proscenium to frame a deep setting; much of the action could transpire on the prominent apron, or forestage. An effective design of movement could be achieved by the actors, as in a celebrated production of Twelfth Night *in which the action occurred on four levels—the main stage, the balcony, the doors at either wing of the stage, and the area below the apron where the dungeon scene was played. In every kind of production, the scenic simplicity favored by Copeau provided much scope for movement and enabled the stage director to achieve a fluidity of action conformable to the pattern of the individual play. This was the case even if the story was as realistic in substance as* The Brothers Karamazov, *adapted for the stage by Jacques Copeau himself in collaboration with Jean Croué. "For," as Waldo Frank declared, "drama is eternally concerned with the planes, colors, metabolic changes of human action."*

FORMALIST STAGE WITH DÉCOR *Copeau's permanent setting is shown here in use at the Théâtre du Vieux-Colombier. Although the stage is supplied with illusionistic details, the formal and theatrical character of the* mise en scène *is quite apparent. Since the stage was shallow, décor, mostly made up of screens and frames, provided a semiformal background for the actor, whose primacy in stage production was constantly affirmed by Copeau. (The actors were expected to create "scenic volume" by their performance; the picture formed by the physical scenery was regarded by Copeau as secondary to the ensemble of their movements even when the stage was supplied with décor.) An effect of formalism was further secured by the use of simple arches, which appeared in various combinations and constituted a pattern. An alcove or inner stage appeared at the back, and the gallery or balcony stage above it was disclosed in some scenes. Moreover, the steps leading from the stage related the playing areas to the auditorium. A peephole stage was an utter impossibility at the Vieux-Colombier. Adaptations of Copeau's kind of stage came into vogue, so that Jules Romains could justifiably associate the art-theatre movement after 1913 with "the multiplication of the Vieux-Colombier."*

treatment have been apparent in stage production, too. Gordon Craig's towering curtains and screens dwarf the individual into insignificance. Symbolist designs express abstract beauty and produce the magic of moods. They serve the actor as a man far less effectively than the actor as a figure. It is not surprising that Craig should have entertained the notion of displacing the live performer with a super-marionette completely subservient to the will of the stage director, for Craig was primarily interested in *design,* and not in the refractory human personality. "Art arrives only by design" was one of his favorite slogans.[14] "Composition" took precedence on the antirealistic stage; and the ultra-esthetic movements characteristically exalted the virtuoso scene designer and stage director.

Stanislavsky's cardinal principle was the development of the actor as a character in the production. In Stanislavsky's view the director's main function was to enable the actor to *live* the character. "Growing" the character, partly by external observation but largely by evoking his own sensory memory and his memory of emotions felt by himself, was and remains the main work of the Stanislavskian actor. And Stanislavskian principles are properly described as "inner realism," for they are an outgrowth of the realistic movement in the theatre. As noted previously, the individual was the central fact of theatre for Stanislavsky after he had passed his early phase of external realism.

Gordon Craig and Max Reinhardt and other leaders of theatrical estheticism inaugurated a counter-movement in which the actor-individual was more or less subordinated to evocative arrangements on the stage. Gordon Craig never saw the fulfillment of his dream of employing the super-marionette. Although he surely did not think that the marionette could replace the actor completely, his longing for a more tractable instrument than the human performer is understandable in the light of his passion for design. Craig's dream was an ambitious one: the *régisseur-*

[14] *On the Art of the Theatre* (Chicago: Browne's Bookstore, 1911), p. 55.

autocrat would rule every aspect of the stage production. It was with this aim in mind that he wrote in 1911, "To make any work of art, it is clear we may only work in those materials with which we can calculate. Man is not one of these materials."

Craig's hope of making use of an *Über-Marionette* was indeed nearly fulfilled, but in a way that could only have distressed his ultrarefined sensibility, when the autocrat-director Meyerhold went through a phase of extreme constructivism during the early years of the Soviet regime. And it must be said that a tendency to mechanize the actor had been present in Meyerhold's work even before the Russian Revolution. The starring actress Komisarjevskaya, in parting company with Meyerhold in 1907, warned him in a letter that he was moving along "the road which leads to the puppet show." [15] After 1918, Meyerhold even attempted to turn the actor into an acrobat. His theatre, as Josef Gregor wrote in Dickinson's *Theatre in a Changing Europe*, "was a theatre peopled with puppets with angular mechanical motions and driven from outside themselves."

And this passion for mechanization, which was also embodied in extreme forms of expressionist staging, was widespread after World War I in Central Europe as well as Soviet Russia. The vogue of machine worship was strong in Italy, too, where mechanistic stylization was dubbed "futurism" because mechanical art was regarded as the inevitable art of the future. Futurism in Italy had its beginnings in the first decade of the century as a cult in painting. It entrenched itself briefly upon the stage under the leadership of the poet F. T. Marinetti, the director Enrico Prampolini, and others. The Futurist Manifesto of 1909 had read in part: "we feel the need of delivering ourselves from old sensibilities, in order to create definitely the new plastic art inspired by the machine."

[15] Anna Irene Miller, *The Independent Theatre in Europe* (New York: Long and Smith, 1927), p. 365.

Antirealism and realism wove tangled skeins in the practice of the constructivists after 1918. The skeletal structure or construction, an outgrowth of Appian strivings for a plastic stage, was adopted in Russia before World War I for the purely esthetic purpose of achieving abstract effects of beauty and universality. With the postwar cult of the machine age and the glorification of a so-called dynamic world, the esthetic construction became an apparatus for developing a muscular theatre and affirming a strenuously materialistic society in symbols of industrial construction. Huntly Carter, reporting from Russia in *The New Spirit in the Russian Theatre,* endeavored to explain the new justification for constructivism.[16] He came close to saying that the post-1918 practitioners of constructivism were trying to serve two apparently incompatible ideals at the same time—those of abstractionism and environmentalism. Dramatic action tended toward abstraction on the ramps and scaffolds, yet the illusion of environment was conveyed by the representative constructions. Carter was unequivocal in declaring that "the constructive form was conceived of in relation to the structure of environmental form," and that constructivism had brought "the ideas of the builder, the architect, the engineer, the mechanic into the theatre" and showed the public "a new conception of the surroundings of social life." Meyerhold's early method of construction "rested, like that of an engineer, on excessive simplification, condensation and conservation." It is hardly surprising that the acting style in productions based on such engineering principles should present the actor as a "tool." Characteristically, Carter's generally enthusiastic description of Meyerhold's acting system included such phrases as "the actor as a social tool," "the influence of Taylorism," "behaviourism, which attempts to cut out mind and to introduce muscular perception and speech," and "Pavlov's reflexology, a theory of reflex action." It is nevertheless quite evident that this mechanical or scientific realism had noth-

[16] London: Brentano, Ltd., 1929; pp. 66-87.

ing in common with the humanistic realism that had modernized
the theatre after 1880.

Symbolism and the Illusion of Unreality

No sooner had realism won its war against vestigial romanticism and the pseudo realism of the mid-nineteenth century than
it was challenged by a rising school of symbolist playwriting, led
by Maurice Maeterlinck, and by symbolist theatrical artists who
formulated programs and founded little art-theatres. The first of
these, the Théâtre d'Art, was established in Paris in 1890 by the
poet Paul Fort. This neo-romantic (or, rather, symbolist) enterprise was significantly dedicated "to the sense of the mysterious."
Before long the sturdy, realistic Ibsen dramas were being el-
bowed in the theatrical world by such "mood" plays as Maeterlinck's *The Blind* and *Pelléas and Mélisande*, by such religious
miracle plays as Paul Claudel's *The Tidings Brought to Mary* and
Karl Vollmöller's religious spectacle *The Miracle*, and such
symbol-threaded poetic pieces as Hauptmann's *The Sunken Bell*.

Indefinite, irrational feelings and visions, allegedly more real
than observed phenomena and issues rationally discussed, became the special province of the art theatres. The drama, according to the symbolist program, was to forego topicality and
deal with the unalterable verities. The symbolists were bent
upon universalizing the theatre, and they succeeded, although
often enough in a void. Universalization by means more musical
than dramatic led, on one hand, to the tone-poem type of dramatic composition favored by Maeterlinck, and, on the other, to
the use of light as a visual equivalent of music. The Swiss designer Adolphe Appia, who has been designated the father of
symbolist lighting, had attended Wagner's famous opera house

at Bayreuth, and his first essay on scenic design, published in 1895, dealt with the *mise en scène* in Wagnerian drama.[17] Like Wagner, Appia thought of opera as a superior drama constituting a synthesis of the arts; and the achievement of such a synthesis was the object of the *avant-garde* stage directors in whose view the stage productions of the realists were crude and incomplete. The new poet-playwrights and visionaries of stage production generally refrained from trying to duplicate the gigantic proportions of Wagnerian music-drama, but they were Wagnerian artists in their mysticism and reliance on verbal mood music. Had not Wagner declared that "Music is the soul of drama"?

Symbolist theatre became fashionable in the 1890's. The movement brought great visual beauty to the stage. Many artists, led by Craig, moreover, labored for the greater glory of a theatre in which visions of universal import, not workaday problems, would be exhibited. The movement brought the poet back into the field of playwriting after his exile by realism. Maeterlinck, Rostand, Hofmannsthal, Claudel, Yeats, and others functioned primarily as poets when they wrote plays, although some symbolists also had a flair for theatre. That the results were in some ways highly gratifying cannot be denied. Nearly everything that has been impressive in American stage design, for example, stems from the introduction of symbolist design for which Robert Edmond Jones was chiefly responsible. In summarizing his views, Jones wrote that "a good scene design should not be a picture but an image," and that he expected the setting to be "an expectancy, a foreboding, a tension." [18] Jones, Lee Simonson, and their successors, as well as their distinguished European colleagues, made of scenery a visual participant, an element that spoke to the eyes often more tellingly than the text of the play spoke to the ear. They were instrumental in causing the setting

[17] *La Mise en scène du drame Wagnerien* (*The Staging of Wagner's Music-Dramas*), Paris, 1895; this study was followed by *Die Musik und die Inszenierung* (*Music and the Stage Setting*), Munich, 1899.
[18] *The Dramatic Imagination* (Duell, Sloan, and Pearce, 1941), p. 25.

to function as an interpretative organ of the stage production. And the working principle behind this accomplishment was invariably *simplification;* art in the theatre, Jones declared, should be "not descriptive, but evocative," and he set at the head of his chapter of advice to young stage designers a sentence by Michelangelo: "Beauty is the purgation of superfluities."

Beauty, of course, was also both the catchword and the consuming passion of the playwrights who came under symbolist influence. John Millington Synge, the greatest of these in the English-speaking world, did not fulfill Yeats's ethereal dreams of an art theatre for Ireland. Instead he gave Dublin's Abbey Theatre more substantial drama in *Riders to the Sea* and other plays than Yeats was able to whip up in his pre-1914 period out of "a little mist, some fairies, and a psaltery," as an unkind critic of Yeats wrote in the Boston *Evening Transcript*. Nevertheless, the exquisite sensibility and language of Synge's folk plays derive from his adherence to the symbolist program in the theatre. He echoed that program in the 1907 preface to the *Playboy of the Western World* when he protested against Ibsen's and Zola's way of "dealing with the reality of life in joyless and pallid words," as a result of which, he claimed, "the intellectual modern drama has failed." He even employed symbolist, almost "decadent," terms in justifying laughter. In the preface to his hilarious farce *The Tinker's Wedding,* he wrote that "Baudelaire calls laughter the greatest sign of the Satanic element in man"—a reference hardly calculated to endear the play to the Irish public, which found it outrageously anticlerical. Perhaps the most appealing element in O'Neill's early realistic plays, especially those dealing with the sea, is their brooding atmospheric quality. And in our own times, Tennessee Williams has brought to the theatre a symbolist sensibility.

Nevertheless, it is difficult not to arrive at the conclusion that the symbolist achievement in playwriting fell short of expectations. Only in the one-act play did the results prove entirely rewarding. The short flight of poetic perception, the brief excursion rather than the exploration of an action or argument, was the symbolist playwrights' main contribution to the modern drama which they set out to transfigure. Except for a rarity like *The Playboy of the Western World,* which is leavened by a folk humor that owes nothing to symbolism, the masterpieces of the movement are short pieces such as Maeterlinck's *The Intruder* and Synge's *Riders to the Sea.* The best of these plays is probably the latter, and the persuasiveness and power of the work derive not so much from the symbolism of the sea as from the reality of ordinary existence conveyed by the play. Synge's justly celebrated poetic dialogue, too, is derived from the dialect of the Aran Islanders, among whom he lived for a time. The dialogue of *Riders to the Sea* is the dramatically shaped speech of real people, so that here again Synge unintentionally gained a victory for realism.

Yeats, who was the sponsor of Synge as well as of Ireland's Abbey Theatre, dreamed of establishing a symbolist theatre, but got instead a realistic one. And if the drama produced by Irish playwrights was poetic, it was essentially realistic peasant drama. It was poetic because the natural speech of the Irish peasantry abounded in imagery and cadence. Yeats himself managed to create impressive poetic theatre in a series of remarkable short plays, such as *A Full Moon in March* and *Purgatory.* But they were written after 1917 when the symbolist movement had receded in Europe and the possibility of giving the Irish national theatre a new antirealistic direction had vanished.

Extreme symbolism in playwriting resulted in a negation, rather than in a new form, of drama whenever the play became static and stopped dead in its tracks or moved in a fog of chiaroscuro impenetrable by any clear dramatic meaning, as was the case in Maeterlinck's *The Seven Princesses* and in his moody passage to nowhere, *The Death of Tintagiles.* Such misty endeavors were usually associated with an ambition to express the inexpressible—an aspiration to which the classic answer remains Samuel Johnson's comment on the mystic Jacob Boehme, "if what Jacob has to say is ineffable, Jacob should not say it." Carried to their logical extreme in the theatre, symbolist principles would have undermined dramatic art, since a play must embody specific action capable of active materialization—that is, of realization on the stage.

The cult of the mysterious and the mystical reached such extremes that the following satirical description by Rémy de Gourmont of the exemplary drama of the "soul state" is hardly exaggerated:

> Hidden in mist somewhere there is an island, and on that island there is a castle, and in that castle there is a great room lit by a little lamp. And in that room people are waiting. Waiting for what? They don't know! They're waiting for somebody to knock at their door, waiting for their lamp to go out, waiting for Fear and Death. They talk. Yes, they speak words that shatter the silence of the moment. And then they listen again, leaving their sentences unfinished, their gestures uncompleted. They are listening. They are waiting. Will she come perhaps, or won't she? Yes, she will come; she always comes. But it is late, and she will not come perhaps until the morrow. The people collected under that little lamp in that great room have, nevertheless, begun to smile; they still have hope. Then there is a knock—a *knock*, and that is all there is: And it is Life Complete, All of Life.[19]

And that is drama complete, all of drama, drama equally remote from pre-Ibsen drama of "action" and modern "drama of ideas"!

The effect, we may add, was not substantially different when the drama was active and dealt with something as specific as social conflict. The subject could be generalized or symbolized away by the idealizing faculty if the playwright happened to be a poetic playwright—say, an Émile Verhaeren, the celebrated

[19] Rémy de Gourmont, *Le Livre des masques.*—Quoted in a slightly different translation in S. J. I. Lawson's translation of *Belphégor* by Julien Benda (New York, 1929), p. 47.

Flemish rhapsode in the Whitman tradition who wrote *Les Aubes* in 1898, or Andreyev, who wrote *King Hunger* in 1907. Poetry or some rhetorical substitute could always be used to abet the process of erosion by generalization and liquification by symbolization. "Poetic drama" became synonymous in the public mind with attenuated drama, and little has happened in recent decades to eradicate that impression. By comparison with the events of history, symbolic literary pieces such as the Nobel Prize winner Lagerkvist's *The Man Without a Soul,* Philip Barry's *Liberty Jones,* and Fry's *A Sleep of Prisoners* were indubitably feeble.

As for moderate symbolist or neo-romantic developments in playwriting, as well as moderately symbolic stage settings, it must be noted that they did not actually transform the theatre. Fantasies such as Maeterlinck's *Blue Bird,* Sutton Vane's *Outward Bound,* and Sir James Barrie's *Dear Brutus* and *Mary Rose* present themselves to us as "real" stories. In these and similar plays we are expected, indeed, to be absorbed or stimulated by the very contrast between the imagined action and its matter-of-fact presentation. Realistic *structure* remained intact in many neo-romantic and symbolist plays, even in those which were written in verse; only the texture of the writing was affected by moderate antirealism. This is equally apparent in Rostand's *Cyrano de Bergerac,* Maxwell Anderson's *Elizabeth the Queen* and *Winterset,* and Christopher Fry's *The Lady's Not for Burning.* The one departure from conventional realistic dramaturgy in many poetic pieces is a reversion to the use of soliloquy.

The realists' idea of theatre as the art of producing an illusion of social and psychological reality and the symbolists' ideal of theatre as the art of producing the illusion of spiritual reality were not actually in conflict, although they sometimes appeared to be. The realists used illusion for one kind of truth, the symbolists, for another. Where the former demanded reality from the theatre, the latter demanded magic. And magic is, of course, entirely dependent upon illusion.

Illusion *per se* was well served by some of the innovations of the Appia-Craig school, so that it became possible to justify the scenic revolution of the symbolist scene designers on grounds entirely agreeable to realists. For one thing, both symbolists and realists opposed the use of the old makeshift and artificial-looking scenery. And if Craig and other advocates of the art theatre wanted a unified, thoroughly supervised stage production, so did the painstaking Stanislavsky and other pioneers of realistic theatre. An able spokesman for the more or less symbolist art theatre was Hiram Kelly Moderwell. In his book *The Theatre of Today*, published in 1914, he called attention to the symbolists' concept of *Inszenierung* not as the mere designing of scenery, but as the complete process of putting a play upon the stage by a single ruling spirit, the super-director or *régisseur*, who was then becoming the autocrat of the theatre. The symbolist school expected the *régisseur* to endow the stage production with a "soul"—that is, with a spiritual and universal meaning. Moderwell also set forth the great improvements in the creation of verisimilitude that had been accomplished by the new plastic staging, improvements that could serve the realists just as well as they were serving the symbolists:

> A landscape in modern *inscenierung* is not a paper and canvas copy of leaves and grass and shrubbery, but the picture of that landscape, the leaves forming a dark mass, the road a cleft of white in the greenery, and the shrubbery a mass of dark at the side. The background is a real solid, not a flimsy panel; it is a real distance, not a flapping sky curtain. . . . Light and shade are not painted on canvas, but are the living consequences of a real light.[20]

Even the mood-inducing lighting effects advocated by Appia promoted illusion. They brought the spectator into intimate relation with the stage action or stage picture; the expressive shadows of Appian lighting could cast a spell on the spectator or draw him emotionally into the scene. The natural light that prevailed in the open-air Greek and Elizabethan theatres must

[20] Pages 65-66.

have had the very opposite (and thus nonillusionistic) effect of "distancing" and "cooling off" the drama on the stage. Irving Pichel was surely right in reminding us that

> light in these ancient theatres—the light of the sun—did not reinforce the "mood" of the play or scene, but mitigated it. Oedipus, his eyes streaming blood; or the wholesale slaughters of Elizabethan tragedies, must have seemed happily less terrible to an audience seated in the sun.[21]

Symbolist playwrights, in the main, merely blurred or softened the outlines of realistic dramaturgy with their mood-drenched style of writing, their mysterious pauses and repetitions, their portentous indefiniteness. The fourth-wall convention, indeed, had an advantage for the devoted symbolist, who preferred indistinct effects to distinct ones. By separating the actor from the audience, the fourth-wall convention "distanced" the dramatic performance; and the romanticism of the symbolists disposed them to favor some means of distancing experience and of keeping reality veiled and at arm's length. The theory of "esthetic distance," propounded for contemporary American theatre practice by John Dolman,[22] is, in a sense, a symbolist ideal,

[21] "Lighting," *Theatre Arts* (March 1934), p. 616.
[22] *The Art of Play Production* (Harper, 1928), pp. 35-62. Dolman referred to the theory developed in Ethel Puffer's book *The Psychology of Beauty* (published in 1905, while the symbolist movement was still in vogue) that "complete aesthetic pleasure is to be found only in perfect repose," and that such repose appeared "only in a perfect balance of emphatic responses, a balance equivalent to neutralization." This view accorded very well, of course, with Maeterlinck's ideal of static drama. Nothing, however, was more remote from the aims of such aggressive realists as Ibsen, Strindberg, and Shaw than a "balance of emphatic responses." Bertram Jessup, in an article entitled "The Play as Esthetic Object" (*Educational Theatre Journal*, October 1952) supplied an admirably lucid description of the theory of esthetic distance, also referred to as "psychic distance," in saying "that a work of art fails as a work when it engages the spectator's real-life interests, practical or theoretical, so intimately that he gets worked up about them." However, Ibsen, Strindberg, and Shaw, as well as many later realists, wanted the spectator to get "worked

but the pathos of distance or remoteness that appears, for instance, in Gordon Craig's settings, is a romantic manifestation independent of the psychology of audience reaction that Dolman had in mind.

A new use was found for the fourth-wall convention by the symbolists; it helped them to create a different kind of illusion than that favored by the realists—namely, the *illusion of unreality*. This illusion reflected the belief that we live in a mysterious, "poetic" universe rather than in a concrete world of facts. At the same time, however, the illusion of reality also acquired a new, practical justification. It was often felt to be a necessity by those who wrote and staged fantasies, fables, miracle plays, and symbolic dramas or allegories. The playwright who composed a fantasy such as *The Sunken Bell* or *The Blue Bird* actually needed more, rather than less, illusion of reality than the author of a thoroughly credible play such as *A Doll's House* or *Uncle Vanya*. The new stagecraft, therefore, had to be just as facile in making the unreal seem real as in making the real seem unreal.

The symbolist movement, it is true, offered one radical dramaturgic concept—namely, the idea of "static drama." But it was a sterile concept, except in the field of the short one-act play, and thus could not generate a new dramatic form. We can observe this best in Maeterlinck's famous one-act plays *The Intruder, Interior,* and *The Blind.* The absence of marked action in these works was explained by Maeterlinck as a profounder sort of

---

up." As a matter of fact, so did a number of expressionists (such as Toller and Hans von Chlumberg, when they wrote anti-war plays after World War I), the epic realists Erwin Piscator and Bertolt Brecht, and the postwar "theatricalist" producer-directors Meyerhold, Tairov, and Nikolai Okhlopkov, the latter a pioneer in central staging. It is worth observing, indeed, that even symbolist playwrights did not consider themselves absolutely committed to esthetic detachment. "Repose" was surely not an objective in such passionate dramas of revolt as Émile Verhaeren's *Les Aubes* (translated as *The Dawn*) and Leonid Andreyev's *King Hunger.*

realism, evocative of "a deeper, more human, more universal life." When he decried action-filled dramas as superficial and inharmonious with modern probings into life, Maeterlinck was actually fighting the same battle against melodrama that had been fought by the realists and, especially, their extremist wing, the naturalists. His "static drama" was not genuinely "new" drama. It was naturalistic playwriting with its teeth drawn.

A sentence that is not usually quoted precedes the famous passage in Maeterlinck's manifesto of 1896, "The Tragical in Daily Life," which begins with his belief that "an old man seated in his armchair . . . giving unconscious ear to all the eternal laws that reign about his house" lives the ideal life for treatment in modern drama.[23] The neglected sentence is: "I admire Othello, but he does not appear to me to live the august life of a Hamlet, who has time to live, inasmuch as he does not act" (p. 105). But the sentence in Maeterlinck's essay containing the key to the symbolist *mystique* is the rhetorical question (p. 99): "Must we indeed roar like the Atrides before the Eternal God will reveal himself in our life?"

Only for purposes of classification, nevertheless, are we obliged to place Maeterlinck in absolute opposition to Ibsen. Maeterlinck perceived no gulf between himself and the master of realism. Like Henry James, Maeterlinck noted a good deal of symbolism and obscurity—an ambiguity or subtlety that used to be called "Northern mist"—in Ibsen's work. He admired this quality, whereas other critics at that time complained that Ibsen was too obscure. Maeterlinck's manifesto concludes with four complimentary paragraphs about *The Wild Duck*. Ibsen, referred to as "the old master," is said to have "freed certain powers of the soul that have never yet been free." Maeterlinck was also impressed with *The Master Builder* and was especially pleased to be able to quote its hero, Solness, who tells his Nordic Lorelei,

[23] Maurice Maeterlinck, *Le Tragique quotidien*, 1896: Translated as "The Tragical in Daily Life," in *The Treasure of the Humble*, New York and London, 1907. Reproduced in part in Barrett H. Clark's *European Theories of the Drama* (New York, Crown Publishers, 1947), pp. 412-413.

'Look you, Hilda, look you! There is sorcery in you, too, as there is in me. It is this sorcery that imposes action on the powers of the beyond. And we *have* to yield to it. Whether we want to or not, we must." According to Maeterlinck, Hilda and Solness are, therefore, "the first characters in drama who feel, for instance, that they are living in the atmosphere of the soul." And for Maeterlinck to say that he found "soul" in a play was, of course, the highest praise.

The temptation to call Chekhov a symbolist was strong among friends of the symbolist movement. Hiram Moderwell, writing in 1914, claimed him for the symbolists by relating Chekhovian playwriting to static drama. Chekhov's plays "are almost completely static" and are written for the sake of character: "For whole acts there may be no sign of plot-action. Acting occurs only when the author needs it for the purpose of producing a change in character." The plays "have no movement, they do not seem to be 'getting anywhere,' " and to appreciate them "you must be content to sit back in your seat with a soul at rest," in "the mood in which one sits for hours before a wood fire, learning to know a friend from remarks dropped at long intervals in the silence." The critic was pleased to add that the dramas of Chekhov's friend Gorki were also "static," especially *The Lower Depths*.[24] Since the original publication of Moderwell's views, hardly any support has been given them. Chekhov himself would have rejected them, for his rejection of symbolist art in general is clear enough in *The Sea-Gull*. Chekhov parodies symbolist writing in the play within the play written by the character Konstantin, the young artist. Chekhov's reflector-character, Doctor Dorn, says of Konstantin's work, "He creates impressions, never more than that, but on mere impressions you don't go far." And Konstantin himself admits, before tearing up all his manuscripts and shooting himself, that "I still move in a chaos of images and dreams." At the beginning of the play he had declared,

[24] *The Theatre of Today* (1914), pp. 190-193.

THE "ELIZABETHAN" PLATFORM STAGE *This scene, from the Shakespearewrights' 1955 production of* The Merchant of Venice *in New York, illustrates the use of a platform and an architectural background of abstract character in contemporary productions. The scene photographed here* presented *Portia's residence more than it* represented *it. Nor could one have determined without hearing the dialogue whether the scene was an interior or an exterior view. For a more or less interior view, as here, the scene was indeed illusionistically adequate, although too abstract for realism. For an exterior scene, the stage, which remained unaltered throughout the production, was distinctly nonillusionistic or formal. (The steps leading from the low platform to the floor of the auditorium might have suggested a descent to a Venetian canal, but such an illusionistic effect in an exterior scene would have been subjective, since nothing in the stage business of the production involved the use of canals.)*

In the 1950's the Shakespearewrights distinguished themselves by the excellence of their economical and vigorous off-Broadway productions. By that time, however, so-called "Elizabethan staging" already had a long history. William Poel's experiments began about sixty years earlier with his staging of Measure for Measure *in 1893, for which he converted the Royalty Theatre of London into a near-replica of the Fortune Theatre of Elizabethan times. The next year Poel founded the Elizabethan Stage Society, which gave Elizabethan productions from 1895 to 1905. (See Robert Speaight's* William Poel and the Elizabethan Revival, *London, 1954.)*

A critical analysis of Elizabethan staging has long been overdue. A Shakespearean production, of course, needs a great deal more than a platform in order to deserve a certificate of merit. For one thing, the actors must be able to make the characters come to life and to speak Shakespeare's music. Furthermore, the absence of all décor is not necessarily a virtue. And it is a question indeed whether the platform may not be treated more imaginatively—perhaps with more creative use of levels—than an antiquarian interest or simple convenience requires. Photograph: Zinn-Arthur. Courtesy of the Shakespearewrights.

THE CONSTRUCTIVIST PLATFORM *This exemplary constructivist setting for Tairov's Kamerny Theatre was designed by Alexandra Exter in 1926. A "vertical construction," distinctly theatrical and rhythmic, it is particularly adapted for dance movement with angular stylization. In Tairov's theatricalism, dramatic art was largely conceived in terms of rhythm, and this involved the actor in movements from level to level. Painted scenery and furniture were displaced at the Kamerny by sculptural volumes by 1916, and were later replaced by constructivist scaffolds and ramps. The stage was "liberated" from humdrum realism by being broken up into angles and multiple levels. For Stanislavskian psychological acting Tairov strove to substitute athletic performances aiming at expressive movement and "rhythmic harmony." After 1918, the Kamerny Theatre began to veer from estheticism to social utilitarianism. But the shift of interest, expedient and indeed compulsory under Soviet rule, did not greatly disagree at first with the Kamerny Theatre's original penchant for broadly generalized external action as contrasted with "inner realism" or psychological art developed by Stanislavsky.*

"We must have new forms. New forms we must have, and if we can't get them we'd better have nothing at all." It is doubtful that Chekhov the realist agreed with him, and Chekhov made his ultimately self-critical hero retract this statement in the last act of the play.[25] Yet Chekhov was a very *flexible* realist.

Much symbolist writing for the theatre sounded as if the authors and their creations were talking around a subject or were trying to attach themselves to an experience constantly undergoing deliquescence. The symbolist plays of Maeterlinck, Hofmannsthal, Hauptmann, the young Yeats (from 1892 to 1917), and Alexander Blok variously provide substitutions of fancy, mood, sentiment, and lyric poetry for the substantial characters and well-marked conflicts of realistic drama. Writing of Ibsen in 1893, Henry James could declare, ". . . I feel in him, to the pitch of almost intolerable boredom, the presence and the insistence of life." No such confession could have been wrung from James by the plays of the symbolists. Their elusive and allusive style fingered life through veils. Ronald Peacock, in *The Poet in the Theatre,*[26] refers to Ibsen's "extraordinary sense of precipitated crisis," and adds that Ibsen's situations "seem to have been shaped under the compulsion of an acute emotional response to the utmost concentration of conflict and tension." In the work of only one notable symbolist dramatist, Andreyev, could this compulsion be found. And in Andreyev, the compulsion nearly always borders on hysteria.

In the field of writing, symbolism was intrinsically a program for poets rather than playwrights. When Mallarmé wrote in an early poem, *Les Fenêtres,* "ici-bas est maître"—that is, "the world below is master"—he indicated the direction of the literary movement of which he himself became the leader. Symbolism was essentially an in-going style, whereas the drama is essentially an out-going art.

Compromises were bound to be made in practice, of course; the alternative would have been for the symbolist theatre to re-

[25] The lines quoted are from Stark Young's translation.
[26] New York, Harcourt, Brace & Co., 1945, p. 79.

main a coterie theatre. Practical playwrights like James M. Barrie and Maeterlinck (in his latter days) became merchandisers of fantasy, mysticism, and saccharine. Symbolism proved to be quite profitable once the cult of beauty and spirituality had been translated into show business. It is surely not an irrelevancy to remark here that the antirealistic theatre proved to be no more invulnerable to commercialization than the realistic theatre. And it must be added that an encounter with the anodynes of Maeterlinck and Barrie was not likely to prove stimulating for someone accustomed to the iconoclasm and remorseless analysis of Ibsen or Shaw. It was not difficult to agree with George Jean Nathan's cross remark in the *American Mercury* that "Symbolism is the child of poetic courage and intellectual cowardice." [27]

Subjectivist Disintegration and Epic Reintegration

If symbolism, in the main, merely softened and attenuated realistic dramatic art, expressionism actually caused its disintegration. For expressionism followed a view of life and art that required the destruction of the external shape of reality. And once the expressionist movement was in full swing in the theatre, other antirealistic styles multiplied, each adding a new corrosive factor or principle (that is, some special idea of theatre), since every new school was convinced that the theatre should be remodeled according to its own standards. For the expressionist, the stage was to be a means of projecting the disintegration of modern man and twentieth-century society. For the futurist and the constructivist, the stage was to express the marvelously dynamic nature of the machine. For the surrealist, the stage was to effect a release of the free fantasy of the unconscious which realism in art rigorously restrained.

[27] *American Mercury Reader* (Garden City, N.Y., 1946), p. 355.

The proponents of the new schools discarded realistic dramaturgy as old-fashioned and unsuitable to their requirements. And at the same time each school claimed that it expressed "reality" better than the others. The expressionist claimed that dramatic action patterned after discontinuous dream formation, as in Strindberg's *The Dream Play*, came closest to the truth about life. The expressionist was also ostensibly making some comment on modern man and the machine age in placing more or less twisted and fragmentary characters on the stage. Society, as described by German expressionists, was often indeed little better than a nightmare. Scenic visualization is needed to supplement the text of such rarely staged plays as Georg Kaiser's *From Morn to Midnight* and *Man and the Masses* if we are to grasp their total effect. Fortunately, one good scenic record of the expressionists' social picture is still available: Fritz Lang's memorable film *Metropolis,* made in Germany in 1926.

The surrealists went even further than the expressionists: they rejected familiar reality, with its orderliness and tidy logic, as a delusion. The façade of reality, according to the surrealists, had to be wrecked if the true life of the unconscious were to become manifest in art. And in order to destroy that façade, it was necessary, of course, to destroy the realistic form of drama. Once the façade was removed, irrational occurrences, such as those in Jean Cocteau's *Orpheus* and E. E. Cummings' *him,* would evoke, if not indeed represent, the anxieties, obsessions, and primitive wishes that constitute the true reality that lies behind the surface of everyday behavior.[28]

Inconsistencies, tricks, enigmas, startling juxtapositions, sophisticated anachronism such as Eurydice's receiving letters delivered by a mailman, and, above all, fantasies, such as Orpheus' passage to Death through a mirror—all these fabrications that may well puzzle an audience seem not only permissi-

[28] We must not, however, always take a solemn view of such dramatic exercises; they are sparked by sheer theatrical exuberance and license, as well as, I believe, by the aggressive bohemianism and the nihilistic spirit of dadaism.

ble but desirable to those who agree with Cocteau and the surrealists that fundamental reality is, as D. H. Lawrence would
have called it, a "fantasia of the unconscious." These devices seem
especially appropriate if it is believed, with Jung and his disciples, that the unconscious contains in the forms of symbols the
archetypal emotions of the human race. Thus Wallace Fowlie
defines Cocteau's treatment of the myth of Orpheus and Eurydice as "a meditation of death." [29] And if we yield ourselves entirely to the fantastic occurrences in Cocteau's *Orpheus,* it is
possible that our sense of death may be powerfully, if irra-
tionally, evoked. We may end with a sense of reality unrelated
to reason—a sense that realism, with its concentration on moral
and social issues and objective data, does not evoke. For Cocteau's disintegrative fantasy parallels the disintegration following
death itself, or the sense of disintegration inherent in our common fear of death. We may apply to our possible experience[30] of
more or less surrealistic work the words of André Breton in his
famous manifesto of surrealism: "What is admirable in the fantastic is that it becomes real."

Finally, it is obvious that the modernistic mechanists,
whether "futurists" or "constructivists," were also convinced that
they served reality. When their plays and stage productions made
automata of the characters and turned acting into acrobatics or
puppeteering, they were calling attention to the partial mechanization of their age and the total mechanization that they predicated for the future. Speed, power, and force epitomized their
idea of theatre.[31]

The emphasis on social reality, however, became most pro-

[29] *The Age of Surrealism* (Denver, 1950), p. 128.
[30] I say "possible experience" because neither the playwright nor
the director can be certain that the playgoer will have the experience he is supposed to have in response to the play, whereas the
realist can be certain that his points will be well understood if
he has acquitted himself with competence.
[31] *Proclama sul teatro futurista,* by F. T. Marinetti (1915).

nounced and effective when the director Erwin Piscator and the poet Bertolt Brecht began in the 1920's to develop the modes of playwriting and stage production now known as "epic realism." In the view of the epic realists, drama and the theatre had to undergo a marked expansion of action and setting. Perhaps no one has stated the case for scenic extension of realism more lucidly than the Group Theatre's scene designer Mordecai Gorelik.[32] He maintained that the modern designer

> faces more and more often the problem of how to show two or more scenes simultaneously taking place. One stage is no longer enough on which to present the many facets of a modern dramatic situation: where formerly dramatists wrote plays in three leisurely acts, modern authors pile scene on scene. . . . For the designer the task becomes that of finding half-a-dozen stages where only one was before.

The wheel, then, now turned full circle, back to the multiple stage of the Middle Ages. Reinhardt had returned to this convention early in our century in staging Hofmannsthal's *The Great World Theatre* on separate little stages or "mansions," set in a row. But a quarter of a century later, in 1934, when the vogue of Hofmannsthal's neo-romantic religiosity had been dispersed by the great storm of the economic depression and the fascism of the 1930's, the theatre was urged by Mr. Gorelik to pass out of its introverted period, "to leave dramatic unity for dramatic simultaneity," not for the sake of poetry, but of realism. Henceforth the stage must be able to accommodate not the reality of the individual bourgeois parlor, with its private interests and problems, but the reality of society, with its collective, multifaceted situations and issues. It is significant that in 1934 this highly gifted designer was speaking the language of stylization or theatrical convention without which the modern form of theatre known as "epic" would be formally indistinguishable from the theatre of nineteenth-century realism. In designing *Men*

[32] "The Conquest of Stage Space," *Theatre Arts*, (March 1934), pp. 213-218.

in White, Sidney Kingsley's Pulitzer Prize-winning drama, Gorelik demonstrated how the principle of multiplicity or simultaneity could be successfully followed. He referred to the "conventionalization" of his setting for *Men in White.* Most of it was permanent, although many different scenes were needed in the production. Gorelik called the setting "a formalized structure which does not represent a hospital, but is, rather, suggested by one," and explained that "within this abstract framework, successive scenes in different parts of the hospital are indicated by means of properties."

In neither his designs nor explanations, however, did Gorelik at that time take the direction which would have brought him into the "epic" school. Instead, he noted how his solution of the problem of space (his "mechanical contrivance for obtaining a stage space," as he called it) was accepted by all types of playgoers: "To the layman this type of setting, which ten years ago would have seemed peculiar, is now 'realism.'" He reflected that "the average conception of what is artistically 'real' depends on the prevailing culture and temper of the times."

Epic theatre, however, is candidly theatrical and, one might even say, joyously so. The epic realists, too, required the theatre and the drama to leave the tight little world of private life to which Ibsen's realism was confined. For the theatre to deal effectively with modern realities, plays would have to become "epic" or extensively narrative again, as they had been in the Romantic and Elizabethan theatres. The drama could be thoroughly episodic, as were Brecht's *Mother Courage* and *The Caucasian Circle of Chalk,* but could nevertheless be unified by the demonstration of some point about men's involvement in an issue that is fundamentally social. Neither the play nor the stage production would be required to maintain any consistent illusion of actuality. On the contrary, such illusion was to be destroyed by fragmentation of scenes and settings, by the interruption of action, and by a deliberate severing of suspense. For the aim of epic theatre was to present a demonstration of some aspect of social reality, and an exposition of how things work takes a mechanism apart instead of simply photographing the machine once all the parts are in place.

The demonstration might deal with the past in order to provide instruction, as does Brecht's *Galileo;* with the recent past, like Piscator's satirical World War I epic *The Good Soldier Schweik,* or Paul Green's rueful satire on the Wilsonian era, *Johnny Johnson;* or with the present, like *The Private Life of the Master Race,* a semidocumentary drama written by Brecht during World War II that reviewed the rise and collapse of Nazism. The play might be pure fiction, like Brecht's *The Caucasian Circle of Chalk* and *The Good Woman of Setzuan;* the latter is, indeed, a fable set in China which calls for Chinese gods to appear in the first and last episodes without offering any rationalistic explanation for their presence. Or the play might be entirely documentary, as were the "living newspapers" developed during the economic depression of the 1930's—plays appropriately entitled *Power* and *One-third of a Nation* and dealing respectively with the development and ownership of electric power and the problem of abolishing slums in accordance with President Roosevelt's statement that one-third of the nation was ill housed. Whatever the specific treatment of a subject, the shape of the epic drama —a web of episodes, with narratives and lyrical interruptions, choral chants and hortatory lectures—was radically different from that of the realistic drama; and the epic productions, even when abounding in realistic detail, did not employ strictly realistic acting, but stylized the performances to various degrees.

A demonstration of the working of social forces cannot rest upon the inwardness of private sensation and the meticulous creation of characters who draw attention to their private selves rather than to the factors operative in the world around them. And the stage, when adapted to the requirements of the demonstration, cannot use the static settings of the realistic theatre. Moving or revolving platforms, treadmills carrying pieces of scenery, charts, cartoons, and projected films were pressed into service by epic stage directors. The stage was made dynamic. It was treated as a constantly operating machine, practical because it provided visual aids to learning. The "stage-as-machine" concept, treated in other instances as a theatrical toy for playful effects, as in one modernist staging of Aristophanes' comedy *Lysistrata,* was used by Piscator, for example, in staging Robert Penn Warren's *All the King's Men,* which had first been written as a play before being turned into a novel. This play was not only epic in its dimensions (it dealt with a political figure whose career involved an entire state and affected an entire nation), but it was compounded in the epic manner of various elements; it had scenes of narration, commentary, and analysis as well as of episodic action. In producing this drama, Piscator employed a constantly (and to the critic Brooks Atkinson, annoyingly) revolving stage structure that looked like a machine with a high rectangular frame. Some scenes were also placed on the platform in front of this "machine," and a neutral area near the wings was occupied by the narrator-character, who analyzed the action or otherwise commented on it.

Perhaps nothing, however, exemplifies the essential theatricality of epic realism so much as the type of acting Brecht has endeavored to develop and on which he has written in some detail. The subject of epic acting requires too much space to be discussed here, but a few points may be noted. For example, Brecht came to rely a great deal on gesture. In an article written for a special issue of *World Theatre,* he declared (in addition to claiming for epic acting "naturalness," "humor," and "earthiness"), that "all emotion must become visible and be developed into gesture," and that the emotion "must free itself, *so that it may be treated in the grand manner."* [33] Brecht also recommended a study of the Chinese theatre, because Chinese acting has been "masterly in the treatment of gesture." It is obvious that he believes that it will never do for the actor *not* to stylize his

[33] *World Theatre,* Vol. IV, No. 1 (1955). The italics are mine.

performance. And it is by stressing theatricalization of the action that Brecht gets the effect he especially wants—the *Verfremdung,* or alienation[34] he believes necessary to his kind of theatre.

Whether factual or imaginative in subject matter as well as treatment, epic theatre represents a revolutionary twentieth-century departure from the essentially settled, individually oriented, emotion-based middle-class world of the realistic drama of the nineteenth century. That drama tended to present the individual as an end in himself; epic realism, however, may be in some jeopardy whenever the sympathy of the playwright (or the actor) creates rounded and moving characterization. Brecht was disturbed, for example, when his Zurich audience identified itself with the "Niobe-heroine" of his *Mother Courage;* therefore he made alterations in the text with the object of reducing the emotional charge of the play. The camp-following mother, who loses all her children, was not to be allowed to interpose her suffering humanity between the public and the author's intention to demonstrate "das rein merkantile Wesen des Kriegs," the "purely commercial nature of war." [35] Brecht has rejected the value of emotional identification and catharsis on the grounds that a play should leave audiences in possession of their critical faculties so that they may learn something conducive to social realism. He has been a strenuous opponent of illusionistic stage production and Stanislavskian acting, which is individualistic "inner realism" based upon the actor's thorough identification with the character he plays. Brecht, calling for *Verfremdung* instead, requires the actor to stand outside the part so that his performance may become a more or less detached comment on the character. Epic theatre is both antirealistic and anti-Aristotelian; and this cool, rationalistic school of neorealism has actually jolted the foundations of Western drama more drastically, because much more effectively, than any of the primarily subjectivistic deviations from realism. After the vogue of subjectivity, epic

[34] See "The Alienation Effect" in *Actors on Acting,* ed. Toby Cole and Helen Krich Chinoy, pp. 281-285.
[35] Brecht's *Versuche 20/21* (Frankfurt am Main, 1949).

objectivity introduced a mode of reintegration into dramatic art; but this reintegration was nothing less than revolutionary when consistently accomplished.

The Expressionist Assault on the Theatre

We may conclude, then, that once expressionists began to violate the realistic form in dramaturgy and stage production (first Strindberg in his late plays, then his followers before and after World War I), it was possible for the character of drama and theatre to be reshaped endlessly. And in each phase of that reshaping, as I have briefly indicated, there were involved concepts of dramatic art or ideas of theatre art that had been developed in reaction to realistic dramaturgy and stagecraft.

To some degree, nearly every school of theatre that departed radically from realism can be described as tending to be more or less expressionistic, and the term "expressionism" has therefore been used rather loosely at times to differentiate from realism all the antirealistic modern styles. There is one advantage in so using the term: it covers a concept of theatre as the comprehensive dramatic *expression*, rather than the more or less literal *representation*, of a subject. Nevertheless, "expressionism" is a confusing term when employed so broadly. Not only have the definitions and claims of its exponents been contradictory, but my generalization has thus far made bedfellows of incompatible schools. The epic realism of Piscator and Brecht, for example, is objective art, whereas expressionism is predominantly subjective; the epic realist considers himself to be an opponent of both naturalism and expressionism.

"Expressionism" is least confusing as a term when used to describe a single, more or less distinct, style of playwriting and theatrical production. It is the general style which, beginning in some of the work of Strindberg at the turn of the century (notably *The Dream Play* and *The Ghost Sonata*) became a theatrical movement in the years from just before to just after World War I. Strindberg struck the keynote of the expressionist theory of theatre when he wrote, in his preface to *The Dream Play* (1902) that in this play, as in his earlier trilogy *To Damascus,*

> Anything may happen; everything is possible and probable. Time and space do not exist. On an insignificant background of reality, Imagination designs and embroiders novel patterns; a medley of memories, experiences, free fantasies, absurdities, and improvisations.

He rightly called this play a *dream play* because, as he declared, "The author has tried to imitate the disconnected but seemingly logical form of the dream." His successors in expressionist experimentation made a veritable cult of morbid introspection and emotionally disturbed pictures of external reality.

Schizophrenic, oedipal, and murder fantasies especially abounded in the Central European literary world that produced explosive pieces such as Walter Hasenclever's *The Son* and Paul Kornfeld's *The Seduction* even before the traumatic experience of World War I.[36] The world of Ibsenism and the world of extreme expressionistic (not to say surrealistic) stylization had nothing in common; or one might say that the world of the former could be found shattered to shards in the nightmare world of the latter. "The intelligent man known to history flourishes within a dullard and holds a lunatic in leash." So says Santayana in *The Life of Reason*. In ultraexpressionistic theatre, the intelli-

---

[36] A few dates should prove helpful here: Strindberg's two most influential expressionistic plays, *The Dream Play* and *The Ghost Sonata*, were published in 1902 and 1907 respectively. The expressionistic drama reached its peak in Europe between 1912 and 1925; it was paralleled in fiction by the work of Kafka and Joyce. The minor vogue of expressionism in the American theatre occurred between 1920, the date of O'Neill's *The Emperor Jones*, and 1924, the date of George S. Kaufman and Marc Connelly's *Beggar on Horseback*.

gent man was never found without the lunatic, and sometimes could not be distinguished from him.

Oskar Kokoschka, one of the early Central European expressionists who was a playwright as well as a painter, plainly declared in a manifesto that "we must harken closely to our inner voice. . . . All that is required of us is to release control. . . . All laws are left behind. One's soul is a reverberation of the universe." [37] Another leader of the movement, Lothar Schreyer, called it "the spiritual movement of a time that places inner experience above external life." Often some social or spiritual problem dealt with in a play was presented in a character's dream. Interest in psychoanalysis gave special support to the dream-technique in the theatre after 1912. But it is a generally subjective orientation rather than dream formation *per se* that is most characteristic of expressionism. And expressionism did, of course, differ in degree and in the manner in which it was used in plays and stage productions. It could permeate a play entirely, so that everything about it was fantastic and expressively distorted, as in *The Dream Play* and *The Ghost Sonata,* or it could share the play, more or less, with the realistic style, as in O'Casey's *The Silver Tassie.* Expressionism could be intensive in some scenes and mild in others. In O'Neill's *The Hairy Ape,* for instance, the Fifth Avenue scene, in which Yank's frustration and disorientation reach a climax, is unmistakably expressionistic. The style of some other scenes (such as Scene 2, on the promenade deck, and Scene 7, in an "I.W.W. local") is not particularly distinguishable from naturalism. Expressionism, moreover, could be either a means towards an end, as when it was employed to underscore some plot situation or some character's state of mind; or it could be an end in itself, as when the entire play and the production were intended to exhibit a chaotic or nihilistic view of reality, as in the previously mentioned Strindberg plays.

[37] Edith Hoffman, *Kokoschka: Life and Work* (London: Faber and Faber, 1947), p. 286.

Whether expressionism was employed partially or completely in playwriting and play production, this much is clear: dramatic form and styles of acting and stage production were more drastically altered by expressionism than by any other style. In the twentieth-century theatre, expressionism introduced the most distinctive modifications of dramatic form and exemplified the most intensive use of free dramatic presentation short of surrealist "free-association" methods. In expressionism could be found the boldest assertion of the artist as the creator of a world independent of objective appearance and the expression of his defiance of a society more inexorable than that of the philistine-Victorian bourgeoisie—namely, the machine-age world whose destructiveness was the theme of such fanciful plays as *Gas* and *R.U.R.*

The expressionist playwright dispensed with the "middle-class" clutter to be found in men's minds and showed only the springs of passion. He did not hesitate to present depersonalized characters, individuals transformed into stark symbols or allegorical types deprived of a personal name—figures called merely Man, Woman, The Unknown, and so on. And the individual was likely to be placed in a truncated scene usually deprived of the padding of "manners" and small talk customary in cup-and-saucer living-room scenes. Only the *dramatic moment* was allowed to matter. This moment was given to the spectator without the familiar preparatory detail of nineteenth-century realism; frequently, it was hurled at him like a missile. In some plays the individual was submerged in the automatism of a milling and shrieking chorus, as in the mob scenes of Kaiser's *Gas*, Toller's *Man and the Masses*, and O'Neill's *The Hairy Ape* (in the firemen's forecastle of Scenes 1 and 4). The expressionist, giving the reins to his own fancy and intensifying his characters' subjective states, felt free to distort all manifestations of character and environment and to shuttle back and forth in time and space. For his purposes the imagination was entirely free to violate the rules of logic and art.

The physical transformations of characters and settings

called for in expressionist dramas offered almost operatic opportunities for the exercise of imagination by the scene designer and the stage electrician. Georg Kaiser calls for the sudden transformation of a snow-laden tree into a skeleton in *From Morn to Midnight*. In Strindberg's *Dream Play* there are such stage directions as the one that reads, rather blithely, "The background is lit up by the burning castle and reveals a wall of human faces, questioning, grieving, despairing. As the castle breaks into flames, the bud on the roof opens into a gigantic chrysanthemum." It is not this sort of Wagnerianism, however, that represents an essential change in form. Fundamental change is to be found in the expressionist treatment of the dramatic action and characterization—that is, in a characteristic fragmentation and distortion of their substance. The distortion, besides, could be motivated either by a character's state of mind (the play being shown through his disturbed sensorium), or by the author's intention to reveal his own disturbed frame of mind or make a figurative appraisal of man and the world. Most of the scenes in *From Morn to Midnight* and *The Emperor Jones* are "subjective" in the sense that the fantastic action and environment are dramatically related to the state of mind of an absconding cashier and an escaping Negro dictator respectively. In other plays, such as *The Dream Play* and *The Ghost Sonata,* the entire work is the phantasmagoria of the author-poet. In still other plays, there is a continual interchange between the real and the unreal that defies analysis, while in some dramas, such as the rather elementary *Beggar on Horseback*, there is a clear distinction between real action and the main character's dream.

Among the changes wrought by expressionism in the structure and the texture of the drama, those that affected dialogue were especially notable. Dialogue was subjected to weird abbreviations and distortions, so that it became frequently violent, telegraphic, and enigmatic. This was particularly true of the work of the German expressionists between 1912 and 1925.

Examples of such dialogue from Ernst Toller's play about the postwar uprising, *Man and the Masses* (1919), read as follows in Louis Untermeyer's translation:

CHORUS
　　Someone tell the doorman:
　　Five hundred
　　gay
　　young girls
　　Wanted here.
　　Meanwhile . . .

　　We donate.
　　We dance!
　　Help
　　The unfortunate.

　　Schools.
　　Barracks.
　　War.
　　Always.
THE GUARDS: To the wall with him.
NAMELESS ONE: Guns loaded?
THE GUARDS: Loaded.
THE PRISONER (*against the wall*): Life! Life!

Even a moderately expressionist play such as *The Hairy Ape,* produced in 1922, employs this kind of telegraphese, as in the chorus of stokers in the first scene, which reads:

　　Gif me a drink dere, you!
　　'Ave a wet!
　　Salute
　　Gesundheit!
　　Skoal!
　　Drunk as a lord, God stiffen you!
　　Luck!

—and so on for 28 consecutive speeches. The action, especially in the Fifth Avenue scene, becomes increasingly frantic as well as unreal, as in the following episode in which Yank, the burly half-animal and half-human stoker, confronts the well-dressed men and women who have come out of church:

> YANK: . . . I'm steel and steam and smoke and de rest of it. It moves—speed—twenty-five stories up—and me at de top and bottom—movin'! Youse simps don't move. You're only dolls I winds up to see 'em spin . . . [*But as they seem neither to see nor hear him, he flies into a fury . . . He turns in a rage on the* Men, *bumping viciously into them but not jarring them the least bit. Rather it is he who recoils after each collision* . . .]

It would be possible to cite many situations and sequences of dialogue much more fantastic than any of O'Neill's. Such German dramatists as Hasenclever, Kaiser, Von Unruh, and Toller were particularly fertile between 1912 and 1925 in evoking violent states of mind, and German stage directors such as Leopold Jessner and Jürgen Fehling were past masters in the art of staging plays with expressive speed, exaggeration and distortion. And it is to be noted that much support for this type of theatre came from a general spread of expressionist views of art, especially in painting. Oskar Kokoschka, considered one of the most gifted of expressionist painters, was also the author of several inchoate plays—*Sphinx* and *Straw Man, The Hope of Women,* and *The Burning Bush*—during the period of 1909-1913 when he also exhibited some of his most daring paintings in Vienna. At the climax of expressionist fervor in Germany, the playwright Kasimir Edschmidt could boast, rather naively but not inaccurately, that "the expressionist believes in a reality which he himself creates against all other reality." [38] A major revolution in the theatre was implied in this statement; if one had taken the expressionists' claims at face value, it could have been assumed that the age of realism was, indeed, over.

[38] Thomas L. Dickinson, *The Theatre in a Changing Europe* (Holt, 1937), p. 23.

Ironically, however, it was expressionism, not realism, that became outmoded. Even in Central Europe the movement was virtually dead by 1925, while the realistic theatre which expressionism was supposed to have extinguished continued to press strong claims. Nor were these claims fundamentally challenged by any great successes in nonrealistic playwriting when the expressionists' efforts were supplemented by those of surrealists in France. Stage production, once greatly enriched by symbolist art, was further enriched (when not utterly disintegrated, of course) by expressionism and by such other experiments in stylization as surrealism and constructivism. But one by one the extremist antirealistic kinds of theatre went out of fashion—perhaps for the reason that they had come *into* fashion. (I believe it was Joyce who said once, "Futurism has no future.") The various revolts against realism in the theatre were fizzling out by 1930.

Nevertheless, one cannot rule out expressionism, both in the general sense of antirealistic dramaturgy and in the specific sense of an extravagantly subjective style, as the *second* radical phase of dramatic modernism.

Although theatrical fashions have come and gone, something indeed remained from each change in dramatic form and style of production. There remained not merely a collection of plays written more or less under the influence of some literary or theatrical program, but also a variety of theatrical practices. The ramps used so freely during the expressionist 1920's are in common use today. Skeletal settings will be found nowadays in productions of realistic plays like Elmer Rice's *Two on an Island*, allegorical ones like Robert Anderson's *All Summer Long*, and semi-expressionistic, semirealistic ones like *Death of a Salesman*. And it is almost everywhere evident that naturalistic clutter of detail on the stage has been displaced by tasteful selectivity, even in dominantly realistic productions. This "selective realism" can be called "imaginative realism" when it is at its freest, as in Elia Kazan's staging of Tennessee Williams' *Cat on a Hot Tin Roof* in 1955. No other term would do justice to room partitions and house walls suggested by wire-like verticals, imaginary doors that have to be "opened" and "closed" with conventional rehearsal movements, and a platform built out beyond the footlight area into the front rows of the theatre. And the imagination was further aroused—or taxed—when Mr. Kazan's actors, standing on this quasi-Elizabethan platform, looked intently into space as though gazing into a mirror hanging on the fourth wall and addressed their thoughts, *treated as both soliloquy and colloquy* at the same time, to characters standing behind them.

In various ways, then, playwriting and stage production were retheatricalized by the various schools of stylization that germinated after 1890. In scenic art, there were even instances of a return to painted scenery; with some modifications, indeed, so that the old perspective wing-and-drop settings have not returned, except in period revivals such as the Theatre Guild production of Molière's *The School for Husbands* in the 1930's. Changes in the training of actors and in styles of performances have also reflected various degrees of retheatricalization. If extreme deviations have become uncommon, modifications of realism continue to appear. Jacques Copeau, a leading figure of the reformation of the postnaturalistic theatre as early as 1913, summed up the minimal modifications in scenery about a quarter of a century later for the 1935 edition of the *Encyclopédie Française:* "Our designers . . . aim at impressions rather than descriptions. . . . They single out a part in order to indicate the whole; a tree instead of a forest, a pillar instead of a temple." [39] As for the art of acting, the most generally held view amounts to perhaps a little more than the statement from Vakhtangov, Stanislavsky's most talented if by no means submissive pupil, that "the actor's inner experience must be conveyed to the auditorium with the help of theatrical means." [40] Vakhtangov made this declaration in 1922; by then, indeed, there was no longer

[39] *Directing the Play*, ed. Toby Cole and Helen Krich Chinoy (Bobbs-Merrill Co., 1952), p. 149.
[40] *Ibid.*, p. 160.

any unmodified realism in the theatre without special reason.

The modern stage, however, has not reached any noticeable equilibrium: conflicts and confusions have abounded, an almost continuous state of crisis has existed in the theatre, and the search for new forms of dramatic art has gone on both with and without fanfare. At the midcentury, all theatrical movements with an antirealistic program, except epic theatre, appear to have exhausted themselves. But the impulse to retheatricalize the art that militant nineteenth-century realism had detheatricalized has continued to make itself felt.

A Note on Romanticism and Symbolism

It is well known, of course, that a particularly strong current of antirealistic modern theatre can be subsumed under the loose heading of "romanticism," just as it can be subsumed under the loose name of "poetic drama." Romanticism was revived in the theatre after 1890 (the revival has been labeled "neo-romanticism"), and the first masterpiece in this mode, *Cyrano de Bergerac,* has been one of the favorite plays of the modern stage. Romanticism has indeed continued to yield attractive and popular plays throughout the century: familiar examples in English are Maxwell Anderson's Elizabethan verse plays *Elizabeth the Queen, Mary of Scotland,* and *Anne of the Thousand Days* and Christopher Fry's verse play *The Lady's Not for Burning.* Neo-romanticism, however, did not by itself introduce any change of dramatic form that cannot be described as a reversion from Ibsen's realistic dramaturgy to the loose Elizabethan dramaturgy of the theatre of Schiller, Goethe, and Hugo. There has been, therefore, no need to discuss neo-romanticism in this essay.

Some confusion results, however, from the fact that the spirit of symbolist drama and stage production was undeniably romantic. Even in treating familiar scenes of life, symbolist dramatic art sought to evoke mystery and wonder and the pathos of romantic isolation. The romantic drama, however, is *explicit,* whereas the symbolist drama is suggestive. The former has the clear outlines of a well-defined action, whereas the latter has an elusive, penumbral content. Romantic drama is insistent—as insistent on the plot and the point of honor as *Hernani*—even when mysterious; symbolist drama is ambiguous—as ambiguous as Maeterlinck's *Interior*—even when its content is simple. The language of a contemporary romantic play such as *The Lady's Not for Burning* may indeed bear the implications of poetry and the innuendo of wit, but there can be no doubt that the author has spoken out and has permitted his characters to speak out even more explicitly than their situation warrants. The neo-romantic poet will undoubtedly employ metaphor in his verse or poetic prose, but in symbolist playwriting the play itself may actually become metaphor. Maeterlinck's *The Blind,* Andreyev's *The Black Maskers,* and Yeats' *A Full Moon in March* are examples of metaphorical drama. Inevitably, too, the symbolist movement was propitious to the return of allegory; thus, different degrees of allegorical abstractness have appeared in such plays as Hugo von Hofmannsthal's *Jedermann* (*Everyman*), Andreyev's *The Life of Man,* and Philip Barry's *Here Come the Clowns.* The treatment of environment is, as usual in the theatre, another test. Briefly, the romanticist *glamorizes* the environment or uses it for effects of horror, but, unlike the symbolist, he does not abstract it into a symbol of the soul of the play or the state of mind of a character.

Symbolism, then, produced more radical, as well as more modern, departures from realistic drama than did neo-romanticism. And symbolist scene design, as well as stage production, was also more radical than neo-romantic art. Vivid and glamorous settings for a bakeshop or a battlefield are the standard requirement for *Cyrano de Bergerac.* A symbolist design by Gordon

Craig is, by contrast, *abstract*. Craig exhorted the readers of his early essay *On the Art of the Theatre:* "Do not first look at Nature, but look in the play of the poet." But this was a very moderate statement for Craig and his disciples. They were more inclined to say "Look into the soul of the play." When Robert Edmond Jones designed the Arthur Hopkins production of *Macbeth* in 1921, he relied mainly on three arches set against a dark background. At one point, they hung over the stage and looked like three baleful masks glaring down at Macbeth. At another point in the play, the arches, which otherwise suggested the interior of a Scottish castle-fortress, were crazily tilted as a symbol of the upheaval in the soul of the characters and in the world they have unbalanced with murder and usurpation of power. And at the close of the tragedy the arches toppled over, signifying that Macbeth's destined end had come. Here, obviously, Jones, functioning as an ultra-symbolist designer in this celebrated production, had no intention of providing an objective environment. Here "setting" became "symbol."

After the appearance of symbolist theatre in the 1890's, it became customary for the various antirealistic movements to take liberties with environment that even the romanticists of the "storm and stress" period had not taken; a climax in the arbitrary fragmentation and phantasmagoric reassembling of environmental detail was reached by the expressionists. Henceforth no school of stylization failed to substitute some degree of abstraction for pictorial realism—not excluding the school of epic realism which gave great ideological importance to environmentalism.

It was the symbolist movement, not neo-romanticism, moreover, that made *metaphor* a cornerstone of antirealistic dramaturgy. Expressionist drama and theatre were distinctly metaphorical; and even the epic realists, who had no use for symbolist and expressionist subjectivity, have tended to present their dramatic action as a partly symbolic epitome of a social situation or a problem in social action. Brecht's parables *The Caucasian Circle of Chalk* and *The Good Woman of Setzuan* and the Piscator version of *An American Tragedy* illustrate the important role of metaphor. In epic-styled stage productions, besides, symbolic scenic elements have appeared frequently, although without the veils of Maeterlinckian soul-fetishism.

Because symbols have been employed not only by symbolist playwrights, but even by the classic realist (in such plays as *The Wild Duck, Rosmersholm, The Master Builder, John Gabriel Borkman, The Sea-Gull, The Cherry Orchard, Golden Boy,* and *All My Sons*), it is ill-advised indeed to lump all kinds of symbolization together. Mordecai Gorelik's statement that metaphors are to be judged qualitatively is highly important. There is a significant difference "between a symbol which is packed with observation and experience, and one which is large and 'simple' only because it is pretentious and lacking in observation and experience." [1]

[1] *New Theatres for Old* (New York: Samuel French, 1940), p. 263.

3

Theatricalism and Crisis

Let it be remembered by all who care for the art of the theatre: the play is a show, but only in the sense that it is not real life but a performance enacted on the stage before an audience.
—ALEXANDER BAKSHY,
The Theatre Unbound

I understood that on the stage truth is that in which the actor sincerely believes . . . that even a palpable lie must become a truth in the theatre so that it may become art. For this it is necessary for the actor to develop to the highest degree his imagination . . . an artistic sensitivity to truth and to the truthful in his soul and body.—CONSTANTIN STANISLAVSKY (My Life in Art.)

What once was expressionism is now the normal way of telling a non-realistic story.
—BROOKS ATKINSON
(The N.Y. Times, February 10, 1956.)

I'm glad we nipped progress in the bud. Somewhere between twenty and thirty years ago there was quite a movement in the theatre to dispense with a species known as people, and to substitute . . . the staccato machinery of telegraphic speech, symbolic zeros on the cyclorama, and assorted zoo-sounds pouring in over the loudspeakers.—WALTER F. KERR (New York Herald Tribune, February 10, 1956.)

Today many people smile at Expressionism; at that time it was a necessary artistic form. It took a stand against the kind of art which was satisfied with lining up impressions side by side, asking no questions about the essence, the responsibility, the idea. The Expressionist wanted to do more than take photographs.
—ERNST TOLLER

All literature tends to be concerned with the question of reality—I mean quite simply the old opposition between reality and appearance, between what really is and what merely seems.
—LIONEL TRILLING

For Pirandello, drama is more than an imitation of an action; it is, equally, response to an action.
—MORRIS FREEDMAN

AN ACCOMMODATION BETWEEN THE REALISTIC AND ANTIREALISTIC modes of theatre has long been apparent in playwriting and play production. Often it has been made as a matter of routine practice, and sometimes it has been the unique achievement of talented artists. Not only do we now accept the *coexistence* of different kinds of drama and stage production, but we observe with equanimity the erosion of distinctions once strongly insisted upon by the proponents of various theatrical movements.

The distinctions have lost their sharpness both in playwriting and in critical jargon. Indeed, the labels "symbolism," "surrealism," and "expressionism" no longer possess much significance for most contemporary plays and performances. This is true of even those plays in which it is possible to detect symbolism (for example, Williams' *Summer and Smoke*) or surrealism (Saroyan's *Sweeney in the Trees*), or expressionism (*Death of a Salesman*). It would be as difficult as it would be useless to find exact labels for such plays as Saroyan's *My Heart's in the Highlands* and *The Time of Your Life,* Giraudoux' *The Madwoman of Chaillot,* and the Anouilh-Fry comedy *Ring 'Round the Moon.* So, with commendable discretion, the authors are apt to be content with calling such dramas "poetic plays," "fantasies," or "improvisations." The Anouilh-Fry piece was subtitled a "charade," and Anouilh called his *Thieves' Carnival* (*Le Bal des voleurs,* 1932) a *comédie-ballet.*

William Saroyan was certainly most thorough, if not necessarily most perceptive, in describing a mode of free dramatic creativity when he described his *Sweeney in the Trees* as "a play, a dream, a poem, a travesty, a fable, a symphony, a parable, a comedy, a tragedy, a farce, a vaudeville, a song and dance, a statement on money, a report on life, an essay on art and religion, a theatrical entertainment, a circus, anything you like, whatever you please." [1] With few emendations one could apply some of these descriptions to Giraudoux' *Intermezzo* and *The Madwoman of Chaillot,* Wilder's *The Skin of Our Teeth,* and other pieces by Saroyan, such as *My Heart's in the Highlands,* and *The Time of Your Life.* Nor are we greatly disturbed when these works are, as Wolcott Gibbs said of *The Time of Your Life,* "occasionally balanced on the thin edge of absurdity." We do not require of such plays the unimpeachable consistency of a drama by Ibsen or Sophocles.

There have also been with us for many decades those more or less unified plays in which contrasting, perhaps theoretically incompatible, modes of drama coexist or intermingle. Even in sociological drama, such as Paul Osborn's dramatization of the Marquand novel *Point of No Return,* the main character's past and present may interweave quite freely. An early example of presenting the same situation both objectively and subjectively was provided by Gerhart Hauptmann in *The Assumption of Hannele* (*Hanneles Himmelfahrt,* 1893). The playwright combined an appallingly naturalistic picture of a child's death in the workhouse with the fairy-tale world of her delirium. The demarcation

[1] *The Beautiful People, Sweeney in the Trees,* and *Across the Board on Tomorrow Morning* (Harcourt, Brace, 1941), p. 106.

between objective reality and fantasy was clearly maintained while the coexistence of the two dramatic modes was justified by the fact that the dying girl's delirium is as "true" as any other element in the play.

Symbolic figures and objects were used in the realistic drama almost from the beginning of the modern theatre, so that it was almost routine procedure for Arthur Miller to use a stunted backyard tree to symbolize the family catastrophe of *All My Sons* in 1947. We may cite *The Wild Duck* and *The Sea-Gull* as early examples of such "natural" use of symbols. The symbolism of the sea gull is particularly striking in its application to Chekhov's heroine, Nina, who is seduced by the middle-aged novelist Trigorin. Trigorin himself implants awareness of the symbol in the playgoer's mind as well as Nina's. The sight of a dead gull shot down near the lake by the frustrated young man Konstantin gives Trigorin an idea for a story about a country girl like Nina who has lived in freedom until one day a man sees her and, being momentarily unoccupied, "destroys her like the sea-gull there." David Magarshack aptly describes the symbolism as "a poetic way of expressing the very common fact of life, namely, the destruction of beauty by people who do not see it and are not aware of the terrible crime they commit." [2] Konstantin kills the bird because he wants to frighten Nina with a threat of suicide, and Nina's lover Trigorin wantonly seduces her because of middle-aged vanity. Magarshack's "the very common fact of life" is the key phrase here: the realist's symbol originates in objective fact and is definite, whereas the symbolists' symbol is by its very nature indeterminate.

Today we do not hesitate to mingle realistic and symbolic styles. A noteworthy recent example was the 1948 Broadway production of *Death of a Salesman,* with its skeletal setting against a background of apartment houses towering over Willy Loman's one-family home. The contrast was clearly designed to serve as a symbol of the "little man's precariously sustained

[2] *Chekhov the Dramatist* (New York: Auverne Publishers, 1952.)

individualism," and there were other details of poetic treatment that were worth noticing—the sudden lyrical transfiguration of the setting when leaves in rich profusion were projected on a screen, for instance, and the strongly contrasting use of the starkly neutral forestage for Willy's burial at the end.

Another notable example was the 1952 New York production of *Desire Under the Elms,* staged by Harold Clurman and designed by Mordecai Gorelik. Neither Clurman nor Gorelik had previously made consistent use of antirealistic stylization; they had been associated with Broadway's most developed realistic producing enterprise, the Group Theatre, during the 1930's. Nevertheless, they did not hesitate to stage O'Neill's farm tragedy in a formally designed setting, essentially a screen with platforms, framed by a cut-out drop of two elms forming an arch. Remembering that Mr. Gorelik was the designer of such plays as Odets' *Awake and Sing!* and *Golden Boy,* we can follow his comments on his scenic treatment of *Desire under the Elms* with special interest:

> The designer has chosen as his dominant theme the idea of "under the elms," as expressed by the silhouette of a house under the silhouettes of two great trees. While the design has a superficial air of naturalism, it is in fact basically theatricalist in style. The silhouette of the house is established by means of a roof-line and chimney, plus the eaves and porch; its interior is influenced by cubism in the relationship of the rooms and by constructivism in the partly curved crosssectioning of the floors. In general, the "house" is merely an elaborate screen enclosing a lower and an upper ledge. . . .
>
> The trees are a cut-out drop, treated as a semi-silhouette. The drop is bordered [drawn on top from the "tree" right to the "tree" left of the "house"] by a curved line which emphasizes its frank theatricalism.[3]

Productions such as these show a pragmatic fusion of realistic and theatrical elements according to the requirements of a

---

[3] John Gassner, *Producing the Play* (New York: The Dryden Press, 1953), pp. 353-354.

play, or according to the stage director's and designer's interpretation. It is obvious from their handling of *Desire Under the
Elms* that Clurman and Gorelik did not consider O'Neill's play
significant as either sociology or genre painting, agreeing in this
respect with the author himself, who had always disavowed naturalism in spite of his penchant for naturalistic situations. It was
the fateful love and hatred, the tragic absolutes, that they found
valuable in *Desire Under the Elms* and that they elected to
represent in the formalistically designed stage setting. No mystique of art enters into the practices described here. Practical artists arrive at craft-judgments; they make decisions based on their
analysis of the play and then proceed to carry them out, hoping
for the best results. Called upon to subscribe to any single principle of creation, they would be likely to agree with Anatole
France's declaration, "There are no other rules than usage, taste,
and passions, our virtues and our vices, all our weaknesses, all
our forces." [4]

One may wonder, indeed, why there has been (since 1940,
let us say) any quarrel over stylization in dramatic art.
Conflict between realism and theatricalization has become
largely theoretical, if not indeed illusory. If realists still look
askance at tub-thumping for theatricalized drama, it is only because they suspect that there is charlatanry, cultural decadence,
or escapism in the opposite camp. They cling to some degree of
literalness or actualism out of a resolve to defend the theatre as
an instrument of the modern rationalistic and scientific mind or
liberal spirit. They can point, as a justification of their wariness,
to the theological or traditionalist character of the revival of
poetic drama in England under T. S. Eliot, the cultivation of a
theatre for the élite by Yeats in Dublin, and the *snobisme*, the
social ambiguity, and the preciosity of other departures from
realism. When the realist encounters work as bizarre as

[4] *French Folly in Maxims,* ed. Henry Pène Du Bois (New York,
1894), p. 111.

BRITISH FORMALISM   A *formalistic, modified constructivist, so-called podium setting was used by Terence Gray for his Cambridge Festival Theatre production of* Antigone. *This theatre, which opened in 1926 and closed in 1933, was the most advanced stage organization in England. It was resolutely antirealistic under the directorship of Gray, who dismissed realistic stage production as "the old game of illusion and glamour and all the rest of nineteenth century hocus pocus and bamboozle." (See Norman Marshall's* The Other Theatre, London, 1948.) *The stage, in Gray's view, should be "a raised platform designed to give the greatest mutual relations of the actors playing their parts in each play, and accordingly for each play there should be a specially designed raised platform, the levels and angles of which fulfil a function in emphasising the dramatic platform" (p. 54). Gray's productions required expert lighting, and his associate Hedley Briggs became England's most important lighting specialist.*

PICTORIAL THEATRICALISM   *The picturesque theatricalism cultivated for simplicity is exemplified by the "Jesus at the Tomb of Lazarus" scene from* Le Mystère de la passion des Théophiliens, *an adaptation of medieval drama by Gustave Cohen, first produced at Rouen, then at Brussels, and then at Paris in 1950. There was a cultivated naiveté in the toylike scenery, partly constructed (in the foreground) and partly painted on a drop in the background. In such theatricalist stage productions it was, naturally, not essential to avoid painted scenery; the theatrical character of the performances actually invited the use of painted scenery in combination with constructions.*

AMATEUR THEATRICALISM   *The "animated house" was used in Fordham University Theatre's playful production of William Saroyan's Sam Ego's House, designed and directed in 1953 by William Riva for arena-stage presentation. Here theatricalism was obviously given full sway.* Courtesy of Edgar Kloten of the Fordham University Theatre. Photograph: Du Rona.

POETIC EXPRESSION AND SYMBOLISM   *The Group Theatre production of William Saroyan's My Heart's in the Highlands used non-realistic scenery which some observers loosely called surrealistic. Robert Lewis, who staged the play in 1939, wrote in John Gassner's Producing the Play (p. 297): "In addition to the usual work on the psychological meaning and development of the performance, it was necessary . . . to find the poetic expression of that content. . . . For example, at one point the old man with the trumpet plays a song for the villagers and they give him food. The feeling I had about this moment was: the people are nourished by art. The image that came to my mind was: a plant flowering as it is watered." Mr. Lewis built up a picture with his actors, as seen in the photograph. This, together with the associated color, stage movement, lighting, and music, constitutes what Mr. Lewis calls "theatre poetry," a translation of Cocteau's poésie de théâtre.* Photo: Alfred Valente. Courtesy of The Group Theatre.

Picasso's surrealistic *Desire Trapped by the Tail,* as formalized and rigidly conventionalized as Yeats's *Full Moon in March,* as involved and introverted as Cummings' *him* and Saroyan's *Jim Dandy,* or, for that matter, as mystifyingly moralistic as Eliot's *The Family Reunion,* he is tempted to damn a good deal of antirealistic stylization as perversity and pretension.

Crisis in the Contemporary Theatre

There has been a general crisis in the theatre, both in America and abroad, that has been more or less distinct from economic and political difficulties. The problem is essentially one of inner disharmony. There has been too much dismal division in the theatre between the humdrum and the showy, between the commonplaceness of realism and the arid "artiness" of antirealism.

The conflicting claims of realism and theatre have seldom been creatively solved in the theatre of recent years. It has been rare for an acting company to work with freshness and a secure sense of style on both the realistic and nonrealistic levels of artistry. By and large, the theatre has been divided between commercial-professional sterility and noncommercial or commercial-experimental futility; and surely an important reason is that theatricalism has been so often misused or used only frivolously, as a rule, when used well. One may, in truth, conclude that the solution of the esthetic crisis depends on our knowing when and how to combine the resources of realistic and theatricalist artistry. And unfortunately the theatre's usual muddle and opportunism are not conducive to the *knowing* of anything. Normally, the commercial theatre just feels its way and hopes for the best, and the academic and community theatres "think out" a production and then are forced to content themselves with inescapable compromises.

We know what realistic technique is in the fields of playwriting, acting, directing, scenic design, lighting, and costuming.

But do we actually know today what we want from the realism of art? It would be patently absurd to assert that *Hamlet* and *The Trojan Women* are deficient in realism because Shakespeare, writing for his platform stage, and Euripides, writing for the hillside theatre of Dionysus, did not employ realistic techniques of the kind developed in the late nineteenth century. They never heard of the fourth-wall convention, which could not at any rate have been maintained on the Elizabethan and Attic stages, but it would be ridiculous not to number these and other poet-playwrights among the theatre's great realists.

We must realize, then, that realism cannot be created by technique alone. Realism was not merely a technique in the work of Strindberg, Shaw, or Chekhov. The idea of realistic theatre has been badly shaken, has been often and seriously called in question, because the "idea" has been confused with technique. Indeed, in many instances, only the technique has been left to realism, while the essence has been allowed to evaporate. This has been the case, no doubt, for reasons that range from indifference to cowardice, from complacency to honest uncertainty. In most latter-day plays and productions, for example, enviroment, although featured in the settings and omnipresent in the small talk of the characters, has borne no relation to the spine of the drama: we are offered realistic form without realistic substance. Such realism, as I have stressed before, is not at all essential to dramatic art and is certainly not indispensable to modern theatre.

Conversely, we must realize, as some of the best artists of the modern theatre have done, that the cause of a true realism has been well served by some degree of stylization. An actual theatricalization of the substance and meaning of the play may reveal more, rather than less, to the playgoer. Numerous writers of problem plays from Dumas *fils* grinding out *La Question d'argent* (*A Question of Money*) on behalf of business honesty in 1857 to, shall we say, Howard Lindsay and Russel Crouse writing *The Prescott Proposals* on behalf of amity at the United Nations in

1953, have dealt with facts, or have pretended to deal with them. But more, rather than less, so did Toller, Georg Kaiser, O'Casey and Jean Giraudoux make vivid and strong use of the life of their times in such nonrealistic pieces as *Man and the Masses, From Morn to Midnight, The Silver Tassie,* and *The Madwoman of Chaillot.* Surely, too, among stage directors, Jessner and Piscator in Germany, Meyerhold and Tairov in Russia, and Elia Kazan in America have sometimes achieved more, rather than less, relatedness when they have resorted to theatricalist stylization.

Why, then, is our theatre not consistently following the dual course of enriching realism with imagination and enriching theatricalism with realism in such degree that the clamor for "new forms" will at last end after some sixty or seventy years? No other period of theatrical history has had so many and so varied stylistic experiments, and none has professed so thorough a devotion to the idea of freedom in theatrical art, as the period from the publication of Hugo's preface to *Cromwell* to the present. Why have the realistic drama and theatre, without radical modifications, remained dominant in spite of the exertions of extremely talented would-be stylizers, theatricalizers, and ultramodernizers? Why has not any particular "modernist" mode—that is, nonrealistic mode—supplanted the "modern"—that is, realistic—one?

Perhaps the most comprehensive answer is that the nonrealistic modes of theatre, often so fascinating in transmutations from symbolism to surrealism, failed to crystallize into an adequate and reliable dramatic form. Realistic dramatic art, whatever its limitations, has been to modern theatre what Shakespearean dramaturgy was to the Elizabethan period and Sophoclean dramaturgy to the Periclean Age. That is the meaning of my previously elaborated argument that realism has been a modern kind of classicism. The nonrealistic modes of theatre fall more or less under the one category of *theatricalism.* But theatricalism has not yet acquired any classical configurations because it has not found a consistent form. The idea of theatricalist art has been with us throughout the century, but its various formal and stylistic manifestations have been tentative, elusive, or fractured—as many an expressionist play, for example, has been fractured. Of theatricalism it may be said that "The One remains, the many change and pass." Its "idea" persists and is, in my opinion, essentially sound, but its forms have been transitory.

Theatricalism: *Pro* and *Con*

Perhaps we shall understand the situation better if we attempt to understand the general character of theatricalism. The fundamental premise of realism is the Aristotelian one that drama is an imitation of an action; realists held, therefore, that the most desirable theatre is that in which imitation is the closest. The fundamental premise of theatricalism is that theatre is not imitation in the narrow sense, which Aristotle himself never could have held, since the Greek drama upon which he based conclusions in his *Poetics* was not realistically imitative.[5] For the theatricalist, the object of action and of all other "imitative" elements is not imitation but *creativeness,* and a special kind

[5] S. H. Butcher, in *Aristotle's Theory of Poetry and Fine Art* (4th ed., Dover Publications, 1951), argues well that "imitation" is a *creative act:* "It is the expression of the concrete thing under an image which answers to its true idea." To reproduce the universal "in a simple and sensuous form is not to reflect a reality already familiar through sense perceptions" (p. 154). It is "rivalry of nature." Certainly esthetic semblance could not have meant slavish imitation for Aristotle, who wrote that the author "ought to prefer probable impossibilities to possible improbabilities" (p. 128). Nevertheless, Aristotle was apparently inclined to place reliance on "imitation" somewhat in our ordinary sense of the term. Art, for Aristotle, involves sensuous perception rather than symbolization. "A work of art," Butcher declares (p. 124), "is a likeness (ὁμοίωμα), and not a symbolic representation of it." Symbolists and other antirealists, then, could draw even less comfort from Aristotle than literal realists.

of creativeness at that. The realists would agree, of course, as to the value of creativeness. But the theatricalist goes one step further, and that step is the truly decisive one for the theory and practice of pure theatricalism. He maintains that there is never any sense in pretending that one is not in the theatre; that no amount of make-believe is reality itself; that in short, theatre is the medium of dramatic art, and effectiveness in art consists in *using* the medium rather than concealing it. In the theatricalist view, concealment of the medium is tantamount to the nullification of art. Therefore, the theatricalist feels that plays should be written and staged in such a manner that there will be no pretense that what is happening on the stage is real. The object of writing and performing for the medium is to create theatre—theatrical actions, characterizations, and images—and nothing else. The object of going to a "show" is nothing else than seeing or experiencing a show, not reality. The appropriate reply to theatricalist extremism is no doubt this: The realists have maintained that the theatrical medium should be made as unobtrusive as possible in order to establish the illusion of reality. The anti-theatricalist can argue that it is surely unnecessary to expose all the strings of a piano in order to play the instrument, and that only infants would need to see the inside wiring in order to be convinced that the instrument is being played.

Even in so distinguished a play as *The Skin of Our Teeth* the intrusion of self-conscious theatricality somewhat blunts the edge of comedy and causes the essential action to mark time. Now and then the play's "playfulness" becomes altogether too arch. But one can go further in criticizing Wilder's theatricality and maintain that the intrusion of "theatre" weakens the power of the play, especially in the last act, which occurs immediately after a world-devastating war. If the human race has survived only by the skin of its teeth, one is tempted to ask, what is the author so cheerful about? In the first and second acts, the audience could be reminded that man has been the same throughout history in his aspirations and contradictions. The humor attendant upon the theatrical blending of life in suburban New Jersey with life during the Ice Age, or the linking of the legend of Noah with an Atlantic City convention, was in accord with the author's comment on the human race. But in the third act, which deals with contemporary disaster, the theatricalism is not only inappropriate because it is played in the wrong key and is perhaps insufficiently climactic for a dramatic masterpiece, but it is evasive as well. The author has apparently nothing to say that he hasn't already told us twice. So he repeats himself again, quotes the right authors, who give us the right schoolbook assurances in a pageant-like procession of the show's backstage personnel; and he reminds us for the third time that *The Skin of Our Teeth* is just a show. Ibsen and Shaw would have scorned to beg off so lightly. Ibsen would have reserved the full power of his meaning for the showdown—what Shaw would have called the element of "discussion" in the play. And if Shaw and Ibsen had had no answer, they would have said so, as Shaw did so eloquently in *Too True To Be Good,* thus turning the very sense of failure into an affirmative passion.

Nevertheless, *The Skin of Our Teeth* is perhaps the best out-and-out theatricalist work of the American theatre.[6] The dangers of theatricalist exploitation of theatre are more striking in such exercises in the construction of the play-within-a-play as Maxwell Anderson's *Joan of Lorraine* and Pirandello's *Tonight We Improvise.* To perceive these dangers we need only compare the first-mentioned with *Saint Joan,* in which Shaw refrains from turning theatricalist somersaults until the epilogue.[7] We could also compare *Tonight We Improvise* with Pirandello's *Six Characters in Search of an Author,* in which the intensity of life routs the artifice of theatre; the reverse is true in *Tonight We Impro-*

[6] Except for Cummings' too esoteric, dadaist-surrealist play *him,* which for all its muddle has a quality of imagination and power of expression absent in many better-built plays.

[7] And even in this fantasy Shaw speaks his mind manfully through the action and Joan's words instead of coyly playing at play-making.

vise, in which the author's theatricality tends to destroy the life of the play.

In stage production, of course, theatricalization has prevailed from time immemorial. The range of theatricalism has been endless. Its manifestations as vaudeville, burlesque, clowning, juggling, and miming have been inexhaustibly delightful. True satire and pathos have come within the orbit of the candidly theatrical artistry for which Max Pallenberg in Germany, Jean-Louis Barrault in France, Beatrice Lillie in England, and Chaplin in America have become celebrated. Also, some theatricalist performers have specialized in more restrained, "serious" modes, as have Cornelia Otis Skinner and Angna Enters and the superbly dramatic Ruth Draper. Others have relied upon the dance, as have Martha Graham and Paul Draper and many others who have performed in a variety of distinctive styles; still others are vocal and instrumental musicians. To rule these and many other virtuosi out of even the most serious discussion of dramatic art is to rule the theatre out of it.

There is no self-consciousness, however, in the theatricality of such performers. In some *avant-garde* endeavors, on the contrary, there appears a disconcerting self-consciousness about theatricality. In one otherwise absorbing off-Broadway production, Genet's *The Maids,* the stage-action consisted of two servant girls pretending that they were mistress and maid respectively. Although both characters were nearly hysterical with snarling and shouting at each other, the director apparently saw fit to remind the public that it was in the theatre by allowing the production's stage manager and an actress waiting for her cues to be visible at one side of the stage. In a Theatre Union production of Brecht's *Mother* in the 1930's, much of the lighting equipment was exposed to the full view of the audience. Although justified by epic-theatre principles and by the anti-illusionist alienation-effect objective, this theatricalist reminder was, from a common-sense view, superfluous. The choral marching and chanting of the actors in this production were also sufficient to inform the audience that the greasepaint of theatre had been laid on with a trowel. In a New York ANTA production of Brecht's *Galileo,* the chief actor, Charles Laughton, stripped to the waist and then costumed himself publicly. The present writer was not alone in considering this expedient neither necessary nor edifying.

Unredundant theatricalist productions are also encountered, of course; these are usually the ones in which the theatricalism is naturally motivated, easily and gaily justified. An example is the delightful Gaston Baty production in 1938 of *Le Chapeau de paille d'Italie* which the present writer saw revived at the Comédie Française in 1950. Labiche's extravagant comedy was appropriately staged as a sort of comic ballet, as an interminable wedding march, and an irrepressible romp across the stage. There could be no question here of awkwardly calling attention to the theatricality of the play and the production.[8]

A theatre freed from all pretense of reproducing reality has been the modern theatricalist ideal. To some theatricalists, even the symbolists of the Craig-Appia school have been vain tricksters. They hold that dramatic action is not an experience offered as a slice of real or imaginary life, but *histrionic reality*. Performance should be openly *histrionic*. In the pure theatricalist style, as explained by its most ardent propagandist, Alexander Bakshy, the performance will be solely "a happening in that real world which is the gathering of actors and spectators come together, the first to practice, and the second to watch, the act of undisguised and glorying make-believe." Love and hatred will be "stage love" and "stage hatred" (the opposite of the love and hatred of Stanislavsky-trained actors), and character will be "stage character." As for the play itself, Bakshy explains:

[8] Tastefulness, of course, cannot be assured by any "production idea" alone. It is possible to overproduce this type of play and to be overstrenuous in directing it, as was Orson Welles, according to some opinions, in staging the play for the Federal Theatre under the title of *Horse Eats Hat.*

The staginess of the play will mean an exhibition of life in terms of the theatre. . . . Nor will the playwright . . . be bound by considerations of realistic, psychological, or some supernatural truth. His aim will be dramatic truth, and in bodying it forth on the stage, he will be free to treat his material—the elements of human character and action—in any fashion he may choose so long as his convention is made intelligible, is theatrical in its nature, and lays no claim to be anything but a method of presentation.[9]

And the ideal stage of theatricalism will, of course, be "a stage and nothing but a stage . . . serving as a pedestal on which the plastic structure of the dramatic show is raised by the actors." It must be a stage freed from the proscenium arch, no longer a picture-frame stage or a peephole stage, but a platform frankly intended for the actor's use. Scenery on such a stage is not pictorial except insofar as the actor's action and dialogue require environmental details; and even these can be theatricalized by the production.

The relation of the spectator to such a theatrical production can be open and independent, says Bakshy, as the spectator knows that he is not supposed to lose himself in an illusion or to succumb to some spell. He is enabled to retain his freedom as an observer; he is treated as the detached critical spectator for whom the show is being put on rather than as a victim of an illusionist's trickery. (The specialist in "illusionism" may be a naturalist who is intent on conjuring up a real environment for the spectator, or a symbolist who tries to make the spectator lose himself in an imaginary world and in a mystical experience.) So much for the generalized aim of the theatricalists!

It must be observed, however, that the theatricalist idea of theatre has been carried out in actual productions in various ways and to various degrees. The question of whether it is, has been, or could be a satisfactory alternative to critical realism in

[9] Alexander Bakshy, *The Theatre Unbound* (London: Cecil Palmer, 1923), p. 18. The essay from which I quote was first published in 1921.

the modern theatre can be answered only in relation to kinds and degrees of achievement. Concerning this question, the following summary conclusions are offered as a basis for further investigation and assessment.

1. Theatricalism ruled the stage in classical times, in the age of Shakespeare, and in the age of Molière, although illusionistic scenic elements provided the illusion of place and although actors surely provided more or less convincing characterizations instead of merely declaiming poetry and prose.[10] In our century, however, theatricalism has commanded the stage consistently and successfully only in the music hall, in vaudeville, and in musical comedies and plays. Theatricalism is indeed the only style that has ever been possible for these forms of entertainment, as well as for opera. Even as realistic a play as Elmer Rice's *Street Scene* had to become a thoroughly theatrical "show," rather than a social document, when turned into a "music-drama" with a score by Kurt Weill.

In so far as theatricalist stylization has improved the composition and staging of musical shows, giving us an *Oklahoma!* instead of *The Student Prince,* the results should satisfy everyone. And insofar as a critical spirit, first brought into modern theatre by Ibsen and his fellow iconoclasts, has found expression in such musical pieces as *The Three-Penny Opera* and *Finian's Rainbow,* theatricalism has proved itself capable of expressing the modern age rather than merely entertaining it. But, obviously, there is nothing remarkable in the success of theatricalism in the musical theatre, which realism has never dominated and cannot be expected to dominate. Obviously, too, plays written for the nonrealistic theatres of the past lend themselves rather well to especially stylized staging. Hence, to deter-

[10] The infiltration of scenic illusionism into the premodern, prerealistic theatres is vividly recounted by Lee Simonson in *The Stage Is Set* (Harcourt, Brace, 1932); see especially Part II, significantly entitled "Myths of Lost Purity."

mine the possibilities of theatricalism for the modern stage we must examine its effectiveness in areas other than musical entertainments and classic revivals.

2. Some degree of theatricalism has been an element in all efforts to depart from realistic playwriting and staging since 1890. Thus, the symbolists, who have been designated earlier as illusionists, theatricalized their presentations to the degree that they transformed experience into symbolic atmosphere or reverie. And the expressionists, who also supported an illusionism of sorts in making their picture of the world conform to the subjective state of some character (or of the author), theatricalized phenomena by "expressively" distorting them. These modernists were not pure or absolute theatricalists. Their motives were essentially extratheatrical. But they did liberate the stage and the drama from humdrum imitations of the humdrum, and they did provide theatricalized pictures and expressions of the individual and the world.

If the symbolists who followed Maeterlinck or Craig failed to establish symbolist drama as *the* modern form of drama and a symbolist style of staging as *the* modern style of theatre, one reason is that it is against the nature of the theatre to exist in a mist and to thrive on vagueness. Drama and theatre are among the most definite of all the arts. It is also against the nature of the drama and theatre to be stationary and meditative. Maeterlinck himself discovered this, and therefore abandoned his theory of static drama. Then, left without a form of drama to support his symbolist idea of theatre, he partially abandoned the idea itself. Writing to the late Barrett H. Clark, he said: "You must not attach too great importance to the expression "Static"; it was an invention, a theory of my youth, worth what most literary theories are worth—that is, almost nothing." [11] And if the expression-

---

[11] Barrett H. Clark, *A Study of Modern Drama* (Appleton-Century, 1938), p. 163. In this letter, indeed, Maeterlinck goes much further; he declares: "Whether a play be static or dynamic, *symbolistic* or *realistic*, is of little consequence." Strange words from the bellwether, program-maker and patron saint of dramatic symbolism. But, then, they were written about 1925, after the virtual

ist playwrights and stage directors failed to establish expressionism as *the* twentieth-century style, one compelling reason is that
although the theatre can take note of a disturbed area of experience, it cannot thrive in it.

Expressionism could *supplement* realism but could not take
its place in the modern theatre. Indeed, expressionism still serves
this supplementary purpose in certain plays, *Death of a Salesman* being a good example. We may well ask ourselves, however, whether *Death of a Salesman* would have been so tre-
mendously effective if it had been thoroughly expressionistic.

Theatricalism, finally, has been freely employed by Piscator,
Brecht, and other epic realists. But they have theatricalized
playwriting and stage production for other than purely theatricalist purposes. They have destroyed the fourth-wall convention in order to demonstrate ideas and ideologies.

3. We have also had in twentieth-century theatre a type of
theatricalist endeavor that has not been associated with some
other, specialized, program and technique such as expressionism
or epic realism. This kind of theatre represents a disposition to
favor the concept of theatre as *an end in itself;* and we may
therefore call it simply "pure theatricalism." To suggest its range
we may refer to four key figures who had formulated their general theories and put them into practice more or less independently by 1914. These men are Alexander Tairov, Vsevolod Meyerhold, Eugene Vakhtangov, and Jacques Copeau; their work is
now well known to students of theatrical history.

Tairov founded his Kamerny ("chamber") Theatre in Moscow in 1914 to express his opposition to Stanislavsky's realistic
methods at the Moscow Art Theatre. Tairov's objective was to
retheatricalize the stage by favoring such nonrealistic plays as
Oscar Wilde's *Salome,* which became one of the outstanding

---

disappearance of specifically symbolist drama—more than a quarter of a century after the writing of *The Intruder, Interior,* and
The Blind, Maeterlinck's three exemplary "static" dramas.

early productions of the Kamerny Theatre. Tairov favored abstract rather than realistic scenic design, and he developed stylized gestures and movements for his actors almost as though he were a ballet-master. As Norris Houghton has declared, "Stanislavski had told his actor to forget that he was on the stage; Tairov told his actor always to remember that he was on the stage." [12] Tairov's approach was one of sophisticated cosmopolitanism and estheticism. When he found it necessary to discard this attitude after the Russian Revolution of 1917, he moderated his absolute or autonomous theatricality and presented plays with realistic subject matter that lent themselves to moderate stylization. He succeeded especially with Eugene O'Neill's plays *All God's Chillun Got Wings* and *Desire Under the Elms*. Tairov's career was, however, especially noteworthy for his efforts to use the related art of the dance as a means of making the theatre theatrical.

Meyerhold left Stanislavsky before World War I in search of a satisfactory nonrealistic convention or style. His quest led him from one experiment to another, ensured him a brilliant career for about two decades, and ended when political reverses lost him his position in 1937; he disappeared sometime after, presumably in one of the Communist purges. Although he came to be considered a spokesman for social revolution after the fall of the Russian monarchy in 1917, his primary interests in the theatre were artistic. Norris Houghton declared, without entertaining derogatory intentions, that "this champion of proletarian art" was "paradoxically enough, a complete aristocrat." [13]

Meyerhold carried his pursuit of new dramatic modes to its most sensational point by developing constructivistic scenery (that is, scenery consisting of ramps, steps, and slides that assured dynamic stage action but established environment only incidentally, if at all) and by evolving a dynamic style of acting that was free from Stanislavskian subjectivity or emotional depth. But "constructivism" was only one phase of the career of

[12] *Moscow Rehearsals* (Harcourt, Brace, 1936), p. 110.
[13] *Ibid.*, p. 96.

a creative director who strove to theatricalize the theatre throughout his career. The audience at a typical Meyerhold performance was never allowed to forget that it was in the theatre. By consciously associating itself with the actors in a game of make-believe, often satiric, the public was expected to participate in the making of theatre instead of submitting passively to the illusion created by the realistic convention. By eliminating the proscenium and removing the front curtain, as well as by flooding the auditorium with light, Meyerhold banished the picture-frame stage from his theatres and bridged the space between the actors and the spectators. (See pp. 192-198.)

A third leader of theatricalist stylization, Eugene Vakhtangov (1883-1922), Stanislavsky's favorite and regrettably short-lived protégé, never completely broke off relations with the Moscow Art Theatre. In comparison with Tairov and Meyerhold, he was a moderate. Declaring that "feeling is the same in theatre and life, but the means and methods of presenting them are different," he endeavored to reconcile the theatrical aims of Stanislavsky and Meyerhold; that is, he tried to reconcile the search for *reality* with the search for *form*, the humanist's interest in realism with the esthete's interest in art for art's sake. Vakhtangov, too, disregarded the fourth-wall convention. He actually ridiculed it in his celebrated 1921 production of *Princess Turandot* when he had the stagehands, who had been shifting scenery in sight of the audience, perform ballets burlesquing the romantic action of Carlo Gozzi's eighteenth-century play. He also had the actors, wearing evening dress, line up on the stage at the beginning of the performance and introduce themselves, after which they costumed themselves in full view of the audience. But Vakhtangov strove for spontaneity and naturalness in acting, and wanted the actor to be thoroughly human, not a robot. He objected, for instance, to Meyerhold's sacrificing of individuality in characterization, and to the assumption that it was impossible to have both emotional truth *and* theatrical reality. But unlike the Stanislav-

"LIVING NEWSPAPER" THEATRICALISM *This scene from the "living newspaper* Power, *produced by the Federal Theatre in New York in 1937, directed by Brett Warren and with settings by Howard Bay, presents a Supreme Court hearing of the arguments on TVA. The judges of the Court were represented by nine masks to which the characters addressed themselves without evoking any recognition or response. Nonillusionistic, theatricalized staging was properly employed for this documentary, "epic" form of drama, which blended journalism and presentational theatre. Hallie Flanagan Davis, director of the Federal Theatre, described this type of drama in her noteworthy history of this theatre* (Arena, New York, 1940, p. 70) *as "factual and formal, musical and acrobatic, abstract and concrete, visual and aural, psychological, economic, and social." She noted that the form was "as American as Walt Disney, the March of Dimes, and the Congressional Record," yet also derivative in some of its features from Aristophanes, the commedia dell' arte, Mei Lan Fang pantomime, and contemporary "epic" and "agit-prop" types of theatre.*

PAGEANT-STYLE THEATRICALISM   *In the banquet scene of Max Reinhardt's open-air production of Hugo von Hofmannsthal's* Everyman (Jedermann), *given annually since 1920, the portals of the Salzburg Cathedral were utilized as a background. One allegorical character actually came out of the cathedral, so that the stage platform and the cathedral were dramatically related, as were other architectural elements in the cathedral square.*

EPIC THEATRICALISM   *In Bertolt Brecht's* The Caucasian Circle of Chalk, *as staged by Robert Schneideman for Northwestern University Theatre, Evanston, Illinois, in 1955, one may note the alienation effect achieved by functional, nonillusionistic scenery, built to reveal the solid brick of the theatre itself; the use of changeable signs and slogans; the participation in the action of a narrator and musicians; exploitation of contrasts; and an attempt at illustrative, cabaret-style gesture in the presentation of a ballad in place of the realistic pantomime used elsewhere in the production. (Settings by Lawrence Goodman, costumes by Ida Mae Goe.)* Photograph: W. B. Nickerson, Evanston, Ill.

skian realistic actor, Vakhtangov's actor was expected to perform two things at one time—both the role in the play and his critical or detached view of that role. Brecht wants the same duality.

Finally, we must refer, though with regretful brevity, to the work of Jacques Copeau, the leader of theatricalism in the West, who was most notably active between 1913 and 1924. Copeau became known chiefly for his Théâtre du Vieux Colombier, founded in 1913 in a small Parisian playhouse, where he built probably the first modern stage for *presentational* (as opposed to *representational,* or peephole) productions. Later he won much admiration as well for the school of acting he established after World War I. But he was perhaps most important to the theatre because of his influence on the brilliant French directors Charles Dullin and Louis Jouvet. Copeau, too, may be described as a reformer rather than a revolutionist in theatrical art. Like Vakhtangov, he emphasized characterization, individuality, and emotional truth even while stressing the histrionic nature of performance and giving primacy to the stage as a platform rather than an environment for pretended living. Much indeed has been made of Copeau's use of a bare platform stage (*un tréteau nu*) consisting of a permanent architectural setting backed by a few screens that could be changed for different plays to suggest different backgrounds. Verisimilitude in scenery had little value for Copeau, who disdained surface realism. Such realism, he protested, "seeks to make us believe in a pasteboard universe."

Copeau and his successors encouraged the development by Obey, Giraudoux, Anouilh, and others of a style of playwriting that made use of theatricality regardless of the intellectual substance, or even the topicality, of the work. The plays written in this style—such as Giraudoux' *Electra* and *The Madwoman of Chaillot*—are presented as constructions, so to speak. The author is thoroughly conscious of creating something for theatrical exhibition. Even in writing *Electra,* his tragedy on the subject of revenge, Giraudoux did not hesitate to employ theatrical devices and to have characters overleap the fourth wall by addressing the audience at length. After we have discarded the fiction that happenings on the stage have an extratheatrical reality, we can indeed let the actors talk to the audience.

Copeau made himself the leader of those who set themselves the objective of *rethéâtrisaler le théâtre*. But he had no use for dazzling stage effects and sheer directorial virtuosity. He encouraged a large measure of humanization in a period and in a country in which artifice was much favored. Because of the nature of retheatricalized playwriting, nevertheless, many French playwrights of the post-realistic school overcultivated artifice; as their contemporary Jean-Jacques Bernard, himself a dramatist of distinction, declared, "in their work, as in that of Giraudoux himself, you find deeply human touches alongside others which are merely exercises in what I might call intellectual tight-rope walking." [14]

It will be observed that each leader of the theatricalist movement made a clear-cut attempt to destroy the realists' "illusion of reality." If the results have been bewildering as well as gratifying, the reason is that theatricalism, like every other method, has suffered from misapplication. Theatricalism offers especially strong seductions to stage directors to display their virtuosity. The process of seduction starts, indeed, the moment they decide to violate the fourth-wall convention.

Those of us who are striving to develop the contemporary theatre should be aware of our danger: We are all parvenus in theatricalism, we who have rediscovered it for ourselves after it

[14] "Art and Artifice," *Drama* (London) (Winter 1952), p. 16. This "tight-rope walking," apparent also in the work of Italian writers such as Pirandello and Ugo Betti, becomes somewhat coy in Giraudoux' *Intermezzo* and *Electra*. It will be found even in so intensely serious and timely a work as his mordant play *La Guerre de Troie n'aura pas lieu* (1935), which contained two unnecessarily fantastic, somewhat sophomorically "literary" scenes omitted by the director Harold Clurman from his production of the play under the title of *Tiger at the Gates*. See the translation by Christopher Fry published by Oxford University Press (New York, 1955).

had been in vogue for some twenty-five centuries before Ibsen. We have embraced it self-consciously, while the clowns and other direct entertainers have been doing their job unostentatiously right under our uplifted noses. So it happens that we must give a little restraining consideration to some of our most ingenious practices and use them with discretion. By all means let us, for example, blow away the imaginary fourth wall for some purposes. Our candid histrionic art may even create a certain charm and establish a certain rapport between actors and audience, both of which results are desirable. Provided, however, that we do not get too much charm and too little else when we aim at more than a simple entertainment, and that we do not get too much "audience participation," which has been known to turn the theatre into a vaudeville show or a kindergarten! Audience participation can be overdone, as, for instance, when the actors go romping through the aisles, nearly barking the shins of the unwary aisle-sitters.

It is also somewhat disconcerting to find that the man sitting in back or in front of you is an actor when he starts yelling "Strike!" or "Hurray!" from his seat. The present writer, who has perhaps too tidy a bourgeois soul, likes to know where he stands in relation to the other people in the auditorium and therefore doesn't want to be startled out of his normal status as a spectator among spectators. But, then, it is usually the object of audience-participation devices to startle sedate persons out of their status of detached observers and make them "participate." The trouble is that there is an amazing number of happenings in which the normal auditor doesn't want to participate, and he may object to being pushed into something he very much wants to stay out of. If the production is "leftist," the playgoer is, of course, expected to feel like a "common man" and a member of the "masses" (that horrible cliché for human beings!). But playgoers do not feel like common men at all; they feel uncommon so long as they are in the theatre. There is nothing more irritatingly "sophisticated" than indicating to the audience that it is now going to participate in a game of make-believe with the actors. Playing at theatre while in the theatre can become preposterous, and that is one of the risks run when the theatricalist idea of theatre is pursued too strenuously.[15]

An illustration of pretentious make-believe is the use of imaginary props, as when the actor turns the nonexistent knobs of nonexistent doors. The habit of using such props persists incongruously even in "hard-boiled" stage direction, as in Kazan's production of Williams' naturalistic drama *Cat on a Hot Tin Roof*. The practice is more natural in the staging of "stylized" plays such as *Our Town* and *The Skin of Our Teeth*. Thornton Wilder built an entire one-act play for amateur production around the rehearsal technique of using imaginary properties, and little-theatre groups have been happy with *The Happy Journey from Camden to Trenton* ever since.

In England, the abolition of properties was one of the aims of the brilliant but unsuccessful theatrician Terence Gray when he headed the experimental Festival Theatre at Cambridge from

[15] Before continuing the account of theatricalist follies, it is only fair to remark that there are mitigating circumstances. These were ably formulated for the present author by Professor Barnard Hewitt of the University of Illinois in a letter, from which I quote with his permission: "I find that I share your irritation, or dissatisfaction, with the self-conscious theatricalism of much modern drama and theatre, but it occurs to me that some playwrights deliberately call attention to the theatricality of their drama not out of coyness or whimsicality, but with serious dramatic purpose. This is certainly true of Brecht. . . . Moreover, until theatricality becomes the expected form of drama and theatre, audiences will continue to be shocked to a degree no matter how unself-conscious the playwright manages to be. And I suppose the playwright cannot be altogether unself-conscious so long as theatricality is not the usual thing." I suppose one should add that the results inevitably differ even in the work of the same author; Pirandello is brilliantly successful with his theatricalist method in *Six Characters in Search of an Author* and *Henry IV*, but awkward and tiresome with the theatricalist flummery of some of his other plays. I myself have found his *Tonight We Improvise* particularly irritating after several readings.

1926 to 1933. Gray's views on "props" stressed the need for stylized performance:

> To hand a man a purse, to open and read a document on the stage, such things must be small when performed with the real objects in the actors' hands. The expressiveness of the action is confined to the dimensions of the object handled. Only by discarding the actual article can the gestures of giving or of reading be rendered really significant.

Norman Marshall, who reports at great length on Gray's experiments,[16] admits that this method was effective in large gestures like crowning a king (the present writer himself doubts this), but otherwise ineffective. Marshall declares that "the result became distractingly like a game of dumb crambo, and far too much of the attention of the audience was spent in guessing what props were indicated by the various gestures of the actors." [17] Gray was also one of the theatricalists who directed their actors to make their entrances and exits through the audience.

Marshall's account of the career of Gray is indeed the best summary of the antirealistic adventure at its extremes in the English-speaking world. Marshall, who had worked with Gray at Cambridge, concluded that "seven years of ceaseless experiment had in the end practically no effect upon the English theatre." Nor was the blame to be laid entirely at the door of British philistinism. Gray's work "was degenerating into mere freakishness and eccentricity." His interest in directing was so all-consuming and his production style so extreme that "he failed to encourage a single author to write a play for production according to the methods practised at the Festival." Even Shakespeare's work was little more than grist for the director's mill when Gray put Sir Toby Belch and Sir Andrew Aguecheek on roller skates and dressed Rosalind in a Boy Scout uniform. When Portia started her "quality of mercy" speech in Gray's production of

[16] *The Other Theatre* (London: John Lehman, 1947), pp. 53-71.
[17] *Ibid.*, p. 61.

The Merchant of Venice, the court lapsed into attitudes of complete boredom and "the judge whiled away the time by playing with a yo-yo," then fashionable in England. Portia, moreover, spoke as perfunctorily as if she had delivered this speech "for the thousandth time." In one scene Shylock was shown fishing in a canal, and in the last scene, having been deprived of his wealth, he passed across the stage playing a barrel organ. Like more recent virtuoso directors, Gray was also so determined to make the theatre theatrical that he removed the "wings" from the stage so that the audience might see the actors waiting at the side to make their entrances, the electrician at his switchboard, the stagehands, the stacked scenery, and the stage manager holding the promptbook.

Ultimately, it was the "idea" of a production that dominated the Festival Theatre, and Gray therefore tended to favor poor actors who would take direction, although from time to time he had such promising young performers as Robert Morley, Maurice Evans, Margaret Rawlings, and Jessica Tandy in his Cambridge company. But the final word on his seven-year-long dedication to "production ideas" was no doubt said by Norman Marshall. The major weakness of Gray's "method of production, like all forms of expressionism [i.e., extreme stylization] in the theatre, was that it oversimplified the play. Subtlety ceased to exist and the attention of the audience was concentrated entirely on the broadest outlines of character and situation."

Marshall was reminded of what Kenneth Macgowan and Robert Edmond Jones wrote of Jessner in their book *Continental Stagecraft,* after having watched his work in the early 1920's: "He appeared to worship the obvious, to believe that the theatre is a place of ABC impressions and reactions . . . He flung out symbols right and left, but they were symbols of the primer. He directed in words of one syllable." Their last sentence may not have been entirely fair to Jessner, but their general criticism has been applicable to other theatricalist directors, not excluding the exponents of epic theatre. It is even applicable to the frequently brilliant playwriting of Bertolt Brecht, as it is a danger inherent in his theories of acting and production. Brecht has been rightly wary of professional productions of his work without "epic-trained" actors and without supervision by himself. The fiasco of the premiere of his *Mother Courage* at the Devon Arts Festival in 1955 justified his worst fears.[18]

"ABC impressions and reactions," unfortunately, have often been the final product of much intellectual maneuvering and stylization, for all ideas are simple enough as ideas; they become complicated only when they have to be applied in a human context. All external stylization becomes obvious and is easily exhausted. Only human nature is complex and affords an interest not easily exhausted by (and for) those who have imagination enough to penetrate surfaces.

It is ironical, alas, that the effort to achieve significant anti-realistic stylization, particularly in the English-speaking countries, should have been made so often on the amateur or semi-professional level, where the actors are so obviously unprepared for it. It is not surprising that back in 1927 so wise a mentor as Stark Young reminded the *avant-garde* that "the reason most of our extremely stylized productions seem so poor and misled is because the actors lack the needed style; and they miss this style because they do not command the simple, straight acting from which the style departs."[19] In working a little with actors at a university, the present writer found it necessary to invent the slogan "Out of reality, into reality": Out of the reality of themselves, into the reality of the characters they were to create on the stage, which, in turn, must be a theatrical reality for both the actor and the audience.

Even the mastery of simple mimicry is not to be overlooked. "A mimetic gift in the actor," said Stark Young, "corresponds to a good ear in the musician. . . . The imitation of others is an instinct born deep in us, and is the source of the actor's art."

[18] See *London Observer,* July 3, 1955.
[19] *The Theater* (New York: George H. Doran, 1927).

And Mr. Young added that the gift for mimicry in the actor is like a gift for likeness in a painter. "Such a knack will not make his drawing fine, but it will give him a kind of solid reality which he can begin with and which he can alter and force to his own ends." [20] When the incompetent actor "stylizes," he lets us see the style rather than the man, the effort rather than the achievement, the silhouette rather than the substance of the part. The nonprofessional companies and directors, however, have not been alone in giving us warning examples.

It is especially easy to turn theatricality to commercial advantage and yet win admiration for artistry from all but a few exceptionally tough-fibered critics. The career of the inventive and eclectic Max Reinhardt, whose memory deserves our respect for some achievements, could have served as a warning that the theatre is not necessarily best served by the specialists in theatricality. A widely experienced and practical man of the stage who had started out as a character actor for the naturalist Otto Brahm, Reinhardt was adept at turning all methods of staging to his advantage. He declared, it is true, that "there is no one form of the theatre that is the only true artistic form." Nevertheless, the passion to exploit the stage as a medium, to make good his contagious slogan that "the theatre belongs to the theatre," trapped even this astute *régisseur* and entrepreneur, whose followers in Central Europe appear to have been legion. Ever the virtuoso director who could commercialize Craig and turn symbolist dreams into world-astounding theatricality, Reinhardt achieved exciting, if not altogether satisfactory, effects at his Grosses Schauspielhaus, a reconstructed circus in Berlin. There he staged mass scenes on a large forestage that extended tongue-like into the audience, much as did the Elizabethan platform stage or a three-quarter arena stage. Reinhardt also planted actors in the audience (a device used many years later in the production of the strike drama *Waiting for Lefty* in 1935) when he

[20] *Ibid.*, pp. 57-71.

staged Romain Rolland's *Danton*. The object was, of course, to make the spectator a participant, as it were, in the historical events.

Theatricalism as employed in these and similar productions could be described as vulgarized illusionism; the vulgarization was acutely noted by the Berlin critic Herbert Ihering in discussing Reinhardt's 1910 production of *Oedipus Rex*, a turgid version of his less spectacular treatment of the same work in 1906. On a ramp or broad stairway leading to a palace front erected on the stage, the director had placed hundreds of extras who represented the Theban populace. The theatricalist "effect" was intensified, moreover, by having the players make their entrances and exits through the audience. Ihering remarked dryly that "When Reinhardt's chorus let loose, several housemaids fainted." [21] And what greater illusionism, actually as repellent to the critical realistic intellect of an Ibsen, Shaw, or Chekhov as to a haughty classicist, than Reinhardt's 1911-1912 staging of *The Miracle*. For that production, the interior of the playhouse was rebuilt as a cathedral, and the playgoers sat in it as make-believe communicants while religious processions went up and down the aisles. It is surely unnecessary to cite further evidence that the theatricalist theatre has indulged freely in illusionism and has cheapened it, too, in the time-honored manner of show business, whether the showman be an art-loving European or a Broadway philistine with faint claims to "culture."

Formalism

Absolute theatricalism was visually engrossing. It became too abstract, however, and developed theatrical form as an absolute experience far more expressive as pantomime than as discourse; and the drama is, after all, discourse. (Let us, indeed, avoid the genetic fallacy of assuming that because the theatre

[21] Mordecai Gorelik, *New Theatres for Old*, p. 219.

started as pantomime several thousand years ago, nonverbal drama is the best drama.) In extreme theatricalism there was too much form without content, just as in a good deal of humdrum realism there has been too much content without form.

Moderate theatricalism, which did not theatricalize humanity out of the theatre, has survived to prove artistically reliable. It influenced the revival of old plays written for the prerealistic stage without encouraging the destruction of the masterpiece in order to make a stage director's holiday. The concept of theatricalist art even encouraged the rise of some very agreeable and provocative playwriting, especially in France. It became apparent, as indicated previously, that it is unnecessary to banish *all* illusionism from the theatre in order to retheatricalize it. It is indeed almost impossible for the stage to avoid conveying some degree of illusion, unless the work is extravagantly playful and not intended to be taken seriously at all.

The effort to use the theatre theatrically but without doctrinaire rigor has continued as a matter of course; nor has the effort been confined to the pragmatic professional undertakings of show business in Paris, London, or New York. In our southeastern states since World War II there has been much work in a relatively new form of pageant-drama that is called "symphonic drama" by Paul Green, a pioneer in the form. Designed as a national or regional celebration revolving around some historical event, symphonic drama has a ritual pattern of sung, danced, and spoken scenes in varying combinations. Such productions as *The Lost Colony* and *The Common Glory* by Paul Green and *Horn in the West* and *Unto These Hills* by Kermit Hunter have exhibited forthright theatricalist stylization. The staging has been characterized by concentration on expressive spectacle and broad performance. Projecting or *presenting*, rather than representing, a story of the American land has been the objective in each production. Any effort to preserve the fourth-wall convention on open-air stages would have been quixotic and disastrous. However, the productions have not been so strongly stylized as to suggest an attempt to create abstract and coterie art.

At the other extreme in the American theatre is the arena-theatre movement that developed after 1940. This development, contrary to Reinhardt's example and the suggestion of bigness in the term "arena," has not favored large-scale production. In the usually very small theatres especially built or modified for arena staging or central staging, the fourth wall of the realistic stage is utterly abolished. The playing area is in the center and is completely surrounded or surrounded on three sides (in so-called "three-quarter-arena" style) by the audience. There can be no imaginary fourth wall in central staging because three real walls are lacking. The arena theatres, usually consisting of two or three tiers of seats, create an atmosphere of extreme intimacy; and the proponents of central staging have, indeed, tended to make "intimacy" their sole esthetic stock in trade.

Actually, arena theatres came into vogue because off-Broadway groups wanted to effect economies in scenery and backstage crew requirements. Intimacy is a deceptive concept and one that must be balanced, now and then, by the need for maintaining esthetic distance. For the spectator, one of the disturbing features of an unsuccessful Greenwich Village Circle-in-the-Square production was having a large, energetic, and deafening chorus of Mississippi Valley townspeople virtually in his lap.

Although this chapter is not the appropriate place for a discussion of the possibilities and limitations of the arena techniques now in use,[22] three points should be made here. First, since arena performances of nonmusical drama have been generally realistic rather than presentational or especially stylized, a blithe inconsistency is being maintained. If logic rather than habit (the habits of directors, players, and playgoers) dictated practice, perform-

[22] A detailed treatment of all aspects of central staging will be found in the present author's *Producing the Play*, 1953 ed., pp. 528-600, and a briefer description combined with provocative criticism is contained in *Principles of Theatre Art* by H. D. Albright, William Halstead, and Lee Mitchell (Houghton Mifflin, 1955), pp. 222-228.

ances on a centrally located stage would be at least as presentational as those that were given in the Elizabethan and Greek
theatres. Without possessing a single real wall, the arena theatre
nonetheless creates the illusion of environment by means of the
furniture, the properties, and the dialogue of the characters. The
second point to be noted is that arena staging, as a rule, is
theatricalist theatre at the start (that is, when the performance
begins) and *realistic* theatre at the end, after the audience has
become accustomed to the convention of having the actors in its
collective lap and after the illusion of reality has established its
hold on the playgoer. As on the proscenium stage, the actors
remain psychologically in their own world and keep out of the
audience's world by studiously ignoring the spectator; they speak
naturally, and they use stage properties naturalistically.

It would seem, indeed, that the theatricalism of arena staging is accidental rather than the result of planning, and that the
best effects may have been fortuitous. An esthetics of arena theatre does not yet exist, and it is not likely to be desired by the
partisans of arena staging so long as they want to produce every
kind of play. In arena theatre, then, we have occasionally engrossing and usually acceptable illustrations of the fusion of
realism and theatricalism by accommodation. In this respect
American arena staging (even by ambitiously experimental
groups) illustrates the characteristic pragmatism and eclecticism of show business, which, as noted previously, has mediated
between realistic and antirealistic modes of theatre more or less
haphazardly rather than by design.

Even moderate theatricalism, however, involves fundamental
modifications of procedure in playwriting and stage production
that must be thought out instead of being haphazardly hit upon.
Many attempts at theatrical realization of a play are weak and
unsuccessful because the authors and producers fail to realize
that they have made a commitment to a new style or form
of theatre. They operate too negatively. They take liberties with

the convention of realism, but do not discover for themselves any other convention that is vital and meaningful. The result, then, is haphazardness in writing and staging.

The principal choice in our century has lain between a great deal of vivacious theatricalism, particularly in musical comedy,[23] and formalism. And an intermediate, elegant theatricality should also be noted, although it has no distinctive form. It has been found everywhere on the commercial stage, but has been especially prevalent in England, where it appears in productions of both old and new plays. Whether applied to Farquhar's *The Beaux' Stratagem* or Fry's *Venus Observed*, *Antony and Cleopatra* or *Caesar and Cleopatra*, "elegant theatricality" is more distinguished by glossiness, glitter, and grace of movement than by incisiveness of meaning and vigor of experience. Laurence Olivier's revolving-stage production of *Caesar and Cleopatra* in the 1950's, for example, was eye-filling rather than mind-filling. The acting in this elegant style of production has no roughness, no crudity, but it also conveys no sense of the grain of the play or of the main characters. The stage production is likely to resolve itself into a succession of group pictures and passages of elocution. In Shakespearean productions, usually approved by academicians as well as by "the carriage trade," songs and dances, along with fetching costumes and attractive scenery, enrich even if they rarely enliven, the proceedings. The New York Theatre Guild's production of *As You Like It*, starring Katharine Hepburn, was duly applauded by the *Shakespeare Quarterly* despite the fact that, as a result of the stringing together of songs, there was more Rudolf Friml than Shakespeare in the proceedings. In

---

[23] Like opera and music-drama, musical comedies are so intrinsically theatricalist in character that there is little need to discuss them here. It is worth noting only that on Broadway the development of musical comedy has been in two opposite directions— toward the realistic character-drama and the problem play, as in Rodgers and Hammerstein musicals such as *South Pacific* and *The King and I*, and toward the use of the formalistic, nonverbal element of ballet, as in Agnes de Mille's *tour de force* at the end of the first act of *Oklahoma!*

productions intended to be "cultural," there is usually a suggestion of ritual in the presentation. The tone is one of gravity,
though it is not infrequently mixed with polite humor; and there
is considerable ceremoniousness in the actors' graceful movement
and good diction, as well as in the settings, the costuming, the
sedate musical accompaniment, and the conventional choreography. This type of patrician theatricalism reached the peak of
elaborateness in the Old Vic's *Midsummer Night's Dream* production of 1953-1954, which simply oozed culture while it
thrummed Mendelssohn.

Formalistic theatre is less likely to be exploited commer-
cially than this mode of theatrical elegance and cultivated ceremonialism. It is also less likely to be the vehicle of star actors,
although it has tended to become the indulgence of star
directors. It is usually characterized by a purity of esthetic aim
such as we associate with Copeau and Yeats, both of whom
retreated from the market place. They had noble aims, these and
other dreamers of stylized, more or less ritualistic, art: The spirit
of man would be liberated by the very process of setting bounds
—the bounds of art—to the imitation of an action and the
imitation of conversation. Man would be magnified to the degree
that action was purified of all but symbolic content, that characterization was refined into typicality, that speech was subjected
to the jeweled yoke of formal utterance. Life on the stage would
recover its antique grandeur to the degree that action was made
ritualistic, characterization sculptural, and language ceremonial.
That was the ideal of formalism virtually from the beginning of
the antinaturalistic reaction of the 1890's. Although it appears
to be an impossible ideal, it proved realizable enough when
formalism was blended with romanticism, as in the work of
Émile Verhaeren, Paul Claudel, and Yeats; and also, later on,
when it was mingled with realism, as in the work of Wilder,
Eliot, Williams, and Brecht.

In order to avoid confusion, it is perhaps also necessary to note that "formalism" has been used in communist propaganda as a loosely defined charge, wantonly applied against "decadent bourgeois culture." Politically, however, formalism is meaningless. *If* the word has any semantic value at all, it is that of signifying conspicuously formal play structure and artificially devised—hence "formal"—characterization, action, and speech. An exponent of Russian formalism, Shklovsky, once declared that "a work of art is the sum total of all the stylistic devices employed in it." He also expressed the extremist view when he wrote that art is always "free of life." [24] In England during the 1930's, Auden, Isherwood, Spender, and others wrote formalist drama from the "left" side of the political fence, and Eliot and others from the "right." [25] Tairov was able to move from a pre-Soviet estheticism to a post-Soviet "social-mindedness," and yet use formalistic elements in his stage productions both before and after 1918. And if Yeats's love of formalism inclined him toward a private type of theatre, there can be no doubt that it has also been possible to employ formalism in mass productions of all kinds, whether religious, patriotic, fascist, or communistic. In 1918 Meyerhold staged an early Bolshevik outdoor mass-spectacle of revolution, *Mystery-Bouffe*, by the "futurist" poet Mayakovsky, along with another "formalistic" drama of revolution, Émile Verhaeren's *The Dawn*.

One may conclude that although formalism *could* have political manifestations, the limitations or dangers of the formalist theatre are not intrinsically political. One may legitimately criticize, instead, the pretentiousness of private appeal or the ostentatiousness of public appeal, the stiffness of action and speech, and the depersonalization of character that appeared in many experiments. Usually, moreover, the formalistic style of making

[24] Victor Erlich, *Russian Formalism-History-Doctrine*, with a Preface by René Wellek (The Hague, 1955).
[25] I refer to "antifascist" or "anti-imperialistic" work such as Auden's *The Dance of Death*, Spender's *The Trial of a Judge*, or Auden and Isherwood's *The Ascent of F6*, on the one hand, and Eliot's *Murder in the Cathedral* and *The Family Reunion*, on the other.

theatre was most deleterious to multi-dimensional acting. Automatism has been the greatest danger, regardless of the political position represented by the play and production. Stiffness and an effect of remoteness have been particularly evident when dramatic treatments have kept the actors from functioning in active communication with each other. "Players who give a clear-cut impression that they are in active communication with each other . . . are likely to seem most real." [26] Characters seem to be isolated or boxed off even in such literary plays as Yeats's *A Full Moon in March* and Eliot's *Murder in the Cathedral* and *Family Reunion,* in which the speakers are notably articulate.

It was probably inevitable that theatricalist and formalist experiments should have also favored the use of masks as in the classic theatre and in primitive rituals. Perhaps the most noteworthy incorporation of the mask as a psychological necessity in the drama was in *The Great God Brown,* in which one character assumed the mask of another to signify an exchange of character. O'Neill, it would seem, renounced the use of masks in his later work rather reluctantly; he included requests for an equivalent fixity of expression and exchange of facial appearance in his stage directions for *Mourning Becomes Electra.* But the first completely nonpsychological and formalistic use of masks in theatrical production appeared at least a decade and a half before *The Great God Brown* when Gordon Craig made some designs in 1911 for Yeats's production of *The Hour Glass* and *On Baile's Strand* at the Abbey Theatre. A formal masking of characters was a feature of productions of such work as Yeats's latter-day one-act plays inspired by the Japanese Noh plays, the Federal Theatre's "living newspaper" *Power,* and the Berliner Ensemble production of Brecht's *The Caucasian Circle of Chalk* that was seen in Paris in the summer of 1955. The motivation varied and will undoubtedly continue to vary: the mask helped

[26] Albright, Halstead, and Mitchell, *Principles of Theatre Art,* p. 120.

to depersonalize characters for one purpose or another. In *Power,* for instance, the motivation was plainly satirical, the nine masks representing the "nine old men," the justices of the U.S. Supreme Court, whom President Franklin D. Roosevelt had denounced for obstructing New Deal legislation. The mask emphasized the ritualistic character of some of Yeats's plays. And, in general, it could distance, elevate, and dignify dramatic experience, freeing it from the temporality and flux of realistic theatre. Craig sensed this, when he designed the mask for the Blind Man in Yeats's *On Baile's Strand.* "The advantage of a mask over a face," he wrote, "is that it is always repeating unerringly the poetic fancy." The theatre must learn the lesson of "durability" from Egyptian art and return to the ancient practice of covering the actor's face "in order that his expression—the visualized expression of the poetic spirit—shall be everlasting." [27]

Formalism is the result of a search for esthetic conventions that will be serviceable to the theatre in general and to the individual dramatist in particular. It is little short of remarkable how deliberately, almost desperately, those who expected a freely inspired or spontaneous art to emerge from theatricalism (which its advocate Alexander Bakshy called "the theatre unbound") turned to the pursuit of convention. Reinhardt, the gifted popularizer, knew which way the wind was blowing when he produced pantomime drama, staged plays against the formal background of a baroque screen in a palace ballroom, used the sets of individual stages which are called "mansions" in the simultaneous staging of one religious production, and presented Hofmannsthal's *Jedermann* (out of our medieval *Everyman*) on a platform in front of the baroque portals of the Salzburg Cathedral. Copeau's permanent architectural stage in Paris and attempts by others to abolish the proscenium arch from the stage reflected the search for formalistic theatre, as did the experiments of Meyerhold and Tairov; Barrault's later development of a miming technique continued the quest for formalistic art; and in playwriting, the search for new "forms" has been continuous.

[27] Janet Leeper, *Edward Gordon Craig: Designs for the Theatre* (Harmondsworth, England: King Penguin Books, 1948), p. 46.

The plays Yeats wrote after 1917 in the style of the Japanese Noh play provide examples of special conventionalization. In *A Full Moon in March,* the Swineherd who is the hero of the piece wears a mask over the upper part of his face, and the heroine, the Queen, is veiled. An inner curtain is drawn when he is to be beheaded at the Queen's order, while an Attendant recites a poem about a legendary beheading of a lover by an Irish queen. Next, the Queen appears, holding the severed head of the Swineherd, and her hands and costume are symbolically red. She begins to mimic the actions of singing, whereupon the Attendant actually sings the words for her while she dances out her feelings to the accompaniment of drum taps. Next, when the Head is supposedly singing, the Second Attendant sings the Head's words, while, as the stage direction reads, *"The Queen in her dance moves away from the head, alluring and refusing."* In the midst of the dance, when the Queen is supposed to laugh, the First Attendant laughs for her. The Second Attendant says: "She is laughing. How can she laugh,/Loving the dead." And the First Attendant replies, "She is crazy. That is why she is laughing," and the stage direction reads *"Laughs again as Queen."* The Queen, then, making no sound, takes up the Head, places her lips against its lips, and dances more and more rapidly. Finally, she sinks slowly down, and the Attendants close the play formally, singing a commentary to the effect that the virginally cruel lack "Their desecration and the lover's night."

A Full Moon in March is an extreme example of formalistic playwriting, but many other twentieth-century plays contain formalistic elements. The high point of T. S. Eliot's *The Cocktail Party* is the second act, in which Dr. Reilly, the psychiatrist-guardian, and his associates, Julia and Alex, assume a religious function. They perform a sort of ritual, reminiscent of the Mass, with their cocktail glasses. Reilly says, "And now we are ready for the libation." Alex calls for "the words for the building of the hearth," referring to the Chamberlaynes, who have been sent home by Dr. Reilly to repair their marriage; and Reilly pronounces a brief prayer for this couple while the "guardians" raise their glasses. Then Alex, referring to the heroine, Celia Copplestone, who is starting her journey toward eventual martyrdom, calls for "the words for those who go on a journey." And the three supernatural "guardians" start the chant "Protector of travellers / Bless the road," the formalism of which is partly established by the parallelism of the lines, as in Julia's stanza:

> Protect her from the Voices
> Protect her from the Visions
> Protect her in the tumult
> Protect her in the silence.

A third simple example is provided by the Spanish poet-playwright Federico García Lorca. In his tragedy of love, *Blood Wedding*, the climax comes when the heroine's lover, who has abducted her from her wedding, fights a fatal duel in a forest with the bridegroom. The most theatrically striking feature of the first scene of the third act is the apparition of the Moon and Death as allegorical figures. Moreover, their speeches are completely formal. The Moon, for example, says:

> Let me in! I come freezing
> down to walls and windows!
> Open roofs, open breasts
> Where I may warm myself!
> I'm cold! [28]

Colors are used formalistically by García Lorca in the costuming and décor of his fantastic play *The Love of Don Perlimpín and Belisa in His Garden*. Masks have been favored in some nonrealistic plays; they are indispensable to the dramatic meaning of O'Neill's *The Great God Brown*. (Masks, it will be remembered, were required in all plays written for the highly formal classic theatre of Athens.) Choruses, another formalistic feature of classic drama, reappear in dramatic modernism. The chorus of Canterbury women is the main structural element in

[28] Translation by Richard L. O'Connell and James Graham-Luján, *Three Tragedies of Lorca* (New Directions, 1947).

Murder in the Cathedral, and choruses play an important part in Giraudoux' *Electra,* in Eliot's *Family Reunion,* in O'Neill's *Lazarus Laughed,* and O'Casey's *Within the Gates.* A single individual, speaking alone or with other characters, may also perform the functions of the classic chorus in a more or less informal manner, as do Seth and the townspeople in O'Neill's *Mourning Becomes Electra.*

A unique formalist device appeared in a modern psychological context when O'Neill restored the old-fashioned "aside" as a recurrent feature of his redundant but successful nine-act drama *Strange Interlude.* The aside was used here as interior monologue, so that it is actually soliloquy. O'Neill's fluent use of this device is comparable to Joyce's employment of stream-of-consciousness writing in *Ulysses,* although the playwright's language is decidedly less imaginative than the novelist's. Progress in modern theatre was once associated with the abolition of the aside and the soliloquy; when this had been achieved, however, progress soon came to be associated with the recovery of these devices for playwriting. Writing in 1910, Clayton Hamilton, in *The Theory of the Theatre,* deplored the aside, especially because the actor delivering it had to step out of the proscenium frame and annihilate the fourth wall. Hamilton was kinder to the soliloquies, distinguishing two kinds: objectionable "constructive soliloquies," in which the plot is explained (as at the beginning of the last act of *Lady Windermere's Fan*) or by which off-stage events are reported, and acceptable "reflective soliloquies." The latter were permissible to the modern playwright, he said, because they reveal a character's train of thought. Hamlet's speeches, for instance, could be made to seem natural because they were psychologically motivated.

Writing in 1939, Clayton Hamilton said that the asides in *Strange Interlude,* which did not at all disturb the public of that highly successful Theatre Guild production, were "reflective soliloquies," for the actor was not "forced out of the stage picture." [29] These analyses of the aside and the soliloquy are likely to be helpful only to someone who cares about the preservation of the "stage picture"—that is, the preservation of the environment established by means of the proscenium arch and the fourth-wall convention. For a mode of theatre in which the illusion of reality is not a desideratum, the playwright and the director may very well *intend* to force the actor out of the stage picture. They may not want to "motivate" the soliloquy, but to startle and stimulate the audience by violating illusion. They will therefore replace psychology with theatricality, and make use of the power (or the charm, or the comic possibilities) of direct address to the spectator. When the theatricalist writers and directors recovered the soliloquy for modern theatre they were certainly not interested in making it "natural"; they wanted it to be "unnatural" —that is, theatrical. Giraudoux obviously had this intention when he wrote his *Electra* in 1937.

Formalism was also well served, of course, by the return of the narrator, who came to be used in a variety of imaginative ways. In *Our Town,* for instance, the narrator (called the Stage Manager) is not merely a townsman of Grover's Corners, New Hampshire; he is the informal master of ceremonies who addresses the audience directly. In Cocteau's modernist retelling of the Oedipus myth, *The Infernal Machine,* the narrator is a disembodied voice. The Voice formally summarizes the plot in advance of the action, as if to say to the audience, "Now that you know the story, I can proceed with demonstrating it to you psychologically and intellectually—and, to be sure, *theatrically.*" And this, in fact, is what the narrator declares, starting with the statement, "He will kill his father. He will marry his mother," and commenting further on, "For the gods really to enjoy themselves, the victim must fall from a great height." The introductory narration concludes with an undisguised public address: "Spectator, this machine you see here wound up to the full in such a way that the spring will slowly unwind the whole length of a human life, is one of the most perfect constructed by the infernal gods for the mathematical destruction of a mortal."

[29] *The Theory of the Theatre* (New York, 1939), pp. 48-51.

An especially candid formalism is achieved by the use of a narrator in Tennessee Williams' delicately written play *The Glass Menagerie*. Here the narrator is an older edition of the boy Tom, who is one of the three important characters in this four-character play. Tom, as the narrator, opens the play by looking back into the past—a past that he now sees in perspective. Dressed as a merchant sailor, he appears out of the darkness, strolls across the front of the stage, and stops at the fire-escape entrance of his remembered home.

Tom becomes, like the narrator in *Our Town*, a man addressing his public in plain violation of the realistic fourth-wall convention. He announces candidly: "Yes, I have tricks in my pocket. I have things up my sleeve. But I am the opposite of a stage magician. He gives you illusion that has the appearance of truth. I give you truth in the pleasant disguise of illusion." After commenting on the depression period of his boyhood and thus establishing the social background of the play, he explains to the audience that it will now see a "memory play." Then, as if the formalism of the work were not already sufficiently apparent, Tom the narrator changes roles; he enters the house and becomes the boy he once was. Finally, at the conclusion of the last vignette of remembered home life, the young Tom once more becomes the narrator. He again addresses the audience as he stands "outside," while the action "inside" is pantomimed by Tom's mother and his sister Laura. His speech ends with his addressing Laura as he watches her across the years. As she bends over the candles in the parlor, Tom says, "Blow out your candles, Laura, and so good-bye. . . ." She does so, and the memory play ends.

From these examples it will be seen, then, that formalism has played an important part in modernist stylization, very much as it did in the great prerealistic periods of the past in which soliloquies, asides, choruses, and narrators were accepted as stage and dramatic conventions. Theatricalism has not, therefore, been merely a swirl of whimsies and fads whipped up in the theatre of our century. It has been a series of revolts and innovations involving alterations of dramatic form and theatrical style. And whether or not these have succeeded completely, they have achieved some liberation of theatrical art, some release of poetic imagination.

The full importance of such changes (or, at least, the fact that they are changes in form) can be realized when we contrast theatricalized dramas with simple fantasies such as *Outward Bound* and *On Borrowed Time*, in which supernatural occurrences are rendered realistically both in the writing and the stage production. Conventional fantasy has been deliberately written and staged as though it were "true," the purpose being to provide the same illusion of reality that common realism affords. At the same time we tend to believe, in the "eat-your-cake-yet-have-it-too" school of commercial theatre, that fantasy will call attention to itself more strongly when the unnatural events occur in an everyday manner and in an environment in which only humdrum occurrences are to be expected. When the present writer produced a Welsh fantasy, Richard Hughes' *Minnie and Mr. Williams,* on Broadway, he debated the question of using either a realistic background distinguished by local color or a predominantly fantastic setting. The latter would have enabled one of the main characters, an imp of Satan, to enter a Welsh preacher's house through the walls. The back wall was to be omitted from the set in at least one scene, and the imp was to appear out of nowhere, as it were, in a blaze of supernatural light laid down by the stage electricians. A realistic style was ultimately selected on the grounds that the presence of an imp of Hell in a preacher's home was eery enough. Eddie Dowling, the stage director of the production, argued that Hell in the shape of an innocent-looking little girl would be considerably more impressive in a natural environment than in a supernatural one.

Not merely imagination, but imagination directed toward the formalization of theatre and drama, has been a decisive factor in the theatricalist revolution. The premise that theatre is art and that art is a tissue of conventions is inherent in the formalistic approach. The aim of theatricality is to create a new reality —*a reality of art*—on the stage. Tennessee Williams, by no means the first writer to favor this view, worded it well in his production notes for *The Glass Menagerie:*

> Everyone should know nowadays the unimportance of the photographic in art: that truth, life or reality is an organic thing which the poetic imagination can represent or suggest, in essence, only through transformation, through changing into other forms than those which were merely present in appearance.

And this definition of art as truth, life, or reality represented in essence and "through changing into other forms" applies as well as any to the artistic reality of great non-naturalistic drama such as *Antigone* or *Hamlet*. Williams' explanation brings us close to Alexander Bakshy's illuminating, though necessarily oversimplified, differentiation between the realistic-naturalistic and the theatricalist ideas of theatre, expressed as a distinction between "representational" and "presentational" art. Representational theatre, said Bakshy, aims for the illusion of actuality, whereas presentational theatre does without that illusion. Dramatic realism, then, can be called "a mode of actuality," and dramatic presentationalism can be called "a mode of theatre."

The Possibilities of a Modern Synthesis

That the makeshift theatricalism of ordinary showmen should have led nowhere except to riches or bankruptcy in the market place is understandable. That the extravagances of abstraction-haunted visionaries should have fizzled out instead of supplying a steady light for creative endeavor is also understandable. The extreme stylizers made promises they could not have kept without either smothering the dramatic medium in symbolism or exploding it with expressionism. But why has not sound and moderate theatricalism, clearly understood and tastefully guided by able stage directors, achieved more than minor renovations of the modern stage? This much is apparent: Although retheatricalization of the theatre after the triumph of realism has been a highly commendable aim, theatricalism has not yet endowed the modern theatre with the power and significance it had when it was served by the pioneering giants of realism.

It is possible, to be sure, to list many charming, imaginative productions in the theatricalist mode, ranging from Vakhtangov's production of *Princess Turandot* in the early 1920's to the Peter Brook production of *Ring 'Round the Moon* in London in 1950. It has been possible to derive much civilized entertainment and stimulation from one or more of the successful plays of Cocteau, Pirandello, Giraudoux, Anouilh, and other writers in the theatricalist mode. Many of the playwrights even give the impression of having felt and thought with some intensity. Yet they have rarely made the theatre seem important to the modern public except when their theatricalist aims have been augmented by others quite distinct from that of presenting "theatre for theatre's sake." We may refer to *The Dybbuk,* which is made "real" by the folk-spirit of Chassidic fantasy; to *Liliom,* which begins as the naturalistic portrait of a misfit; to *Six Characters in Search of an Author,* which derives its dramatic power from the paradoxically real emotions of fanciful characters as well as from the polarization of life and theatre in the text; to *Our Town,* which has the quality of a genre painting of an actual New England town; to *The Madwoman of Chaillot,* in which fantasy is treated in a matter-of-fact fashion and has the immediacy of social drama; or to Jean Anouilh's drama *The Lark,* which consists of realistic episodes from the life of Joan of Arc and is, at the same time, "theatricalist" in treatment—mainly in the formalism of the frame of the play and the unchronological sequence of its episodes.

Theatricalism has made—or has given a realistically disposed public the impression of making—significant contributions to the modern drama mainly in association with some quality of realism. Good theatre has, however, also been frequently defeated by the serious intentions that accompany realism, and the theatre of our century has been littered with the lumpy wreckage of imaginations that should never have been required to carry much freight. I believe I am not alone in considering Ugo Betti's brooding fantasy *The Gambler,* one example of overextended theatricality, a far less satisfactory work of art than such pieces of frivolous legerdemain as Molnar's *The Play's the Thing* or, for that matter, any number of farces from *Charley's Aunt* and *The Importance of Being Earnest* to *Private Lives* and *Blithe Spirit.* And the reverse has also been true—the theatricality of a work has negated or diminished its claims to significant meaning. Theatricality made many a German play, from Hauptmann's *And Pippa Dances* in 1906 to Wolfgang Borchert's *Outside the Door* forty years later, embarrassingly frantic rather then genuinely serious, and brought confusion into even the urbane French theatre in the work of Paul Claudel and Armand Salacrou. Giraudoux, too, was not always immune to an undulant fever of theatricality, as in *Ondine* and in two mythological scenes omitted from the New York production of *Tiger at the Gates;* and *The Lark,* as written by Anouilh rather than as adapted by Lillian Hellman, was made more specious by Anouilh's fondness for jumping through theatrical hoops than most New York reviewers realized.

Theatricalists have generally been most secure when governed by a sure sense of comedy and least secure when impelled to write "seriously." The tact and urbanity of Giraudoux have been rare among theatricalist playwrights. Nor is the taste of a Jouvet or Barrault commonly to be found in the field of stage production. Some artists have known how to be playful, and that knowledge is indispensable for anyone who elects to be theatrical. A clodhopper should not dance in ballet, and a dray-horse should not run in the Kentucky Derby. Some subjects and moods, moreover, do not usually lend themselves to successful theatricalization or formalization. The brassy theatricalism of John Howard Lawson's *Processional* suited the materials of the play and served the author's satirical purpose. A charade such as the Fry-Anouilh *Ring 'Round the Moon* is comic and frothy, and theatricality is appropriate in both the writing and performance of such a play. But theatricality was curiously inappropriate in *Camino Real,* Tennessee Williams' fantasy on the failure of modern society and the miseries of modern man. Theatricality, indeed, ran amok in the busy Broadway production of this work when actors pranced about in the auditorium, even up to the box seats. Eddie Dowling, the producer of Williams' earlier play *The Glass Menagerie,* was better advised when he dispensed with the author's rather redundant theatricalism which the reader will find incorporated in the stage directions of the published play.

Formalism, too, has often betrayed its devotees, who have been mostly poets bent upon avoiding contamination by the commercial theatre. Yeats, the most gifted of modern mandarin playwrights, staged his Japanese-inspired pieces in his own or a friend's living room with all the ceremoniousness of a ritual. One such performance of the formalist little play *The Hawk's Well* made O'Casey nostalgic for his own boozy character Fluther in *The Plough and the Stars:* "What headlines his visit would make in the morrow's newspaper! Fluther runs wild in Yeats's drawing room." O'Casey reflected farther that "the people's theatre can never be successfully turned into a poetical conventicle," and he put his finger on a major limitation of any formalism created by fiat or by imitation—the danger of sterile artificiality:

> Yeats had read in a big book all about the Noh Plays . . .
> and had seized on the idea that he could do in an hour what
> had taken a thousand years to create. And so . . . Yeats'
> idea of a Noh Play blossomed for a brief moment, then the

artificial petals faded and dropped lonely to the floor, because a Japanese spirit had failed to climb into the soul of
a Kelt.[30]

The conventions of modern nonrealistic theatre have not
developed in a stable cultural context. In earlier ages, the development of presentational or formalistic theatre had paralleled a development toward cultural climaxes; this was true in
Periclean Athens, in Elizabethan England, and in France in the
age of Louis XIV. The course of our century's nonrealistic theatre
has paralleled only a flux of tensions, passions, and reactions.
Modern theatricalism has not been, perhaps could not have
been, an organic style. The theatricalist form of theatre has not
grown up naturally. It has been invented or willed into existence
by talented idealists like Craig and Copeau and talented op-
portunists like Reinhardt. On the one hand, then, we have had
much routinized realism; on the other, much footless theatricality. It is not surprising that at the midcentury we have found
ourselves in Matthew Arnold's uncomfortable situation of wandering between two worlds—one dead, the other powerless to be
born.

At first glance there seems to be no possibility of breaking
this impasse. Yet the situation is not at all desperate wherever
the theatre artist and the playwright can create without intimida-
tion and official control. Realism has survived as a vital mode of
theatrical art in our century precisely because theatricalism has
challenged it continually and because the realists have been able
to learn from the theatricalists. The great realists of the past
were antitheatrical, after all, only to the degree that they opposed false and question-begging drama and empty showmanship.

There appears to be a way out of the artistic impasse in
which the contemporary theatre finds itself. It is for the realists

[30] *Inishfallen, Fare Thee Well* (Macmillan, 1949), p. 373.

to tap the dramatic resources of theatricalism, but to use them in order to *advance essential realism.* And this would demand integrity, not opportunism. There can be no real gain in merely tidying up or prettifying realism, as the British especially have been trying to do for decades. We must respect the fact that not all things have to be fluent, graceful, and glossy in order to attract and stimulate. The true artist and the intelligent critic can only endorse Santayana's statement in the preface to his poems: "The owl hooting from his wintry bough cannot be chanticleer crowing in the barnyard, yet he is sacred to Minerva."

Imagination is the link between all schools of modern art. It is clear that there need be no conflict between the leading realists and their opponents over the importance of imagination. This is made evident by such developments as the crystallization of Stanislavsky's so-called system, which had for its objective the stimulation of the actor's imagination or "magical, creative *if,*" and the rise of the Musical Studio of the Moscow Art Theatre, which startled the Western world with superb productions of Charles Lecocq's *The Daughter of Madame Angot,* Offenbach's *La Périchole,* Aristophanes' *Lysistrata,* and Bizet's *Carmen,* the last presented in the memorable gypsy version entitled *Carmencita and the Soldier.* It is noteworthy that these imaginative contributions to the lyric theatre came not out of the *avant-garde,* antirealistic theatres, but out of the Moscow Art Theatre, that center of realism. Also, the director of the Musical Studio was none other than Stanislavsky's celebrated cofounder and codirector of the Art Theatre, Vladimir Nemirovich-Danchenko. To historians of modern theatre it may indeed seem ironic that the greatest service to the romantic or Wagnerian ideal of "synthetic theatre" made since Wagner's day should have come in the twentieth century from the theatrical organization that gave the realistic stage its highest status. Far from allowing experience with the realistic stage to lead him into "the barren field of realistic opera," [31] Danchenko turned to the great fusion that has

[31] *Inside the Moscow Art Theatre,* by Oliver M. Sayler (New York: Brentano's, 1925), p. 148.

been dreamed of by Western artists ever since they began, during the Renaissance, to look back to the Greek theatre as a lost ideal of synthesis. We may certify it, as Wagner did in his *Art Work of the Future,* the "great united art-work," in which the play is regarded as only one element of a totality which is theatre. Wagner described this synthesis as one that must embrace all the genres of art *and in some degree undo each of them in order to use it as a means to an end.*[32] It is plain, then, that one of the great theatres of realism, if not indeed the greatest, was entirely willing to accept the *theatrical nature* of theatre by 1919.

Only at the Moscow Art Theatre, declared Danchenko,[33] could he have achieved the results he had visualized, because there "the atmosphere of triviality is an utter impossibility." But he also understood a more important point, of which he made use in practice—namely, that a productive merger, so to speak, is possible when the realistic and the theatricalist approaches to theatre are allowed to *complement* rather than destroy each other. "It would be the greatest mistake, and disastrous for the music, to construct an operatic performance according to the naturalistic methods of the drama," declared his associate Sergei Berthensson, the Musical Studio's acting director in 1924.[34] Without a doubt, however, it is possible to establish a link between the presentational form of music-drama and that quintessence of realistic performance which Stanislavsky and his followers called "inner justification." Berthensson declared that "if a wonderful singer is not first of all an actor" he should not be used except at a concert; only a singer-actor "can create a performance instead of a concert." He expressed the possibility of a merger of realism and theatricalism when he spoke as follows:

A singer must not, like a dramatic actor, live his role realistically. A singer cannot cry because a sincere tear would

[32] *Ibid.,* p. 146.
[33] *Ibid.,* p. 54.
[34] *Ibid.,* p. 55.

FORMALIST PLATFORM STAGE FOR A SHAKESPEAREAN PRODUC-
TION *Teo Otto designed this setting for a Zurich Schauspielhaus production of* Romeo and Juliet *in 1950. Teo Otto's own statement may
serve as both justification and unintentional self-criticism: "Naturalism
may be bad as a programme, but it can be an excellent means of expression. So can abstract representation, though carried to the point
of a system it will kill art."* From *World Theatre* magazine.

THEATRICALIST USE OF THE PLATFORM STAGE *An extreme example of the theatricalist approach to staging a play was furnished by
the Zurich Schauspielhaus production of* The Taming of the Shrew *in
1952, designed by Teo Otto.* Photograph: W. E. Baur, from *World
Theatre* magazine.

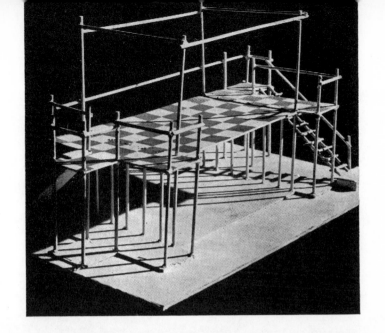

THEATRICALIST DÉCOR, OR "ELEGANT THEATRICALISM" *The 1950 American production of the Anouilh-Fry "charade" Ring 'Round the Moon was a replica of the British production directed by Peter Brook and designed by Oliver Messel. The playful theatricalist quality of the production, marked by an elegance not inappropriate to the social background, is particularly apparent in the skeletal form of the hothouse and the free—that is, "theatrical"—treatment of the striped awnings at the right and the left.* Photograph: Eileen Darby for Graphic House. A Gilbert Miller production; courtesy of the producer.

contract his larynx; he cannot laugh without the risk of spoiling his tone. But with a flexible artistic fantasy, he can detect an inner problem, embracing the musical foundations of the subject matter, the psychological background and the plastic form. Without the "inner justification," all so-called "play" results in nothing but stencils, frauds—all that which creates tasteless and unconvincing "theatricality." [35]

It should be added here only that, as Danchenko declared concerning his work on Charles Lecocq's opera, "music helps to make immense psychological leaps." And ballet, when properly associated with drama, also introduces psychological leaps. In *Oklahoma!*, for example, the superb ballet created by Agnes de Mille for the end of the first act expressed the heroine's mental conflict far more impressively than a dramatic discussion could have done. The realistic theatre's ideals of analysis, motivation, and conviction were attained here by the expressive employment (or shall we say deployment) of music and the dance. "Realism," as understood in terms of these ideals, becomes impossible only when, as in ordinary practice, there is no true interfusion of arts, but a haphazard or routine mingling of elements; for musical theatre and opera are usually treated as "an omelet of the arts of the theatres." [36] Inner justification of action certainly can appear only when considerations of theatrical spectacle or musical virtuosity do not prevail so strongly that human motivation above the kindergarten level is eliminated.

It was the striving for a theatricalism that agrees with essential realism, instead of conflicting with it, that kept the aims of the two original leaders of the Moscow Art Theatre from clashing. Stanislavsky was never an enemy of the imagination: he staged Maeterlinck's fantasy *The Blue Bird*, as well as some of the Belgian writer's early symbolistic one-act pieces, before World War I and indeed had a symbolist phase himself, as did many leaders of Russian literature, between 1905 and 1916.

[35] *Ibid.*, p. 55.
[36] A. Kugel, a Russian critic, quoted in Sayler, *Inside the Moscow Art Theatre,* p. 139.

Stanislavsky's concern was with making the imagined action real for theatrical purposes through the proper use of the actor. After a quarter of a century of intensive work, Stanislavsky spoke clearly enough on this particular point in 1924 when he described his "system" as a means for promoting "the creation of the creative mood," or producing "a favorable condition for the appearance of inspiration by means of the will, that condition in the presence of which inspiration was most likely to descend into the actor's soul." Stanislavsky added that he came to understand that the actor becomes a creator by virtue of the "magical, creative *if.*" The actor believes in this "imagined truth" more ardently than he believed in "practical truth": "From the moment of the appearance of *if,* the actor passes from the plane of actual reality into a plane of another life, created and imagined by himself. Believing in this life, the actor can begin to create." [37]

Stanislavsky and the imaginative realists could require no less of the actor than Wordsworth required of the poet, who was in turn Wordsworth's romantic hero:

> . . . a disposition to be affected more than other men by absent things as if they were present; an ability of conjuring up in himself passions, which are indeed far from being the same as those produced by real events, yet . . . do more nearly resemble the passions produced by real events than anything which, from the notions of their own minds merely, other men are accustomed to feel in themselves. (Preface to *Lyrical Ballads,* 1800.)

We may conclude that the creative act was one of *imagination* for Stanislavsky, whether he was concerned with realistic or nonrealistic plays. It is nonsense to say that realistic artists have been unimaginative. If they had been unimaginative, they would not have been artists. And this is true whether the individual happened to write, stage, design, or act in a play. It would be

[37] Sayler, *op. cit.,* pp. 176-177.

absurd, for example, to say that there is no imagination at work in *Ghosts, Rosmersholm, The Wild Duck,* and *John Gabriel Borkman,* or that this imagination is of a lower order than that which created, let us say, *Cyrano de Bergerac.* I am surely not alone in attributing a stronger imagination to Ibsen than to Rostand. And taking our cue from Coleridge's distinction between imagination and fancy, we could profitably pursue the question of whether good realistic writing, staging, or acting is not more profoundly imaginative than a great deal that has passed for imagination in the nonrealistic theatre.

By no means has a feeling for theatre been the exclusive attribute of those who like to play at making theatre or those who elect to perform literary or nonliterary legerdemain in dramatic writing and on the stage. There is surely as much sense of theatre (and, indeed, a *power* of theatre) in *Hedda Gabler* as in, let us say, Molnar's *The Play's the Thing,* or, for that matter, *Liliom.* Maxwell Anderson's *Joan of Lorraine* is an ingenious theatricalist play about an actress rehearsing in a play about Joan of Arc and learning to understand the role. Thus Joan's idealism is elucidated for the audience in discussions of scenes with the stage director, who is also a character in the play. It does not follow, however, that *Joan of Lorraine* is more dramatically and theatrically effective than Shaw's *Saint Joan,* which is just a play about Joan of Arc herself that calls no attention to the theatre, or to itself as make-believe, until we reach the epilogue. And surely Shaw knew as well as Maxwell Anderson that what he was writing about Joan of Arc would be performed in the theatre and would not be merely studied in the reading room of the British Museum. Stanislavsky, in staging *The Lower Depths,* was just as concerned with making Gorki's play vibrate as an experience of theatre as in making us feel that the characters lived and suffered. And the great actor Ivan Moskvin, who played the pilgrim Luka in this masterpiece of naturalism, was triumphantly *both* that character and an actor bent upon giving theatrical definition, rhythm, and accent to the performance. We may say, then, that in so far as realists and naturalists were supremely effective in the theatre, they were distinctly theatrical as well as imaginative. Strictly speaking, we should not call their work realism or naturalism, but *theatrical realism* and *theatrical naturalism.*

How richly theatrical some essentially realistic productions of the past have been cannot be conveyed to anyone who did not see the Moscow Art Theatre's productions of *The Cherry Orchard* and *The Lower Depths* in New York in the mid-1920's, or for that matter, the Group Theatre's production of *Awake and Sing!* in the mid-1930's. How supremely theatrical, without being specious, some realistic plays have already been will be evident to anyone who takes the trouble to give careful study to O'Casey's *Juno and the Paycock* and *The Plough and the Stars,* written in the 1920's, or to Chekhov's *The Three Sisters,* written at the beginning of this century. And a more immediate example is *A Streetcar Named Desire,* which actually contains considerably more theatre in its fabric of characterization, atmosphere and action (this in spite of Williams' naturalism) than many nonrealistic plays, not excluding poetic ones such as *The Cocktail Party* and *The Lady's Not for Burning.*

That self-consciously sensational jumping of the fourth wall, trick effects, and other kinds of theatricalism that are destructive of conviction and depth in playwriting are unnecessary to the production of powerful theatre by a playwright was, surely, best demonstrated by Chekhov, in whose works realism and the sense of theatre merged perfectly. Not only is the structure of *The Three Sisters* superbly symphonic, not only do the action and speech of the characters appear in continual counterpoint, but the pantomime and sound effects, a fire in the town, the playing of a military band, and other nonliterary details produce the crackle of theatre in this drama. Theatre is constantly created, moreover, in details of action that are at once *characterizing* in a realistic mode and *symbolic* in a theatrical mode. One cannot fail to realize this in considering the character Solyony, who wantonly kills the youngest sister's fiancé at the end of the play. Throughout the play, Solyony pours perfume on his death-dealing hands; this mentally twisted man cannot stand the smell of mortality that he imagines them to have. Throughout this play, objects are used theatrically—that is, as theatrical extensions and symbols of Chekhov's realistic action and characterization. And, of course, there is nothing more honestly theatrical in Chekhov's work, as well as more realistically characterizing, than the ridiculous ball in that other Chekhovian masterpiece, *The Cherry Orchard*—a ball staged so inappropriately just when the family has lost its estate. That dramatic realism can fuse with theatricalism and can thereby increase rather than lose its persuasiveness is, indeed, too apparent to justify despair of prospects for revitalizing the realistic theatre.

The leaders of theatrical stylization, too, can play an increasingly effective role in facilitating a merger of the rival modes. In 1941, after having staged *My Heart's in the Highlands,* Robert Lewis, who later directed other fanciful productions such as *Brigadoon* and *The Teahouse of the August Moon,* was moved to protest that there had been a mistaken distinction between so-called stylization and naturalism—"the implication being that the former has problems of form and the latter hasn't." Any satisfactory production, as well as any play, whether it is satisfactory or not, must have form. "To be sure," Mr. Lewis declared, "*realism,* too, is a form; one of the theatrical forms. In realistic drama and theatre, too, the life presented on the stage has been arranged—that is, 'formed.' " But from his experience as a member of the Group Theatre and as teacher of acting, he went on to remind us that in the realistic mode the emphasis is more markedly on the "inner movement" of the play. Everything important in it is determined by what the character wants—that is, by psychological justification.[38] A fusion of theatricalism and realism was, besides, the aim of Jacques Copeau, the most dedicated leader of the theatricalist movement of Western Europe, whose disciples kept theatrical art alive in France. Copeau formalized

[38] Gassner, *Producing the Play,* pp. 294-300.

his scenery because he wanted to simplify it; and he simplified it in order to prevent the décor from overshadowing the dramatic text. Nor did Copeau want to slight character creation. He gave close attention to acting style at his theatre and school with a view to making the actor achieve convincing characterization. Copeau cultivated the histrionic sensibility of the actor as thoroughly as possible, teaching him to *act out* and underscore or punctuate characterization. But he also expected the actor to enact his role with virtually the same "inner realism" that Stanislavsky cultivated at the Moscow Art Theatre. (See pp. 197-202, and pp. 202-205.)

The mixed effect on playwriting of Copeau's work is perhaps best exemplified by André Obey's biblical play *Noah,* written in 1931 for the Company of Fifteen directed by Copeau's talented nephew and disciple Michel Saint-Denis, who became head of the Old Vic School. In Obey's play will be found both universality of theme and concreteness of characterization. In *Noah,* theatricalism is advanced by means of spectacle, pantomime, and dance. And, at the same time, the major requirement of realism is met by orderly sequences of credibly motivated human behavior. (Pierre Fresnay in New York and John Gielgud in London found the title role a thoroughly gratifying one in 1935.) Both the poetry and prose of the human condition are evoked in this work. And Obey requires the actors to provide both realistic portraiture and theatrical action—the latter in the miming of animal roles (for Obey makes charming use of the animals in the ark), and in the dancing of a primitive "earth-greeting" when Noah's children emerge from the ark and touch land at last.

Noah is fundamentally a piece for the little art theatre, and is incapable of affording a gripping experience or sustaining a keen adventure or combat of the mind. Obey, who reached his apogee with this play, has remained a distinctly minor figure in the modern theatre. I believe that even his sturdier colleagues, including Giraudoux and Anouilh, who also emerged from the Copeau-influenced French theatre, have lacked stature commensurate with their talents, not to say with their reputation. Political and financial weather permitting, we may expect a renascence of modern theatre as a result of the intelligent synthesizing of realism and theatricalism. But we shall have only the shadow of a renascence unless there is also a *revitalization* of the drama itself. Imaginative and theatricalized dramatic writing will have to attain at least some of the depth and force with which Ibsen and the other pioneers modernized the drama. By itself, neither the poetic simplicity of an Obey nor the theatrical sophistication or finesse of an Anouilh, nor any of the other histrionic and formalistic qualities to be found in theatricalist writing, can create a very vital stage.

Glimmerings of a renascence of modern theatre have been discovered from time to time since the 1930's whenever a Giraudoux, Anouilh, Brecht, or O'Casey has married theatricalist dramaturgy to contemporary reality or to contemporary realizations of legend and history, as in Giraudoux' *The Trojan War Will Not Take Place*[39] and Brecht's best work. If a vital, non-coterie theatre is to be created it is, however, still imperative that we overcome the tendency to associate theatrical imagination predominantly with absolute emotional states (as in Yeats's *The Player Queen* and *A Full Moon in March*) or with exquisite poetic experience (as in Obey's *Venus and Adonis*) rather than with commitments to the contemporary world. It is especially important to go beyond commitments to theatricality alone even when these are as entrancing as Anouilh's youthful play *Le Bal des voleurs* (*Thieves' Carnival*). So far as significant theatre for the twentieth century is concerned, theatricalism for its own sake, or theatre-for-theatre's sake, is a blind alley. It is the blind alley of amateurism, on the one hand, and of decadent sophistication on the other.

[39] Now to be known in English forever as *Tiger at the Gates,* the title of Christopher Fry's excellent translation and Harold Clurman's superb London and Broadway productions in 1955.

In the theatricalist-realist synthesis there must be a suitable mediation between *immediacy* and *universality*, between the specificity of a subject and the imaginative projections that lead us out of time and place into the realms of essence. And at the same time, the synthesis must be predicated on a sense of the present. For effective drama we need a grasp of events, emotion, and thought transpiring in an environment rather than in the vast inane that romanticism began to sanction after 1770. If we disavow topical or journalistic realism as an ideal, we must also repudiate the idealization of absolutes and the dream of arriving at universals by means of inspired leaps into the void.

Before 1919, Julien Benda sensibly warned writers about "this aesthetic of the elementary soul" which tends to lead to exploitation of the simplicities until art becomes vacuous. Idealized naiveté, the special passion of the sophisticated, has littered the stage with fragile women possessed of inexpressible yearnings, pure Mélisandes and Mary Roses, as well as with "between-wars" Magdalens like the prostitutes of Simon Gantillon's *Maya* and the amoral heroine of John Van Druten's *I Am a Camera*. And inevitably, of course, with beatified degenerates and idiots. *Der reine Tor,* the Wagnerian "pure fool," is a romantic creation; the "impure fool" of our own times, who exhibits the surface naturalism that outrages censors, is merely the obverse side of the same idealization of mindlessness. He is produced by the romanticization of the dungheap, whereas his counterpart emerged from the flower garden. The overvaluation of the "instinctive life" results in the depiction of the same character feeling the same things over and over again, yet understanding nothing but his own impulse.

Without contesting the right of the purely instinctive to a place among the materials of art,[40] Benda protested against the

---

[40] Julien Benda, *Belphégor* (New York, 1929), pp. 77-85. The essays in this abrasive volume, published in French in 1919, were written before 1914.

doctrine that it is "sole material of art, the material *par excellence*. . . . As though intelligence were not just as great a reality. As though Goethe's soul were less real than Mélisande's." Goethe's soul would, of course, reintroduce complexity, take us beyond primitive levels of sensation, and point in the direction of the "drama of ideas" which first invigorated realistic theatre.

All these caveats are especially needed in view of the insubstantiality of the writing of many playwrights, even tough-fibered ones, when they leave their realistic moorings. And warnings may be in order, too, against the search for profundity through indistinctness—the profundity-fetishism which, unlike the cultivation of the "play of ideas," is a foe to light and a friend to darkness. The obscurities of the soul, the inscrutability of fate, the mystery of faith may well provide matter for meditative poetry, but, unless aided by strong plot and characterization, they are likely to prove soporific on the stage. "Profundity" is the special delusion of poets and poetasters of the theatre that makes an effective fusion of realism and theatricality particularly difficult. This delusion was first powerfully fostered by Maeterlinck and Andreyev, those sentimentalists of the universal and hierophants of an unintelligible universe. The mirage of profundity, however, has become particularly seductive in recent decades for those who write in English; Fry and Eliot are only the best known, they are not the worst, of the deluded. Nor do all the deluded write formal poetry, as O'Neill proved in *Dynamo* and *Lazarus Laughed* and as Williams did in *Camino Real*. In the theatre, it would seem, the imagination outruns, and sometimes overwhelms, the creative faculty.

Our reasonable expectations for a realist-theatricalist synthesis by no means place dramatic poetry under interdict, however. Indeed, the full resonance of dramatic art will have to come from more than a mere *poésie de théâtre*. However greatly indebted the playwright who makes use of such a synthesis may be to his own theatrical imagination and that of his stage director, he will need language. The art of the mime, the subtleties of stage movement, the most expressive scenery and stage lighting, all technical and histrionic skills, may well be deplored if they should tend to reduce the artist of words to a cipher in the theatre. Visions of a fusion of realistic and theatricalist art, indeed, light ultimately upon a poetic drama that is the creation of the writer rather than the technician, the mere showman, and the play-carpenter. Dramatic poets cannot of course be created by fiat from a critic's pen or by a general clamor for songbirds in the modern playhouses. But a theatre that gives the poet an opportunity to develop his skill may ultimately be rewarded with a vital poetic drama.

SOME FURTHER OBSERVATIONS

A Chronology of Meyerhold's War
Against Realism

A blow-by-blow account of Meyerhold's assault on realism as recounted by Huntly Carter (*The New Spirit in the Russian Theatre, 1917–1928*) is instructive. It indicates that (1) Meyerhold's nonrealistic experimentation started long before the Russian political revolution of November 1917; (2) his art, like that of the dramatic and nondramatic writers of the prerevolutionary period (Andreyev, Evreinov, Sologub, Blok, Pasternak, Ivanov, and others), was not exclusively Russian but was part of a wave of the antinaturalistic, symbolist, and formalistic movement diffused throughout Europe; (3) the revolution in Russia merely accelerated his imaginativeness and theatricalizing disposition; (4) constructivism, as noted previously, was only one phase of his career and one that he had abandoned by the middle 1930's, so that "formalistic" excesses could no longer honestly be charged against him when he fell afoul of Stalinist reaction in the arts; and (5) constructivism was not simply a naive form of mimesis, a response to industrial architecture and modern machinery, but a fairly self-sufficient program for arriving at esthetic ends. Also, Meyerhold's arbitrary treatment of the classics was not barbarity or mere whim on his part. He had to take drastic liberties with the text in order to assert his own time-conditioned creativeness. Nor was Meyerhold alone in tailoring the text to the director's creative vision or to his political passion. In support of this statement, we need only recall the free handling of plays by Reinhardt, Piscator, and Orson Welles.

Below is an abbreviated chronology of Meyerhold's search for form in the years 1898–1920.

1898   Meyerhold joins the Moscow Art Theatre at its formation and becomes steeped in realism, creating the roles of Treplev in *The Sea-Gull* and Baron Tusenbach in *The Three Sisters*.

1902   Meyerhold leaves the Moscow Art Theatre and goes in search of new forms of theatre in opposition to Stanislavsky's realistic doctrine of ignoring the audience—*i.e.*, of observing the fourth-wall convention. He travels to Italy next year.

1904–1905   He adopts "conventionalism," then called "conditionalism" in Russia. He strives to punctuate his productions with some ruling accent or notion of a somewhat abstract character.

1905   He tries to create a "mystic theatre" and responds to Maeterlinckian symbolism in producing Maeterlinck's nebulous drama *The Death of Tintagiles*.

1906   Staging plays in Tiflis, he uses some indefinite kind of formalism, apparently under the influence of Greek theatre. "He now turned to develop the idea of music applied to dramatic form . . . [producing Maeterlinck's mystic

1906 *(Continued)*

drama *Sister Beatrice* and Schnitzler's *The Call of Life*].
. . . He sought to make the actors' movements resemble
those of a dance." In a provincial theatre, Meyerhold
next removes the proscenium and the act-drop in producing *Ghosts,* which had been written for representational, "fourth-wall" performance. "Take away the act-
drop and the spectator is immediately saturated by the
stage and its contents, and is thus prepared for the act of
dramatic communication," says Carter, approvingly.

(November) Meyerhold becomes associated with the successful actress-manager Vera Fedorovna Komisarjevskaya
(1864–1910), who had come under the influence of the
symbolist movement. His aim in directing *Sister Beatrice*
for her in St. Petersburg was "to dematerialize [sic] the
stage in order to express the mystery . . . in the play. So
he gave it the air of a religious service." To abolish the
separation of the actor and the spectator, he used the
shallow-stage technique (as used in the Künstlertheater in
Munich) "by playing on the forepart of the stage against
flat decorative church-like scenery." He also used "mel-
odic speech, and plain, precise, carved-out gesture." He
showed the actor "carved, as it were, in relief" against the
flat decorative scenery.

Meyerhold successfully produces, in association with Komisarjevskaya, Andreyev's symbolist morality play *The
Life of Man.* "The make-up of the actors was mask-like.
Their beards were as though sculptured. Here the aim
was to communicate the sentiments and feelings of a
dream."

1907 Meyerhold goes to Berlin with Komisarjevskaya and studies the work of Reinhardt there. He now moves toward
giving the actor the roundness of sculptural form in space,
treating the actor like free-standing sculpture instead of
presenting him against the scenery like a figure in relief.

1907   (*Continued*)
Back in Moscow, Meyerhold stages Wedekind's natural-ist-expressionist drama of adolescence *The Awakening of Spring*, using different stage levels for presenting the actor in the round. He also introduces stairs across the stage that raise the actors to different heights.

1908   After Meyerhold's rupture with Komisarjevskaya, because (as she alleged) she opposed his interest in marionettes and his tendency to turn the actors into puppets, he stages plays in Minsk. He continues his theatricalist experimentation, using screens instead of sets and using full light on the audience, because he thought "it heightened the mood of the spectator, while enabling the actor to see, as in a looking-glass, the effect which he was communicating." Also, in staging opera, he uses the actor more and more sculpturally on bare levels, emphasizing the contours of the body, arms, and legs. This practice probably marks the beginning of Meyerhold's celebrated principle of "bio-mechanics" in acting.

1910   He develops other theatricalist methods, as well as those sketched above, especially in staging Molière's *Don Juan* as a spectacle and in using masks for another production. Japanese and Greek influences are strongly present in his work as a director at this time. He also produces a harlequinade.

1912–1913   He goes to Paris and stages a play by D'Annunzio with décor by the celebrated Léon Bakst. He also organizes a studio for the teaching of the technique of the *commedia dell' arte*.

1914   In producing the poet Alexander Blok's symbolistic-poetic play *The Unknown*, he uses a "construction," instead of "decoration," for the first time. This marks the beginning

This multiple setting was designed by Jo Mielziner for the 1948 Broadway production of Tennessee Williams' realistic drama Summer and Smoke. *The production made use of simultaneous mansion-like settings (an extension of medieval staging) for the homes of the principal characters, with symbolism introduced in the centered statue of Eternity. The steps in the center were serviceable as playing levels, but they were not used as a major production element. The screen-like skeletal flats at the right and left provided a lyrical tracery of exteriors. Imaginative design settings have been greatly admired in the English and American commercial theatre even when the story, as in this case, has possessed strong naturalistic elements.* Photograph: Eileen Darby for Graphic House. Courtesy of Margo Jones.

1914 (*Continued*)

of his break with the symbolist technique of esthetic unity or "synthesis." Now begins his use of open theatricalization: "eccentric accessories, jugglers, Chinese boys throwing oranges among the audience, quaint things and human figures were interwoven in a fantastic manner."

1918 With the Bolshevik revolution, Meyerhold begins a search for dynamic form that will express collectivist aims and the industrialization of society along with a depersonalization of the individual.

1919 He stages open-air productions of such works as the poet Mayakovsky's revolutionary rhapsody *Mystery-Bouffe,* which was presented as a "mass spectacle." He develops the technique of "construction" or "constructivism," which represents an evolution of his use of levels and plastic acting. He had at first used acting levels for the purely esthetic or Appian purpose of liberating the actor from décor and giving him sculptural dimensionality. But now the scenic construction has the mechanical qualities of a machine, for Meyerhold brought "the ideas of the builder, the engineer, the mechanic into the theatre . . . a new conception of the surroundings of social life."

1920 Meyerhold now fully develops his acting system of bio-mechanics or bio-dynamics, which tends to turn the actor into an athlete, acrobat, and animated machine; the system showed the influence of behaviorism and of Pavlov's studies of conditioned reflexes. He also begins to use vertical constructions—frames divided into floors and compartments joined by platforms, staircases, and gangways, which made it possible for a large number of scenes to be played without pause. He also begins to use film strips with stage productions, as Piscator and Brecht were to do later in their style of epic theatre. Next, he uses movable constructions, and begins to employ movable walls and a revolving stage divided into concentric rings which move separately, so that many scenes can follow in rapid suc-

1920   (*Continued*)

cession: "he was able to stage the 35 or more scenes into which he divided a play with a film-like speed and continuity"—a system of producing a play for which, indeed, perhaps only acrobatic acting was appropriate.

Meyerhold continued his experiments for another 17 years. Of his later productions, the most notable for its bold inventions was his brilliant staging of Gogol's *The Inspector-General.* The scene presenting the return of the hero from a drunken spree while people appeared at the numerous doors of the background and rustled paper money at him was particularly outstanding. The scene was plainly a projection, on a fantastic scale, of bribery under the old Czarist regime.

The variety of this director's creative output taxes the imagination and makes adequate description impossible. A director's creations exist only on the stage, and Meyerhold's work was so completely of the theatre that the text of a play, even of a classic like Gogol's comedy, was to him only the libretto for an essentially nonverbal creation. Charles Dullin, Copeau's disciple and a great stage director himself, paying homage to Meyerhold in 1931, called him a creator of form and a poet of theatre—"un créateur de formes, un poète de la scène"—who wrote with gestures, rhythms, and a theatrical language invented for his needs, and who addressed himself to the eyes as much as the text of the play addressed itself to the ears: "Il écrit avec des gestes, des rhythmes, avec toute une langue théâtrale qu'il invente pour les besoins de sa cause et qui parle aux yeux autant que le texte s'addresse à l'oreille." [1] Without doubt this master of *la poésie de théâtre* entranced all who saw his productions, even if they could not be entirely certain he was not confounding art with artifice and making them connive in his misdemeanor.

This brief review of Meyerhold's ventures up to 1920

[1] Charles Dullin, *Souvenirs et notes de travail d'un acteur*, Paris, 1946.

should be sufficient to indicate the nature of his quest, which epitomized the search for antinaturalistic form that has characterized the theatre in our century. Perhaps this summary will also serve as a reminder that virtually every device or system of theatrical stylization has been tried, so that the problem is no longer one of *inventing* theatricalist methods, but of using them organically and meaningfully.

Theatricalism and the Actor

Competent acting is, indeed, essential to truly gratifying theatricalism. Thus, a great deal of the theatricalist staging in our college and university theatres is unsuccessful, despite admirable work by the directors and designers, because the performance of individual roles is inadequate. Few students have succeeded in creating characters rather than character types, animated cartoons, and automatons, and even among the best of the student actors and amateurs will be found few who are capable of sustaining a long role. Understandably, then, the directors endeavor to compensate for the deficiency by tolerating, if not indeed encouraging, such mechanical tricks as gesticulating, stamping, shouting, leaping, and mugging.

Encouraged by local success, the directors may think up more and more ways of turning their actors' inadequacies to theatrical advantage. And being persons who are in general better educated than most professional producers and directors, they have no difficulty in finding esthetic justifications for their practices. They are, understandably, the most ardent exponents of theatricalism, to which they are greatly indebted for tolerable productions, just as they are greatly beholden to Gordon Craig. With him, they place reliance on "directors' design" and give it priority over acting. Their productions are usually superior in design to Broadway and Shaftesbury Avenue productions. But the productions rarely penetrate to the living core of a good play precisely because they are based on design rather than on character realization. Nor is the result appreciably better when the play to be staged stems from a historically conventional theatre, such as that of Louis XIV, the Restoration period, or the eighteenth century—that is, when the play is "artificial" by historical sanction. The tendency, in some academic dramatics, is to assume that a production of *Love for Love, She Stoops to Conquer, The School for Scandal,* or *The Importance of Being Earnest* needs only to be theatrical in order to be successful. The resulting productions are often full of clever stage business, including such extraneous feats as an actor's pretending to light candles in chandeliers or in eighteenth-century footlights, but often leave an impression of style pursued for the sake of style rather than employed as a means to some further end.

If plays are to survive theatricalist treatment, they need acting that is *better* rather than worse than that required by ordinary realistic drama; they need character building *and* style. We ought not to forget that comic characterization is still characterization, and that a Molière and a Congreve stand out among numerous forgotten playwrights not because they were "artificial" but because they had something to say through such character-creations as Millamant, Mirabell, Alceste, and Harpagon. When John Gielgud produced a memorable *Importance of Being Earnest* and played John Worthing in it, he showed his awareness of the importance of comic characterization even in farce by supplying a John Worthing who had more substantiality and was more "real" than a run-of-the-mill performer's realistic portraits. Gielgud's Jack had reality *with* style. The mediocre realist thinks that he can be real without style; the mediocre theatricalist, that he can have style without reality. The results are equally inadequate for both realism and theatricalism. A theatricalism of pat and transparent artifice, far from being "progressive," is retrogressive; it brings us back to the bankrupt prerealistic theatre of pasteboard dramatics and ham acting.

It is not surprising, then, that some leaders of stylization have paid close attention to the training of actors. Copeau, at the height of his fame, gave up producing in order to establish a school for acting; and his associates and their disciples—Jouvet, Dullin, and Barrault—gave most of their attention to the creation of character within the ambience of a particular style and the limits of a particular type of play. It is characteristic of their regard for character realization that Christian Bérard's setting for the celebrated Jouvet production of *L'École des femmes* was a highly theatricalist, toylike construction (Arnolphe's house was surrounded by a collapsible fence), but that Jouvet's Arnolphe was a total creation—a foolish and obsessed but *complete* man. One could even feel somewhat sorry for him.

Brecht, too, has formulated a theory of acting. It has been set forth in his *Kleines Organon für das Theater* and other writings, including "A Short Description of a New Technique of the Art of Acting Which Produces an Effect of Estrangement," written for the International Theatre Institute's quarterly publication, *World Theatre* (Vol. LV, No. 1). The views of Brecht, like those of Meyerhold, Barrault, and other proponents of stylization, can mislead the inexperienced. There are pitfalls in his writings for those who might adopt his anti-Stanislavskian methods without realizing that Brecht, like other leaders of the European theatre, assumes that his actors will be competent enough to create character and get *inside* a role. Having made that assumption, he then considers how he can teach the actor to get *outside* the role as well. There is, of course, no point in training an actor to get out of his role if he cannot get into it. In playwriting, too, Brecht's principle of breaking the illusion is meaningless for the playwright who is not capable of creating an illusion, just as there isn't much point in telling a playwright or actor to guard against emotionalism if he lacks a capacity for feeling.

The mature Brecht has created true characters in his plays perhaps more frequently than he himself has realized. A character, of course, is not a reproduction of a person in the street, but a playwright's and actor's creation, which makes him a work of art. This involves selectivity, intensification, special perspective, composition or design, and a certain abstractness along with the obvious attention to creating a resemblance to persons. At one time Shaw was accused of failing to create characters, too; yet today few dramatic characters are as well known as Shaw's in the English-speaking world. It was a mistaken view of both realism and character reality that inspired the charge against Shaw, who became the modern theatre's greatest "realist-theatricalist." But we can make the same mistake about the work of older playwrights if we fail to realize that the effective theatricalism of the great ages has been memorable for its characterizations: Otherwise the great actors and dramatists of the pre-realistic stage could never have attained their reputation for carrying conviction ("holding up a mirror to nature"), and all the famous dramatic characters from Antigone and Oedipus to Hamlet would have been mere two-dimensional cartoons. In a sense, acting *is* characterization, and the soundest theatricalist artists know only what realists also have known—namely, that there are both "round" and "flat" characters in a play, just as in novels. The theatricalist merely deploys the characters, especially the flat ones, more "theatrically"—with more or less "theatricalist" objectives in mind.

It is this deployment that is implicit in the introduction written by Michel Saint-Denis for the publication of Arthur Wilmurt's translation of Obey's *Noah*. On the one hand, Saint-Denis stresses the importance of having a good actor for Noah and "a sensitive actress of wit and personality" for Mrs. Noah; on the other hand, he calls for the "theatrical" treatment of Noah's children and the animals. The important thing in producing the play is to make them act as choruses: "There is nothing complex about their individual psychology—it is the movement which they do together which must be thought out and combined so that they give shape and rhythm to the action."

And he is right in sounding a warning against "complex psychology," which tends to be overused as a result of misapplied realism and misunderstood Stanislavskian training until each actor plays his part as though he were a case history.

Saint-Denis defines a vivid histrionic method when he writes that "it is through their movements together that the children mime the rain as it begins to fall, that they make us feel the roll of the boat during the storm . . . , that they enable us to follow the flight of the dove in the sky; and finally, before going their separate ways, it is together they first set foot on dry land and fight to possess it." It is work of this kind that is soundly threatrical, and Saint-Denis gives a good description when, in writing of his Compagnie des Quinze, he declared that the actors were capable of "showing life rather than explaining it, relying more on sound and physical movement than on talking, used to singing and dancing, able to build up from choral work to the invention of simple, clearly defined characters." Nevertheless, it is plain that even the best ensemble of this kind would have little power to engross our attention for an evening of theatre in the absence of character creation by the chief actors, as *Noah* wouldn't be much of a play if it were all chorus and no character. It is possible, indeed, to prefer Odets' not entirely clear version of the biblical theme *The Flowering Peach* precisely because less "artiness" stands in the way of characterization.

The Realists, Copeau, and the Possibilities of Synthesis

We can readily understand that some rapprochement between realistic and theatricalist views of theatre should have taken place in our century. Even Antoine had not intended to make his *Théâtre Libre* an exclusive citadel of naturalism. Stanislavsky sought theatrical effects wherever he could attain them without sacrificing truth of environment and truth of character.

About forty years after he had founded it, the Moscow Art Theatre could make a theatrical romp out of a dramatization of *The Pickwick Papers* without feeling that it had betrayed its ideals. (This celebrated production even combined painted and three-dimensional scenery, and used both live actors and painted figures.) Nor is there any evidence that Stanislavsky was in the least disturbed when his favorite pupil, Eugene Vakhtangov, gave the modern theatre two of its most famous early theatricalist productions, *Princess Turandot* and *The Dybbuk,* after World War I. Stanislavsky, who staged several plays by Maeterlinck and exercised patience and humility in working with Gordon Craig on the latter's Moscow Art Theatre *Hamlet* production in 1911, had indeed given abundant proof of his regard for theatrical imaginativeness before 1918, as had other pioneers in realism. For example, it was none other than the pioneer of German naturalistic theatre, Otto Brahm, who gave Craig his first opportunity to design a production on the Continent. Craig was utterly stalemated in England in 1904 when Brahm, then managing the Lessing Theatre in Berlin, invited him to design the Hugo von Hofmannsthal version of Thomas Otway's *Venice Preserved.*

A greater fusion of realism and theatricalism east of the Rhine was made difficult, however, by the turbulence of the theatre after World War I. The revolutionary postwar situation in Central Europe favored the wild excesses of the expressionists which made the gulf between realism and theatricalism altogether too wide to be bridged. And in Russia during the 1920's and early 1930's the Moscow Art Theatre came to be regarded as a stodgily academic organization by those who combined political revolutionism with revolutionism in the arts. Vakhtangov, who could have perhaps mediated between Stanislavskian realism and extreme theatricalism, died in 1922.

In Western Europe, the possibilities of mediation depended largely upon the teachings and example of Copeau. These bore fruit in some highly regarded productions by Dullin, Jouvet, and others, and in plays by Giraudoux and a few other playwrights. Copeau, unlike some other Parisian *avant-garde* producers, could esteem the work of Antoine, Becque, and Stanislavsky while at the same time developing his art of simplified and theatricalized acting and staging. Unfortunately, however, Copeau's career in the Parisian theatre was interrupted by World War I and then disorganized by his own temperament—or, rather, by the defects of his virtues. He succumbed to religio-esthetic mysticism and to that last infirmity of noble minds called perfectionism. His Théâtre du Vieux Colombier had closed its doors by 1924. He was no longer a practicing producer-director during the last decades of his life except for a few disturbed years between 1936 and the fall of Paris when he had limited scope as one of four stage directors at the Comédie Française. Copeau died at the age of seventy in 1949, but the important part of his career in the public theatre was over by the time he had reached his forty-fifth year. Gide noted, regretfully, in the third volume of his *Journals*, that "Copeau, though claiming not to do so, was working for a select few," and wanted "to lead to perfection, to style, to purity, an essentially impure art." Gide charged Copeau with having allowed himself to be deluded into inactivity by a vision of holiness "which misleads only the holiest."

It was with good reason, too, that Granville-Barker pleaded with Copeau in 1928 "to spend no more time kissing the earth [Copeau had retired to the countryside in order "to kiss the soil" and regain spiritual strength] or laying foundations, but to go ahead with your building; that is to say, with the interpreting of one good play after another, letting the art of one beget the better art of the next." He warned Copeau that "all the virtue goes out of simplicity that is guarded too carefully and too long. . . ." [1]

Waldo Frank, referring to Copeau's refusal to perform many successful modern plays at the Vieux Colombier, reported in

[1] Harley Granville-Barker, "A Letter to Jacques Copeau," *Theatre Arts Monthly* (October 1929), p. 755.

1925 that a "legend grew that Copeau's purity was a Puritan madness against living merit." [2] Copeau allowed the work of Pirandello, O'Neill, Crommelynck, and other candidates for his attention to pass out of his hands. The men he encouraged most, Gide and Jules Romains (and he lost the latter, too) were chiefly novelists by vocation.

More than other men, Copeau could have reconciled the aims of realism and antirealism. But a man who rejected the possibility of having a strong, immediate effect on living playwrights could not resolve the conflict between styles. To influence stage production and the training of actors, as he unquestionably did, was not enough.

[2] *Theatre Arts* (September 1925), p. 586.

4

The Plurality of
Theatre

In dramatic art the eye is more easily deceived than the mind. —JULES JANIN

. . . the aim and object of all true art is the skillful blending of the real and the ideal. —WILLIAM CHARLES MACREADY

I am for nature and against naturalism.—CONSTANT COQUELIN

The stage is a lie; make it as truthful as possible.—VOLTAIRE

A work of art which serves life cannot at the same time be independent of life. —ALEXANDER BAKSHY

. . . the theatre, as Huysmans said of schools of literature, is neither realistic nor poetic; it is only good or bad, true or false. —STARK YOUNG

The actor 'forgets' himself in his role, yet always knows that he is playing, and that the object of his performance is to entertain. —HAROLD CLURMAN

Once the Characters [in Pirandello's play-within-the-play theatricalist drama Six Characters in Search of an Author] are in action . . . they are "real" people involved in terrible human problems. They at once seem more "real" than the actors, because only they are engaged in an intense, determined struggle for identity. It is the actors who turn out not to have the "reality" of being; while the Characters, in their urgency, and in the sense— as soon as their flashbacks begin—of their struggling in the present, absorb audiences in an experience of a continuing life action; and this experience accumulates up to the climactic shouting at the end. The attempt by Pirandello to cancel out with irony this mounting linear crisis fails because the Characters are too "life-like" . . . —MARVIN ROSENBERG

. . . in the stress of a too violent feeling, we can find relief from the illusion of the moment, and then give way to it again at will. —SCHOPENHAUER

The Idea of Duality

THE COMBINATION OF REALISTIC AND THEATRICALIST TECHNIQUES IN the writing and staging of a play or the acting of a part can never be a simple matter. It requires a great deal of understanding, taste, and tact at all times, and the *ad hoc* decisions that have to be made (and often revised) cannot be discussed abstrusely. Certainly, there is no rule of thumb by which the playwright, the actor, and the *régisseur* can infallibly mingle realism and theatricalism. It is important, however, to make it possible for them to function without inhibition and with a minimum of confusion; and to this end, it is essential to formulate principles upon which their creativity in the theatre can rest securely. In other ages these principles apparently did not need to be formulated, but clarifications of theory are generally desirable in a self-conscious age like our own, and they are especially needed by self-conscious contemporary students of theatre who have been exposed to the seductions and obfuscations of the rival theatrical programs of our century. The fuzzy acceptance of eclecticism so often associated with decadence in art and the "anything-goes" attitude so characteristic of show business cannot satisfy the needs of responsible artistry. These needs will be met only by a view of theatre that recognizes the ambivalent character of all representation on the stage. It is a view that cannot accept any rigidly monistic attitude toward the making and experiencing of theatre.

Since the vogue of the symbolists, we have been greatly under the influence of the unity-minded, design-minded leaders of the Craig-Appia school. These leaders have felt that one central design or style of treatment must bring all elements of a given stage production into a single focus, that one tone must dominate it, and that one vision must rule it if the theatre is to be taken seriously as an art. This prescript agrees so well with esthetic principle in general, and has indeed been so effective in preventing many productions from disintegrating into chaos, that the principle of *design* should not be rashly discarded. Nor has esthetic unity been challenged in our time except on special principle, Erwin Piscator, Bertolt Brecht, and their associates in epic theatre having violated it only on the grounds that unbroken identification with stage characters and complete immersion in an emotional situation can work on the mind of the spectator as a soporific.

Nevertheless, it does not follow that the *sense of reality* must be violated by theatricality, for the play in the theatre can be served by a factor that operates strongly in theatrical practice and in the response of audiences—namely, a factor of *duality*. Duality of experience exists to some degree in every theatre and for both the performer and his audience: action in the theatre is both make-believe and actual for them.

As spectators in the theatre, we make use of a built-in mechanism comparable to a shuttle, which enables us to move back and forth between the planes of reality and theatre. Or this faculty may be described as double vision, which enables us to experience a stage performance in such a way that it is both reality and theatre at the same moment. We can focus on

"real life" (that is, succumb to the *illusion* of reality), at one
point in the performance, and soon thereafter respond to a thoroughly theatrical effect which we *know* to be "theatre" rather
than "real life." Also, we can have the experience of feeling an
action to be "real" and "theatrical" *at the same time,* just as we
are simultaneously aware of "real" time and "theatrical" time,
which may be much longer and may even consume decades during the actual lapse of minutes.

When theoreticians of play production speak of "esthetic
distance" they surely imply such a fusion of the real and the
unreal, of reality and theatre. When esthetic distance has been
established at a performance of *Hamlet,* I may feel the death of
Hamlet deeply, tragically; but I do not feel it with the immediacy (or, if you like, reality) that would make me want to run
up onto the stage and administer first aid. I sympathize with
Hamlet as though he were more real to me than most people,
but I also know that I am in the theatre.

One may go somewhat further and maintain that the esthetic distance was there from the moment the curtain rose because the mechanism that established the distance already existed in my sensorium. I came to the theatre prepared to give
myself up to the experience on the stage, but also wary of total
involvement. I was prepared to *detach* myself from the experience lest it engross me to the point where my capacity for criticism, my physical safety, or my sense of personal dignity might
suffer. There is much to be said for Samuel Johnson's assertion "the spectators are always in their senses, and know, from
the first act to the last, that the stage is only a stage, and the
players are only players." The spectator can turn his empathy
on and off, so to speak. He can derive gratification both from
identification with the actor as a momentarily real person in a
real-life action, and from observation of the actor as the performer of a feat of acting. (Almost, indeed, as though the actor
were supplying the intellectual-emotional equivalent of bareback

riding and of acrobatics on a flying trapeze.) Our response to many a favorite of the stage has been of this nature: We wait for Alfred Lunt and Lynn Fontanne to deliver an inflection "just so," for Helen Hayes to establish a character detail with her characteristic piquancy, and for Mary Martin to "put across" a certain song. These things belong legitimately to the experience of theatre. Moreover, enjoyment of this sort need not hamper appreciation of characterization. At all times, the good actor functions both as an *actor* and a *character,* and there is no reason to believe that histrionic duality was ever absent, even when the actor was a masked Greek protagonist or a masked *commedia dell' arte* harlequin.

The experience of the theatre is always a dual one, if for no other reason than that the playgoer brings with him his double consciousness or focus, his ability to experience theatre on two planes. Therefore, it is always possible for the stage to achieve a satisfactory synthesis of realism and theatricalism. Audiences (at least today's audiences) are remarkably ready to feel themselves into the major roles, to identify themselves with the characters. Vicariousness seems to be the particular passion of entertainment in our century. And the ability to achieve identification makes the playgoer and the player much alike. To some degree, they both employ "affective memory." There is probably no immoderate manifestation of naïveté to be discovered in all this illusion-seeking, which intellectual and formalist artistry has endeavored to moderate or "cool down." Perhaps even the urbane playgoer is never completely "out" of illusion except while functioning as a specialist whose business it is to judge the performance technically. (As is the case, for instance, when a producer and his associates go "out of town" with the show with a view to improving it during the try-out period.) Perhaps it is even more accurate to say that the playgoer is usually both "in" and "out" of a stage production at the same time, and that the play is an *extratheatrical* and a *theatrical* experience for him at the same time.

It is noteworthy how easily an effect that is distinctly realistic or naturalistic can be converted into its opposite, into something grotesque or symbolic. On the basis of this fact, we may postulate for the theatre the existence of some sort of *law of conversion.* Extreme effects have a tendency to undergo some transformation for the spectator into an effect of a different, perhaps opposite, character.

A case in point is *Tobacco Road,* as produced on Broadway in 1933. For those whom its sensualism and brutish naturalism repelled, the production, of course, lost effect. For other play-goers, the naturalism tended to be transformed into social comment; the play induced pity and aroused the social conscience, and so the brutishness of the production underwent a transformation. That was the present writer's experience, and it induced him to include the play in one of his anthologies of American plays.[1] The reasons for including *Tobacco Road* could probably never have been made clear to the elderly Louisiana lady who burned the book because she was outraged by the "indecency" of the play; she could not have understood that for playgoers who had been conditioned by the depression of the 'thirties to look for "social significance" *Tobacco Road* was no more pornographic than a scalpel stuck in a tumor.

At the other extreme, there was the response of an older and wiser critic, Joseph Wood Krutch, for whom the naturalism of *Tobacco Road* underwent conversion into grotesque humor. Mr. Krutch attributed this humor to Erskine Caldwell's novel, upon which the play was based; however, one may wonder whether it was not actually the stage production that sharpened this distinguished theatre critic's awareness of the grotesque. Caldwell's "peculiar effects" were made possible for Mr. Krutch

> only by the assumption of an exaggerated detachment from all the ordinary prejudices of either morality or taste and a consequent tendency to present the most violent and repul-

---

[1] *Twenty Best Plays of the Modern American Theatre* (New York: Crown Publishers, 1939), now a volume in *John Gassner's Library of Best American Plays.*

sive scenes with the elaborate casualness of a careful pseudo-naiveté . . . the mood which dominates his writing is the mood of a grotesque and horrible humor.[2]

He could have said of Caldwell's story what W. C. Brownell once wrote about some of Maupassant's work: "Every detail is real, but the implication of the whole is fantastic."[3] I should go on to say that Mr. Krutch, who considered the play "scarcely more than a parody on humanity," nevertheless found the work entertaining and expressed considerable approbation for it. And so it happened that the two drama critics of the 1930's who approved, in the main, of *Tobacco Road* were critics who would normally have been least inclined to do so. The flagrantly naturalistic production became transmuted into a mordant poem of pity for the present writer and into a sort of comedy of the grotesque for Mr. Krutch.

Perhaps the best example of the working of this process of conversion—or of the ease with which reality may become unreality in the theatre—is provided by Mordecai Gorelik's comments on the Broadway production of *Street Scene*. Although Alan Downer could call Elmer Rice's play "selective realism at its best,"[4] the slum tenement setting would ordinarily impress us as a naturalistic one. But a curious transmutation takes place as one studies that setting: (1) we start with an *artifice*—namely, the artificially constructed setting, a thing mainly made up of frames and canvas to simulate a brownstone tenement house; (2) the first result is the naturalistic illusion of the house, a dreary achievement of verisimilitude, of fidelity to ugly fact; (3) we end up experiencing this scenic construction as a "theatrically immediate," rather than "actual," reality, and as a symbol of sorts. Gorelik's view was that

> while the setting for *Street Scene* is at first glance almost in the style of Belasco, it shortly becomes evident that the

[2] *The American Drama Since 1918* (New York: Random House, 1939), pp. 122-128.
[3] *William Crary Brownell: An Anthology of His Writings* (New York: Scribner's, 1933), p. 150.
[4] *Fifty Years of American Drama* (Regnery, 1951), pp. 63-65.

apartment house façade is first of all a theatrical convention which permits the play to be staged in a new and arresting way. *The longer the setting remains on the stage* (in this case it remains throughout the play), *the less an audience identifies it as an actual place.* Instead, the audience sees and accepts it as *a sheer theatrical device.*[5]

Those who have had much experience in the theatre could undoubtedly report many arresting instances of conversion, although one must concede, of course, that conversion is a subjective phenomenon. John Mason Brown found the horrifying laundry scene in Sidney Kingsley's play *The World We Make* objectionably naturalistic. For the present writer, however, the steam laundry was an effective theatrical realization of the reality the rich young heroine of the play must learn to accept before she can be freed from her neurosis. But surely the point need not be labored; it is sufficiently familiar to artists in diverse fields. It is perhaps necessary only to remind ourselves that the law of conversion works both ways: not only may the apparently real become the apparently unreal or symbolic, but the reverse may happen—the apparently symbolic may become the apparently real, and the theatrical construction may take on (or give off) an effect of naturalistic verisimilitude.

A symbolist-impressionist setting, such as Mielziner's famous Williamsburg Bridge design for *Winterset,* may well convey the reality of New York's East Side more convincingly than a photograph. It may be said, then, that *environment,* too, is not at all as simple a thing as it seemed to be when the naturalists gave painstaking attention to realizing it on the stage with solid settings and the symbolists to dissolving it with space stages and atmospheric lighting. The environment may become a symbol, and the symbol may become an environment, once the total experience of theatre begins to be sought by writers and directors. Many a constructivist setting used by such theatricalist

[5] "The Conquest of Stage Space," *Theatre Arts* (March 1934). Italics mine.

director-producers as Tairov and Meyerhold underwent transformation in the spectator's mind from theatrical abstractness into the reality of factory catwalks, girders, bricklayers' scaffolds, and other structural elements.

Meaningless, finally, becomes the idea of "presentational" staging as the panacea for modern dramatic art. Unless the producer is prepared to make a carnival out of every modern play, or unless the playwright has included a narrator, choruses, and soliloquies or other presentational elements, the audience may well turn the presentational production into a representational or realistic one. Let us suppose we staged Shaw's *Don Juan in Hell* interlude "presentationally." What does this really mean? Unless the director orders each actor to carry on the Shavian conversation while hanging head downwards from a trapeze, isn't it likely that the audience will soon feel itself into the situation by identifying itself with the characters? (The spectator does not identify himself with a character's ideas; he identifies himself with the *character*, once he is sufficiently interested in the thoughts.) The actors performed on a bare stage and faced the audience directly in the Paul Gregory "reading" that was successfully given in the early 1950's. How long did it take the audience to make persons out of the actors and push them into a "real" environment (a little corner of Hell), instead of saying to themselves how delightfully unreal, how charmingly theatrical, everything is? And conversely, suppose *Don Juan in Hell* were staged, as was Sartre's existentialist conversation-piece *No Exit* (*Huis Clos*), in a realistic environment. In view of the character of Shaw's interlude, isn't it highly probable that the spectator would at times resist fourth-wall illusionism to the extent of receiving various portions of the dialogue, such as Don Juan's great apologia, as rhetorical displays or arias out of an "opera" by that Mozart of the spoken theatre, Shaw? (In this connection, it is perhaps wise to quote what Shaw said about casting plays: "The four principals should be soprano, alto, tenor, and bass . . . take care that every speech contrasts as strongly as possible in speed, tone, manner, and pitch with the one which provokes it, as if coming unexpectedly as a shock, surprise, stimulant, offense, amusement, or what not." [6]) The audience, then, may *restore* the fourth wall to the presentational production and abolish it in the representational production. A *law of conversion* or transmutation in the theatre, it is apparent, discourages an "either-or" effect. It induces fluctuations between presentationalism and representationalism, illusionism and theatricalism.

A "theatricalist-realist" or "realist-theatricalist" synthesis indeed must have always been experienced by audiences because of the spectator's capacity for adjusting himself to stage convention and yielding to an illusion of reality, and the actor's capacity for creating and nourishing that illusion. The actor has always been a powerful maker of illusion, whether masked or not, and whether standing on the platform of the Globe Theatre or under a chandelier on the abbreviated forestage of a seventeenth- or eighteenth-century playhouse. He has the two indispensable qualifications for engendering an illusion of the real—namely, the actuality of the human body in posture, gesture, and movement, which not all the pomp and stylization of costume can nullify, and the actuality of the human voice, that penetrating *vox humana* that comes out of a mask as well as out of the uncovered face. Where illusion is maintained, however, there convention also prevails: the illusion is illusion only because it is maintained within some artificial framework of art. And the frame-of-reference of dramatic reality, as well as its physical framework, can only be the theatre. We may say, then, that in the theatre an experience is not reality unless it is, first of all, theatre. Mrs. Alving's story, no less than the great debate between philanderer and devil in Shaw's *Don Juan in Hell* interlude, has existence only as theatrical reality—and the greater the theatrical reality of play and performance, the greater the illusion of reality.

[6] *Theatre Arts* (August 1949), p. 9.

Bearing in mind such an obvious fact (not obvious, however, to doctrinaire theatricalists any more than to doctrinaire naturalists), we can find it easy to understand why fidelity to nature has been claimed for favorite playwrights and players from the time of Shakespeare. No one received more praise than Garrick for introducing naturalness in acting on the English stage; yet Garrick's naturalness, which obviously carried a great deal of conviction for audiences in 1750, was theatrically realized at Drury Lane on an apron stage extending 13 feet from the proscenium arch and the front lines of the stage setting. And Garrick's "realism" was lit by chandeliers suspended from the ceiling of the playhouse. "The candles once lit at the beginning of each act remained so for all its scenes, and thus suspended in the midst of a moonlit grove, a dark forest, or a street at midnight, were always inevitably those six chandeliers in the foreground." [7]

In all periods, playwrights and players have been realistic *for their times* and within dramaturgic and theatrical conventions —that is, within limits more or less agreed to by their audiences. A present-day American audience would not agree with an Athenian audience of the fifth century B.C. that the making of theatre must be limited by the requirements of open-air production, by taboos, and by vestiges of ritual. The theatre we use as a frame of reference makes demands for the sake of "reality" that radically distinguish our plays and performances from those of the Greeks. In the twentieth century, the "realism" of Garrick's age would be either valueless or it would be incongruously "theatricalist." And if the "realism" of another period is theatrical in ours, it cannot function as the nontheatricalist element in a realist-theatricalist synthesis.

It follows, then, that such a synthesis requires a full realization, rather than any adulteration, of truly modern realism, and especially of the inner realism with which the actor is concerned.

[7] Mary Barton, *Garrick* (Macmillan, 1949), p. 81. I say nothing here about the incongruous costuming in that century. "The subjects of Queen Anne saw nothing incongruous in the full-bottomed wig worn with breast-plate and helmet by Booth as a noble Roman" (p. 82).

Realism and theatricalism should serve as checks on each other, but the greater check should be exerted by the former, for conviction remains the main desideratum in the dramatic experience. Chicanery and skittishness are the particular dangers of any theatricalist mode that is not rooted in national culture; Athenian theatricalism was so rooted, because the mask, the chorus, and the epiphany, or *deus ex machina,* were inherited from ritualism.

With respect to creating suitable stage settings there has been no serious difficulty ever since selective realism came into vogue as a result of the revolt against naturalism inspired by Appia and Craig; and today acting performances that are both realistically and theatrically based can be developed further. Even so Stanislavskian a school as the Actors' Studio of New York was able to turn out young actors after World War II who could create convincing characterizations and at the same time play their parts in a pattern of theatrical presence, pose, and movement. The present writer was particularly aware of this duality in the performances of Ben Gazzara, who played leading roles in *End as a Man* and *Cat on a Hot Tin Roof* between 1953 and 1955. The actors in Copeau's and Vakhtangov's type of theatre were particularly noted for this double faculty of creating a convincing character and theatricalizing it at the same time. Some remarkable notes in Vakhtangov's diary[8] present Stanislavsky's own teachings with exceptional clarity. They indicate that the Stanislavskian-trained actor would by no means be unfitted for a "theatricalist" performance. Critics of Stanislavsky, according to Vakhtangov, tended to neglect "the statement which takes first place in the system"—namely, "that the actor should not be concerned about his feeling during a play." Feeling will come of itself, if the actor thinks first of all about what he, as a character, wants to obtain. The diarist re-

[8] *Acting: A Handbook of the Stanislavski Method* (New York: Lear Publishers, 1947), pp. 116-124.

calls that Stanislavsky said to his pupils, "Don't wait for emotions —act immediately," and there is surely no better advice for the actor serving a theatre unfettered to naturalism. But it is plain, of course, in Vakhtangov's notations, that Stanislavsky did not dream of fostering mechanical acting. The attentive pupil, who was later going to develop his own style of production, made such familiar notes as "you must proceed from yourself . . . place yourself in the position or the situation of the character. . . . To create and not to be oneself is impossible."

In developing the style required by the synthesis we seek it is necessary to guard against extravagant Stanislavskian (or, shall we say, pseudo-Stanislavskian) overmotivation, on the one hand, and overtheatricalization on the other. The former is usually apparent in the work of earnest professionals, which is likely to be hobbled by a finicky treatment of characterizing detail. It is a serious error to overextend characterization greatly beyond the needs of a scene and so withdraw attention from the dominant dramatic action, thus retarding the evolution, obscuring the point, and dulling the edge of a play. So talented an actor as John Garfield, for example, played an early scene in *Peer Gynt* with such twisting of his body and such constant rubbing of his haunches on a ladder that he subverted the style and spirit of the play. The overconscientious actor was bent on giving us a total characterization at a point at which it was vastly more important to get ahead with Ibsen's symbolic and satiric fable. The error of overtheatricalization is more characteristic of the untrained or ill-trained nonprofessional actor who has learned to spark his movements with all the kinetic energy of an athletic young body and all the lack of restraint of ignorance. In one university production, the performer's footwork was so energetic that the present writer watched it with trepidation, expecting the young man to slip and break his neck at any moment. So efficient was his stamping that he came through the performance with nary a mishap. But if the footwork was excellent, the "face-work" was virtually unnoticeable. It would have been better to clap a mask on this actor's face, so that the spectator would have stopped expecting more than one carved expression from him.

Even in professional performances, however, the theatricalizing impulse can easily get out of hand. The actor may elect to play the virtuoso, and the result may be the superficiality and thinness that can keep a theatre solvent without making it significant. Some distinguished performers of our time have succumbed to the temptation of dramatizing *themselves* rather than the part. And the temptation to strive for effect alone has been even greater for those virtuoso directors who impose a theatrical style on the play instead of letting its "theatre" grow out of its dramatic substance and idiom. European directors such as Reinhardt, Jessner, and Meyerhold tended to take liberties that amounted to drastic adaptation.

At the very source of these dangers will be found an imperfect understanding of the theatre's duality. This misunderstanding comes from failure to realize the fact that there is no "either-or" principle at work in dramaturgy and stage production, that the theatrical experience can be both real and stylized, both real and theatrical. Only when this possibility is clearly realized or deeply sensed can a play be written, as well as staged of course, so that it will be most notably real when it is most theatrical, and most notably theatrical when it is most real. The ability to achieve both the illusion of reality and the ideality of art, both realism and theatricalism, in the same play has characterized the greatest playwrights of all previous ages. This dual power is the glory of Sophocles and Shakespeare. It was never entirely absent in the best work of such modern dramatists as Ibsen, Strindberg, Shaw, Chekhov, O'Casey, and O'Neill.

It is not suggested that a gratifying synthesis is to be achieved by combining incompletely realized elements—that is, by taking a pinch of adulterated realism and a pinch of diluted theatricalism and then shaking well. On the contrary, a fruitful synthesis can come only from realizing fully the possibilities inherent in both realism and stylization, within the limits of the author's intent and the conditions that rule the theatre for which the play was written. This is illustrated by such master-pieces as *Oedipus the King, Phèdre,* and *Macbeth.* In the first mentioned, the personal anguish of Oedipus and Jocasta, on the one hand, and the formal collective role of the chorus, on the other, are never inhibited or offered stingily in order to effect a compromise between the realistic (I should say, rather, natural-istic) situation of the characters and the formal dramatic pattern. In *Phèdre,* the neoclassic formalism of the writing is not in the least incompatible with the convincing reality and obsessive ur-gency of the Queen's emotions. In *Macbeth* the quality we nowa-days call "psychology" is never sacrificed to the theatrical at-mosphere and action, and neither are theatrical atmosphere and action stinted in order to thrust the psychological element into the foreground. Shakespeare moves here from "psychology" to "theatre," back and forth; there is no evidence that he was aware of any incompatibility between the two. There are, in point of fact, very great scenes, such as the murder of Duncan and the appearance of Banquo's ghost, in which the "psychology" of the work (the state of mind of Macbeth and his wife) is "theatre," and conversely, the "theatre" of the work (what we should other-wise call melodramatic action) is "psychology." It can be seen, therefore, that the word "psychology," used in so many discus-sions of modern theatre, has little meaning. Great drama (great performance, too) is neither psychological nor unpsychological.

The blending of realistic characterization and formal or in-formal theatricality also produces a good deal of the charm, dra-matic scope, and imaginative vigor of plays regardless of their dramatic magnitude. This mingling of modes of presenting a dra-matic story produces vivid contrasts of formalism and feeling, pageantry and pain, preciosity and naturalness in *Romeo and Juliet.* In *Richard II* there is an especially noteworthy contrast of styles of presentation in the difference between the actuality of the scene before Flint Castle (Act III, Scene 3), in which

Richard yields to Bolingbroke, and the morality-play effect of the very next scene, in which the Duke of York's Gardener, addressing his helpers, delivers his formal speech on good kingship:

> Go bind thou up yon dangling apricocks,
> Which, like unruly children, make their sire
> Stoop with oppression of their prodigal weight.
> Give some supportance to the bending twigs.
> Go thou and, like an executioner,
> Cut off the heads of too fast growing sprays
> That look too lofty in our commonwealth.
> All must be even in our government. (III, 4, 29-36)

In the celebrated abdication scene (Act IV, Scene 1) there is, besides, a provocative blending of psychological and rhetorical elements or qualities. Realism in the characterization of Richard and Bolingbroke and theatricalism in the ceremonialism of the scene are superbly interfused here.

Richard the character, besides, is his own actor, so that there is a fusion of characterization and theatricality in the hero himself. It can be noted, indeed, that other Shakespearean characters are intrinsically actors. Richard III, Iago, Benedick, Beatrice, Mercutio, Falstaff, Hotspur, and Henry V, not to mention Hamlet, are some of these. Shakespeare, like every true dramatist, wrote for actors; and to express humanity in the theatre, he needed "actor-characters" in his plays—characters who are highly articulate, histrionic, self-dramatizing. Henry V is the "actor-as-character" in Act IV, Scene 1, when he walks through the English camp at night casually conversing with the common soldiers, and primarily the "character-as-actor" or as "actor-orator" in the Saint Crispin's Day address to the troops two scenes later (IV, 3). The first scene is heightened realism (the key to it, perhaps, is the line "I am afeard few die well that die in battle"), and the later scene is motivated theatricalism, since the king's aim is to inspire his followers.

We may make similar observations concerning modern

plays. The mad countess in Giraudoux' *Madwoman of Chaillot* is a good example of the character that exists simultaneously on the planes of reality and theatricality. And the scene of weird discourse with her mad cronies, too, is surely both a theatrical *tour de force* and a scene full of the spontaneity and immediacy of life.

All things point to the possibility of advances in modern dramatic art along the lines of a realist-theatricalist fusion. The greatest promise lies in the nature of theatre itself—that is, in its dual aspects as illusion and theatre. The principle of duality —of bifocality or double functioning—appears in all aspects of theatre. It appears in the spectator's double vision or dualism of response, so that a performance can be simultaneously or alternately reality *and* theatre. It also exists in playwriting and play production. And there is, of course, considerable interaction between the kind of playwriting and the kind of stage production that develops at any particular time. Whether the first moves are made by playwrights or stage directors, the results are likely to be the same.

We have been moving for some time toward a realistic-theatricalist theatre. In the century's rarely satisfactory, usually inconclusive search for new dramatic forms, nothing else has held out so much promise. We may, then, hope for a resolution of the crisis in dramatic art that has existed ever since nineteenth-century realism began to show diminishing returns. It cannot be true that the modern drama has lost the power to develop, and we have had ample evidence that modern stagecraft *has* developed. Realism without theatrical intensification generally has proved dull. And theatricality without a realistic foundation frequently has proved trivial. But a judicious fusion of the potentialities of both modes of theatre may legitimately arouse the highest expectations. In order that the possibilities of success may be increased and the possibilities of failure reduced, it is imperative to resolve, once and for all, the conflicts between realism and theatricalism. These were never esthetically necessary; and if they were once historically necessary, they are so no longer in any modern theatre of the West.

The Multiple Stage and Plurality of Forms

The *duality* of stage experience for actor and audience, if sufficiently realized, will serve as a liberating principle in the modern theatre. It should help to reconcile the opposites of realism and antirealism—of so-called naturalness and stylization, although it is obviously impossible not to have some degree of stylization if there is to be art. It is largely a matter of *degree* of stylization, and of the facility with which the author and the production manage to conceal stylization (as Chekhov does by indirection and other means) or to disclose and accentuate it.

At the same time it would be well to strongly avow a principle of *multiplicity* as a catalytic concept of modernity. It is important to openly accept rather than to simply deplore or desperately conceal the fact that modernity in the theatre is by its very nature, or by virtual necessity, multifaceted. And therein resides a good deal of its special interest to critic and creator alike, as well as its confusion, waywardness, and instability. On any level except that of blank mediocrity or bland commercialism, whether it be Broadway, the West End of London, or the boulevard theatres of Paris, the modern drama and stage have had staggering potentialities and partial achievements.

It may be maintained, of course, that there is nothing extraordinary about multiplicity of styles and genres; that other important theatrical periods have also manifested considerable variety, concerning which we would know more but for our insufficient knowledge of their productions. But this much is true: Insofar as our knowledge extends, no *other* period has revealed so much variety, and no other has manifested as much latitude of critical assessment and interpretation, which has greatly enlarged our consciousness of varieties of genre, style, and point of view. In the early part of the modern period (say, from 1875 to 1900) critical discourse in the theatre seemed simple, often to the point of naivete or delusion whenever such matters as "realism," "naturalism," "drama of ideas," "thesis drama," or social theatre were discussed by critics and scholars, theatrical leaders, and playwrights. This tendency has lingered on, indeed, in discourse on "social drama" (as in the 1930's in the United States), "socialist realism," and early Epic Theatre. In the main, however, discussion has moved toward increasing complexity and emphasis on differentiation of styles and genres.

If our prime criterion for naturalism is "objectivity," can we be justified in regarding Strindberg's profoundly personal work in *The Father, Creditors, The Dance of Death,* and even *Miss Julie,* which was painstakingly self-endorsed by the author as the very acme of naturalistic principles, as authentic masterpieces of naturalistic drama? Must we then posit a genre of patently *subjective* naturalism? Theoretically, this is a contradiction in terms. And if we go that far toward relaxing our guard with respect to scrupulous objectivity shall we not recognize also a patently propagandistic variant? In the case of Brieux's once highly touted pieces, for example, Shaw even wrote a preface to three translated by Mrs. Shaw endorsing their propaganda as virtual naturalism. And is not Hauptmann's *The Weavers* an example of the same commodity, which justifiably gained the support of the Social Democratic party in Germany?

Surely, then, we have here a radically different type of play than that envisioned by Zola and crudely demonstrated in his dramatization of his novel *Thérèse Raquin,* for which Zola provided his famous "Preface." In such instances the emphasis rests on the quasi-scientific premises of determinism by biological factors. Strindberg, it is true, tried to drag them into his work, too. He treated the "sex duel" as a central biological factor aggravated in modern times by feminism, thereby erecting upon the foundations of his own neurosis a veritable theory of instinct and a sociology—indisputably crude, though not cruder than other nineteenth-century formulations for which scientific validity was claimed on the basis of insufficient evidence. But in his case the subjectivity was plainly in conflict with the aim of scientific detachment. Also in conflict with this ideal, of course, was the propagandism of his antifeminist campaign or its attendant—

postures, including the dubious superiority of the male in all respects except venality and guile. And this is the case in virtually every dramatic work in which an author endeavored to demonstrate or formulate some scientific and sociological point—as in Hauptmann's early drama *Before Sunrise* (1889) in which the young author advanced the then fashionable simplistic principles of eugenics. Zolaist naturalism is a genre *per se*, and may be observed in its purest form in Wedekind's dramas of sex, particularly *Earth Spirit* and *Pandora's Box*, and perhaps most satisfactorily encountered in *Reigen* (*La Ronde*), thanks to Schnitzler's Viennese urbanity, which secured him against vulgarizations of naturalistic biology. Throughout the present century biological or biopsychological Zolaism has continued to attract attention from time to time, most fashionably in more or less sensational excursions into homosexuality or Lesbianism, as in Bourdet's well-known *The Captive*. Freudian and crypto-Freudian drama has virtually become a distinct genre of twentieth-century theatre.

There has also been a genre of *regional* naturalism, in which local color, with attendant dialect, customs, and manners, constitutes the primary interest. Peasant tragedy, as in Tolstoy's *The Power of Darkness* and John Masefield's *Tragedy of Nan,* and village comedy, as in Hauptmann's *The Beaver Coat* and Lady Gregory's comedies of Irish life, has also abounded. This genre has often also incorporated poetic elements, as in D'Annunzio's *Daughter of Jorio,* Benavente's *The Passion Flower,* and Lorca's *The House of Bernarda Alba,* as well as *Blood-Wedding* (notably in the wedding scene) and *Yerma.* Moreover, there has also been a genre of distinctly urban naturalism, noteworthy examples of which have appeared in many places. (For example, St. John Ervine's *Jane Clegg,* John Galsworthy's *Justice* and *The Pigeon,* O'Casey's early masterpieces, Elmer Rice's *Street Scene,* and Odets' *Awake and Sing!*)

In brief, we had a number of naturalistic genres, each with its distinctive as well as overlapping features. And this not only in the play text but in the subtext realized in stage production and performance. We can observe the same variety in other styles that acquired a program, a critical label, even the semblance of a philosophy.

Symbolism in drama and theatre, for example, is not really a single "style," even though it was propagandized as such by an entire array of would-be saviors of the theatre for poetry and the imagination from Appia and Craig to Robert Edmond Jones and others after 1914 in our American theatre. Here, too, aside from the uniqueness of genuine creativeness, there have been essential distinctions. First there has been the artistry, chiefly in the staging and designing of plays, that consists mainly of *simplification,* as in a return to various degrees of Shakespearian production in noteworthy attempts by William Poel in England and Jocza Savits at the Court Theatre in Munich. Like Poel, Savits used curtains for the background. (The latter did not, in fact, confine the principle of simplified staging to Shakespearian drama, but opposed all but frugal décor for all types of drama.) Orson Welles pursued this principle brilliantly at the Mercury Theatre in the late 1930's in staging *Julius Caesar.* For this type of symbolic production the Globe and other "public" theatres of the Elizabethan period provided the example. (See pages 247-258 on Elizabethan staging.)

At the opposite extreme we can refer to Max Reinhardt's use of *decorative symbolism,* as in his staging of *The Winter's Tale* at the Deutsches Theatre in Berlin when he turned from a simple though lofty décor for Leontes' palace to the rural scene in "Bohemia," designed like a page from a "child's picture book" (p. 87, Huntly Carter's *The Theatre of Max Reinhardt,* 1914). The grass, Huntly Carter reported, "was bright green velvet, spangled with conventional flowers. A blossoming fruit tree shadowed a toy cottage; and in the background some quaint masts and pennons showed the proximity of the sea," presumably suggesting "the seacoast of Bohemia." In this production, Reinhardt combined the curtain technique with décor to indicate the folk-tale quality of the latter half of this play. From this procedure it is but a step to many playful and fantastic stage pictures effected by means of design, color, and light used symbolically as well as picturesquely.

But we are in a different world altogether when we move with Gordon Craig in a mystical world which dwarfs the actors and mankind with huge, essentially undifferentiated, masses of blackness or shadow, portentous spaces, and an abstruse atmosphere that must be described, to all intents and purposes, as *contentless*. Here symbolism is a mystique and virtually an end in itself. The parallel in literature is "pure" poetic drama as written by a Mallarmé, Valéry or Gertrude Stein. Also a parallel is mime drama as conceived by Etienne Decroux, Marcel Marceau, and Samuel Beckett in *Act without Words*—the equivalent in Craig's words that "Über-marionettes and wordless plays and actorless dramas are the obvious steps to a far deeper mystery" as the next steps in an enlargement of "Cosmic" consciousness. With works like these we are in a world of dramatic art radically different from allegorical plays such as Maeterlinck's *The Blind* and *The Blue Bird*, Andreyev's *The Life of Man*, or Percy McKaye's *The Scarecrow*, and fancies such as James M. Barrie's *Dear Brutus* or *Mary Rose* with which symbolist drama enjoyed popularity early in the century.

Still another mode of symbolist drama appears when the symbolic dimension is merely supplementary, as in Ibsen's *Rosmersholm, The Wild Duck*, and *The Master Builder*. This tendency, which also appears effectively in the work of Chekhov, has continued to exert a justifiable attraction up to the present day by providing a poetic dimension and significance to what would otherwise constitute only humdrum drama or argument. Clifford Odets supplied several moderate examples of this realistic-symbolist fusion in *Paradise Lost, Golden Boy, Night Music*, and *Clash by Night*. More extreme examples of symbolization and therefore "borderline cases," would be O'Casey's *Cock-a-doodle-Dandy* and Marcel Aymé's *Clérambard* (1950). We must conclude, then, that symbolism, too, manifested more diversity than unity of purpose and character, not to mention manifestations in various branches of musical theatre where fancy has been allied with symbolization of mime and dance and "production numbers," as in *Oklahoma!* and *West Side Story.*

"Expressionism" has also manifested considerable variety, as have Epic Theatre and Theatre of the Absurd in more recent decades. And what is more significant in any practical sense is not that we can multiply categories for the arid purpose of classification but that many uses have been found for the techniques and styles of expressive exaggeration, ranging from relatively simple fantasy to extreme distortion; from simple invention of a story or notion, in *R.U.R.* and *The Makropoulos Affair*, which involved the discovery of indefinite longevity, to distinct exemplifications of disturbed states of mind. Moreover, vital differences are observable between schools of extreme subjectivity which dramatized private anguish or conflict in the case of Sophie Tread-well's *Machinal* (or even in an American "musical" such as Moss Hart's pseudopsychoanalytical play *Lady in the Dark*) to "social drama," in which objective social conflict was more or less subjectively exemplified, as in Kaiser's *Gas*, Toller's *Man and the Masses*, and Elmer Rice's *The Adding Machine.*

In some instances we have not been far from the old morality play pattern of allegory, whether in the relatively subtle form of the Capek brothers' *Insect Comedy* or the distinctly unsubtle form of Philip Barry's *Miss Liberty.* In other instances we have approached the radically different pattern of psychological or, if you will, psychoanalytic drama, as in Lawson's *Roger Bloomer* and Moss Hart's *Christopher Blake.* Other points of differentiation are tenable, if not indeed necessary, as between Strindberg's highly personal *To Damascus* plays and his *Dream Play*, which, for all its vaunted dream-technique (emphasized in his brief prefatory note to the play) and whatever its roots in the playwright's personal experience, is largely a philosophical demonstration of the hellishness of life and the fallen state of mankind, virtually a Buddhist "morality." Lumping these and other kinds of plays in one single category of expressionism, as the present writer along with other critics and historians have done, may obscure an essential multiplicity of resources. And we must also take into account other supplementary uses of expressionistic detail in unmistakable association with primarily realistic aims, as in Odets' *Waiting for Lefty* and Miller's *Death of a Salesman*.

For the varieties of Epic Theatre, a brief summary is offered on pages 281-308; and the modes of Theatre of the Absurd, with all dadaist and surrealist and Italian "school of the grotesque" (Pirandello, Rosso de San Secondo, Ugo Betti) anticipations and variants could easily fill a volume, and has indeed filled one, by Martin Esslin's *The Theatre of the Absurd*. There are certainly marked differences between the plays of Ionesco and Genet, Beckett and Pinter, and Artaud and N. F. Simpson. And there are obvious distinctions of degree of fantasy even in the work of a single author—for example between Albee's *The Zoo Story* and *The American Dream*.

In summary, then, it is quite apparent that regardless of questions of ultimate merit, modern theatre comprised a vast flux and reflux of experiments superimposed on a base of commonplace theatre and accommodation to largely middle-class perceptions and interests. (And so-called Socialist Realism in Eastern Europe has been no less "middle-class" in orientation and sensibility regardless of any propaganda for the "workers' states" and ideals of collectivity.) Moreover, since the realism has been pushed further and further away from any center of artistic conscious-ness, except in the case of unquestionably private drama such as O'Neill's *Long Day's Journey into Night* and Robert Bolt's *Flow-ering Cherry*, experimentation in other areas of theatre has been essential.

We have, in fact, been increasingly reluctant to grant even the "objective" master-realists, Ibsen and Chekhov, any straight-forward representation of reality. We are often indeed rather recklessly inclined nowadays to claim them all for the "theatre of the absurd." Under the surface of the work we are apt to locate symbolic and grotesque elements, farcical or bizarrely melodramatic dimensions or accents. The programs or principles under which they first attracted attention have lost their attraction after many decades of disillusion. The realism for which Ibsen and others became famous or infamous in their own time has undergone a transformation in our avant-garde consciousness of more sophisticated or subtle styles and of orientation toward nonreformist and pessimistic attitudes considered "existentialist" and "absurdist."

An effort to corral even Shakespeare for "the theatre of the absurd" was made in *Shakespeare Our Contemporary* by the Polish scholar Jan Kott, and put into theatre practice in 1964 when the distinguished director Peter Brook staged *King Lear* for the Royal Shakespeare Company. And with the accent on other levels of interest than surface values, "symbolism," which had very limited success in the European theatre when it constituted a "movement" between 1890 and 1914, belatedly acquired an augmented, though not always "officially" recognized, status. Not "reality" but metaphors for reality achieved a vogue after 1950; chiefly in theatre-of-the-absurd experiments. They abounded in such bizarre but more or less well aimed imaginings as Beckett's *Waiting for Godot* and *Endgame* and Ionesco's *The Chairs* and *Rhinoceros* (even the Communist countries have taken note of the "absurd," as in the case of a 1964 production of *King Ubu* in Prague), as well as in allegorical works such as Max Frisch's *Biedermann and the Firebugs* and Friedrich Duerrenmatt's *The Visit*, augmented by Brechtian "Epic" theatrical didacticism and irony.

Still, it does not follow that recent playwrights, any more than recent actors and stage directors, have suddenly discovered some magical substitutes for human experience or that mere metaphors can now stride across the stage in place of embodied feeling. There can be no greater illusion than the notion entertained by callow would-be creators, and encouraged by equally callow would-be critics, that plays can be improvised rather than organized (*organically* organized, if you will!), or created by asserting one's superiority to drama as an Aristotelian "imitation of an action" by merely *destroying* illusion and flouting realistic dramatic structure and uncongenial reality. It is far better to adhere to a *fundamental* naturalism or realism as the beginning, *though not the end*, of wisdom in matters of dramatic art. It is the practical wisdom John Galsworthy defined in three sentences: 1. "A Drama must be shaped so as to have a spire of meaning." 2. "The aim of the dramatist employing it is evidently to create such an illusion of actual life passing on the stage as to compel the spectator to pass through an experience of his own, to think and talk and move with the people he sees thinking, talking and moving in front of him. . . ." (The recommendation may be modified, as in Brechtian theory and practice, but Brecht knew better than to banish illusion and the possibilities of identification with characters altogether or continuously. That way lies suicide for playwrights and actors, except in the case of necessary farce and caricature.) 3. "A good plot is that sure edifice which rises out of the interplay of circumstances on temperament, or of temperament on circumstance, within the enclosing atmosphere of an idea." ("Some Platitudes Concerning Drama.")

The following chapter presents a melánge of considerations that pertain to the manifestation of forms and styles that have been at issue, and is organized as a sort of anthology of essays and reflections by myself and other writers, with myself performing the functions of master of ceremonies. This chapter could have been extended to book-length proportions, and perhaps should be. Every serious student of modern theatre will have no difficulty in supplementing it with material in the form of criticism, explanations or explications, and programs proffered by individual playwrights (there are many such as in Toby Cole's *Playwrights on Playwriting*, Hill and Wang), and producers and stage directors from Antoine and Stanislavsky to Jouvet and Barrault. But such plenitude of discourse unless kept within narrow bounds here, could also overcomplicate the issues that have arisen in our time. I am concerned here only with broad attempts to put order in the modern theatre and direct its strivings into significant channels.

5

Perspectives on Modern Drama and the Theatre

. . . at the period at which we have arrived the predominance of the grotesque over the sublime in literature is clearly indicated.
—VICTOR HUGO

. . . naturalism has regenerated criticism and history by submitting man and his works to a precise analysis, taking into account circumstances, environment and organic cases. . . .—ÉMILE ZOLA

". . . all human behavior tells of absurdity and all history of absolute futility . . . I had the impression I could do anything I wished with the language and the people of a world that no longer seemed to me anything but a baseless and ridiculous sham."—EUGENE IONESCO

Art is meant to enlighten us, not to increase the chances of chaos.
—PAUL WEST (The Modern Novel.)

. . . man must affirm justice in order to struggle against eternal injustice, create happiness in order to protest against a universe of evil.—ALBERT CAMUS

Camus sees the absurd as a clash between the world's irrationality and the desperate hunger for clarity which cries out in man's deepest soul. "The absurd depends as much upon man as upon the world."—JAMES H. CLANCY

. . . I never know how to finish a play. There are no last acts any more in life, so how can we find any in the theatre? There are no easy solutions.—JOHN OSBORNE (New York Post, Leonard Lyon's column, November 12, 1963.)

. . . to learn gives the liveliest pleasure, not only to philosophers but to men in general.—ARISTOTLE

Selective Realism and a View of Open-Stage Acting

THE FOLLOWING DESCRIPTION OF ELIZABETHAN THEATRICAL PRAC-
tice is taken from Bertram Joseph's essay, "The Elizabethan
Stage and Acting," included in "The Age of Shakespeare." It
suggests how a modern poetic drama could be made to prevail
in the theatre instead of being engulfed by second-rate illusion
and having its expressive language timidly slurred over or deprived of its imagery and justifiable rhetoric.

Two important points have great bearing upon the possibilities of modern realism. One is that *rhetoric* can be regarded as
an essential ingredient of theatre. As long as a play offers a histrionic view of character and situation, rhetoric is its natural concomitant and means of expression. It is natural, that is, for characters to speak eloquently when they take an exalted or excited
view of themselves and others, when they dramatize themselves
to themselves and to others (as does Hamlet), and when they see
themselves as significant characters in some perspective of history, politics, or simple worth. Rhetoric in all such instances is

actually more "natural" than incoherence dignified as art under the rubric of naturalism. Articulateness and inarticulateness, it is to be noted, are not necessarily associated with social status; characters rise or fall in expressiveness in accordance with the sensibility imparted to them by a playwright. Thus Tolstoy's peasants and Synge's have a status in dramatic art considerably above their status in society.

Shakespeare is by consensus the great master of character creation, and a number of his fellow Elizabethans have also created memorable characters. This means primarily that they had a strong hold on character reality despite the crudity of official Elizabethan psychology. Yet this masterful realism of characterization that gives life to all conditions of men is imbued with the rhetoric appropriate to each state of mind, so that Poins is no less eloquent to the purpose of Falstaff, Falstaff no less than Prince Hal, and Prince Hal no less than Hotspur or Henry IV.

Equating realism with inarticulateness is "unrealistic" in the order of nature and of art and is unnatural to the stage—which is a place for action only by convention, and to performance on the stage—which is histrionic whenever effective. Even good "underplaying" is *"playing."* To postnaturalistic stylization there can be no leaven more natural than the expressiveness intrinsic to the theatre—that is, to the art of conveying thought and feeling in public by means of verbal as well as nonverbal mimesis. Mature theatricalism consists of utilizing expressiveness instead of repressing or concealing it; or, for that matter, keeping it submerged in feeling as in *bad* "Method" acting by actors insufficiently trained in voice control and stage movement. Dumb-show or mime, moreover, seems less natural to us today than verbalization. I suspect indeed that this has always been the case, since man is a talking animal. Ever since the birth of comedy and tragedy in civilized communities, pure mime has been an attention-arresting device rather than an ordinary, taken-for-granted activity. The speaking actor has become the norm. The mime is, so to speak, the gifted freak; or, when he is a Barrault or a Marceau, the justifiably applauded genius-freak.

A problem related to that of the reclamation of rhetoric by both realists and theatricalists is *the reclamation of imaginary space* by both. Elizabethan stage production is significantly suggestive in this respect. Shakespeare could sustain a realistic view of political as well as private character and action, and he could convey a local habitation for this purpose, without substantial assistance from illusionistic detail. Elizabethan actors localized their space by defining, with the author's help, their station, purpose, and action; whereas in the modern realistic theatre, after about 1850, it was the scenic artist who defined space for the actor and for the beholder.

In Shakespeare's theatre it was the actor who defined the space for himself and his public. Was this not a "real" enough environment, especially when further distinguished by stage properties such as banners, thrones, and stage levels on which "discoveries" could be made, cities besieged, and ladyloves wooed? The nineteenth-century realists, including the Victorian actor-managers did not think so; otherwise, they would not have cluttered their productions of Shakespeare's plays with ponderous scenery. Since Poel, Craig, and Copeau set us their examples, we have thought otherwise, even though we now look doubtfully on avant-garde stage productions that dissolved space itself (which an open-air Elizabethan public playhouse production without artificial lighting could never do) and gave us atmosphere instead. Today our playwrights and directors no longer think they must do more than suggest the environment by means of so-called selective realism; and if that method is satisfactory, as it was in Harold Clurman's staging of Inge's *Bus Stop* (see illustration), is not environment largely a state of mind? Establish the right state of mind and you may establish all the environment you need. And if naturalness is a desideratum, we can but reflect that nowadays it is the naturalistically solid and detailed setting that seems unnatural, because it calls attention to itself as a feat; it becomes downright theatrical rather than natural.

The idea, drawn notably from the Elizabethan theatre, that the actor defines his environment, or that he can do so when given a sufficient degree of assistance from the author's text, is a *liberating one.* To be liberated from environment, in the narrow sense of the term, is by now almost as important as to be liberated from prose, or rather prosiness and, what is more, it is no less important to the determined twentieth-century realist than to the antirealistic "theatre for theatre's sake" devotee. The progress of modern theatre has been from nineteenth-century efforts to *bind* ourselves to environment for the sake of external and *literal* truth to twentieth-century efforts to liberate ourselves from environment for the sake of internal or *imaginative* truth.

Latter-day efforts have been much involved with this subject in several ways. There is the way of the would-be fantasists, or "escapists." This happy, at times "picture-happy," breed goes about abolishing environment as a functional reality. It is apt to favor pretty ("visually gratifying") scenery *sui generis,* and to think almost exclusively in terms of visual color and pictorial composition. The practitioners and propagators of this view in the United States are to be found, for the most part, in the academic world. Their audiences usually applaud this estheticism, if for no other reason than that the effect is pleasantly decorative. Their opponents accuse them of ineffectualness, if not indeed effeteness. Whether these charges can be sustained or refuted in particular instances, it is plain that environment usually carries little weight, if any, with these proponents of "pictorialization"; they evince little taste for realism and deplore its prevalence in the modern, post-1850 theatre as a distressing interlude. They hanker for poetic drama and abstract or neutral, as against topical and didactic playwriting.

There is the somewhat different way of the symbolists, for whom the life of man is a mystery. They aspire to an *o altitudo* of artistry or elevated state of feeling, and to intimations of immortality amidst the greasepaint, the gluepots, and the paint and flats of the stage, hoping to "get away from it all" through the magic of light under the inspiration of a prophetic Wagner disciple, Adolphe Appia, whose interest lay primarily in opera, music, or "music-drama." Owing a great deal, too, to the vatic estheticism of Ellen Terry's son, Gordon Craig, they look to the "soul" of a play and move "inward", understandably then, they hesitate to speak out when they can whisper, or to define a situation whenever they can intimate one. They disdain environment as a social factor, accept it only as a subjective or psychological one, and take pride only in rendering an "environment of the soul." The languidly spiritual interpretation of a Shakespearean play used to be, and may still be, the peak of their aspiration. It may be argued that all spirit and no flesh makes Shakespeare a dull boy, but this is no matter if they can ensure profundity for him by making the work vague enough. Their happy hunting grounds used to be the bohemias of the gay nineties and the first decade or so of the present century. Today they are too genteel for bohemia and are more likely to be delighting their soul in the shaded walks of a campus usually removed by considerable mileage from the madding metropolitan centers.

Then there are the "Epic" neorealists, notably Piscator, Brecht, and their followers (they are not unknown in vigorous community and university theatres) who disdain environment as local detail even while stressing it as a determinative factor in the drama of individuals and societies. Insofar as environment is used in these plays and productions, it is conjured up as a factor in an argument rather than as pictorial reality. In the interests of a staged demonstration they will not indeed spurn a pictorial element, but in that case it becomes more of a *stage property* (like the properties of an Elizabethan court scene with a throne placed on the platform stage) than an environmental setting. The scene in such instances offers ocular assistance to the spectator, but provides no complete "illusion" of environment. The latter is cancelled out, to a degree, by the fact that the setting for a particular scene in an "Epic" production is partial rather than complete, or completely illusioned, and by the equally anti-illusionist factor that such a scene does not occupy the entire stage visible to the public. The setting, if indeed it may be called such without substantial qualification, is apt to seem virtually suspended in the space faced by the audience.

My mental picture is that of a peasant's hut, in an excellent 1962 production of *The Caucasian Chalk Circle* at the Aldwych Theatre in London. Brecht's heroine, the kitchen maid, Grusha, takes refuge in her married brother's home in such a cottage, and in another one she marries a presumably dying man to stifle the scandal caused by her possession of a fatherless child. Empty space was visible above this stage setting or, rather, stage property, because no *teaser*, no dark-colored border or drapery, was used to cut down the proscenium opening on top; there was nothing but space in front, on both sides, and back of this property. In some Epic productions, such as Piscator's *War and Peace* adaptation, as given by the Bristol Old Vic (transferred to London in 1962, and bound for New York in the season of 1964-1965), even such a fragmentary special setting for a scene was deemed unnecessary; the stage was treated frankly as a platform consisting of several levels for presenting the argument in narrative and hortatory scenes. Even in private scenes taken from Tolstoy's novel, pictorialism was confined to a few properties such as the old Prince's desk and chair.

"Epic Theatre," we may say, is thoroughly realistic as a form of social drama, but exhibits no allegiance to nineteenth-century pictorialism and its attendant realistic play-structure. It actually invites the reverse, because in demonstrating a socially relevant point it uses imaginative dramaturgy and actually provides opportunities for the poet. Its various manifestations in the work of Piscator, Brecht and others (such as the authors of the Federal Theatre "Living Newspapers" of the 1930's; W. H. Auden, in *The Ascent of F6*, and Robert Bolt, in his St. Thomas More drama, *A Man for All Seasons*) are modern examples of how pictorial realism can be violated for the sake of critical or analytical realism, and of how physical environment can be minimized in the very effort to deal with society or social reality. It provides proof that the modern theatre can have as much realism of content as it wants without confining the imagination and limiting expression to the commonplaces of conversation. We can have realism and eloquence, too.

Those who have been eager to banish "realism," making it their whipping boy for all of the theatre's woes and attributing these, as Walter Kerr has sometimes done, to the bad example of Ibsen and Chekhov, have been making an identification between realism and illusionism that has been growing less and less tenable to anyone familiar with the possibilities of selective realism even without adherence to Epic Theatre doctrine.

An excellent example of "selective realism" appeared in Jo Mielziner's design for Arthur Miller's *Death of a Salesman*. The designer provided a brief description of his approach in the lecture-essay, "The Future of Theatre Architecture," in *Futures in American Theatre* (The University of Texas). Among the settings called for by the play were Willy Loman's home, its backyard and garden, its background of neighboring suburban brick homes, two business offices, a hotel room in Boston where Willy has a brief affair with a female buyer, a restaurant, and a graveyard. Jo Mielziner concluded that an episodic play consisting of many short scenes that shuttled back and forth in time needed to be unified physically. Unification in this case meant simplification and the elimination of impediments to the flow of events. The scenic artist, therefore, developed a design that would make it possible for *Death of a Salesman* to be staged without lowering the curtain on any of the episodes except where an intermission was required.

Since the action in the house occurs in several areas and on two levels, the designer, the director, and the author agreed on using a skeletal unit setting. Because the action spilled out into the yard, and since Willy's home underwent changes in the course of the recollected chronicle of his life, Mielziner decided to achieve the effect purely by projecting light on a cyclorama painted on both sides. On one side he painted "the shut-in bricks of the neighboring houses keeping out the sunlight and showing only the half-living tree trunks" to indicate the condition of the house and the neighborhood late in Willy's life. On the other side he represented the same scene with leaves sprouting and a feeling of light and air when Willy was still a hopeful young husband and father. By rearranging the furniture on the porch of the house and relighting the scene it was possible to represent an office scene. The hotel room in Boston was conveyed "purely by projecting the image of a faded wallpaper design in the wire mesh near the garden wall on Stage Left": and the graveyard scene of Willy's interment was created on a bare stage or "space stage," with nary a gravestone and nothing more than autumnal lighting and a wreath of flowers.[1]

In this type of selective experience we obviously encounter the imagination at work with space, light, and color. The scenic experience is as sensuous or as abstract as one wishes it to be, and it can be sensuous at one point in a play, and intellectual or discursive at another point. By not allowing oneself to be hamstrung by the conventional requirements of proscenium theatre, it is possible to achieve selectivity and to emancipate the actor from irrelevant or hampering physical objects that slow up his performance and the pace of the entire production.

With open-stage *mise en scène* what can suitable acting accomplish? What can it not? Epic theatre practice provides some examples that bring us back indeed to the Elizabethan theatre. Open-stage acting in Epic speaks out boldly, addresses audiences, and provides the right flourishes of rhetoric when the occasion calls for them, as in the antiwar harangues of the aforementioned *War and Peace* dramatization comparable to the pro-war harangues in *Henry V*. It defines character by means of an accumulation of characterizing comments, actions, and reactions. It states and analyzes motivation. It does not tease us into making desired conclusions; instead it *makes* the conclusions with us or for us—which is often Shakespeare's procedure in assigning

[1] *Futures in American Theatre*, p. 15.

ruminative soliloquies to Hamlet or declarations of intention to Iago. It tells us what a character thinks, instead of challenging us to find out what he thinks. And it nullifies or minimizes suspense in plot development, since the plot is a demonstration rather than a strung-out yarn or an intrigue in the manner of a well-contrived story-drama, the *pièce-bien-faîte* of nineteenth-century Parisian bourgeois realism. There is an affinity in this with Shaw's concept of the "drama of ideas" when he maintained that since the time of *A Doll's House* "the discussion has expanded far beyond the limits of the last ten minutes of an otherwise 'well-made' play . . . in which the discussion interpenetrates the action from beginning to end," to which Shaw added that "the action of such plays consists of a case to be argued."

The following description, which offers a much-needed corrective to many a Shakespearean production, may provide us here with a key to present-day efforts by no means confined to Epic Theatre, to reconstitute realism in "open-stage" theatres, and reconcile it with poetic theatre on thrust out stages that promise recovered freedom and fresh opportunities for the actor.

People are beginning to understand in our day that exact localization is one of the first elements of reality. —VICTOR HUGO

The task of the scene designer is to search all sorts of new and direct and unhackneyed ways whereby he may establish the sense of place . . . a true stage-setting is an invocation to the genius loci— a gesture "enforcing us to this place"—and nothing more. The theatre we know [*in 1941*] *occupies itself with creating stage "illusion." What we are now interested in, however, is not illusion, but allusion.*

. . . A mere indication of place can send our imagination leaping. —ROBERT EDMOND JONES (The Dramatic Imagination.)

We are less conscious of the artificiality of the stage when a few well-understood conventions, adroitly handled, are submitted for attempts at an impossible scenic veri-similitude. —BERNARD SHAW, (On Theatre in the Nineties, II, 191.)

Where others plan their works, I intend to do nothing but reveal my spirit. —ANTONIN ARTAUD

◊   The Elizabethan Stage and Acting
                                          by Bertram Joseph

First, we must realize that consistent naturalism as we understand it, even in its most rudimentary form, had not touched the English theatre. Consistent naturalism, as distinct from sporadic realism, dates from the publication in 1570 of a commentary on Arisotle's *Poetics* written by the Italian, Ludovico Castelvetro. There for the first time we find a consistent deployment of reasoning with which the next three centuries became more and more familiar: in essence the argument depends on our accept-

◊ Volume 2 of the *Pelican Guide to English Literature*, edited by Boris Ford, 1956. Reprinted by permission of Penguin Books, Ltd.

ing Aristotle's doctrine of *mimesis* as a declaration that it is the duty of an artist to imitate the phenomena of nature as closely as possible in his medium. It then follows that drama, with its staging and actors as well as dialogue, is the art in which *mimesis* can be most effectively achieved. It is thus the duty of the dramatist, the argument continues, to present on the stage a picture of men and women behaving as they would in real life; or, in other words, the dramatist is to ask us to imagine a story as the result of watching and listening to human beings who appear and sound exactly as would their counterparts if the same situations were to take place off the stage in real life.

In Castelvetro's day, however, theatrical taste would not tolerate plain naturalistic prose; we do not find that even in the popular English theatres, for the prose of Shakespeare and his fellows is far from plain or naturalistic. Nevertheless, the Italian critic started the consistent development of the theatre to the point at which in the later nineteenth century it became normal to use words on the stage apparently only as they are used off the stage in contemporary life. And at the bottom of centuries of theorizing and of the resultant practice lies the insistence that nothing less than Aristotle's authority demands that art shall imitate life as closely as possible, the artist aiming always to induce his audience to respond as if they were witnessing the natural phenomenon and not the imitation.

But there existed another theory of art, both in Renaissance Europe and in the England in which Shakespeare and Marlowe were educated and learnt and mastered their art of drama; according to this the dramatist—like any other artist—used his medium to express what was in his mind. The play is an imagined story which also records his own individual reaction towards the persons and situations he was imagining; not merely the emotions which he imagined in their minds, but his own emotions as he imagined theirs. Once this was done, if it was done properly, we, the audiences, could be inspired by the words in which he has recorded his thoughts and feelings to imagine in turn, with reactions as close to his as our individual personalities and the interpretation of the performers will permit.

Obviously the quality of performance is an important element for success; but even before they can start to communicate the poet's imaginings, performers are defeated if their audience has been conditioned to expect anything but the speech and behaviour which the dramatist's work demands. And it is very evident that Elizabethan drama demands that an audience be prepared to imagine with the poet as the result of seeing and hearing a great deal on the stage that is unlike what happens off it. The Elizabethans responded to plays in which some parts are like life as we know it outside theatres, but in which there is much that cannot be experienced except in the performance or reading of a play. Characters soliloquize, indulge in apostrophe, and other 'unrealistic' behaviour as it suits the needs of the author to express and communicate his play. It was because the Elizabethans were untouched by theories of art which prevented their responding that their stages were suitable to the needs of the playwrights. . . .

It is now clear to us today that rhetorical delivery, known as 'action' and 'pronunciation', was more than a mere technique of flamboyant expression; to the centuries in which it was practised, it was as much a part of full expression and communication on thought and emotion as the voice alone to us in modern days. The Elizabethans held that if what is in our minds is to be communicated to others, it is not enough only to pick the perfect style of expression as we compose our thoughts into words; we must also ensure that these words are received by those to whom we speak in such a manner that they are able to share our individual sensibilities. It was for this reason that boys were taught to 'pronounce' in Renaissance schools and universities, not simply for the professional use of those who were to be lawyers, preachers, actors, and other public speakers, but as an essential accomplishment for everybody who aspired to become as completely articulate as befitted a civilized man.

To master rhetorical delivery meant an arduous and lengthy

training in the control of every limb, of the voice and breathing, of the face and features. From what is written about the art in all ages we can distinguish two separate techniques, which were, however—and this must be emphasized—fused inseparably in practice. First, the speaker who was to express emotion must be able to mime; and second, he had to enable his listeners to experience the literary quality of what was pronounced, for only through that experience was it possible for them to become completely aware of the exact nature of what he was actually saying. Similarly, we today are enabled to experience the musical quality of what is played and sung in opera, no matter how full of incident the story may happen to be.

As emotion is fused with, or rather is expressed in, the quality of a writer's style, the two techniques of Renaissance acting are equally fused in practice, when they extend and support one another. And it would be correct to say that so close is the fusion that it is impossible to express adequately the emotion recorded in Elizabethan verse and prose, in and out of drama, unless you are aware of the fashioning of the structure of words as a relationship of thought, emotion, and want, which is also a relationship of articulate sound.

This statement ought not to be regarded as an attack on modern acting; but acting as we know it at the moment must be adapted if it is to deal adequately with Renaissance drama; both our ear and our delivery need polishing if we are to do justice to any prose or verse written in England before 1800. But here we are not considering what an Elizabethan actor actually did; it is not possible to reconstruct the individual details into the continuous flow of sustained acting; yet by looking at the text of any Elizabethan play and following Renaissance directions such as are to be found in Abraham Fraunce's *Arcadian Rhetoric* (1588), we can distinguish within the literary structure the words which are to be emphasized, so that we can produce their musical, rhythmic, and emotional qualities, but in a modern way.

The closet scene in *Hamlet* (III. iv) shows the Prince opening his mother's eyes to the real quality of her second husband. Hamlet tells her sarcastically to warn Claudius if she likes to risk her own neck, and she replies:

> Be thou assur'd, if words be made of breath,
> And breath of life, I have no life to breathe
> What thou hast said to me.

The urgency of her assurance, the breathless resolution, the desperate insistence that her son must believe her now that her eyes are opened, all this meaning and emotion has been composed into the figure of climax: step by step it rises with 'words' balanced against 'breath' 'breath' is repeated to be balanced against 'life' to bring us to the top of the ascent; and then with the repetition of 'life' one swift, forceful denial speaks from the Queen's very soul. But the words are none the less sincere and natural in their emotion for the fact that another figure is employed to vary the music of the line, with 'breathe' substituted for 'breath'; and instead of words with which the pattern began, we have at its close the far more expressive periphrasis 'What thou hast said to me'.

Exactly what the boy actor did, or exactly how he sounded as he spoke these lines, we cannot say; yet we can be certain that as a result of his 'action' or 'pronunciation' of his speaking and his gesture, the audience responded to the presence of the figurative pattern, including those who were unable to identify it. Elizabethan acting was not an esoteric art; there was no need to learn any mysteries of symbolism to respond to it; its symbols are plain and obvious to all who behold them, even today. And in Elizabeth's day, we are assured by Renaissance authorities, it was possible for people who did not understand an author's words completely to respond satisfactorily none the less, thanks to the style of acting. This made the spectators aware of everything that is latent in the text, the quality of the literature, and the strength and variety of emotion.

It was, then, as the result of Elizabethan acting that Shakespeare, Marlowe, and their fellows could rely on a response to literature in the playhouse; but this does not mean that the passions and characterization were sacrificed. Works on the subject in the Renaissance stress repeatedly the essential importance of a life-like representation of the passions without which, they argue, it is impossible for an orator to sway his listeners and for an actor to affect his audience. The whole style was more flamboyantly expressive than we commonly find on our modern stage. In anger the brows were gathered in a menacing frown, teeth clenched, the right fist shaken, the feet stamped to reinforce the violence of emotion; yet here again is nothing that a modern audience would find obscure, and so it is with the other emotions. The great difference between modern and Elizabethan emotional acting lies in the greater expressiveness of the old style; its gesture and speaking were often incompatible with modern notions of civilized adult behaviour.

What an Elizabethan actor—Burbage or Taylor—could do with a passionate speech is described for us by Shakespeare in one of Hamlet's soliloquies:

> Is it not monstrous that this player here,
> But in a fiction, in a dream of passion,
> Could force his soul so to his own conceit
> That from her working all his visage wanned;
> Tears in his eyes, distraction in's aspect,
> A broken voice, and his whole function suiting
> With forms to his conceit?
>
> (II. ii)

Today we might wonder whether all these things could in fact occur, especially the change of colour, the face going wan. But descriptions of acting continue to have such details well into the nineteenth century, and the present author knows of actors to whom these things happen today.[2]

[2] See, however, J. L. Hotson, *The First Night of Twelfth Night* (1954), *Shakespeare's Wooden O* (1959); R. Watkins, *On Producing Shakespeare* (1950); G. W. Wickham, *Early English Stages* (1959).

In this soliloquy Hamlet touches upon another aspect of stageplaying which is often mentioned in the Renaissance. He asks 'Is it not monstrous' that the player can do all this when he suits his 'forms' to what he is imagining? And there is something uncanny in the Elizabethan actor's power to turn himself into something imaginary with such utter conviction and lack of restraint. As Hamlet says:

> . . . And all for nothing!
> For Hecuba?
> What's Hecuba to him or he to Hecuba,
> That he should weep for her?

In real life the Elizabethans believed that it was literally monstrous, unnatural, for a man to show in his 'action' a spirit which was not really within. In an age which believed in the teachings of physiognomy, it was held natural to express in outer show the true quality of spirit, of thought and feeling, that lay within. Evil ought to be visible in the appearance and deeds of an evil man, and goodness similarly in the good. To express in outer show a goodness or an evil which is not really in the character was to the Elizabethan way of thinking to be a hypocrite. But that is just what an actor has to do; he has to suit his forms to his own conceit, to the conceptions of his imagination; the imagination, which is liberated in dreams, is also set free when a player acts a passion 'in a dream of passion'. The actor shows feelings which are supposed to be those of an imaginary character; they are his own and they come from an inner reality; but he is not what he gives out to be, the character come to life; he is appearing to be what he is not. That is why opponents of the theatre in the Renaissance often refer to stage-players as hypocrites.

Where the enemies of the stage went astray was in assuming that it is the business of the actor to deceive; for in actual fact the Elizabethan actor, at his most passionate, was doing nothing more than inducing his spectators to respond to what the dramatist had recorded in the text of the play. Everything depended on suiting the action to the word; that is why this point is

stressed when Hamlet gives the famous instructions to the players. By 'action' Shakespeare meant that use of the voice and body
which Baker, as we have seen, called 'the greatest pleasure of a
Play: seeing it is the greatest pleasure of (the Art of pleasure)
Rhetoric'. And what Hamlet tells the players about acting can be
found over and over again in works on rhetorical delivery from
the time of Cicero until the late nineteenth century. The art was
practised as the result of a consistent attitude towards the problem involved in expressing and communicating thought in every
age. What we call composition today, the art of expressing oneself in language, was known throughout the Middle Ages and
Renaissance as 'rhetoric'; moreover, that was the name under
which composition was taught; and the teaching included all
kinds of literary composition, fiction and non-fiction, history-
writing and oratory, poetry—both dramatic and non-dramatic—
of every type. Teaching included the learning of the various figures, the acquiring of an ability to recognize and respond to
them in others' work, and to use them in one's own writing in practice. As a result of this teaching, we find the various figures already remarked upon in Gertrude's speech, figures which would
not go unnoticed when the play was performed by the original
Shakespeare company.

There is again nothing mysterious, obscure, or esoteric about
Shakespeare's use of figures, or about their use by any other popular dramatist. It is what we should expect once we realize what
the Renaissance meant by 'rhetoric'. Style, which includes the
figures, is the result of expressing ideas perfectly, but it must itself be transmitted to the audience if they are to appreciate exactly what is being expressed; and here delivery becomes the link,
both in oratory and in acting.

Renaissance treatments commonly divide delivery into voice
and gesture, a convenient division for us to follow. The voice was
carefully trained by means of exercises similar to those used by
modern opera singers. Nothing can be said dogmatically of the

quality of sound produced. But one of the points made by Hamlet is often found in the usual authorities of the time—that the words should be spoken 'trippingly on the tongue'. To do this it was necessary to preserve the quality of rising and falling inflections inherent in the nature of the English language; and one important result was that the individual words and syllables of Elizabethan verse received the correct emotional and meaningful stresses and emphases, without any sacrifice of metrical variation. Verse is thus spoken as verse without becoming monotonous or meaningless.

When we come to the details of gesture, the position is far simpler. Numerous Renaissance works supply accounts of the use of head, face, trunk, legs, feet, and especially of hand, arm, and fingers. The gesture of the hand or 'manual rhetoric' was considered to be essential to good acting. We can often read that without the hand the gesture is nothing; and so important was the technique that the physician, John Bulwer, included in his two treatises, *Chirologia* and *Chironomia* (1644), plates showing individual gestures to illustrate his copious accounts of what ought to be done.

A very important point that emerges from a study of the Elizabethan attitude to drama and the Renaissance art of acting is that there was no possibility of interpreting a part in the modern sense. The position was much the same as with the performance of music and with singing today; the performer in each case puts his technical ability at the disposal of the artist; like musicians and singers, the stylized Elizabethan actor had to use his imagination to understand the artist's intention but that can be easily perceived in the work of art. Once a part was set it could have been played with exactly the same end in view by any number of actors; and the available evidence suggests very strongly that this was the usual practice.

When we consider the implications of the term 'stylized' as used of Elizabethan acting, we see more clearly why it was possible for a boy to give a satisfactory rendering of a woman's part. He had only to perform, to 'pronounce' the text correctly; that means to communicate in his voice and gesture the thought, emotion, and objective expressed in the words. Then character formed itself automatically; it was already recorded in the author's text. A trained actor who understood the principles of speaking and punctuation could run over a piece of dialogue in the way that a musician runs over a score; the directions were plain and easily followed. That is probably the reason why Ben Jonson continually corrected his plays, improving his punctuation until it could give the actors clear guidance for 'pronunciation' which would always preserve those qualities of his style in which he felt he excelled the other popular dramatists.

In this theatre, with these techniques and the Renaissance attitude to drama alive in all who had to do with the stage, it is no wonder that boys were able to perform adult male as well as female parts in serious drama. There is nothing particularly juvenile about *Bussy D'Ambois*, *The Fawn*, or *The Malcontent*, yet these full-blooded adult dramas, with their atmospheres of violence, horror, and evil passions, were played by boys. It is possible, as Shakespeare suggests in *Hamlet*, that the boy companies were more of a passing fashion than an adequate artistic alternative to the adult companies; but we must remember that the gibe about 'little eyases' was probably occasioned by a sudden surge of popular interest when the children's companies were resuscitated at the end of the sixteenth century, after about ten years in which there is little record of their having attracted attention.

There are good grounds for any study of the Elizabethan stage to begin with the child actors. As soon as we consider their art we are brought into immediate contact with the essential quality of Elizabethan drama as a whole: it seeks not to deceive but to make others conceive; it is the actor's part to represent, to suggest, to stimulate, not to imitate a real person but to represent an imaginary one. All that was needed was a text, some bodies and voices trained to make us imagine what was in it, and a space on which the voices and bodies could be used. The essence of the play was recorded in the author's text, and 'Pronunciation', with its traditional techniques, translated that essence into living flesh and blood and voices, into what was then called 'lively action'. The stage and the scenery were incidentals, the actors, whether boys or men, were instruments and instrumentalists at the same time; and everything was subordinated to one end, to making the audience realize the quality and all the implications of a dramatic text in the theatre. It was for that reason that a schoolmaster like Thomas Godwin of Abingdon could say of scenery and dancing that they 'are not so truly parts, as accidental ornaments added to beautify the plays'. He adds, talking of tragedy and comedy:

> The *partes circumstantes,* or accidental ornaments were four, common to both, Titulus, Cantus, Saltatio, Apparatus, i. the title of the play, Music, Dancing and the beautifying of the scene. By the Scene in this place, I understand the partition between the players' vestry, and the stage or scaffold.

Although the title of Godwin's work, published in 1614, is *Roman Antiquities,* he seems to be thinking in terms of Elizabethan theatrical architecture with his reference to 'the partition between the players' vestry, and the stage or scaffold'. For in the various Elizabethan theatres, the players acted on a stage or scaffold, with the partition behind them, and the 'vestry' or 'tiring-house' behind that. This is the basis of Elizabethan staging[2] whatever variations may have been elaborated upon it; and they were many, for what we call 'the Elizabethan platform stage' refers to a number of different stages in the open air and indoors, public and private. All, however, agree in one particular—they were neither designed nor used in such a way that they impeded the actor's performance of his real duty, the 'enlivening' of words with 'action'.

The greater difference between a platform stage and a picture-frame stage lies in the relationship of the actor to his audience. It is not merely a matter of realism or lack of realism: unrealistic techniques behind a proscenium arch still do not expose the actor to the same tests, nor give him the same opportunities, as a position in which he can be observed from all sides simultaneously. The result is that spectators in different positions are given quite a different picture, although they hear the same words. The actor's technique must therefore become mobile and uninhibited enough to extend the qualities of the text instead of presenting the appearance of speaking as a man might off the stage in real life. Whether performance took place in public theatres, indoor or outdoor, in private theatres, at Court, or in noblemen's halls, the primary duty of the actor was to induce the aucience to imagine an equivalent of what the author had himself imagined and recorded in his text.

In all types of Elizabethan places of performance certain conditions were the same. The scenery represented and suggested, it did not imitate to deceive. The scene of action could change without holding up the play; indoor and outdoor scenes could follow one another swiftly and without confusion, and acting could take place on more than one level. The great difference between the outdoor theatres and the 'private houses' and halls was one of lighting. At the Globe, the Curtain, the Red Bull, and other playhouses open to the sky, natural light was used; but at theatres like the Blackfriars and at Court it was necessary to use artificial light.

Strindberg and "Surnaturalism"

Exactly what a major playwright meant by the extreme form of realism called Naturalism is perhaps best conveyed by "The Author's Preface" to *Miss Julie* by August Strindberg. It follows below in Arvid Paulson's translation with comments in the form of annotations that refer to the over-all subject of modern drama and theatre. The importance of this Preface has been universally acknowledged, even if the full meaning appears to have eluded many of its readers. In Germany, it was read to the audience on the occasion of the premiere of *Miss Julie* at Berlin's famous avant-garde theatre, the *Freie Bühne*, by one of its founders and directors, the noted journalist and critic, Paul Schlenther. And copies of a French translation were distributed at the Théâtre Libre in Paris when Antoine staged this work.

Yet it is anything but certain that even Strindberg's program does not raise more questions than it answers. And when we match his play against his program two things at least seem clear. Its dramatic action is not less, but actually *more*, theatrical than many plays never publicized as even moderately naturalistic dramas; and the least convincing elements in the play are those that would require "naturalistic" explanations from nineteenth-century scientism. The real interest lies in the play's driving power and feeling for character—and in its grim irony. The same sources of strength are to be found in the author's earlier drama of the sex duel, *The Father,* which again owes its fascination to Strindberg's passionate extremism rather than to any rigidly held naturalistic ideal or program. In both instances the ideal of scientific detachment or, if you will, impartiality, the cornerstone of naturalistic ideology, is absent despite attempts at "naturalness" of speech and external appearance, and the avoidance of romantic fripperies. Also noteworthy is Strindberg's ambivalence toward the masculinity and "health," or biological superiority, of the valet Jean to the representatives of aristocracy; and we can also sense ambivalence toward even the Captain in *The Father* for whom we are expected to feel the deepest sympathy (he is such a weak and petty would-be master of his household). In short, it is dramatic complexity that provides the really valuable naturalistic texture of these plays; and this is something deeply imbedded in both the genius and the disturbed state of mind of the author, rather than in any superficial, real or factitious, scientism.

I chose ridiculous and ordinary minor characters to show the banality of everyday life behind the grim anguish of my heroes. In staging the play [Thérèse Raquin] I tried to stress continually the ordinary occupations of my characters, in order that they might not seem to be "acting" but "living" before the audience. —ÉMILE ZOLA

Realist means laying bare society's causal network. . . . there are sensuously written works which are not realist, and realist works which are not sensuously written. —BERTOLT BRECHT ("The Popular and the Realistic," in John Willett's "Brecht on Theatre"—Hill and Wang.)

I might have written a play of ideas and flattered the taste of the contemporary public which likes to think that it thinks. I have preferred to give free rein to fantasy, which is my way of interpreting nature. —GUILLAUME APOLLINAIRE (on his "Surrealist Drama" *The Breasts of Tiresias*, 1903, 1916; first produced, 1917.)

◊

The Author's Preface to *Miss Julie*
by *August Strindberg*
translated by Arvid Paulson

In common with art generally, the theatre has long seemed to me to be a *biblia pauperum*, i.e. a bible in pictures for those who cannot read the written or printed word. Similarly, the playwright has the semblance of being a lay preacher presenting the views and sentiments of his time in popular form—and in a form sufficiently popular so that the middle classes, from which theatre audiences are chiefly drawn, can understand what it is all about without racking their brains.

◊ Reprinted by permission of Arvid Paulson from his translations, *Seven Plays by August Strindberg*, Bantam Books, New York, 1960.

Thus the theatre has long been a public school for the young, for people not too well educated, and for women who still possess that primitive faculty of deceiving themselves and letting themselves be deceived, or, in brief, who are impressionable to illusion and susceptible to the suggestions of the author. For the self-same reason it has seemed to me as if, in our time—when the rudimentary, immature way of thinking (which is a process of the imagination) appears to be developing into reflection, inquiry and analysis—the theatre, like religion, is in the throes of being abandoned as a moribund form of art for which we lack the conditions requisite to enjoyment. The profound crisis now sweeping through the whole of Europe gives credence to this assumption, and not least the fact that in those countries of culture which have given us the greatest thinkers of the age, namely England and Germany, the drama, in common with most of the other fine arts, is dead.

In other countries, however, efforts have been made to create a new form of drama by employing elements reflecting the ideas of modern times within the framework of the old forms. But, on the one hand, there has not been sufficient time for these new ideas to have been so generally accepted that the audiences can fathom their purport and implication; on the other hand, some of the audiences have been so impassioned by partisan polemics and propaganda that it has been impossible to enjoy the play in a purely objective manner while one's innermost feelings and convictions are being assailed, and when an applauding or hissing majority displays a tyranny so openly as only a theatre affords an opportunity for. And, furthermore, the new content has as yet been given no fresh form; as a result, the new wine has burst the old bottles.

In the present drama I have not attempted to create anything new (for that is an impossibility) but merely to modernize the form to meet the demands which, it occurs to me, people of our time are likely to make upon this art. To this end I have chosen (or rather, been captured by) a theme which may be said to lie outside the partisan and controversial issues of the day. The problem of social rise or downfall, of who is higher or lower, or who is better or worse, whether man or woman, is, has been and shall be of enduring interest. When I chose this theme from real life—as I heard it related a number of years ago, at which time I was greatly moved by the story—I saw in it the ingredients of a tragic drama. To see an individual on whom fortune has heaped an abundance of gifts go to her ruin and destruction, leaves us with a tragic feeling; to see a whole line die out is still more tragic. But perhaps there will come a time when we will be so enlightened that we will view with indifference the brutal, cynical and heartless spectacle that life has to offer—perhaps when we have done with our imperfect, unreliable thought mechanisms which we call feelings, and which may be superfluous when our reflective organs have developed(1).

The fact that the heroine in this play arouses our pity and compassion is due solely to our weakness and inability to resist such a feeling for fear that we ourselves may meet with the self-same fate. And the over-sensitive spectator may still not be content with feeling pity and compassion; the man with faith in the future may demand some sort of positive action or suggestion for doing away with the evil—in short, some stroke of policy. But, first of all, there is nothing absolutely evil; for the extinction of one family is nothing short of luck for another family that gets a chance to rise in the world. And the succession of rise and fall is one of life's greatest fascination as luck is only relative. And to the man with a program who desires to rectify the unfortunate fact that the bird of prey devours the dove and that the lice eat the bird of prey, I wish to put this question: "Why should it be rectified?" Life is not so mathematically idiotic that it allows only the big to eat the small, for it happens just as often that the bee kills the lion or at least drives it mad(2).

That my tragedy has a depressing effect upon the many is the fault of these many. When we have grown as hardened as the first French revolutionaries were, then it will without question produce only a happy and wholesome impression to see the royal forests weeded out and cleared of rotting, super-annuated trees that too long have stood in the way of others, equally entitled to their day of vegetation—the kind of impression one experiences when one sees somebody with an incurable disease taken by death.

Not long ago I was upbraided by someone who thought my tragedy *The Father* was too sad. As if a tragedy were meant to be amusing! People are constantly clamoring pretentiously for *the joy of life*, and play producers keep demanding farces— as if the joy of life consisted in being ludicrous and in depicting all human beings as if they were suffering from St. Vitus' dance, or idiocy. For my part, I find the joy of life in the hard and cruel battles of life; and to be able to add to my store of knowledge, to learn something, is enjoyment to me. It is for that reason I have chosen an unusual situation—yet one that teaches a moral; an exception, in brief,—but a rare exception that proves the rule and that no doubt will make all those who love the commonplace, feel offended. The next thing that will offend the simple-minded is the fact that my motivation for the action is not a simple one and that the *raison d'ère* is not a single one. A happening in life—and this is a fairly recent discovery!—is generally brought about by a whole series of more or less deep-lying motives; but as a rule the spectator selects the one which in his opinion seems the easiest to understand or that is most flattering to his own best judgment. A suicide takes place. "Bad business!" says the burgher. "Unrequited love!" say the women. "Physical illness!" says the invalid. "Crushed hopes!" says the human derelict. But now it is possible that the motive may be all or none of these things, and that the deceased may have concealed the actual motive by letting another be known that would cast a more favorable light over his memory! (3).

The sad fate of Miss Julie I have motivated by a host of circumstances: the mother's fundamental instincts, the father's wrong upbringing of the girl, her own strange nature, and the suggestive influence of her fiancé upon an insipid, vapid and degenerated mind. In addition, and more directly, the festal mood of Midsummer Eve, the absence of her father, her monthly period, her preoccupancy with animals, the excitement of the dance, the long twilight of the night, the strongly aphrodisiac influence of the flowers, and lastly, the chance bringing together of the two alone in a secluded room—not to mention the aroused passion of a bold and aggressive man. Consequently my mode of procedure has been neither one-sidedly physiological nor psychological: I have neither placed the blame exclusively on traits inherited from the mother nor have I cast the blame on the girl's physical indisposition. By the same token, I have not put the blame solely on "immorality," and I have not merely preached a moral. For want of a priest, I have left this task to the cook.

I recommend myself for the introduction of this multiplicity of motives; they are in keeping with the times. And if others have done the same thing before me, I will acknowledge with pride that I was not alone in my paradoxes—as all discoveries are called.

With regard to the delineation of the characters, I have made them somewhat lacking in character for the following reasons:

In the course of time the word *character* has been given many meanings. Originally it no doubt denoted the dominant trait in the soul-complex and was confused with temperament. With time it became the middle-class term for any antomaton, an individual who had become so fixed in his nature—or who had adapted himself to a particular role in life and who, in a word, had ceased to grow—that people called him *a character*. On the other hand, a man who continued to develop, an able navigator on the river of life, who sailed not with sheets set fast but who veered down the wind to steer closer to the wind again—this man was called lacking in character. And this, of course, in a derogatory sense—because he was so hard to capture, to categorize, to keep an eye on.

This bourgeois notion of the fixed state of the soul was transmitted to the stage, where the middle-class element has always been in dominance. There a character became synonymous with a man permanently settled and finished, one who at all times appeared as a drunkard, a jolly jester, or a deplorable, miserable figure. And for the purpose of characterization nothing more was needed than some physical defect such as a clubfoot, a wooden leg, a red nose—or that the actor in the role be given some repetitious phrase such as: "That's splendid!" or "Barkis will be glad to do it!", and so forth.

This one-sided manner of looking at human beings still survives in the great Molière. Harpagon is a miser and nothing else, although he could have been both in a miser and an excellent financier, a fine father, a good man in his community. And what is worse, his infirmity is precisely of utmost advantage to his son-in-law and daughter who are his heirs. For that reason they ought not to take him to task, even if they have to wait a little before they take to their nuptial bed. I do not believe, therefore, in simplified characters for the stage. An author's summary judgment upon men (this man is a fool; that one brutal; this one is jealous; that one stingy, etc.) ought to be challenged and rejected by the Naturalists who are aware of the richness of the human soul and who know that vice has another side to it that is very like virtue(4).

I have depicted my characters as modern characters, living in an age of transition at least more breathlessly hysterical than the period immediately preceding it. Thus I have made them more vacillating, disjointed: a blending of the old and the new. And it seems not improbable to me that modern ideas, absorbed through conversations and newspapers, could have filtered down to the domain of the domestics.

My souls (characters) are conglomerates of a past stage of civilization and our present one, scraps from books and newspapers, pieces of humanity, torn-off tatters of holiday clothes that have disintegrated and become rags—exactly as the soul is patched together. I have, besides, contributed a small fragment of evolutionary history by having the weaker character parrot words purloined from the stronger one, and by having the souls (the characters) borrow "ideas" (or suggestions, as they are called) from one another.

Miss Julie is a modern character. Not that the half-woman, the man-hater, has not existed since time immemorial but because she has now been discovered, has trod into the open and begun to create a stir. The half-woman of today is a type who pushes herself forward; today she is selling herself for power, decorations, aggrandizement, diplomas, as she did formerly for money; and the type is indicative of degeneration. It is not a wholesome type and it is not enduring, but unfortunately it can reproduce and transplant its misery in another generation. And degenerate men seem instinctively to choose their mates from among such women; and so they multiply and bring into the world progeny of indeterminate sex, to whom life becomes a torture. Fortunately, however, they come to an end, either from being unable to face and withstand life, or from the irresistible rebellion of their suppressed desires, or because their hope of coming up to men has been thwarted. It is a tragic type, revealing the spectacle of a desperate struggle against nature; tragic also as a Romantic inheritance now being put to fight by Naturalism, whose aim is only for happiness; for in order to achieve happiness, strong, virile and wholesome types are required(5).

But Miss Julie is also a remnant of the old war nobility, which is now giving way to the new aristocracy of the mind with its nervous driving force. She is a victim of the discord which a mother's "crime" produces in a family; a victim also of the delusions and deceptions of her time, of circumstances, of her own defective constitution—all of which adds up to the "fate" or "universal law" of days now past. The Naturalist has done away with the idea of guilt, as well as God; but the consequences of the act: punishment, imprisonment (or the fear of it)—*that* he cannot do away with for the simple reason that they are bound to remain.

They will remain whether he (the Naturalist) lets the protagonists go free or not; for the injured parties are never so good-natured as outsiders (who have not been wronged) can be—at a price.

Even if the father for compelling reasons should take no vengeance, the daughter would avenge herself—as she does here—from that innate or acquired sense of honor which the upper classes have as their inheritance. From where? From the barbarian ages, from the original homeland of the Aryans, or from the chivalry of the Middle Ages? It is a beautiful thing, but these days it has become somewhat of a disadvantage to the preservation of the race. It is the nobleman's hara-kiri—which is the law of the Japanese, of his innermost conscience, that bids him cut open his own abdomen after receiving an insult from another man. The custom survives, in modified form, in the duel, also a privilege of the upper classes. And that is why Jean, the valet, remains alive; but Miss Julie cannot go on living once she has lost her honor. This is the advantage the serf has over the earl: that he is without this deadly superstition about honor. In all of us Aryans there is something of the nobleman, or Don Quixote, which makes us sympathize with the man who takes his own life after he has committed a dishonorable deed and so lost his honor. And we are noblemen enough to suffer when we see a person once considered great, suddenly topple and then be looked upon as dead and a nuisance. Yes—even if he should raise himself up again and make up for the past by performing an act of nobility. Jean, the valet, is a procreator, and he has acquired a distinct and separate character. He was born the son of a farmhand and has gradually taken on the characteristics of a gentleman. He finds it easy to learn, his senses are well developed (smell, taste, vision), and he has a feeling for beauty. He has already come up in the world; and he is hard and unscrupulous enough not to allow sensitiveness to interfere when it comes to using others for his purposes. He is already a stranger to those around him (the servants and farmhands) whom he looks down upon, as he does upon the life he has turned his back on. He avoids the menials and fears them because they know his secrets, pry into his schemings, watch with envy as he betters himself, and anticipate his downfall with glee. This accounts for the duality of his indeterminate character, which vacillates between love of power and glory and hatred against those who have it. He thinks of himself as an aristocrat. He has learned the secrets of good society. He is polished on the surface, but the inside is uncouth and vulgar. He has learned to wear formal clothes with taste, but one cannot be so certain that his body is clean.

He has respect for Miss Julie but is timid and apprehensive about Kristin (the cook), for she knows his precarious secrets. He is also sufficiently callous not to let the night's happenings interfere with his plans for the future. With the brutality of the serf and the lack of squeamishness of the ruler he can see blood without losing consciousness, and he can throw off any hardship or adversity. Consequently he emerges from the battlefield unscarred, and no doubt he will end up as a hotelkeeper; and if he fails to become a Roumanian count, his son will probably attend a university and may end up as a petty official.

For the rest, Jean gives a rather enlightening insight into the lower classes' conception of life—of life as they see it—when he speaks the truth, which he infrequently does; for rather than adhere to the truth he asks what will do him most good. When Miss Julie suggests that the lower classes must feel oppressed by those above them, Jean naturally agrees with her because his aim is to gain sympathy. But when he realizes that it is to his advantage to place himself apart from the common herd, he quickly takes back his words.

Aside from the fact that Jean is well on his way up in the world, he possesses an advantage over Miss Julie because of being a man. Sexually he is the aristocrat because of his male strength, his more acutely developed senses, and his capacity for taking the initiative.

His feeling of inferiority can principally be ascribed to the temporary social environment in which he lives, and he can probably rid himself of it when he sheds his servant's livery.

The mental attitude of the slave manifests itself in his inordinate respect for the count (as exemplified in the scene with the boots), and in his religious superstition. But his respectfulness is chiefly inspired by the fact that the count occupies a position of rank which he himself would like to attain. And this deference remains with him after he has won the affections of the count's daughter and seen the emptiness within the shell.

I find it hard to believe that a relationship of love in a higher sense could exist between two souls so different in nature. For this reason I have made Miss Julie imagine that she is in love—to justify her behavior, to blot out her transgression; and I let Jean think that if social conditions were different, he might be able to love her. I imagine love is much like the hyacinth: it has to strike roots in darkness *before* it can produce a healthy, hardy flower. In this instance, it shoots up instantaneously—and therefore the plant withers and dies so soon.

Finally there is Kristin. She is a female slave, obsequious and dull (from standing at the hot stove) and laden with morality and religion that serve as a cloak for her own immorality, and as a scapegoat. Her church-going is a means of lightheartedly and glibly unloading on Jesus her household thieveries and taking on a new lease of guiltlessness. Otherwise she is a subordinate figure, and therefore intentionally sketched much in the manner of the Pastor and the Doctor in *The Father*—the reason for this being that I wanted to have precisely this type of ordinary human being (such as country clergymen and country doctors usually are). If these subordinate figures of mine have appeared as abstractions to some, it is because everyday people go about their work in a somewhat detached manner. By that I mean that they are impersonal and that they show only *one* side of their personality. And as long as the spectator feels no need of seeing the other sides of their personality, my abstract characterization of them is quite correct.

As far as the dialogue is concerned, I have, to a certain degree, broken with tradition by not making catechists out of my characters; that is, they do not keep asking silly questions merely for the sake of bringing forth a clever or jocular retort. I have avoided the symmetrical, mathematical construction commonly used by the French in their dialogue. Instead I have had my characters use their brains only intermittently as people do in real life where, during a conversation, one cog in a person's brain may find itself, more or less by chance, geared into another cog; and where no topic is completely exhausted. That is the very reason that the dialogue rambles. In the early scenes it piles up material which is later worked up, gone over, repeated, expanded, rearranged and developed much like the theme in a musical composition(6).

The plot is tolerable enough, and as it is really concerned with only two persons, I have concentrated my attention on them. I have added only one other character, a minor one: Kristin (the cook), and have kept the spirit of the unfortunate father hovering over and in the background of the entire action. I have done this because I seem to have observed that the psychological course of events is what interests the people of our time most. I have also noticed that our souls, so hungry for knowledge, find no satisfaction in merely seeing something done; we want to know *how* and *why* it is done! What we want to see are the wires—the machinery! We want to examine the box with the false bottom, take hold of and feel the magic ring in an attempt to find where it is joined together; we want to scrutinize the cards and try to discover how they are marked(7).

In this attempt of mine I have had in mind the brothers de Goncourt's monographic novels which, among all literature of modern times, have appealed to me most.

As far as the technical side is concerned, I have, as an experiment, done away with the division into acts. This I have done because I seem to have found that our decreasing capacity for illusion might be disturbed by intermissions, during which the theatregoer would have time to engage in reflection and thereby escape the author-mesmerizer's suggestive influence. The performance of Miss Julie will probably last one hour and a half. As people can listen to a lecture, a sermon, or a parliamentary proceeding lasting that length of time or longer, it has struck me that a theatrical piece ought not to fatigue an audience in a similar space of time. Already in 1872, in one of my earlier playwriting experiments, *The Outlaw,* I tried using this concentrated form, although without much success. The play was originally written in five acts, and when it was completed, I was cognizant of the chaotic and alarming effect it had upon me. I burned the manuscript and from out of the ashes roses a single, well-constructed act, fifty printed pages in length, that took one hour to perform. While the form of *Miss Julie* is not absolutely original, it nevertheless seems to be my own innovation; and as public taste appears to be changing, there may be prospects for its being accepted in our time.

My hope is that we may some day have audiences so educated that they will sit through a whole evening's performance of a play consisting only in one act. But to attain this, tests would have to be made.

In order, however, to provide momentary interludes (or rest stops) for the audience and the actors without allowing the spectators to lose the illusion that the play has created, I have included three art forms, all integral parts of the drama, namely: the monologue, the pantomime, and the ballet. Originally they were part of the tragedies of antiquity, the monologue having been derived from the monody and the ballet from the chorus.

The monologue has now been condemned by our realists as not being true to life; but if its motivation is sound, it can be made believable, and consequently it can be used to good advantage. It is, for instance, quite natural that an orator should walk up and down in his home practising aloud his speech by himself; not at all improbable that an actor should rehearse the lines of his role in a stage voice; that a servant girl should babble to her cat; that a mother should prattle to her little child; that an old spinster should chatter with her parrot; that anyone might talk in his sleep. And in order that the actor, for once, may have an opportunity to do some independent work, free from any interference, suggestions or directions from the author, it may be preferable that the monologue scenes not be written out (in so many words) but merely indicated. For it is of small importance what is being said by a person in his sleep, or to a parrot, or a cat—it has no influence on the action in the play. A gifted actor may, however, improvise such a scene better than the author can, because the actor has become part and parcel of the situation and is imbued with the mood of it. In short, the author has no way of determining in advance how much small talk may be used and how long it should last without having the audience awakened from the spell it is under.

It is general knowledge that certain theatres in Italy have gone back to the art of improvising—and as a result have produced some creative artists. They follow, however, the author's general outline and suggestions; and this may well prove to be a step forward, not to say a new art form which may truly be said to be *creative*.

Wherever the monologue, on the other hand, has made for improbability, I have resorted to the pantomime; and there I have given the actors still wider scope for creating imagery—and to win individual acclaim. To prevent the audience from being strained to the utmost, I have designated that the music—for which there is ample justification owing to the fact that it is Midsummer Eve, with its traditional dancing—exert its seductive influence while the pantomime is going on. And I address a plea to the musical director that he consider carefully his choice of music selections, lest he conjure forth an atmosphere foreign to the play and lest he induce remembrances of strains from current operettas, or reminders of popular dance music, or of primitive folk airs which are too pronouncedly ethnographic.

The ballet which I have introduced could not have been replaced by a so-called mob (or ensemble) scene. Such scenes are generally badly acted and afford a lot of grinning fools, bent on attracting attention to themselves, an opportunity to shatter the illusion. As rustics usually do not improvise into ditties their derision and jeers, but make use of already existing material (which frequently carries a double meaning) I have not composed their scurrilous innuendo but have chosen a little-known dance game, which I came across in the vicinity of Stockholm and wrote down. The words fit the actual happenings only to a degree and not entirely; but that is exactly my intention—for the wiliness and insidiousness in the slave makes him shrink from attacking in the open. Thus there must be no cackling buffoons in a serious drama such as this, no exhibition of coarse grinning in a situation which forever places the lid on the coffin of a family lineage.

With regard to the scenery, I have borrowed from impressionistic painting its asymmetry, its terse and pregnant concision, and in this way I think I have increased the possibilities for creating illusion. The very fact that the room is not seen in its entirety (nor all of its furnishings), gives us the incentive to conjecture. In brief, our imagination is set to work and fills in what is lacking before our eyes. I have also gained something by getting rid of the tiresome exits through doors, primarily because the doors in a stage set are made of canvas and move at the slightest touch. They can not even give expression to an angry father's temper when he, after an execrable dinner, gets up and leaves, slamming the door after him "so that the whole house shakes." On the stage "the whole house" (of canvas!) moves unsteadily from one side to the other. Similarly, I have used only one single setting, and this for two purposes: to blend the figures into the environment, and to break with the habit of using extravagant scenery. And with only one setting, one can expect it to be realistic in appearance. Yet there is nothing so hard to find on the stage as an interior set that comes close to looking as a room *should* look, no matter how convincingly the scenic artist otherwise can produce a volcano in eruption, or a waterfall. We may have to tolerate walls made of canvas, but it is about time that we stopped having shelves and kitchen utensils painted on it. There are so many other conventions on the stage that strain our imagination; certainly we might be freed from overexerting ourselves in an effort to believe that pots and pans painted on the scenery are real.

I have placed the rear wall and the table obliquely across the stage for the purpose of showing the actors full face and in half-profile while they face each other across the table. I once saw a setting in the opera *Aïda* that had a slanting backdrop, and it opened up to the eye unknown perspectives; and this arrangement did not have the look of having been made in a spirit of rebellion against the trying straight line.

Another innovation that is much needed is the removal of the footlights. The lighting is designed to make the actors appear plumper of face. But now let me ask: Why must all actors have plump faces? Does not the light from below tend to erase many of the sensitive, subtle character traits of the lower part of the face, and especially round the mouth? And does it not change the shape of the nose and cast a shadow effect above the eyes? Even if this were not so, there is one thing that is certain: that the eyes of the actors are suffering under a strain, making it difficult for them fully and effectively to project the varying expressions of the eyes across the footlights. For the light strikes the retina in places that under ordinary circumstances are protected (except in the case of sailors: they get the glare of the sun from the water), and consequently one seldom witnesses anything but a glare, a stare, or a crude rolling of the eyes—in the direction of the wings or upward toward the balconies—so that the whites of the eyes show. Very likely this also accounts for the tiresome habit of blinking with the eyelashes, especially by actresses. And whenever anyone on the stage has to speak with his eyes, there is only one way in which he can do it (and that a bad one): to gaze straight out into the audience, and so come in close contact with it from the stage apron outside the curtain line.

Rightly or wrongly, this nuisance has been referred to as: "Greeting one's acquaintances!"

Would not sufficiently powerful lighting from the sides (with parabolas or similar devices, for instance) be of help to the actor and enable him to project more completely the sensibility of expression and mobility of the eyes, which are the most important means of facial expression?

I have no illusions about being able to persuade the actors to play *for* the audience and not *to* it, although this would be highly desirable. Nor do I look forward with much hope to the day when I shall see an actor turn his back completely to the audience throughout an important scene; but I do wish that crucial scenes would not be given close to the prompter's box (in the center of the stage) as though the actors were performing a duet and expected it to be received by applause. I would like to have each scene played at the very place where the situation demands it to be played.

And so there must be no revolutionary changes, only minor modifications. To transform the stage into a room with the fourth wall removed, and to carry out the effect of realism by placing some pieces of furniture with their backs to the audience would, for the present, provoke an outcry(8).

And I would also like to say a word about the make-up, although I dare not hope that the actresses will pay much attention to me. They much prefer to look beautiful rather than look their part in the play. But it might be well to give a thought to whether it is expedient and becoming for the actor to smear his face with make-up until it becomes an abstraction and its character is obliterated by a mask. Let us imagine an actor who—in order to achieve an irascible, choleric look—applies a couple of bold, black lines between the eyes and that he, still looking wrathful with his ineradicable expression, has to smile in response to somebody's remark! What a horrible grimace it will result in! And again, how can the old man possibly wrinkle the false forehead of his wig (which is smooth as a billiard ball!) when he flies into a rage?

Presented on a small stage, a modern psychological drama, in which the most subtle reactions of the soul must be reflected by facial expression rather than by gesture, shouting and meaningless sound, would be the most practicable testing ground for the use of powerful lighting from the sides, with the participating actors using no make-up, or at least very little.

If, in addition, the visible orchestra with the disturbing glare from the lamps (on the music stands), and with the faces of orchestra members turned toward the audience, could be made invisible; and if the parquet ("orchestra") could be elevated so that the eyes of the spectators focused on a level higher than the actors' knees; if the stage boxes, with their giggling, snickering late dinner and supper party arrivals, could be got rid of; and if, in addition, we could have absolute darkness in the auditorium while the play is in progress; and if we, first and foremost, could have an intimate stage and an intimate theatre—then we may see the inception of a new drama, and the theatre could again become an institution for the entertainment of the cultured.

While waiting for this kind of theatre to come into being, we may as well continue our writing and file it away in preparation for the repertory that is to come.

I have made an attempt! If I have not succeeded, there is time enough to make another!

NOTES: 1. If Strindberg appears to be sarcastic at this point, his dismissive attitude toward those who are disinclined to consider *Miss Julie* a tragedy does not effectively close the subject. It may be possible to play the eponymous heroine tragically. Eleanora Duse would probably have done so, and Strindberg must have had a performance in mind that would bear out his description of this daughter of the aristocracy in referring to Miss Julie as "an individual on whom fortune has heaped an abundance of gifts." There is hardly anything in the play itself, however, to bear out this attribution of "an abundance of gifts," and there is little evidence of it in the heroine's sensibility. (In this respect, Tennessee Williams did better by his Blanche Du Bois than Strindberg by his Julie.) It is the neurotic, not the tragic heroine, that makes *Miss Julie* an early masterpiece of psychological realism or naturalism. As for seeing "a whole line die out" in the play, the interest we take in that family line and the concern we feel for its extinction is surely exaggerated by Strindberg's ambivalence with respect to his own social status as the son of a gentleman who married below his station. A struggle between the upper and lower classes is undoubtedly present in this affair between a nobleman's daughter and his valet, but that it is "tragic" is dubious.

Neither as "psychological drama" nor as "social drama," and Strindberg conceived *Miss Julie* as both psychological and social, is the play tragic. Strindberg started the great academic struggle over genre-identification with this *Preface* to a play written as early as 1888. Has the vogue of psychological and social drama deprived the modern theatre of producing genuine tragedy? Joseph Wood Krutch treated the subject in his chapter *The Tragic Fallacy*, and arrived at the conclusion that it did; and although he later granted the possibility of tragedy being written in our times, particularly in the case of O'Neill, the question still stands. Controversy raged over *Mourning Becomes Electra* in this respect; was it tragedy or melodrama? The same controversy was possible over Tennessee Williams' *A Streetcar Named Desire,* and was waged with some vehemence over Arthur Miller's *Death of a Salesman.*

2. Here Strindberg associates himself with the vaunted objectivity and scientism of Zolaist naturalism. It is the *Weltanschauung* conspicuous in turn of the century drama as written by the young Hauptmann (*Before Sunrise,* 1889), Schnitzler (*Reigen,* or *La Ronde,* 1896), and Wedekind (*The Earth Spirit,* 1895), as well as in fiction such as *Sister Carrie* (1900) by Theodore Dreiser, and *The Pit* (1903) by Frank Norris.

3. In the above paragraph Strindberg is referring to what the Viennese psychoanalyst Robert Wälder later called The Law of

Multiple Causation, and sets down a principle for psychological drama. Great dramatists, of course, followed this principle without fanfare or formula long before Strindberg. *Hamlet* is the inevitable example.

4. In calling for multisided characterization as an article of naturalistic dogma, Strindberg actually proposed a naturalism more ample and subtle than routine naturalism. With complex and surcharged plays such as *Miss Julie, The Father, Creditors, The Bond* (or *The Link*), and *The Dance of Death* to his credit, Strindberg could have justifiably called himself a *surnaturalist* rather than naturalist. The work is too personally felt and too fluid in feeling to conform to cool naturalistic scientism. It can be argued that all first-rate naturalistic work is "surnaturalistic." The term would help us in defining the fascination and power of such disparate plays as Becque's *Les Corbeaux,* Ibsen's *Hedda Gabler,* Strindberg's *Miss Julie,* Chekhov's *The Three Sisters* and *The Cherry Orchard,* O'Casey's *Juno and the Paycock,* and O'Neill's *The Iceman Cometh.*

5. In the next eight paragraphs Strindberg mingles social drama with psychology, or draws upon the social situation to illuminate the private one. Determination by environment, it is well to remember, is combined with determinism by heredity and instinct in the naturalist's view of *la condition humaine.* These forces comprise the constellation of Fate under which men live, desire, act, and suffer or cause others to suffer, and provide an equivalent to the Greek idea of Necessity or *ananké.*

6. Compare the major works of Chekhov—all nominally naturalistic but all fluid, imaginative and, in a special sense, poetic.

7. See Note 3. In the above paragraph, we find some apt references to psychological drama, then still in its infancy.

8. All these things were to occur within a generation of the writing of this seminal essay.

◊　　◊　　◊

Epic Theatricalism and Epic Realism

Of all the modes of modern theatre in recent decades the one that has received the greatest attention in intellectual circles, both academic and nonacademic, is "Epic Theatre." The literature on the subject is immense and is utterly disproportionate to the actual practice of the commercial theatre anywhere in the world. The reason is not far to seek. There are, in the main, only four forms of theatricality that have proved viable in the theatre proper.

The most popular is the musical theatre, ranging from light revues and musical comedies to music-dramas of the calibre of *Porgy and Bess* and *West Side Story* which infringe on the preserves of opera. Their success in the United States has been paralleled by their popularity, no doubt under American influence, in England and Western Europe. (And elsewhere, too, if one may judge from the fact that *South Pacific* was the most successful entertainment in Istanbul when the present writer visited Turkey in 1962.) Popular, within geographical and climatic limits, is the theatricality of open-air pageant plays produced mostly in the South during the summer months, such as Paul Green's *The Lost Colony* and Kermit Hunter's *Unto These Hills*. They are capable of further artistic development as well as enrichment of subject matter. Thus far, however, pageant drama has been more "inspirational" than "critical," and to that degree alien to the sceptical and rebellious spirit of the urban intellectualism that pervades the theatrical capitals of the West. A third use of "theatrical theatre" has been particularly noteworthy in France and won the adherence of the French intelligentsia virtually from the beginning of the century. Inspired by the rare genius of Jacques Copeau, and encouraged by the successful practice of imaginative director-managers such as Jouvet, Dullin, Pitoëff, Barrault, and Jean Villar, a number of playwrights wrote plays noteworthy for both virtuosity and literary sophistication. Two of these, Giraudoux and Jean Anouilh, manifested a high degree of polish and urbanity from the beginning and acquired much reputation in other lands. Others who gained repute abroad were André Obey, Cocteau, Salacrou, and Marcel Aymé, and their number was increased by existentialist playwrights, the best known of whom became Jean-Paul Sartre and Albert Camus. They did not greatly revolutionize dramatic form, but they did avail themselves of fantasy and myth (as in Sartre's *No Exit* and *The Flies*) as a convenient means for expressing existentialist philosophy. Nevertheless, French theatricalism *per se* rarely rose above a rueful passiveness or wry withdrawal from the realities and challenges of the times. (*The Flies* is one of the rare exceptions.)

In the art of Giraudoux and Anouilh there have been few departures from a more or less poised estheticism, even in such socially "engaged" plays as the former's *The Madwoman of Chaillot* and the latter's *Antigone*. Their work has been most appealing to "cultivated" members of the middle classes, and has served them chiefly as an anodyne. The only kind of theatricalism that has stirred the mind and spirit of the young and rebellious has been that which exposed and ridiculed or openly defied conventional life and received values. This was apparent in expressionism, immediately before and after World War I, dadaism, surrealism, "The Theatre of the Absurd" and "Epic Theatre." But expressionism expired by about 1925 from its own frenzy, and dadaism dissolved in its self-created chaos.

Only Epic Theatre has thus far proved to have staying power and possibility of growth, and the reason probably is that its negativism with respect to the world as it is was coupled with a positive purpose and posture. In fact, the evolution of Epic's greatest playwright, Bertolt Brecht, was precisely a progression from anarchistic dadaism (in *Baal*, for example, and in *The Three-Penny Opera* and *Mahagonny*) to Epic criticism and challenge. Thus in *Mann ist Mann* we are shown that men can be transformed into machines for destruction, in *Mother Courage* that war is destructive to the common people who endeavor to thrive by it, in *The Good Woman of Setzuan* that unalloyed good-ness is simply not possible in a rapacious world, and in *The Caucasian Chalk Circle* that things belong morally to the people who are good for them.

What is perhaps insufficiently realized, however, when new-comers to Epic theatre theory speak in generalities, is that this style has evolved and is capable of evolving further, and that subsumed under it are many kinds of theatre rather than just one kind—and that the dubious one of "propaganda." It is to ex-pand somewhat on the evolution and the multifariousness of "Epic" that I proffer the ensuing remarks.[3] And I also offer them as an attempt to observe the degree to which "Epic" is a mode of realism that should be differentiated from romantic variants.

[3] Originally, a paper delivered at the first meeting of the American Association of Comparative Literature, at Columbia University, in September 1962. Reprinted from Comparative Literature Studies. Special Advance Issue, 1963.

*Since it is their aim to forge
myths, to project for the
audience an enlarged and
enhanced image of its own
sufferings, our playwrights
[i.e., the French existentialist
playwrights] turn their backs
on the constant preoccupation
of the realists, which is to
reduce as far as possible the
distance which separates the
spectator from the spectacle.*
—JEAN-PAUL SARTRE

*Au siècle où nous vivons,
l'horizon de l'art est bien*

*élargi. Autrefois le poète disait:
le public; aujourd'hui le poète
dit: le peuple.*—VICTOR HUGO
(Preface d' "Angelo", 1835.)

*The real paradox of acting, it
seems to me, resolves into the
paradox of dual consciousness.
. . . Why should stage
emotions be supposed to
absorb all of a man's faculties
when the most poignant
emotion in real life does
nothing of the sort?*
—WILLIAM ARCHER

◊

Varieties of Epic Drama
by John Gassner

Interest in the nature and value of Epic Theatre has mounted with the growing vogue of Bertolt Brecht since World War II, and the literature on Brecht himself has been piling up impressively for the past decade and a half. But it is still necessary for us to locate the subject of "Epic Drama" in the stream of efforts to enlarge the scope of modern dramatic art and to release its energies. To this end it is essential to start with the realization that Brecht did not originate modern Epic Theatre; although Brecht's

◊ Revised version of *Varieties of Epic Theatre in the Modern Drama* given at the first meeting of the American Comparative Literature Association (Special Advance Issue of Comparative Literature Studies, 1963), by courtesy of the editors of *Comparative Literature Studies.*

practice and theory have recently given "Epic Theatre" virtually all of the prestige it possesses in our universities or university theatres, he was not alone in moving in this direction and drawing attention to it.

Erwin Piscator, born at Marburg, Germany, in 1893, revolting against three years' military service in World War I, exchanged a brief engagement to dadaism for a permanent marriage to politically oriented theatre when he established a short-lived theatre in 1919 at Koenigsberg. It was characteristically called the Tribunal (*Die Tribüne*), and it was there that the director Karlheinz Martin staged Ernst Toller's first play *Die Wandlung*, a lyrical antiwar drama in thirteen rapidly moving, more or less fragmentary, scenes that culminated in a mass scene in which the returning soldier Friedrich, repulsed by his mother and uncle for his conversion to radicalism, starts a revolt with such revolutionary ejaculations as *"Marschiert! Marschiert am lichten Tag!"* and *"zertrümmert die Burgen, zertrümmert, lachend die falschen Burgen."* Piscator next started short-lived ventures such as the Proletarisches Theatre in Berlin which lasted until April 1921, and after a year of producing naturalistic plays such as Gorky's *Small Citizen* and Tolstoy's *The Power of Darkness* at the Central-Theatre in Berlin in 1921-24, he became the director of the long-established and influential Berlin Volksbühne in 1924 and produced plays of political content and more or less Epic form until he broke with that organization in 1927 over his production of Ehm Welk's historical drama, *Storm over Gothland,* an account of a medieval revolt to which Piscator added a politically inspired film sequence. Piscator was accused of arbitrarily injecting propaganda into the work and the film strip was removed by the governing body of the Volksbühne.

Piscator's blending of film and stage drama in this production appears to have been the first successful experiment in giving historical dimension to a play by this means. The author had indicated his intention with a statement on the title page reading "This play does not occur merely in the year 1400," but since he had composed a conventional drama he failed to realize this intention in dramatic scenes. Piscator, in staging the work, resorted to the device of providing contemporary parallels by means of a film-strip. This was to remain a Piscator "Epic-theatre" device, and was employed by him during his period of exile in the United States in a provocative production of Sartre's *The Flies* (*Les Mouches*) at the President Theatre, New York, in 1947. After his conflict with the Volksbühne management, Piscator renovated an old theatre in West Berlin, the Theater am Nollendorfplatz, and opened his *Piscator-Bühne* in 1927 with a production of Ernst Toller's *Hoppla! Wir Leben* in which he again made considerable use of synchronized filmstrips with staged episodes. The object was to document the traumatic experience of a revolutionary idealist who emerges from eight years of imprisonment into a world run by his socialist comrades that he finds so intolerable that he commits suicide. Since Toller had not done so, Piscator set out to demonstrate what had happened during those eight years to destroy the hopes his hero had once entertained for a "better" world. The premiere on September 3, 1927 ended in a political demonstration and resulted in a sharp denunciation of the production as political agitation rather than art.

Important sectors of the press, however, credited Piscator with the creation of a new and extraordinarily vivid mode of dramatic art, while cautioning him to resist the temptations of propaganda. Insisting upon the cause-and-effect relationship between dramatic form and political content, Piscator continued to explore the possibilities of imparting political instruction or criticism in other noteworthy *Piscator-Bühne* productions. From November 1927 to January 1928 he presented a new play, *Rasputin*, by Leo Lania, and as usual, Piscator was not content with the circumscribed—that is, non-epic—character of the play he was going to produce. He saw in it another and more important subject, which he has described as quite simply the destiny of Europe between the years 1914 and 1917. He had been called the real author of *Hoppla! Wir Leben,* and there is indeed hardly a play produced by him in the 1920's that he did not recreate or amplify to such a degree that he could be credited with coauthorship. If Brecht can be called a playwright-director, Piscator may be almost as justifiably described as a director-playwright.

In staging *Rasputin,* Piscator's Epic-theatre leanings led him to take all of Europe for his subject, and to connect the private Rasputin story with the intertwining political and economic factors of the world conflict. To explain the stage production that ensued—an imaginative presentation of multiple action on a globe-like stage—Piscator's play editor Leo Lania, who was apparently the chief author of the final version of the play originally by Alexei Tolstoy, wrote in the program that the aim had been not to present the tragic destiny of a particular hero, but rather to produce a political document about the era. Lania insisted that history could not be divorced from politics and maintained that playgoers wished to see the documents of the past that would illuminate the immediate present. To meet this need, Piscator and his associates added no less than 19 new scenes depicting imperialist machinations to the original seven scenes of Alexei Tolstoy's play. A film strip and a globe-like stage, segments of which were opened to present scenes transpiring in different European capitals, fulfilled Piscator's desire to convert a private tragedy into a public document. And the document was enlarged into a commentary, particularly in the case of the filmstrip, which performed the function of a chorus and addressed the audience directly, calling attention to important historical details, explaining or interpreting them, criticizing the characters' actions, or even haranguing the spectators. The production led to a trial as a result of which Piscator was obliged to eliminate the character "Kaiser Wilhelm II" from the play.

Having carried out the project of an epic documentary with *Rasputin,* Piscator went on to develop an *Epic satire* in *The Good Soldier Schweik,* a dramatization of composite authorship based on an uncompleted novel by the then already deceased Czech writer Jaroslav Hašek. (I shall not attempt to unscramble the authorship of the dramatization, originally made by Max Brod and

Hans Reimann, modified and augmented by Brecht,[4] Piscator's playreader Gasbarra, Lania, and Piscator himself. There is no complete and definitive text in existence, so far as I know.) This was the first time that Piscator took his material from a novel—a novel of adventure, definable indeed as a picaresque novel except for the fact that its hero Schweik gets into numerous scrapes not as an unmitigated rascal but as a lovable innocent. Schweik's inspired idiocy when he is assigned as an orderly to a lieutenant wreaks havoc with the Austrian army during the World War and makes a hollow mockery of the entire war and of a good deal else besides. Recognizing the satiric possibilities of the work, Piscator allowed it to assume its natural non-Aristotelian character, producing a thoroughly horizontal pattern of incidents strung on the thread of Schweik's comic gaucheness. Since Hašek had not completed the novel, Piscator did not even strain for a conclusion— the play as it stood without a dramatic ending (and it had no Aristotelian "beginning" and "middle" either) was all the action that was needed to expose the absurdities of the Austrian-Hungarian empire and the confusing futility of the first World War.

The dramatic action lay entirely in the movement of the production rather than in any destination sought and arrived at; neither Schweik nor the war had any distinct destination anyway, and that was indeed the point of the satire. Since Schweik, moreover, was a mere cork bobbing on the surface of a world cataclysm concerning which he could have no perspective, movement *alone*—movement without clearly perceived destination—was the essence of this travesty of the state of the war-torn world be-

[4] Brecht wrote a variant version in the early 1940's *Schweyk im Zweiten Weltkrieg* (Schweyk in the Second World War) first produced at Warsaw in Polish in 1958, and a year later in Germany, with music by Hanns Eisler. The chief attractions of this play are the lyrics—*Und was bekam des Soldaten Weib?, Das Lied vom kleinen Wind,* and *Das Lied von der Moldau.* The theme was the rejection of Hitler by the "Little Man" Schweyk.

tween 1914 and 1918. The resulting play was inevitably "Epic" rather than dramatic in the Aristotelian sense of having a beginning, a middle, and an end. The horizontality of the play was intrinsic—as intrinsic as it is in *Mother Courage*, at the close of which the heroine, who has lost all her children to the war, is still bent upon following camp and hawking her wares. At the same time, Piscator's *Schweik* was no more static than Brecht's *Mother Courage*, since the agitation of the war is a constant pulsation in the play, the individual sections are *events*, and the characters act and are acted upon by individuals and forces. Piscator also achieved a theatrical equivalent in constant stage movement and found both the right technical device and a suitable symbol for it —namely, the treadmill. By means of the treadmill, everything was kept in movement; and keeping everything in proper flux necessitated expressive curtailments of realistic scenery. Piscator deployed, as Brecht would have done, only partial settings on the stage. He also used film projections, such as the famous caricature drawn by Georg Grosz to represent the army physician who diffidently examines the crippled Schweik and pronounces him fit for military service.

Both as a director and play adapter (and in his case the two roles tended to be indistinguishable), Piscator was, then, once more involved in Epic dramaturgy by the exigencies of his material and the requirements of his socially engaged art. He was to be attracted henceforth to the novel as a springboard for socially engaged drama, and this interest was later apparent in two dramatizations, with collaborators—namely, Dreiser's *An American Tragedy*, which the Group Theatre produced in New York in the mid-thirties under the title of *The Case of Clyde Griffiths*, and Tolstoy's *War and Peace*, which Piscator first presented at his Dramatic Workshop in New York and subsequently, after returning to Europe in 1951, in France, Germany, and Scandinavia. (It is noteworthy that one of the most highly and deservedly praised productions of the year 1962 in London was Piscator's *War and Peace*, reworked by an English writer and staged by an English director.) Piscator's penchant for the novelistic stage was also apparent in his New York production of Robert Penn Warren's *All the King's Men* at the President Theatre in January 1948, in which he made continual use of a tiny revolving stage and several ramps for constantly shifting the playing areas.

Each of the first two of these Epic plays, however, had a distinctive shape that distinguishes them from both the forced historicity of the *Storm over Gothland*· and *Rasputin* productions and the Epic comedy of *The Good Soldier Schweik*. *The Case of Clyde Griffiths* assumes the form of a demonstration by means of a court trial. In this dramatization of Dreiser's novel, a Narrator acting as the lawyer for the defense and treating the audience as the jury endeavored to extenuate Clyde's guilt by demonstrating the nature and effect of the forces that collaborated with the immature hero's weak character in encompassing his ruin. The outer form of the play was a trial, but with a difference: Whereas the ordinary trial drama zealously maintains the illusion of a court trial, Piscator's treatment broke that illusion with the Narrator's speeches to the audience and with the devices of an illustrated lecture; and whereas the average trial play presents a tightly knit action of conflict and discovery in the manner of the *pièce bien faite,* the Piscator dramatization presented a string of episodes as case-history data in the Epic-novelist manner. *The Case of Clyde Griffiths* amounted to an opening up of the trial-drama genre in two senses—in letting the action and the argument spill over the proscenium arch into the audience, thus breaking the tight structure of the well-made-play type of realism, and in visualizing on the stage a series of episodes intended to enlarge Clyde's trial of his milieu, if not indeed of·society as a whole.

Piscator's *War and Peace,* as presented in its final form in London by the Bristol Old Vic, is a radically different type of play. It is a chronicle combining the fate of a single noble family with Napoleon's invasion of Russia. In *War and Peace* we find an intermingling of a novel about individuals with history. But these artfully arranged snippets from Tolstoy's epic novel became more than a mere adaptation because the episodes were not simply strung together, as they are in a novel. Tolstoy's book underwent a formal modification in agreement with the content of the dramatization, which amounted to an antiwar lecture demonstration. The play had the usual didactic narrator who assumed the character of a master-of-ceremonies as he defined different playing areas for the private drama and the public action, commented on events, and drew the inevitable antiwar conclusion from his demonstration in an eloquent address to the audience. An additional feature of the work, both as a play and a stage production, was the forthright yet tasteful and dignified way in which the proscenium arch was abolished and the fourth-wall convention ignored. If the genre of *War and Peace* is to be closely defined, we may describe it as a fused private and historical chronicle in the form of a demonstration conducted with complete transparency. We may call the play a complex example of open dramaturgy openly arrived at.

Piscator continued to experiment with Epic-theatre techniques both in the choice and treatment of plays when he maintained his Dramatic Workshop in New York from 1940 to 1950. One of his most successful productions was *Winter Soldiers,* a drama of resistance to the Nazis in various parts of Europe which contributed to the ultimate defeat of the German army on Russian territory. Written by a young American playwright, Dan James, who was awarded the Sidney Howard Prize by the then flourishing Playwrights' Company, *Winter Soldiers* was an effective Epic drama in conveying the action in short scenes occurring either successively or simultaneously in different parts of the European continent. It had the comprehensiveness that Piscator, like Brecht, sought for the theatre. In this case the comprehensiveness was extensive and cinematic; this sequence of episodes constituted a "horizontal Epic drama" in the sense in which *Mother Courage* is a "horizontal Epic" drama, though a more tightly knit one. *Winter Soldiers* was a *moderate* example of the genre, however, because neither the author of the play nor its stage director, James Light, the former Provincetown Players director then an instructor at Piscator's "Workshop," made any effort to theatricalize the production with conspicuous violations of the fourth-wall convention and interpolations of song, chorus, a narrator, or a lecture. And the moderateness of the technique was perhaps all to the good, since the representation of the resistance movement on the stage was sufficiently "instructive" without further Epic theatricalization and sufficiently "interrupted" by the jaggedness of the resistance-movement scenes not to require additional "distancing" of "alienating" devices; and exhortations in the form of speeches, lectures, or songs would have been quite redundant in the anti-Hitler period of the 1940's.

Winter Soldiers would have been less well received if Piscator had not refrained from overstressing the didacticism to which he was prone. The greater resistance to Epic theatre in New York was to Brecht's early didacticism in the *Lehrstück* genre, which was brilliantly parodied in a skit contributed by the left-wing publicist, Emanuel Eisenberg, to the International Ladies Garment Workers' celebrated musical revue *Pins and Needles*. Piscator's addition of a documentary film on the Nazification of Germany to his 1947 production of Sartre's *The Flies,* staged under his supervision by a member of his staff, Paul Ransom, was deplored as a redundancy. Piscator had resorted to the film sequence in order to draw a contemporary political parallel to Sartre's existentialist *Oresteia.* Piscator's tendency to employ stage machinery as far as his slender means would allow also invited criticism, from his first New York production of *King Lear* on an overworked turntable in 1940 to his staging of *All the King's Men* eight years later. It was one of the characteristics of both Piscator and Brecht to want to cross all *t's* and dot all *i's* in a script and a production in order to ensure complete comprehension of their argument—a fault against which Piscator was rarely secured by his theatrical talent and from which Brecht was frequently saved by his combination of poetic talent and penchant for irony. Piscator had a strong penchant for stage machinery, although it is only fair to report that he was not indissolubly wedded to heavily mechanized productions; one of his most successful productions in New York was a *Twelfth Night,* staged under his supervision by Chouteau Dyer, with exemplary simplicity on a virtually bare stage. It was Piscator's ambition to force through an agreement between modern theatre and the machine age and to make full use of its mechanical resources. A statement of this vision of a regisseur-engineer appears in a note contributed by Piscator to my book *Producing the Play,* first published in 1941.

In sum, Piscator, who in his sixty-ninth year in 1962 was made the director of a new theatre, the *Freie Volksbühne,* in West Berlin, which was to rival the Brechtian Theatre am Schiffbauerdam in the Eastern zone, (one of his first productions was the anti-Nazi drama, *The Deputy,* by Rolf Hochhuth, which attained international notoriety with its accusation of papal opportunism) contributed a variety of dramatic forms of Epic theatre and was, to a degree, Brecht's predecessor. It is significant that his book, *Das politische Theatre,* published in 1929, was reissued in Germany in 1962, and that it should have been put out somewhat earlier in the year in Paris. The translation *Le Théâtre politique* was made by the avant-garde playwright, Arthur Adamov, who had abandoned "The Theatre of the Absurd" school for "Epic Theatre" with a play about the Paris commune: it was produced in the summer of 1962 under the title of *Spring '71* by the left-wing Unity Theatre of London. Largely unsuccessful in text as well as in the London production, *Spring '71* bears considerable resemblance to Piscator's experiments. It exemplifies a characteristic distinction between Epic-theatre technique and the usual history play. An allegorical personage played by a young actress wearing the traditional red cap of Liberty appears at the beginning of the play as well as throughout the text to harangue the audience and inform it about the course of the revolt, to symbolize the conflict and to participate in it at the same time. Thus the fragments of scene are used not in a commonplace narrative sequence, but as projections of partisan fervor.

Until Brecht came to write his major works after 1940, Brecht's chief contribution to Epic drama was *lyrical* rather than dramatic. This is most apparent, of course, in his collaborations with the composer Kurt Weill, *Die Dreigroschenoper* and *Aufstieg und Fall der Stadt Mahagonny*. In this area of the theatre, to which Piscator made no particular contribution and for which Brecht was uniquely qualified by his poetic talent, he had no peers. A special lyrical realization of "Epic" also appeared in the *Lehrstücke,* notably, *Der Jasager, Der Neinsager, Die Massnahme,* and *Die Ausnahme und die Regel.* These, too, were Epic pieces despite their brevity. They illustrated or demonstrated some social idea or some question of tactics with episodes presented singly, as in *Der Jasager* (which should be coupled, however, with *Der Neinsager*), or collectively, as in *Die Ausnahme und die Regel;* Brecht's short plays had in view some issue invoking a larger political sphere of action than the constricted plot of these little plays.

At the same time the crispness of their structure and texture assured the proper esthetic relationship between form and content; the acuteness of the author's argument accorded well with its embodiment in the action and dialogue of the play. The little *Lehrstücke* were miniature Epic dramas. They are distinguishable by their compression and telescopic dramaturgy from the "chronicle Epic" and the "novelistic" genre represented by Piscator's *Schweik* and Brecht's *Die Mutter,* his dramatization in 1933 of Maxim Gorky's famous novel of the same title.

In this work, too, however, Brecht created a *Lehrstück* of sorts, and a distinctive dramatic form; for instead of merely dramatizing the novel, Brecht inserted lyrical interludes known as "mass chants," with special music composed by Hanns Eisler. In the Theatre Union production given in downtown New York in 1936 the imaginary fourth-wall framed by the proscenium arch was pierced not from within, as when an actor addresses the audience from the stage, but from *without*—that is, from the auditorium. At strategic points in the action a group of actor-singers filed up the stage and delivered appropriate sentiments or comments in unison. These mass chants comprised the choral portions of Brecht's *Mother*, and they served the *Lehrstück* purpose of instructing the audience along with the general "Epic-theatre" objective of widening the range of a play beyond mere plot. At the same time, they were instrumental in promoting the "alienation effect" of Brechtian drama, lowering the emotional temperature of the scenes and reducing identification with Gorky's sympathetic mother whose love for her son turns her into a revolutionary heroine.

That Brecht, as was also the case with later American productions of *Galileo* and *The Good Woman of Setzuan,* paid too dearly for the alienation effect and lost some of the effect on New York audiences was easily noted. The production of *Die Mutter* was not a success even with critics and audiences of the left, and the play appears to have been relegated to an inconspicuous place in the Brecht canon. But the form of the play was fascinating to some observers including myself, then drama critic for *New Theatre* magazine, and Archibald MacLeish. Both of us read papers at a symposium on the play praising the experiment as a means of reintroducing poetry into the modern drama *en bloc* in a novel and viable manner. By comparison with this more or less aborted drama, *Frau Flintz,* by Helmut Baierl, a recent Berliner Ensemble treatment of the conversion of another old-fashioned woman to collectivist ideals in East Germany after World War II, produced in the summer of 1962, was decidedly moderate; the episodes followed each other successively without any pattern of antiplot and anti-illusionistic interruptions. The structure of Brecht's *Mother* was a veritable blueprint for chorally augmented Epic drama and is another example of its author's important lyrical enrichment of the theatre. Other examples can be cited. It would be especially profitable to return here to Brecht's *Fears and Miseries of the Third Reich,* because some of the most telling dramatic effects are produced by the singing of the famous *Lied der Moorsoldaten* in a prison scene and by parodies of the "Horst Wessel Song" throughout the play. Here the reliance on the lyrical element is anything but flight from dramatic scenes, because this work contains many good scenes. It includes *The Jewish Wife* and *The Informer*, two superb episodes that have been presented as self-contained one-act plays.

The retention of the lyrical element in Brecht's later work is a well-known feature of his technique. I found it tiresome in one, not necessarily conclusive, production of *Der gute Mensch von Setzuan*, the music for which was composed by Paul Dessau, but I found it fairly effective in Washington and London productions of *The Caucasian Chalk Circle* in 1962; and Eric Bentley, who translated *Mother Courage* for a Broadway production, made out an interesting case for the importance of the "Songs" in *Mother Courage*. In an essay in Stanley Burnshaw's *Varieties of Literary Experience* (New York University Press, 1962, pp. 60-61), Mr. Bentley points out that "the Brechtian song is an individual item, clearly marked off from its content, like an individual number in vaudeville," and repeats his belief that it would be less misleading to declare that in Brecht's plays "the dialogue is an interruption of the songs" than to say that the songs are interruptions of the dialogue. Even if it may be too much to claim that "Epic Theatre is lyric theatre," it is indisputable that Brecht's most characteristic contribution to Epic drama was lyrical.

That contribution was at the same time also dramatic and theatrical, and with respect to the forms of Epic drama developed by Brecht and others we are obliged to note that in *Galileo*, for instance, Brecht transformed the conventional genre of biographical drama quite radically. This is apparent when one compares his treatment of Galileo with another well regarded play, Barrie Stavis's *Lamp at Midnight*, the New Stages production which Brooks Atkinson reviewed favorably in the *New York Times* in the 1940's. Atkinson and other New York drama critics, with the exception of Louis Kronenberger then reviewing for the newspaper *PM*, saw little merit in Brecht's play, which was by its author's design the very antithesis of a simple narration and a eulogy. By means of calculated violations of the fourth-wall convention, the use of song as well as demonstration of scientific data, and other "alienating" or "anti-illusionistic" elements in the play, Brecht created a genre of biographical drama in which narrational biography is secondary to demonstration, analysis, and argument.

With this in mind, we are justified in referring to a genre of "Epic biography," formally distinguishable from a simple and sentimental chronicle such as Laurence Housman's *Victoria Regina,* which was originally a haphazard collection of one-act plays about Queen Victoria, and from a more complex play such as Robert Sherwood's *Abe Lincoln in Illinois* which, for all its seeming documentary character in a Lincoln-Douglas debate scene, remains a sequence of biographical scenes rather than an argument for which the author has found an expressive form.

By comparison with *Abe Lincoln in Illinois,* John Drinkwater's *Abraham Lincoln,* though written twenty years earlier, and Norman Corwin's Lincoln-Douglas debate-drama, *The Rivalry,* presented in New York twenty years later, were closer to Epic play-structure. The Drinkwater play alternated episodes and a chorus of "Two Chroniclers" speaking verse in unison, and Corwin's play had the Lincoln-Douglas debates as their main dramatic feature. Brecht's *Galileo,* nevertheless, is a decidedly more ample and penetrating work than either *Abraham Lincoln* or *The Rivalry;* and Brecht must be credited with having brought biographical drama into the theatre as an *Epic* form. *Galileo* is a more fluid, varied, and theatrically original drama than Drinkwater's stiffly patterned play; and *Galileo* combines richer characterization with more penetrating theatricality than Corwin's résumé of Lincoln's political debates.

Mother Courage also constitutes a unique genre. Although it belongs to the quasi-historical genre of Epic Theatre in dealing with *The Thirty Years' War,* it is personalized in its emphasis. It deals primarily with the human beings who both live by war and are destroyed by it. This work, perhaps the most penetrating antiwar play in any language since *The Trojan Women,* expresses the fundamental ambivalence or duality of human nature in an alternation of scenes exposing greed and cowardice with scenes depicting human perseverance and sympathy. The essence of Brecht's chronicle resides in this dramatic pattern or rhythm. And this rhythm is theatrically punctuated by the projections on a front curtain and especially by the "Songs."

It is because of its special structure that *Mother Courage* is distinguishable from the ordinary chronicle play. It differs from a work such as Gerhart Hauptmann's naturalistic Peasants' Revolt drama *Florian Geyer* written in 1896. In Hauptmann's play, the size of the cast and the extensiveness of the action result in an inchoate mass of matter, because there is nothing in the structure of this loose work to hold the parts together. *Florian Geyer* is a much simpler work than the concern with ambivalence allows *Mother Courage* to be, yet Brecht's also loosely tied episodes constitute a comprehensible whole because the dramatic form is a demonstration by strong dramatic and theatrical means. In this work, then, Brecht produced an exemplary Epic drama rather than an epic by mere extensiveness or by mere default in failing to observe the Aristotelian dramatic form of a beginning, a middle, and an end. Adamov's *Spring '71*, written almost a quarter of a century later than *Mother Courage*, represents another endeavor to match form and substance; if it is a poor play, it simply proves that it is possible to make a mess of things in *any* form or genre. And if Hauptmann's *The Weavers* and O'Casey's *The Plough and the Stars* are impressive works without benefit of Brechtian theatricalism, if both works have dramatic power and illumination without the dramatic machinery of a Piscator or Brecht, it is an obvious conclusion that there has been no Piscator-Brecht monopoly in Epic Theatre. This reflection does not, however, invalidate the view that the presentational, theatricalist, organization of *Mother Courage* does constitute a special form suitable for a dialectical demonstration and dramatic showing, rather than discussion, of its subject. *Mother Courage* is a "pure showing" whereas Giraudoux' non-Epic treatment of the Trojan

War, *La Guerre de Troie n'aura pas lieu* (*Tiger at the Gates* is the title of the English adaptation), for example, is mainly a discussion along urbane Parisian lines; and Shaw's *Saint Joan* is essentially a story which has intellect irradiated with the superb dialectics of the famous tent scene. Anouilh's *The Lark*, it is true, is replete with theatricalist devices, but Anouilh is chiefly playing with theatre while presenting a serious and painful subject. At the other extreme, however, we may find consistency of naturalism, as in *The Weavers*, depriving a play of both a rich texture of characterization (Brecht's is vastly richer in *Mother Courage* than Hauptmann's) and the discussion element Shaw employed so brilliantly in *Saint Joan* and upon which he placed so much emphasis in acclaiming Ibsen as the creator of discussion drama or so-called drama of ideas in *The Quintessence of Ibsenism*.

Brecht's other two major works, *The Good Woman of Setzuan* and *The Caucasian Chalk Circle* also comprise distinct modes of "Epic." They are collectively designated as "parables." *The Good Woman*, written between 1938 and 1941, is a dramatic tale exemplifying the problem of being virtuous in a predatory world. *The Caucasian Chalk Circle*, written in 1944-45, is presented as a legend to illustrate the moral that, as the Singer or Narrator put it, "what there is shall belong to those who are good for it." Both parables, however, are not fortuitous mutations in the Brecht canon but are extensions of the earlier *Lehrstücke*, which also illustrated a point by means of a theatrically presented instance. A problematical subject is raised. It is not necessarily answered. It is both raised and answered in *The Caucasian Chalk Circle*. The question raised in *The Good Woman of Setzuan*—the extremely complex problem of goodness in the world as it is—is not answered; it is passed on to the audience.

Two somewhat separate types of drama appear in these parables. We may conclude that *The Caucasian Chalk Circle* is an "Epic" Morality; *The Good Woman of Setzuan* is an "Epic" Problem Play. It is not, of course, a well-made play like Ibsen's *Pillars of Society* because of its theatricalist, quasi-oriental, features, the most striking of which is the heroine's nonnaturalistic transformation into her male cousin. It is a shrewdly designed *ill-made* play, and this makes it possible for the play to be truly problematical and ensures the artistic agreement of content and form. If we should call *The Caucasian Chalk Circle* a *Lesson Play* we should have to define *The Good Woman of Setzuan* as a *Question Play*.

Both are modern Epic dramas. And both have their limitations or dangers, too. Brecht overcame the chief danger of Morality drama—that of single-tracked, lesson-giving in *The Caucasian Chalk Circle* through the open dramatic form of that play. The structural looseness averted the effect of narrow didacticism, as did also the comic and folksy line of the action. Brecht also successfully combined vivid caricature in depicting the ruling class with affecting characterizations in the case of his humble heroine and her soldier lover, thus avoiding Morality-Play abstractionism, which is not unknown in Epic Theatre. He also lightened his didacticism by giving it exuberance and folksy theatricality. He did not blend caricature and character, realistic illusion and anti-illusionist detail, but, rather, set these elements side by side, very much as the *pointilliste* dabs one dot of color on the canvas next to a different dot of color instead of mixing them on his palette. Brecht followed the same procedure in his production scheme when he required masks for some characters, such as the Governor's Wife, who is not created as a real person, and dispensed with masks for the servant girl whose simple human reality is essential to the action and the argument. Brecht, however, was not always so successful in escaping the pitfalls of didacticism, which is apparent in the constricted character of the one-act play *Die Massnahme,* or *The Measure Taken,* written in 1930, and the choppy overinsistence that vitiates the chorus-punctuated dramatization of Gorky's *Mother* and partly accounted for the failure of the Theatre Union production of the mid-thirties. This "weakness from strength," so to speak, accounted for the inadequacy of many an American left-wing drama of the 'thirties that suffered from a so-called *conversion ending,* and also weakened the Berlin Ensemble's recent drama *Frau Flintz,* which has the additional faults of diffuseness and failure to make the conversion of its elderly heroine either clear or convincing.

The Good Woman of Setzuan may well leave its audience "hung up," so to speak, so that the play itself becomes problematical, and if it is that for audiences it can prove the same for the venturesome director who stages it. I do not in fact know of any conspicuously successful professional production of this almost a quarter-of-a-century old play in the West; and Brecht himself was apparently troubled by its quizzical character and lack of resolution in dutifully noting the advent of Communist China and declaring that "the province of Setzuan in this parable, which stood for all places where men are exploited by men, is such a place no longer." Nevertheless, it is a genuinely modern type of play in its very inconclusiveness. It is a quizzical drama of failed idealism, of which Ibsen's *Brand* is an epic prototype, Chekhov's *Ivanov* is a naturalistic variant, and Paul Green's *Johnny Johnson,* a play about a Schweik-like American innocent, produced in 1936, is a later "Epic" example. To a degree, however, it is the challenge intrinsic to the unresolved or suspended ending that is important. This is the case in Brecht's play; in Ibsen's lumberingly splendid "epic," *Emperor and Galilean,* in which the reconciliation of the opposites of paganism and Christianity is left for the future; in *Johnny Johnson,* in which the supposed madness of its Wilsonian pacifist puts to shame the unsound sanity of normal men who make war; and in Irwin Shaw's one-act play of the same year (1936), *Bury the Dead,* in which the dead soldiers of a future war step out of their graves in order to seek a fuller life than they had ever had while alive. The range of the suspended, essentially unresolved, epic type of drama seems large, indeed.

In concluding this summary of Epic forms and the problems of dramaturgy encountered in them, it is necessary to observe, of course, that the review is partial and sketchy. For one thing, both Piscator and Brecht insisted that they were following a long-established tradition, evident in the oriental theatre, the classic

Greek drama, the medieval mystery-play cycles, the Elizabethan drama, and the romantic theatre that adopted the open Shakespearean drama from the eighteenth-century *Sturm und Drang* period of *Goetz von Berlichingen* and *Die Räuber* to the late romantic period of Büchner and Gutzkow. This is too large a subject to be treated here. It would also be essential to differentiate between what is and what is not truly modern Epic Theatre; we would have to observe, for instance, that mere Epic extension does not make a play an Epic drama in the Brechtian sense. Thus Büchner's chronicle of the French Revolution, *Danton's Death,* is a prototype of modern Epic and *Oedipus Rex,* Aristotle's example of a perfect tragedy, is *not* an Epic drama despite the presence of the choruses. *Oedipus* has a closed structure, *Danton's Death* an open one; it is also "narrative" in the manner of Piscator's *War and Peace* and "documentary" in the manner of *Rasputin* in so far as it gives a kaleidoscopic view of a critical period in history. *Danton's Death* is a composite Epic drama possessing the merit of provocativeness and the defect of spottiness and diffuseness. It tells or, rather, shows a many-faceted story, it depicts an historical situation in a variety of scenes, and it flares up into critical scenes of accusation and defense—as in an Epic trial drama. There is no *a priori* reason, of course, why an Epic play should not have a composite structure and style; an "Epic" playwright cheerfully dispenses with the Aristotelian and neoclassic unities. The "composite" Epic play is an obviously acceptable form of modern drama.

Since the advent of Piscator, Brecht, and their associates the leaders of Epic Theatre on the European continent, various degrees and modes of "Epic" have continued to appear in many places—notably in France, where existentialist plays by Sartre and Camus, such as *The Devil and the Good Lord* and *Caligula,* have had marked Epic-Theatre features. Successful productions in English are Robert Bolt's Thomas More biography *A Man for All Seasons* and the *War and Peace* London production, in 1962. In the English-speaking theatre, two distinct developments of Epic can be noted in stage drama (aside from musical-comedy chronicles such as Kurt Weill's Broadway failure *Love Life* and Lionel Bart's London success *Blitz*), although attention may also be given to documentary films, which reached their peak in the United States during World War II as well as television documentaries and Epic radio plays, which attained literary distinction in Archibald MacLeish's *The Fall of the City* in 1937 and had rhetorical effectiveness in Norman Corwin's *On a Note of Triumph* produced at the conclusion of World War II.

One type of Epic drama intended directly for the stage has been the stage spectacle. In its weakest form, it came into fashion in the 1900's in European countries under the general title of *Son et Lumière*. It was indeed very little more than "Sound and Light" and comprised an open-air historical pageant based on the annals of a particular place such as Notre Dame de Paris or the City of Bruges. A less vulgarized form has been the plainly political one represented probably at its worst by staged Nazi demonstrations and perhaps at its best, in literary and theatrical afflatus, by *Mystery-Bouffe*, a mass-spectacle celebrating the Bolshevik Revolution written by the poet Mayakovsky, and staged in 1919 by the pioneer antinaturalistic director, Meyerhold. And a moderate form of dramatic history has been steadily developing in the United States, chiefly in the South, ever since the production, in 1937, of *The Lost Colony*, the first of Paul Green's pageant-plays. Since then Paul Green has written many other pageant-plays, some more Epic in quality than others, and he has been joined in this enterprise in outdoor summer theater by other Southern writers, notably Kermit Hunter, the author of the successful Cherokee Indian chronicle *Unto These Hills*, given annually before large audiences at Cherokee (North Carolina), in the Smoky Mountains. The results have been uneven, although Paul Green has maintained a high standard of literary taste in producing these amalgams of historical episodes, recitations, choruses, songs, dances, and spectacles for which Green's generic term "symphonic drama" is not inappropriate.

But if this experiment in American Epic Theatre has been the most continuous, it is the documentary form that made the greatest impression as a new and vital art form. It materialized as the so-called Living Newspaper and while one cannot urge literary claims for it, it amounted to remarkably dramatic journalism and special pleading. Developed during the Depression period of the 1930's in the work relief program known as The Federal Theatre, it brought journalists, actors, and technicians together in an endeavor to express the period's analysis of social ills and zeal for social reform. The producers of the "living newspapers" blended narration, action, demonstration, song, and dance; they used both naturalistic and symbolic details at will. They reproduced the façade of a New York slum tenement in *One-Third of a Nation* that could have done justice to David Belasco's spectacular naturalism, and they used nine masks to symbolize the Supreme Court in another production, *Power*. The "living newspapers" favored other formal features, including a sort of minstrel-show interlocutor or "Little Man" who wants to know why he cannot have decent housing or why electric power is so expensive and a Narrator-lecturer who provides an explanation by means of slides, demonstrations, and scraps of illustrated scenes. The greatest impression that native Epic theatre ever made on the American stage came from these "living newspaper" experiments of the Federal Theatre under the supervision of Hallie Flanagan Davis from Vassar, who later prepared a "living newspaper" of her own, $E = Mc_2$, on the subject of the atom bomb, at Smith College and presented it briefly in New York as well. If the "Living Newspaper" came to an untimely end as an Epic genre, the reason was not esthetic but economic. It earned high critical praise as a form of theatre despite its slight literary value, but it could not be produced on any impressive scale without federal subsidy. Only one fully implemented "living newspaper," *Medicine Show*, appeared on the New York stage after Congress liquidated the Federal Theatre along with other New Deal welfare projects in

1938. It was also from the Federal Theatre during its last slender lease on life that the American drama acquired its outstanding, if narrowly circumscribed, lyrical Epic drama, Marc Blitzstein's song-and-dance satire and paean to social militancy, *The Cradle Will Rock*, which was presented by Orson Welles' Mercury Theatre after the Federal Theatre found it expedient to drop the project it had nursed along.

In England Epic drama attracts more attention than it ever did, the attraction resulting in nothing more original, on the one hand, than the biographical chronicle exemplified by John Osborne's *Luther* and Chrstopher Fry's *Curtmantle*, and, on the other hand, the effective, theatrically invigorated, drama of *A Man for All Seasons*, which strict proponents of Epic Theatre would be reluctant to endorse wholeheartedly because it does not actually go far enough toward illuminating social reality. We are given the sense of the character, Thomas More, but not the issue itself in more than the general terms of his Roman Catholic loyalties and other peoples' opportunism. In Germany, Brecht, who died in 1956, lacked a worthy successor; the East German author of *Frau Flintz* has made no particular contribution to Epic drama and the West German Carl Zuckmayer's *Das kalte Licht* (1955), an account of the treason and detection of Klaus Fuchs, the physicist who spied for the Communists, was but a pale reflection of Epic drama and was considerably inferior to his earlier drama of the Nazi period, *Des Teufels General*. In Switzerland, however, Epic drama has recently had noteworthy variants in the work of Friedrich Duerrenmatt and Max Frisch (especially in the ironic tragedy of antisemitism *Andorra* and the Morality drama of *The Visit* and the parable-comedy of *Biedermann*), so that the further development of Epic forms seems probable even if talent such as Brecht himself possessed is too rare in any period to be anticipated.

In summary it is possible to list the following conclusions: Epic drama derives from a tradition that predates the modern period and won new prestige after the neoclassical period with the vogue of Shakespearean open dramaturgy and the rise of Romanticism. But it lacked modern definition and direction until the advent of Piscator and Brecht. It also acquired a dynamic quality in social Expressionism that had some vogue between 1910 and 1925, chiefly in Germany. But the Epic element in such earnest plays as Kaiser's *Gas* and Toller's *Masse-Mensch,* was scattered by expressionist explosions of violence and dissolved in expressionist subjectivity; and the same thing may be observed in more or less dadaist expressions of cynicism and satirical protest, of which Brecht's early plays *Baal* and *In the Jungle of the Cities* (*Im Dickicht der Städte*) and E. E. Cummings' *him* are perhaps the most meritorious examples. When the expressionist wave subsided, Epic Theatre forged ahead with its characteristic forms and found a genius with a dual talent for literature and theatre in Bertolt Brecht. Piscator, Brecht, and others who have been mentioned or unmentioned in this paper produced a number of dramatic forms that have enlarged the scope and enriched the possibilities of modern drama. The end of these ventures has been by no means reached, and they have already been too numerous to be subsumed under a single definition or associated with the single ideological trend of Marxism. Perhaps we can even associate Epic Theatre with religious drama, as once was the case when the Middle Ages of Faith produced the *mystery* cycles or Passion Plays. Perhaps the Age of Doubt can also produce Epic religious drama, and that this has been the case, in some respects, is suggested by Claudel's Christian chronicle *The Satin Slipper* and Christopher Fry's *A Sleep of Prisoners.* And if these reflections tend to minimize some distinctions and to obfuscate the subject of Epic Theatre with their inclusiveness, such obfuscation may actually be a first step toward clarification. The alternative of limiting application of the adjective "Epic" to a single dramatic form is plainly untenable. Certainly, Epic drama, in its widest allowable range of open dramaturgy, has proved to be the only viable nonromantic and unskittish alternative to the constricting structure of ordinary realism and naturalism.

To arrive at this conclusion, however, is to invite a number of questions. The first is whether "Epic Theatre" does not become meaningless unless its application is restricted in one or more respects. That danger is considerable when the term is allowed to embrace premodern as well as modern drama because nearly every historical play and non-neoclassic tragedy before Hebbel's mid-nineteenth century *Maria Magdalena* can be designated as "Epic drama" in so far as the dramaturgy is presentational, the scope of the presentation is large and varied, and the subject matter is the fate of a ruler, dynasty or nation. Brecht tacitly acknowledged a link with the past when he adapted Sophocles' *Antigone* and Marlowe's *Edward II* or used John Gay's *The Beggar's Opera* as a basis for his *Dreigroschenoper*, and it is worth noting that Piscator chose *King Lear* for his debut as an Epic-Theatre producer-director in New York in 1940. As a matter of fact, Piscator and Brecht *preferred* to identify themselves with the mainsteam of the theatre and the great tradition of presentational drama, which has sanctioned all known styles of open dramaturgy and Epic Theatre ever since the time of Aeschylus.

The contention that Epic Theatre is anti-Aristotelian did not disturb proponents of "Epic" when they related themselves to the presentational theatre of the past and should not have troubled them, for a good deal of Greek drama, including Aeschylus' Oresteian trilogy, is not particularly "Aristotelian" either. The real difference between the Piscator-Brecht school and the older theatre is ideological rather than esthetic. Even the emphasis on *Verfremdung*, or the "alienation principle, in Brecht's theoretical writings can be misleading, for presentational comedy has always been more or less "alienating," except in emphatic pastoral or romantic scenes; and the formalism of tragedy, in general, not to mention presentational devices such as the Chorus, the *deus ex machina* and the Messenger, has been a "distancing" factor. Therefore, Brecht's term "Epic *Realism*," with its implication of a materialistic and more or less Marxist viewpoint, is helpful in distinguishing between the Piscator-Brecht type of Epic theatre and older presentational styles.

The term is also helpful in distinguishing the open dramaturgy of a Claudel from that of Brecht. In such baroque work as
the chronicle play *Le Soulier de Satin* (1919-1924) and the biographical drama *Le Livre de Christophe Colomb* (1927), undoubtedly uninfluenced by the dramatic art of Piscator and
Brecht, the effect is Wagnerian, symbolist, and "magical." If we
say that Brecht's *Galileo* and Claudel's *Christopher Columbus* are
both Epic biographies, we are not saying what *kind* of plays they
are except that they are "Epic" in certain formal features. Yet it is
obvious that the two aforementioned plays "work" on us quite
divergently and *affect us* altogether differently. An attempt to
take Claudel's plays, as well as those of sundry symbolists, ritual-
ists, and subjective expressionists (Verhaeren, Andreyev, Eliot,
Strindberg, O'Neill, Lenormand, et al.), into "Epic Theatre" on
purely formal grounds (and such an effort is made rather strenuously in Marianne Kesting's *Das epische Theater,* Kohlhammer,
Stuttgart, 1959),may, in the last analysis, be commended for
comprehensiveness rather than for discrimination.[5] The mystical

[5] Marianne Kesting, it is only fair to say, acknowledges some distinctions. In her chapter on Claudel, for example (pp. 88-105),
she says that *"das Zeitliche wird unter dem Blickpunkt des
Ewigen betrachtet"* (p. 99) in *Christopher Columbus.* She admits
that *"Claudel bediente sich des epischen Theaters, ausser zum
Kommentar, um innere Visionen zu vergegenwärtigen"* (p. 105)
and correctly applies the same qualification to Strindberg's *Dream
Play.* She also takes note of Claudel's lavish use of atmospheric
spectacle, which is actually a characteristic of *symbolist* rather
than of Epic theatre; and concerning Claudel's heavy reliance on
musical effect, a *Wagnerian* rather than Epic realistic procedure,
she observes that in contrast to Brecht, *"baut Claudel die Musik
als 'Fil du récit' ein, welche die Kontinuität der Bühnenhandlung
wahrt, während Brecht diese Kontinuität durch die Musik unter-
brechen will"*—in order, she might have added, to allow or enable
the playgoer's analytical and critical faculty to take over, which is
hardly a Claudelian objective. But Marianne Kesting concedes too
much similarity in not differentiating sharply enough, in the final
analysis, between Epic realism and Epic symbolism or Epic idealism. Herbert Ihering's protest against Claudel's *"Anwendung des*

impetus of Claudel's art, his poetic afflatus (one might call his orotund poetry a form of poetic as well as religious intoxication by comparison with the powerful and ironic "*Sachlichkeit*" of lines by Brecht such as "*Der Grosskönig muss eine neue Provinz haben, der Bauer muss sein Milchgeld hergeben./Damit das Dach der Welt erobert wird, werden die Hüttendecher abgetragen./Die Schlacht ist verloren, aber die Helme sind bezahlt worden*"), and the baroque imagination that disposed Claudel toward the grandiose and the grandiloquent alters the essential form of the play. It is not just the surface content, but the inner form of the work that is affected by his mystique; a Claudel Epic play becomes in successive parts or as a whole an ecstasy, a plangent oratorio, a solemn rite, or a majestic procession, whereas a Piscator or Brecht drama is essentially a *demonstration* of an idea or point of view. To say that *The Satin Slipper* and *Mother Courage* are chronicle and Epic plays may be technically correct but tells very little about the distinctive character of these works. Claudel's Epic *idealism* produces a work that is essentially an extension of a Calderón *auto sacramentale*. It is fundamentally a different kind of drama than a play produced by Piscator's or Brecht's Epic *realism*, despite the similarity of presentational devices, interruption of plot, violation of "fourth-wall" illusionism, structural anti-Aristotelianism, and narrative comprehensiveness.

Efforts to bring other types of work, such as Thornton Wil-

---

epischen Dramaturgie" is doctrinaire in its rationalism, but has the merit of calling attention to the contrast with Epic realism: "*Er . . . verwendet alle Mittel eines revolutionären, eines harten, eines wirklichen Theaters, um religiös zu mystifizieren. Was gesschaffen war, um aufzuklären, wird hier dem Glauben unterstellt. Was desillusionnierend gedacht war, dient einer neuen Illusion.*" (Quoted in Kesting, p. 89). *The Coral* and the two parts of *Gas* by Georg Kaiser, the expressionist playwright to whom Brecht was rather partial, and Shaw's *St. Joan*, especially in the great discussion tent scene between Warwick and the Bishop when they decide to destroy Joan because she is a premature "Nationalist" and "Protestant," are obviously much closer to Epic *realism* than Strindberg's *Dream Play* and Claudel's *Satin Slipper* or *Christopher Columbus* despite their patently open structure.

der's *Our Town* and *The Skin of Our Teeth* and Tennessee Williams' *Camino Real*, within the orbit of "Epic Theatre" must also be viewed with suspicion or hedged about with strong qualifications. They may constitute Epic *theatre*, but they are not Epic *realism*, and the difference is not simply one of content but of form. Williams' play is merely a "dream-play" analogue to reality, as is indeed Strindberg's *Dream Play* itself. And if we call Wilder's two plays chronicles, which they technically are, we do not touch upon their unique character at all. *The Skin of Our Teeth*, for example, would be more accurately described as two acts of benign extravaganza and one act of domestic drama augmented by *Lehrstück* features, such as the procession of the placard-carrying figures in Act III. By virtue of its extensive coverage of time and space, its non-Aristotelian structure, and its presentational devices, such as Sabina's address to the audience in Act I, *The Skin of Our Teeth* may be "Epic theatre" but is not "Epic realism." To a large degree, the play relates itself by means of ingenious anachronisms to vague universals rather than to the particulars of society. Its "Finnegan's Wake" type of comic and (in Act II) vaudeville synthesis of the past and present subordinates content to theatricality. A large part of the play (two out of three acts) operates as a theatrical *tour de force,* and verges on a "theatre for theatre's sake" type of composition. A work of Epic realism such as *Mother Courage* differs radically in expressive form from *The Skin of Our Teeth.*

We may conclude, then, that Epic plays can be *organically* very different despite their common non-Aristotelian and "open" structure, depending on the author's organizing principle—that is, on whether the plays are idealistically or materialistically, magically or analytically, romantically or realistically oriented. Claudel actually subordinates the written drama to mime, dance, and spectacle to produce an effect of uncritical and submissive ecstasy or hypnosis. It is precisely because the possibilities of Epic theatre have been ample that discrimination among them is important. And in this connection the operative word *realism* in the term "Epic realism" should prove especially useful.

◇   ◇   ◇

To supplement the above review of observable variants of Epic Theatre, it may be instructive to turn to a British "Third Programme" lecture by Mr. Henry Adler that provides a useful summary of Brechtian theatrical technique and, at the same time, enters a demurrer against Brechtian theory and practice. It is possible to take exception to Mr. Adler's exceptions; for instance, did the author of Grusha, Asdak, Galileo, Mother Courage, and her companion the Cook, actually desiccate his characters as much as his disdain for empathy would suggest? But the question of "the reality which springs from the roots of character" will ultimately have to enter into our judgment of Brecht's plays, even more so than in the case of the French theatricalists, who can be taken more lightly. In so far as "Epic" moves toward realism, albeit "theatrically," it must move toward character drama, too. Or, is this but a deduction of time-conditioned "bourgeois humanism" and does realism require us to give priority to social rather than individual interests and to social rather than private reality? "Epic realism" implies the latter, I think, and might do so even without its customary Marxian *parti pris*, through sheer sociological orientation. It should not surprise us, then, that Brecht's career as a dramatist culminated in the "parables" of *The Good Woman of Setzuan* and *The Caucasian Chalk Circle*. Allegories and parables are least dependent on individual characterization, impressing characters into the service of an idea or lesson. And in two other major plays, *Mother Courage* and *Galileo*, Brecht's protagonists were respectively a quasi-historical character and a famous biographical subject. The one was set against the historical background of *The Thirty Years' War* and the other against the Counter-Reformation in Italy cutting athwart the post-Renaissance wave of scientific progress. If both *Mother Courage* and *Galileo* escape diminution by the social background, they represent the triumph of Brecht's personal genius rather than of the genre of Epic Drama.

I have the profound conviction . . . that the experimental and scientific spirit of the century is going to reach the theatre. And what is the future? It is the human problem studied within the bounds of reality, it is the casting aside of all fable; it is the living drama . . . free from fairy tales, historical fragments, bombast, trivialities, and conventional blusterings. . . . The well known tricks for tying and untying a plot have had them. —ÉMILE ZOLA (Preface to Thérèse Raquin.)

The drama . . . must be a concentrating mirror, which instead of weakening, concentrates and condenses the colored rays . . . —VICTOR HUGO (Preface to Cromwell, 1827.)

The drama is complete poetry . . . true poetry, complete poetry, consists in the harmony of contraries . . . the grotesque is one of the supreme beauties of the drama.—VICTOR HUGO

◇   Bertolt Brecht's Contribution to Epic Drama
by Henry Adler

During the days of the Weimar Republic, Bertolt Brecht and Erwin Piscator lacked the money to stage one of their socialist propaganda plays at their Berlin theatre. Instead, the actors gave a play-reading. Sitting at a table on the bare stage, they perfunctorily read their lines, sometimes making a gesture, sometimes rising to indicate a move. But, although the actors made no pretence of being 'in character,' as we say, the audience were more completely held than by the plays which attempted full theatrical illusion. Suddenly Brecht saw that what held them was

◇ First published in *The Listener*, January 12, 1956, pp. 51-52. Reprinted by permission of the author and the British Broadcasting Corporation.

not character, not illusion, but the moral relationship between the characters, the moral argument of the play. The actor was quoting the words, imitating the actions; he was estranged from the character. The moral conflict was seen isolated, at a distance, as history. This is the effect of 'estrangement', of 'alienation', which is Brecht's particular contribution to the theatre. He calls it the *Verfremdungseffekt*.

This is not altogether new. Two hundred years ago Diderot was propounding the same principles, and indeed Brecht has formed a society which he calls the Diderot Society. Diderot complained that 'the audience leaves its vices in the cloakroom and collects them on the way out'. And he urged that the actor must not be lost in his part but detached from it. He must not be overwhelmed by emotions but interpret them and present them in intellectual terms. Diderot quotes with approval the case of an actor in a dying scene who was so much in control of himself that he could arrange the position of a chair without losing his effect on the audience. In the same way Brecht points to the Chinese actor who, in his opinion, does not enter into his part but demonstrates it, who looks at the audience as though saying: 'Doesn't it happen like this?'

The actor in Brecht's own company is estranged from his part. He relates what the character said, describes what he did, with a kind of deliberation as though he realises that the character could have acted or spoken otherwise—and yet did not. As a marxist, Brecht is aware that every action has its alternative, that history depends on the correct choice of action. That is why he divides his play 'Mother Courage' into short scenes, each of which is a stage in her life. There is no climax. Each stage is determined by the previous stage, just as it determines the next stage; we know from the start that her degradation is inevitable. We are estranged from her because it is not her we see but only the actress who is telling us about her and who depicts her. . . . She stands monumental in her rags against the gaunt, hooded *doppelgänger*, her wagon which is her means to livelihood. The huge, bare stage is her lifetime, the battlefields she treks through, the years she lives through, as she turns and turns about. She is doomed because, as Brecht says over and over again, an individual cannot be good in an evil society. The war which gives her a living destroys her children. But she is too degraded to understand how it all happened. She is inside the war, we are outside, estranged, listening to her story. Therefore there is no catharsis of pity and indignation, no empathy. She goes off singing harshly the same hopeful song with which the play began, and, in case this sounds plaintive, Brecht cuts across it with some jeering military music. This contrast is used often and sometimes becomes a trick, an inverted sentimentalism, but Brecht does this deliberately so that the easy emotion may be stored up, may set up what he calls 'atmospherics', be translated into thought and moral decision.

Brecht's theatre is thus like an operating theatre. The human beings are exposed on that stage, beneath the white light poured down from a battery of lamps which are clearly visible and create no illusion. We watch it, not enthralled by illusion but, in Brecht's own words, like a man smoking, so that sometimes, despite our detachment, we may give an angry laugh, or a grunt of recognition at the incontrovertible truth of what we see. You are not made to forget that you are in a theatre but reminded of it. With a kind of preternatural clarity the actors are revealed, pathetic as animals blinking in the headlamps, caught at a moment of history. Each scene is announced by a large poster, like a clinical scientific label. For instance: 'General Tilly wins a victory and Mother Courage loses four shirts'. As a matter of fact, the shirts are wrested from her to bandage soldiers wounded in the victory. Mother Courage is at once related to and estranged from the war. She is not allowed to be pathetic. When a critic compared her to Niobe, Brecht withdrew the script and made her more unsympathetic.

Estrangement—the *Verfremdungseffekt*—is also the keyword in Brecht's theory of 'epic drama'. Epic drama, so-called, was not new in Germany at that time: the Aristotelian definition of epic, as 'a narrative poem unrestricted by the unities of place and time and capable of dealing with many events', had already been applied by Piscator to the dramatisation of the savage social conflicts in Germany. He used a technique of short episodes, clearly influenced by the film, in order to bring out the contrasts between the lives of rich and poor. But while Piscator saw epic drama as a dramatisation only of social forces.[6] Brecht introduced a more personal note. He combined with his marxism a belief in the individual, a strange awareness of the power of the irrational moral choice. He has proclaimed his admiration for Brueghel and I believe that it is not only the big, group paintings which attract him, but the more subtle 'Fall of Icarus'. In this picture the ploughman in the foreground gets on unconcernedly with his ploughing, the shepherd stolidly watches his sheep: no one notices the catastrophe taking place in the distance over the sea. Far away, the tremendous event makes its tiny splash. So, throughout his plays, Brecht is trying to isolate the inconspicuous moral drama, to estrange it, to set it in a sharp light, so that it is not taken for granted before it falls, dragged down by the weight of society. His own analogy for what he means by estrangement is a watch. A watch is a familiar object. But, he says, take it apart, and all the pieces seem strange and small: they are unfamiliar in their estrangement from the functioning timepiece, almost irreconcilable with it. There is the same sort of strangeness, of irreconcilability, about an individual who is naturally good in a society which is evil. To understand, we must watch his path through society. We must stand at a distance and judge him; we are powerless to help him but we can recognise where he goes wrong.

[6] I do not think this was the case in Piscator's adaptation and production of *The Good Soldier Schweik* with its extremely individualized "little man" hero Schweik, nor is it the case, as the author of this article points out in *War and Peace,* a late Piscator dramatization.—J. G.

A New Classicism

Therefore, the theatre must change. We must achieve a new classicism. No longer the Greek hero doomed by an enigmatic Fate; no longer the Shakespearean hero isolated in his conflict with right and wrong; and no longer Stanislavski's theories of empathy, nor the Chekhov play with its illusion of shared emotions and its inconclusiveness. Not fate, but human intelligence. Not individual isolation but the individual in terms of society. Not the rapid tying up of a problem through climax and *dénouement* but the working out of a moral relationship between an individual life and the world. Above all, not intimacy with the character but a distance from which the audience can judge. But we shall have to remember that when Brecht says we must judge, he does not mean that we must consider the facts objectively, as Zola and the social realists do, but judge from the standpoint of the marxist faith to which he is committed. That is why, although the method produces exciting drama, you realise afterwards that the issues of the play are rigged, that everything that happens to Mother Courage is an illustration of marxian economics and that the play which pretends to judgement is animated by a veiled didacticism.

Indeed Brecht calls some of his plays 'parables.' Now a parable is surely a means of referring something unknown to something known. For example, the parable of the Prodigal Son suggested the behaviour of the heavenly Father by comparing it to the hehaviour of a human father. 'The Good Woman of Sezuan' and 'The Caucasian Circle of Chalk' are parables of the necessity for a balance between heart and head; but the larger truth which the parables represent is nothing but a marxist preconception. In 'The Good Woman of Sezuan' Shen-Te, a good-hearted prostitute, finds that all her kindness is exploited and turned to evil. Therefore she disguises herself as a shrewd, ruthless cousin, whose hard dealings put things right. The head comes to the rescue of the heart. And when the gods, whom Brecht sees as amiable old fogeys, descend from Heaven advocating a change of heart, they get badly knocked about by the tough world of men.

'The Caucasian Circle of Chalk' is a still more explicit parable. At the beginning, we see two groups of shabbily dressed people squabbling almost inaudibly. They are members of two Russian communes disputing the ownership of a farm. Which group has the most right to it? The group which reared goats on it until ordered to leave before the invading nazis, or the group which later took it over and made it agriculturally prosperous? To interpret the ethics involved, a story-teller sits at the side of the stage, and as he reads the old legend of 'The Caucasian Circle of Chalk' it comes to life on the stage. Sketched on the backcloth are the pyramids of oriental hovels. On the stage a baroque arch. The little world lives before you although you know it is dead. There is a squalid little revolution going on, in which the Governor gets deposed. You watch it as though through the wrong end of a telescope. The characters are wearing wooden masks and their naive, painted expressions emphasise their distance away in history. The sensitive, sweet, silly face of the Governor looks out unseeingly at the twentieth-century audience on this fine summer's day, when he is being led in cords to sudden death. The face of his consort is haughty and wooden as she flees; she saves her dresses and deserts her child.

Epic Form

But Grusha, the girl who saves the child, is a peasant and therefore does not wear a mask but shows us her nice, healthy, wholesome, human face. Upon her decision the rest of her life very nearly depends. 'Terrible is the temptation of goodness', is the comment of the story-teller, and as he speaks, so she acts. She saves the child and persists in her moral decision despite hunger, cruelty, danger, and, finally, arrest by the Iron Guard. Her adventures are told in a series of short scenes. Brecht uses this epic form precisely because it is not continued in time; it can trace the implementation of a moral decision through a lifetime. Her ordeals, however, seem contrived, for she has no inner life, there is no opportunity for empathy. Yet the drama of the staging is undeniable. We seem to see the world at our feet. From a seat in the circle the revolving stage seems to undulate, and one sees the girl and the pursuers who overtake her steadily through the play as though glimpsed through a break in the clouds, related in a sinister tension.

Grusha is caught and brought to trial for protecting the aristocratic child. But now the leader of the chorus who has been commenting on the play steps into it, as so often happens in Chinese morality plays. His name is Asdak and he dominates the second half of the play. He is head as Grusha is heart. He has suddenly become a judge in the topsy-turvy world of revolution. He sees that in a crooked world the good-hearted must use their wits and rise so that legalised injustice may be replaced by illegal justice. When the Governor's wife seeks to reclaim her child, he submits the two women to the test of the Chalk Circle. The child is put in the centre of it. Which woman can pull him out of it? Grusha gives up from fear of hurting him, and Asdak awards the child to her because her love is the greater. The moral, according to the epilogue, is that fields belong to those who look after them best, which apparently refers to Grusha and peasants who do not wear masks.

Superb Staging

But this celebration of a moral act withstands the hobnailed marxist interpretation which Brecht imposes on it. The staging is superb. One remembers the wedding ceremony in the peasants' hovel which is straight out of Brueghel. And Asdak comes to life in a rich, rumbustious way through his sheer vitality and through that empathy which Brecht pretends to disdain. There we have the root of the matter. He gives us a wonderful new dimension which could be used by playwrights and producers and tries to cram it into a narrow political angle. He disdains the reality which springs from the roots of character and imposes his schematic marxian preconceptions. The result is that what might be a rich, dramatic orchestra becomes in his hands a one-string fiddle. If the theatre of illusion can make you believe what is false, the trouble about Brecht's classical approach, which disdains empathy and illusion, is that it cannot make you believe what is true. Brecht does, after all, say that we may use a little empathy—rather like a chef advocating a pinch of salt. For there is no incompatibility between the epic survey and the presentation of individual character. *War and Peace* proves it.[7] That is to say, it is possible to blend the classical approach from the outside, which formulates the emotions in intellectual terms, with a sense of the living creature understood from within. And, indeed, one questions whether the classical model is quite as detached as Brecht claims. After seeing the Chinese actors, and particularly the play 'The Favourite Bids Farewell to the Doomed Warrior', I personally feel that the method is highly realistic inside a convention accepted by the Chinese as easily as we accept naturalism. What Brecht has failed to recognise is that it is possible to present a moral argument without desiccating the characters.

Shaw once claimed, it is true, that Bunyan was a greater poet than Shakespeare because Bunyan possessed a moral background which gave him a hard, spare, moral vocabulary, which Shakespeare, the word-spinner, lacked. But the fact remains that the vast and untidy characters which Shakespeare gave flesh and blood to had a unity in their diversity. We can see a moral meaning in their apparently formless experience. Even Shaw in his didacticism recognised that there are many approaches to the truth. But Shaw was capable of seeing both sides of a question. Compare the appalling intellectual naivety with which Brecht presents the story of Galileo as a simple conflict between scientific enlightenment and obscurantism with Shaw's preface to 'Saint Joan,' and you can see the difference between a rationalist hide-

[7] The dramatization of Tolstoy's famous novel by Piscator and others.

bound by dogma and a first-class, independent intellect. It is because Brecht's new classicism is unilinear, marxist, external in approach, that it can depict with such beautiful precision the estrangement between the unity of the individual and the diversity of the world—but also that it lacks the complex human reality which arises from a sense of the estrangement between the unity and the diversity of the individual himself.—*Third Programme*

We can no longer avoid asking ourselves what we are doing here on earth, and how, having no deep sense of our destiny, we can endure the crushing weight of the material world. This is the eternal problem, if there ever was one; for living means alienation.
—EUGENE IONESCO

Ubu is a liberation of the greed and aggression of the average man, an anarcho-realist onslaught on the French anal-erotic bourgeois whose subconscious united him to the tycoons and dictators of the future—CYRIL CONNOLLY (The London Magazine, February 1964.)

◇   They Also Serve

No new play on the London stage has had a more unexpected and exciting success in recent years than Mr. Samuel Beckett's *Waiting for Godot*. Audiences and critics have, in this country, immediately apprehended its appeal, but there has been no serious attempt to define its theme. Any discussion about what *Waiting for Godot* "means" soon loses itself in a tangle of cross-purposes. Nor do Mr. Beckett's novels, such as *Molloy* and *Watt*, throw much light on the appeal of the play. In one sense, indeed, they do not share that appeal. In his narrative prose, Mr. Beckett presents the paradoxical picture of a man of very great talent, and possibly even of genius, using all his gifts with enormous skill for the purpose of reducing his readers to a state of tired disgust and exasperated boredom. But *Waiting for Godot* is not, except to the most squeamishly fastidious of playgoers, in the least disgusting. It is anything but boring, it instead extracts from the *idea* of boredom the most genuine pathos and enchanting comedy. Again, the message of Mr. Beckett as a novelist is perhaps a mes-

◇ Reprinted by permission of *The Times Literary Supplement*, February 10, 1956.

sage of blank despair. The message of *Waiting for Godot* is perhaps something nearer a message of religious consolation. Audiences do not leave the theatre, after seeing his play, feeling that life has been deprived of meaning. They feel rather that a new light has been cast on life's meaning, at several deep levels.

What sort of light, however? That is what so far eluded critics of the play as performed. Mr. Beckett is rumoured to have instructed his English producer not, by any manner of means, to tell the actors what the theme of the play was. Yet unless Mr. Beckett whispered his central secret in the producer's ear, the warning was probably unnecessary. The elusiveness of the core has, indeed, led some critics to contend that there is no core; that the whole startling effect of the play on the stage depended on excellent production and acting and on Mr. Beckett's own mastery of the mechanics of stage-craft. The play, on this theory, would resemble the machine recently invented by an ingenious Californian, which works perfectly, with the minimum of friction, but does no "work," performs no function. Or, to put this with more dignity, the theory might be that Mr. Beckett in *Waiting for Godot* dramatizes the notion of emptiness. This, or something like this, was the reaction of the French dramatist Jean Anouilh to the first performance of *En Attendant Godot* in Paris. "Nothing happens. Nobody comes, nobody goes, it's awful! But," M. Anouilh added, "I think the evening at the Babylone is as important as the première of Pirandello, put on in Paris by Pitoeff in 1923." And from what we know of Mr. Beckett's other work, we might assume that to dramatize emptiness, to have his much ado literally about nothing, may have been his conscious intention. Yet, with a play even more than a poem, we have to consider not the author's conscious intention—not what the author, in a conversation, might say he believed about "life"—but the whole complex significance, the valid levels of meaning, of a coherent structure. What *Waiting for Godot* essentially is is a prolonged and sustained metaphor about the nature of human life. It is a metaphor also which makes a particular appeal to the mood of liberal uncertainty which is the prevailing mood of modern Western Europe; and which makes (to judge by the play's failure in Miami) much less appeal to the strenuous and pragmatic temper of the contemporary American mind. It is also a play by an Irishman, by a friend and disciple of James Joyce; a play, therefore, by a man whose imagination (in the sense in which Mr. Eliot used this phrase of Joyce himself) is orthodox. In other words, we should consider where Mr. Beckett springs from and what he is reacting against in his roots. Even at his most nihilistic he will come under Mr. Eliot's category of the Christian blasphemer.

The fundamental imagery of *Waiting for Godot* is Christian; for, at the depth of experience into which Mr. Beckett is probing, there is no other source of imagery for him to draw on. His heroes are two tramps, who have come from nowhere in particular and have nowhere in particular to go. Their life is a state of apparently fruitless expectation. They receive messages, through a little boy, from the local landowner, Godot, who is always going to come in person to-morrow, but never does come. Their attitude towards Godot is one partly of hope, partly of fear. The orthodoxy of this symbolism, from a Christian point of view, is obvious. The tramps with their rags and their misery represent the fallen state of man. The squalor of their surroundings, their lack of a "stake in the world," represents the idea that here in this world we can build no abiding city. The ambiguity of their attitude towards Godot, their mingled hope and fear, the doubtful tone of the boy's messages, represents the state of tension and uncertainty in which the average Christian must live in this world, avoiding presumption, and also avoiding despair. Yet the two tramps, Didi and Gogo, as they call each other, represent something far higher than the other two characters in the play, the masterful and ridiculous Pozzo and his terrifying slave, Lucky. Didi and Gogo stand for the contemplative life. Pozzo and Lucky stand for the life of practical action taken, mistakenly, as an end in itself. Pozzo's blindness and Lucky's dumbness in the second act rub this point in. The so-called practical man, the man of action, has to be set on his feet and put on his way by the contemplative man. He depends—as becomes clear, in the first act, from Pozzo's genuine though absurd gratitude for the chance of a little conversation—on the contemplative man for such moments of insight, of spiritual communication, as occur in his life. The mere and pure man of action, the comic caricature of the Nietzschean superman, Pozzo, is like an actor who does not properly exist without his audience; but his audience are also, in a sense, his judges. Pozzo and Lucky, in fact, have the same sort of function in *Waiting for Godot* as Vanity Fair in *The Pilgrim's Progress*. But they are, as it were, a perambulating Vanity Fair; Didi and Gogo are static pilgrims. It is worth noting, also, that Didi and Gogo are bound to each other by something that it is not absurd to call charity. They treat each other with consideration and compunction (their odd relationship, always tugging away from each other, but always drawn together again, is among other things an emblem of marriage). Pozzo and Lucky are drawn together by hate and fear. Their lot is increasing misery; but if Didi and Gogo are not obviously any better off at the end of the play than they were at the beginning, neither are they obviously any worse off. Their state remains one of expectation.

Waiting for Godot—one might sum up these remarks—is thus a modern morality play, on permanent Christian themes. But, even if the Christian basis of the structure were not obvious, Mr. Beckett is constantly underlining it for us in the incidental symbolism and the dialogue. The first piece of serious dialogue in the play, the first statement, as it were, of a theme, is about the "two thieves, crucified at the same time as our Saviour."

> VLADIMIR: And yet . . . (*pause*) . . . how is it—this is not boring you I hope—how is that of the four evangelists only one speaks of a thief being saved? The four of them were there—or thereabouts, and only one speaks of a thief being saved. (*Pause.*) Come on Gogo, return the ball, can't you, once in a way?
> ESTRAGON: (*with exaggerated enthusiasm*). I find this really most extraordinarily interesting.

The discussion goes on to canvas the melancholy possibility that perhaps both thieves were damned. And the effect of the dialogue on the stage is, momentarily, to make us identify the glib Didi and the resentful and inarticulate Gogo with the two thieves, and to see, in each of them, an overmastering concern with the other's salvation. There is also towards the end of the first act a discussion about whether their human affection for each other may have stood in the way of that salvation:

> ESTRAGON: Wait! (*He moves away from Vladimir.*) I wonder if we wouldn't have been better off alone, each one for himself. (*He crosses the stage and sits down on the mound.*) We weren't made for the same road.
> VLADIMIR: (*without anger*). It's not certain.
> ESTRAGON: No, nothing is certain.

The tree on the stage, though it is a willow, obviously stands both for the Tree of the Knowledge of Good and Evil (and, when it puts on green leaves, for the Tree of Life) and for the Cross. When Didi and Gogo are frightened in the second act, the best thing they can think of doing is to shelter under its base. But it gives no concealment, and it is perhaps partly from God's wrath that they are hiding; for it is also the Tree of Judas, on which they are recurrently tempted to hang themselves.

Here, in fact, we have the subtle novelty, the differentiating quality, of *Waiting for Godot,* when we compare it with *Everyman* or with *The Pilgrim's Progress.* Didi and Gogo do not complete their pilgrimage nor are we meant to be clear that they will complete it successfully. The angel who appears to them at the end of the first act is an ambiguous angel: the angel who keeps the goats, not the angel who keeps the sheep. And Godot—one remembers that God chastises those whom he loves, while hardening the hearts of impenitent sinners by allowing them a term of apparent-impunity—does not beat him but beats his brother who keeps the sheep:

> VLADIMIR: Whom does he beat?
> BOY: He beats my brother, sir.
> VLADIMIR: What does he do?

BOY: He minds the sheep, sir.
VLADIMIR: And why doesn't he beat you?
BOY: I don't know, sir.
VLADIMIR: He must be fond of you.
BOY: I don't know, sir.

Are Didi and Gogo in the end to be among the goats? The boy who appears as a messenger at the end of the second act looks like the same boy, but is not, or at least does not recognize them. He may be, this time, the angel who keeps the sheep. That Godot himself stands for an anthropomorphic image of God is obvious. That is why Vladimir—if he had a blonde or a black beard he might be more reassuringly man or devil—is so alarmed in the second act when he hears that Godot, Ancient of Days, has a white beard.

VLADIMIR (*softly*): Has he a beard, Mr. Godot?
BOY: Yes, sir.
VLADIMIR: Fair or . . . (*he hesitates*) . . . or black?
BOY: I think it's white, sir.
                    Silence.
VLADIMIR: Christ have mercy on us!

The peculiar bitter ambiguity of the use of the Christian material is most obvious, perhaps, in the dialogue about Gogo's boots towards the end of the first act:

VLADIMIR: But you can't go barefoot!
ESTRAGON: Christ did.
VLADIMIR: Christ! What's Christ got to do with it? You're not going to compare yourself with Christ!
ESTRAGON: All my life I've compared myself to him.
VLADIMIR: But where he was it was warm, it was dry!
ESTRAGON: Yes. And they crucified quick.

One main function of Pozzo and Lucky in the play is to present, and to be the occasion of the dismissal of, what might be called "alternative philosophies." Pozzo, in the first act, is a man of power, who eloquently—too consciously eloquently, as he knows—expounds Nietzschean pessimism:

> But—(*hand raised in admonition*)—but—behind this veil of gentleness and peace (*he raises his eyes to the sky, the others imitate him, except Lucky*) night is charging (*vibrantly*) and will burst upon us (*he snaps his fingers*) pop! like that! (*his inspiration leaves him*) just when we least expect it. (*Silence. Gloomy.*) That's how it is on this bitch of an earth.

Like an actor, he asks for applause:

> ESTRAGON: Oh, tray bong, tray tray tray bong.
> POZZO: (*fervently*) Bless you, gentlemen, bless you! (*Pause.*) I have such need of encouragement! (*Pause.*) I weakened a little towards the end, you didn't notice?
> VLADIMIR: Oh, perhaps just a teeny weeny little bit.

In the second act, in his far more genuinely desperate state, his pessimistic eloquence is less obviously "theatrical":

> (*Calmer*). They give birth astride of a grave, the light gleams an instant, then it's night once more. (*He jerks the rope.*) On!

There is an echo in the rhythm and idiom of the first sentence, there, of Synge. And since it is the only overtly "poetical" sentence which Mr. Beckett allows himself in this play, and since he is the most calculatingly skilful of writers, one may take it that the echo is meant as a criticism of Pozzo—a criticism of romantic stylized pessimism. If the Nietzschean attitude is dismissed in Pozzo, it is harder to suggest just what is dismissed in Lucky. He is the proletarian, who used to be the peasant. He used to dance "the farandole, the fling, the brawl, the jig, the fandango, and even the hornpipe." Now all he can dance are a few awkward steps of a dance called "the Net." But in Lucky's long speech— the most terrifyingly effective single sustained episode in the play —he stands for a contemporary reality, composite, perhaps, but when presented to us immediately recognizable. He stands for half-baked knowledge, undigested knowledge, the plain man's naive belief in a Goddess called Science, his muddled appeals to unreal authorities:

> . . . but not so fast for reasons unknown that as result of the public works of Puncher and Wattman it is established beyond all doubt that in view of the labours of Popov and Belcher left unfinished for reasons unknown of Testew and Cunard left unfinished it is established what many deny that man in Possy of Testew and Cunard that man in Essy that man in short that man in brief in spite of the progress of alimentation and defecation wastes and pines wastes and pines and concurrently simultaneously what is more for reasons unknown in spite of the strides of physical culture the practice of sports such as tennis football running cycling swimming flying floating. . . .

And so on to the length of almost two complete pages! Lucky's speech is the great bravura piece of writing in the play. Mr. Beckett has never been more brilliantly unreadable; not only Didi, Gogo, and Pozzo but the audience want to scream. What is dismissed in Lucky's speech is perhaps Liberalism, Progress, Popular Education, what Thomas Love Peacock used to call, sardonically, "the March of Mind." The Nietzschean and the Liberal hypotheses being put out of court, the Christian hypothesis is left holding the stage. It is at least a more comprehensive and profound hypothesis, whatever Mr. Beckett may personally think of it; and the total effect of his play, therefore—since most of us, in the ordinary affairs of the world, have more of Pozzo or Lucky in us, than of Didi or Gogo—is not to lower but unexpectedly to raise our idea of our human dignity. Questioning and expectation do give life dignity, even though expectations are never satisfied, and even though the most fundamentally important questions can expect, perhaps, at the most an implicit answer. [*Thus, the London Times tried to make sense of the masterpiece of Absurdism!* J.G.]

Theatre of the Absurd and Dramatic Form

A proper *historical* perspective on Absurdist theatre cannot be formed without some familiarity with the plays written more or less under the influence of the preceding dadaist and surrealist movement. The boundaries between these and the plays designated as Absurdist cannot, in fact, be strictly defined. Both groups of work are, in the main, products of postwar periods of disenchantment and constitute a reaction against the relatively stable orientation of "middle-class" realism. Both pay little heed to social and psychological matters except in the spirit of parody or mockery. Both use antibourgeois bohemian shock-tactics that include a deliberate resort to coarse, even scatological, speech, childish or freakish simplifications and exaggerations, clowning and acrobatic circus feats, mock-heroic passages, brusque transitions from apparent realism to the wildest kinds of farce, cultivated naïveté, and calculated incredibility.

Some of the most characteristic early avant-garde pieces, moreover, have their structure determined by a process of "free association" and "automatic writing." Some are plainly unstageable; four of these available in translation (see *Modern French Theatre*, edited and translated by Michael Benedikt and George E. Wellwarth, 1964) are Armand Salacrou's *A Circus Story* (1922), which nevertheless could become an engaging film, René Daumal's *en gggarde!* (1924), Gilbert-Lecomte's *The Odyssey of Ulysses the Palmiped* (1924), and Antonin Artaud's *Jet of Blood* (1927). Some of these (among which Jarry's *Ubu Roi*, 1896, and Apollinaire's *The Breasts of Tiresias*, 1917, are the earliest examples), on the contrary, bloom vividly on the stage; and extraordinarily lively are such later products as Cocteau's *Les mariés de la Tour Eiffel* (1921) and Cummings' *Him* (1927); and extraordinarily beautiful *in the theatre* is Gertrude Stein's *Four Saints in Three Acts* with a score by Virgil Thompson. Some pieces have exceptional humanity, and blend irony with pathos and poetry; among those available in English are Jean Anouilh and Jean Aurenche's *Humulus the Mute* (1929), Robert Desnos' *La Place de l'étoile* (1944), and Robert Pinget's *Architruc* (1961). Closely related to this genre are a number of Saroyan plays, two of which *My Heart's in the Highlands* (1939) and *The Beautiful People* (1941), were notably appealing. A singular feature of some of these pieces is the animation of physical objects; thus, Apollinaire has a newspaper kiosk in *The Breasts of Tiresias* that talks, dances, and sings, and Cocteau employs in *Les mariés . . .* two Narrators costumed as phonographs with old-fashioned "His-Master's-Voice" type of amplifier horns substituting for the mouth.

"The Theatre of the Absurd" looms large as a movement in contemporary theatre not merely because it has been in fashion recently but because it reflects a shared state of mind. Undoubtedly talented writers (Ionesco, Beckett, Genet, Pinter, and Albee) have contributed variously intriguing or powerful plays under this general designation.

The so-called Absurdists are scions of a long lineage. Their forerunners expressed various shades or degrees of antipathy to the organized Western world, to the chief representatives of its superficial contentment and optimism—the middle classes or bourgeoisie, and its popular literature and art. The history of dramatic nihilism can be traced by the conscientious historian through the work of mavericks like Alfred Jarry whose scabrous masterpiece *Ubu Roi* delighted *fin de siècle* bohemians, of authors of raw and amoral comedies known as *comédies rosses* and naturalistic studies of the sexual instinct such as Wedekind's *The Earth Spirit*, of expressionist explosions of sexuality and hostility even before the start of World War I (1914), and of postwar dadaist and surrealist experiments such as E. E. Cummings' *Him*, and Brecht's *Baal*.

It might also be noted that the absurdist outlook was not greatly removed from Zolaist, deterministic naturalism which, in viewing the individual's behavior as the result of his instincts and environment denied man's freedom of choices. And only the dogma of progress in the dynamics of dialectical materialism could counteract the tendency in Marxist thought to subordinate the individual to sociological determinism. If this tendency were pushed so far as the Marxist critic, Christopher Caudwell, pushed it on one occasion, it could almost be possible to arrange a marriage of the minds between naturalists, absurdists and Marxists; the naturalistic-absurdist formulation, in Caudwell's *George Bernard Shaw: A Study of the Bourgeois Superman,* reads as follows: "Human beings are mountains of unconscious being, walking the old grooves of instinct and simple life, with a kind of occasional phosphorescence of consciousness at the summit."

To the critic of dramatic art, moreover, "Theatre of the Absurd" experimentation suggests noteworthy efforts to contend with the problems and possibilities of dramatic form. It is especially this last-mentioned matter with which we must concern ourselves. But before we do so, it is necessary to ascertain what "The Theatre of the Absurd" actually has meant to its proponents whose first theoretical exponent was Antonin Artaud, author of the apocalyptic book, *The Theatre and Its Double,* which became the bible of the absurdist movement, and whose most able American exponent has been the gifted playwright Edward Albee. The latter's critical justification of "absurdism," exemplified by his one-act plays, *The Zoo Story, The Sandbox,* and *The American Dream,* follows.

In The Bald Soprano . . . some people have seen a satire on bourgeois society, a criticism of life in England, and heaven knows what. In actual fact, if it is criticism of anything, it must be of all societies, of language, of clichés—a parody of human behavior, and therefore a parody of the theatre too . . . if man is not tragic, he is ridiculous and painful, "comic" in fact, and by revealing his absurdity one can achieve a sort of tragedy.
—EUGENE IONESCO

Which of us is not forever a stranger and alone?
—THOMAS WOLFE

Is man no more than this?
—KING LEAR

The absurd is felt when man's desire that the world should be explicable is seen to be opposed by the fact that the world cannot be made explicable in human terms.
—JAMES H. CLANCY

Ubu: We won't have demolished anything at all if we don't demolish even the ruins.—ALFRED JARRY (*King Ubu,* first produced in 1896.)

Measured by the scale of eternity, all activity is futile. . . . Every product of disgust capable of becoming a negation of the family is Dada; . . . absolute and unquestioned faith in every god that is the immediate product of spontaneity [*is* Dada].*—TRISTAN TZARA (1918)

◇

Which Theatre Is the Absurd One?
by Edward Albee

A theatre person of my acquaintance—a man whose judgment must be respected, though more for the infallibility of his intuition than for his reasoning—remarked just the other week, "The

Theatre of the Absurd has had it; it's on its way out; it's through."

Now this, on the surface of it, seems to be a pretty funny attitude to be taking toward a theatre movement which has, only in the past couple of years, been impressing itself on the American public consciousness. Or is it? Must we judge that a theatre of such plays as Samuel Beckett's "Krapp's Last Tape." Jean Genet's "The Balcony" (both long, long runners off-Broadway) and Eugene Ionesco's "Rhinoceros"—which, albeit in a hoked-up production, had a substantial season *on* Broadway—has been judged by the theatre public and found wanting?

And shall we have to assume that The Theatre of the Absurd Repertory Company, currently playing at New York's off-Broadway Cherry Lane Theatre—presenting works by Beckett, Ionesco, Genet, Arrabal, Jack Richardson, Kenneth Koch and myself—being the first such collective representation of the movement in the United States, is also a kind of farewell to the movement? For that matter, just what *is* The Theatre of the Absurd?

Well, let me come at it obliquely. When I was told, about a year ago, that I was considered a member in good standing of The Theatre of the Absurd I was deeply offended. I was deeply offended because I had never heard the term before and I immediately assumed that it applied to the theatre uptown—Broadway.

What (I was reasoning to myself) could be more absurd than a theatre in which the esthetic criterion is something like this: A "good" play is one which makes money; a "bad" play (in the sense of "Naughty! Naughty!" I guess) is one which does not; a theatre in which performers have plays rewritten to correspond to the public relations image of themselves; a theatre in which playwrights are encouraged (what a funny word!) to think of themselves as little cogs in a great big wheel; a theatre in which imitation has given way to imitation of imitation; a theatre in which London "hits" are, willy-nilly, in a kind of reverse of chauvinism, greeted in a manner not unlike a colony's obeisance to the Crown; a theatre in which real estate owners and theatre party managements predetermine the success of unknown quantities; a theatre in which everybody scratches and bites for billing as though it meant access to the last bomb shelter on earth; a theatre in which, in a given season, there was not a single performance of a play by Beckett, Brecht, Chekhov, Genet, Ibsen, O'Casey, Pirandello, Shaw, Strindberg—or Shakespeare? What, indeed, I thought, could be more absurd than that? (My conclusions . . . obviously.)

For it emerged that The Theatre of the Absurd, aside from being the title of an excellent book by Martin Esslin on what is loosely called the avant-garde theatre, was a somewhat less than fortunate catch-all phrase to describe the philosophical attitudes and theatre methods of a number of Europe's finest and most adventurous playwrights and their followers.

I was less offended, but still a little dubious. Simply: I don't like labels; they can be facile and can lead to non-think on the part of the public. And unless it is understood that the playwrights of The Theatre of the Absurd represent a group only in the sense that they seem to be doing something of the same thing in vaguely similar ways at approximately the same time—unless this is understood, then the labeling itself will be more absurd than the label.

Playwrights, by nature, are grouchy, withdrawn, envious, greedy, suspicious and, in general, quite nice people—and the majority of them wouldn't be caught dead in a colloquy remotely resembling the following:

IONESCO (*At a Left Bank café table, spying Beckett and Genet strolling past in animated conversation*): Hey! Sam! Jean!

GENET: Hey, it's Eugene! Sam, it's Eugene!

BECKETT: Well, I'll be damned. Hi there, Eugene boy.

IONESCO: Sit down, kids.

GENET: Sure thing.

IONESCO (*Rubbing his hands together*): Well, what's new in The Theatre of the Absurd?

BECKETT: Oh, less than a lot of people think. (*They all laugh.*)

Etc. No. Not very likely. Get a playwright alone sometime, get a few drinks in him, and maybe he'll be persuaded to sound off about his "intention" and the like—and hate himself for it the next day. But put a group of playwrights together in a room, and the conversation—if there is any—will, more likely than not, concern itself with sex, restaurants and the movies.

Very briefly, then—and reluctantly, because I am a playwright and would much rather talk about sex, restaurants and the movies—and stumblingly, because I do not pretend to understand it entirely, I will try to define The Theatre of the Absurd. As I get it, The Theatre of the Absurd is an absorption-in-art of certain existentialist and post-existentialist philosophical concepts having to do, in the main, with man's attempts to make sense for himself out of his senseless position in a world which makes no sense—which makes no sense because the moral, religious, political and social structures man has erected to "illusion" himself have collapsed.

Albert Camus put it this way: "A world that can be explained by reasoning, however faulty, is a familiar world. But in a universe that is suddenly deprived of illusions and of light, man feels a stranger. His is an irremediable exile, because he is deprived of memories of a lost homeland as much as he lacks the hope of a promised land to come. This divorce between man and his life, the actor and his setting, truly constitutes the feeling of Absurdity."

And Eugene Ionesco says this: "Absurd is that which is devoid of purpose * * * Cut off from his religious metaphysical, and transcendental roots, man is lost; all his actions become senseless, absurd, useless."

And to sum up the movement, Martin Esslin writes, in his book "The Theatre of the Absurd": "Ultimately, a phenomenon like The Theatre of the Absurd does not reflect despair or a return to dark irrational forces but expresses modern man's en-

deavor to come to terms with the world in which he lives. It attempts to make him face up to the human condition as it really
is, to free him from illusions that are bound to cause constant
maladjustment and disappointment * * * For the dignity of
man lies in his ability to face reality in all its senselessness; to accept it freely, without fear, without illusions—and to laugh at it."

Amen.

(And while we're on the subject of Amen, one wearies of the
complaint that The Theatre of the Absurd playwrights alone are
having at God these days. The notion that God is dead, indifferent, or insane—a notion blasphemous, premature, or academic
depending on your persuasion—while surely a tenet of some of
the playwrights under discussion, is, it seems to me, of a piece
with Mr. Tennessee Williams' description of the Deity, in "The
Night of the Iguana," as *a senile delinquent.*")

So much for the attempt to define terms. Now, what of this
theatre? What of this theatre in which, for example, a legless old
couple live out their lives in twin ashcans, surfacing occasionally
for food or conversation (Samuel Beckett's *"Endgame"*); in
which a man is seduced, and rather easily, by a girl with three
well-formed and functioning noses (Eugene Ionesco's *"Jack, or
The Submission"*); in which, on the same stage, one group of Negro actors is playing at pretending to be white, and another
group of Negro actors is playing at pretending to be Negro
(Jean Genet's "The Blacks")?

What of this theatre? Is it, as it has been accused of being,
obscure, sordid, destructive, anti-theatre, perverse and absurd (in
the sense of foolish)? Or is it merely, as I have so often heard it
put, that, "This sort of stuff is too depressing, too . . . too mixed-
up; I go to the theatre to relax and have a good time."

I would submit that it is this latter attitude—that the theatre
is a place to relax and have a good time—in conflict with the
purpose of The Theatre of the Absurd—which is to make a man
face up to the human condition as it really is—that has produced

all the brouhaha and the dissent. I would submit that The Theatre of the Absurd, in the sense that it is truly the contemporary theatre, facing as it does man's condition as it is, is the Realistic theatre of our time; and that the supposed Realistic theatre—the term used here to mean most of what is done on Broadway—in the sense that it panders to the public need for self-congratulation and reassurance and presents a false picture of ourselves to ourselves is, with an occasional very lovely exception, really and truly The Theatre of the Absurd.

And I would submit further that the health of a nation, a society, can be determined by the art it demands. We have insisted of television and our movies that they not have anything to do with anything, that they be our never-never land; and if we demand this same function of our live theatre, what will be left of the visual-auditory arts—save the dance (in which nobody talks) and music (to which nobody listens)?

It has been my fortune, the past two or three years, to travel around a good deal, in pursuit of my career—Berlin, London, Buenos Aires, for example; and I have discovered a couple of interesting things. I have discovered that audiences in these and other major cities demand of their commercial theatre—and get— a season of plays in which the froth and junk are the exception and not the rule. To take a case: in Berlin, in 1959, Adamov, Genet, Beckett and Brecht (naturally) were playing the big houses; this past fall, Beckett again, Genet again, Pinter twice, etc. To take another case: in Buenos Aires there are over a hundred experimental theatres.

These plays cannot be put on in Berlin over the head of a protesting or an indifferent audience; these experimental theatres cannot exist in Buenos Aires without subscription. In the end— and it must always come down to this, no matter what other failings a theatre may have—in the end a public will get what it deserves, and no better.

I have also discovered, in my wanderings, that young people throng to what is new and fresh in the theatre. Happily, this holds true in the United States as well. At the various colleges I have gone to to speak I have found an eager, friendly and knowl-edgeable audience, an audience which is as dismayed by the Broadway scene as any proselytizer for the avant-garde. I have found among young people an audience which is not so precondi-tioned by pap as to have cut off half of its responses. (It is inter-esting to note, by the way, that if an off-Broadway play has a sub-stantial run, its audiences will begin young and grow older; as the run goes on, cloth coats give way to furs, walkers and subway rid-ers to taxi-takers. Exactly the opposite is true on Broadway.)

The young, of course, are always questioning values, knock-ing the status quo about, considering shibboleths to see if they are pronounceable. In time, it is to be regretted, most of them—the kids—will settle down to their own version of the easy, the standard; but in the meanwhile . . . in the meanwhile they are a wonderful, alert, alive, accepting audience.

And I would go so far as to say that it is the responsibility of everyone who pretends any interest at all in the theatre to get up off their six-ninety seats and find out what the theatre is *really* about. For it is a lazy public which produces a slothful and irre-sponsible theatre.

Now, I would suspect that my theatre-friend with the infalli-ble intuition is probably right when he suggests that The Theatre of the Absurd (or the avant-garde theatre, or whatever you want to call it) as it now stands is on its way out. Or at least is undergoing change. All living organisms undergo constant change. And while it is certain that the nature of this theatre will remain constant, its forms, its methods—its devices, if you will—most nec-essarily will undergo mutation.

This theatre has no intention of running downhill; and the younger playwrights will make use of the immediate past and mould it to their own needs. (Harold Pinter, for example, could not have written "The Caretaker" had Samuel Beckett not existed, but Pinter is, nonetheless, moving in his own direction.) And it is my guess that the theatre in the United States will always hew more closely to the post-Ibsen/Chekhov tradition than does the theatre in France, let us say. It is our nature as a country, a society. But we will experiment, and we will expect your attention.

For just as it is true that our response to color and form was forever altered once the impressionist painters put their minds to canvas, it is just as true that the playwrights of The Theatre of the Absurd have forever altered our response to the theatre.

And one more point: The avant-garde theatre is fun; it is free-swinging, bold, iconoclastic and often wildly, wildly funny. If you will approach it with childlike innocence—putting your standard responses aside, for they do not apply—if you will approach it—on its own terms, I think you will be in for a liberating surprise. I think you may no longer be content with plays that you can't remember halfway down the block. You will not only be doing yourself some good, but you will be having a great time, to boot. And even though it occurs to me that such a fine combination must be sinful, I still recommend it.

Communication by Form

It may be observed that absurdist theatre has often been represented without portentousness ever since *Ubu Roi,* which was itself more of a lark than anything else. The dadaist-oriented avant-garde after World War I in France was known not only for its antics in general but its penchant for ultra sophisticated revues like *Parade,* acrobatics, and the circus. (Faint reflections appeared in the American theatre, notably in *The Grand Street Follies* of the Neighborhood Playhouse and the Rodgers and Hart *Garrick Gaieties* produced in New York during the early 'twenties by the Theatre Guild.) And after World War II, the English theatre began to exhibit a growing fondness for satirical café-style revues, such as *The Establishment* and *Oh, What a Lovely War,* while America developed similar irreverences such as *The Premise* and *The Second City*. In England, the vogue culminated in full-length plays that were first and last extravaganzas presumably reducing the workaday world or the world of logic and serious purpose to sheer nonsense, exhibiting the playful inconsequentiality of N. F. Simpson's *One Way Pendulum* (1959), originally subtitled "An Evening of High Drung and Slarrit" to define its nonsensicality, or disguising negativistic content with the dégagé lightheartedness of Ann Jellicoe's zany, if also slightly ominous romp, *The Knack*. Carried too far in this direction lighteartedness can, and has, become lightmindedness, which is hardly offensive or objectionable but hardly significant, either. It ceases to be an issue of dramatic criticism altogether, and may be left to the dilettante spirit of any age.

But an issue does arise from a trend toward the reduction of logical communication to the nonlanguage of cries and screams that is especially marked in this movement which has endeavored to be meaningful by being meaningless. It succeeded a few times for the present writer, most notably with Lucky's breathless harangue in Beckett's *Waiting for Godot*, a nocturnal animal nuptial scene in Ionesco's *Jack*, and the oration of gibberish at the conclusion of the same author's *The Chairs*. The dangers of failure are vastly greater, however, than the possibilities of success when a working principle is made, without very special warrant and limited use, of Artaud's rhapsody on nonverbal elements—on cries, groans, apparitions, incantations, theatricalities of all kinds, dance movements, musical effects, masks, and the rest. Artaud's very defense of his position points to his radical departure from Western humanism when he declared that he was well aware that the language of gestures and postures, dance and music was less capable of analyzing a character and revealing a man's thoughts or elucidating states of consciousness clearly and precisely than verbal language, but asked rhetorically "whoever said the theatre was created to analyze a character, resolve the conflicts of love and duty [see *The Cid,* and *Bérénice!*], to wrestle with all the problems of a topical [social] and psychological nature that monopolize our contemporary stage." (*Encore,* Vol. 8, No. 4, July-August 1961, p. 19.) And so fine a director as Peter Brook was moved to support Artaud with equally revealing sentences when he wrote: "I believe in the word in classical drama, because the word was their tool. I don't believe in the word much today because it has outlived its purpose. Words don't communicate, they don't express much, and most of the time they fail abysmally to define." He went on to say that there have been great theatres "with a concrete language of their own that is not the language of the streets nor the language of books," (*Ibid.*), and we can only wonder what theatres of the Occident he could cite unless he meant the *commedia dell' arte* with its extremely limited content of intrigues and stereotypes.

Ritual is another matter, of course, and calls for an interpenetration of physical movement and verbal context. This has been extraordinarily effective in Jean Genet's stunning rite of hate *The Blacks* (*Les Négres*), a *Götterdämmerung,* so to speak, of white colonialism in Africa. In such a play, Western dramatic structure is distinctly altered. It is multileveled, fluctuating, and mock-serious in *The Blacks,* so that if this sort of drama were to become a norm of "absurdism," we would be justified in ascribing to its influence a return to primitive pantomime or the creation of a new form. This has not been the case thus far, just as we could not posit the victorious arrival of new ritualistic form on the strength of Yeats' ultraformalistic short plays of the second decade of the century or a later ritualistic type of drama after the success of *Murder in the Cathedral* and other Canterbury Festival poetic plays.

Absurdist works have actually been distributed among long-established types of drama to such a degree that we do well to refrain from identifying "Theatre of the Absurd" drama with any single dramatic form. Thus Beckett's *Waiting for Godot, Endgame* and *Happy Days* may be described as symbolist dramas with a naturalistic base, while Beckett's moving one-acter *Krapp's Last Tape* could pass for any impressionist memory play; Ionesco's *The Bald Soprano* could be described as zany vaudeville, *The Chairs* as a symbolic extravaganza, *The Lesson* as a mordant grand-guignol, and *Rhinoceros* as a symbolic fantasy; Genet's *The Blacks* as a symbolist ritual drama, but *The Balcony* as phantasmagoric satire, and *The Maids* and *Deathwatch* as naturalistic melodrama. The most that could be said in attempting to find a common denominator for most absurdist plays is that they are histrionically structured, and this is significantly attributable to only about half of the plays in the case of those mentioned above. Specifically, to *Krapp's Last Tape*, in that Krapp reconstructs his memories from recordings made by him at various times; to *The Chairs*, in which an elderly couple sets up an imaginary audience to receive an incomprehensible valedictory message; and to *The Blacks*, *The Balcony* and *The Maids*, in which the plot consists of the action of variable make-believe identities.

It is necessary to reflect, moreover, that a histrionic orientation has appeared in the modern theatre ever since the beginning of a reaction to naturalism. It is variously present in Edmond Rostand's neoromantic plays, *Cyrano de Bergerac*, *Les Romanesques* (a play within a play now known to the American public in its delightful musical comedy transformation as *The Fantastiks*), beast-fable comedy *Chantecler*, and *The Last Night of Don Juan*. It appears in *The Player Queen* and other poetic plays by Yeats; in Lorca's *The Love of Don Perlimpín and Belisa in the Garden;* in the Piscator adaptation of Dreiser's *American Tragedy* under the title of *The Case of Clyde Griffiths,* and Brecht's parable of *The Good Woman of Setzuan,* in which the good Shen Te impersonates a harsh cousin, Shui Ta, in order to defend herself against exploitation by rich and poor alike; and, of course, in plays by Pirandello, such as *Six Characters in Search of an Author* and *Tonight We Improvise*.

Sometimes the technique is one of "the play within a play," already familiar to the Elizabethans in *The Spanish Tragedy* and

Hamlet, and metaphysically extended in Calderón's *Life is a Dream* (*La Vida es Sueño*), and Grillparzer's *The Dream is a Life* (*Der Traum ein Leben,* 1834), long before Pirandello's *Henry IV.* Sometimes the histrionic drama is based on an impersonation, such as that of the queen in Betti's *The Queen and the Rebels,* a device already used abundantly in the Renaissance theatre, as in the case of Shakespeare's girls in the disguise of pages. And sometimes the staging of a play is the essence of the work as a whole, as in the case of Jean Anouilh's Joan of Arc drama *The Lark* (*L'Alouette*), although this type of dramatic strategy cannot be regarded as a "Theatre-of-the-Absurd" discovery when we can cite examples from the older dramatic literature such as *The Knight of the Burning Pestle, The Rehearsal,* and *The Critic.* Still, the histrionic mode may be especially linked with absurdist playwrights because it reflects the absurdists' inclination to treat truth as relative and to reduce life to illusion.

Another structural development associated with absurdist avant-gardism is a circularity of movement conveying a cyclical view of drama. It expresses the absurdity of man's mores, aspirations, and metaphysical situation, and discounts the possibility of any real amelioration of his lot. It is tantamount to a radical total renunciation of the twin doctrines of the "idea of progress" and the "perfectibility of man" which attended the birth of the modern age. This technical development, as radical a break with the Aristotelian concept of drama as Brecht's rejection of empathy, is formulated by Professor Marvin Rosenberg in the following essay, and it will be noted that his formulations concern the modern drama as a whole.

My own creed as a playwright is fairly close to that expressed by the painter in Shaw's play The Doctor's Dilemma: "I believe in Michelangelo, Velasquez, and Rembrandt; in the might of design, the mystery of color, the redemption of all things by beauty everlasting . . ."
—TENNESSEE WILLIAMS

I defy the remaining romantics to put a heroic drama on the stage. Playgoers shrug their shoulders at medieval scrap-iron [armor], secret doors, poisoned wines, and the rest. Melodrama, the middle-class offspring of the Romantic Movement, is even more outmoded and lifeless than its predecessor. . . . The great [romantic] efforts of the 1830's

stand as preliminary works . . . which helped to over-throw the old classical [neoclassical] heritage. . . .
—ÉMILE ZOLA

I can't deny that I use a lot of those things called symbols but being a self-defensive creature, I say that symbols are nothing but the natural speech of drama.—TENNESSEE WILLIAMS

Only poets can give coherence to drama.
—PIRANDELLO

The poet must bring objects and feelings from behind their veils and their mist; he must show them suddenly, so nakedly and so swiftly, that it hurts me to recognize them.
—JEAN COCTEAU

◊

A Metaphor for Dramatic Form
by Marvin Rosenberg

I suggest that the form of conventional drama is linear—that, while it takes place in a continuing present, it moves as it were from left to right, from a beginning through a chain of chronologi-

◊ In *The Journal of Aesthetics and Art Criticism* Vol. XVII, No. 2, December 1958, pp. 174-180. Reprinted by permission of the author.

cal sequences toward an end. This traditional form in modern times has been distorted and shattered by adventuring playwrights trying to hold time at bay, to circumscribe the present, to isolate non-narrative felt life. I propose to develop a metaphor to describe their adventures in form.

In the traditional mode, the line of forward movement organizes the drama. Every important speech or action is an arrow pointing to a next speech or action, all merging into the sequential Aristotelian beginning-middle-end pattern. It is an economical mode, and ideally every element has some significance for the forward progress; nothing is aimless, as it so often is in life. A thousand times in life a man will say, "What a miserable day," and nothing follows, nor do we expect anything; let one in the theatre say, "So foul and fair a day I have not seen," and we sense this to be part of the man's special history and future; it must point forward to a development in mood, character, action. Life is a ground on which random figures momentarily emerge to a threshold of perception, and then fade, coalesce with new figures, or dissolve into the ground as our gestalts change. In conventional drama the gestalt is fixed, the ground is a controlled field for the movement of a clearly defined figure across it.

In the simplest dramatic type, the melodrama, the forward line is the essence of the play. A dead body has been discovered; some two hours later successively linked events will have led to the discovery of the killer. For purposes of tension the flow of the line will be interrupted by titillating reversals, but the momentary blocks will only increase the force by which the audience is rushed toward the predestined stop. All dispensable elements— character, language—that slow the line must be stripped away.

The same linear form can be beautifully complex—as in *Oedipus*. Basically the story is the same: the finding of a murderer. The end is known in the beginning; and speeches and action point to the end with a force and directness that melodrama can only envy. Creon, Teiresias, the messenger come pat; the old shepherd is in the wings. The linear pace toward destiny is almost intolerable. But unlike melodrama, and its thin hypnotic line, *Oedipus* moves forward in breadth. What happens is only important because of what happens in Oedipus, what happens in the others, the meaning of what happens, the language and spectacle. These broad scarves braid about the central line of the play, and the whole unrolls in a wide, firm texture that will bear the weight of our full scrutiny, sensual, emotional, intellectual.

Analogically, the simple action melodrama is like a popular melody: it moves thinly from a beginning to an end, setting up little arches of expectation, completing them, bringing them toward a final terminus—a satisfying, unmistakable end we have been led to anticipate. Chords play around the line of melody, but are submerged in it—unless improvising musicians, tired of the thin forward movement, thicken it with complementary themes that often only disguise or destroy the thread of song, which is too light to bear them. Similarly, in pretentious melodrama, heavily laden with pompous language and character, the action line is often smothered, and the play grinds on pointlessly. A musical parallel to the complex progression of *Oedipus* would be a classical symphony—a Beethoven. Musicians themselves call this form "dramatic"; its straightforward line carries the hearer along, arousing expectations, satisfying them, while leading forward to new expectations, all building to a peak of excitement released in the finale. But the musical line is dense with counterpoint; supporting themes, like supporting characters in a play, oppose the main theme or submit to it, and the whole moves on a broad front toward the climactic suspense. The end of a classical symphony is an absolute terminus; few things end so completely: thump crash crash THUMP CRASH *THUMP!* There is no mistake about it: this is the end of the line. Complex plays usually break off less sharply, may leave a suggestion that life goes on; but normally their end, too, is unmistakable, and sometimes close to excessive (as in the repeated fortissimos of death in *Hamlet,* or the long bravura of Cyrano), since the playwright also has a passion to wring us tight before he lets us go.

There is good reason for the linear form in drama. It promises the precious catharsis that life can rarely offer. The crises of life don't end; as one subsides, another—many another—builds up in the wings. Mortality is inexorably continuous. In drama we can experience the ultimate torment of joy and have done with it, we can participate in the wildest forbidden passions and hostilities, titanic externalizations of the fantasies that shake us privately—and at play's end we are through with them, for the moment purified and free of them, as the expiating curtain scene washes them clean.

The deep satisfactions inherent in this sequential tension-release pattern have made it the dominant dramatic form, so much so that a sensitive modern aesthetician, Susanne Langer, has seen in the "movement toward destiny"—what to me is a manifestation of the "linear pattern"—the *only* form. "It is only a present filled with its own future that is really dramatic. A sheer immediacy, an imperishable direct experience without the ominous forward movement of consequential forward action, would not be so . . . This tension between past and future is what gives to acts, situations, and even such constituent elements as gestures and attitudes and tones the peculiar intensity known as dramatic quality . . ."

Tragedy is an advance toward destiny, a self-consummation, Mrs. Langer says; and these phrases have themselves the lure of the cathartic terminal form, of the act committed, punished, and eternally expiated. A great trouble must be met, a great crisis against which the spirit hurls itself, and discovers its fate and final end. Herein lies a technical secret of the linear form: an advance toward tragic fate is always over a rocky road, guarded by one or more great obstacles or enemies, and the more truly fearful the course, the more the audience is enlisted emotionally in its champion's journey. Forward action develops more friction if it must beat down counter-action; and so we have the beguiling Hegelian theories that drama is conflict, that purposeful will must drive ahead against anti-will, and out of the clash will come synthesis—in other equations recognition or rebirth.

But to many modern artists, in all art forms, the easy hypnotic power of the neat linear form has seemed insufficient to convey the raggedness of existence. They are trying to break from the representation of smooth, unlifelike, closed experience, and suggest the incompleteness, the discontinuous continuity, the confused emotional tone of living. In the linear form, as mind follows movement, there is often—to use Sypher's phrase about narrative painting—"shallow-seeing," a gliding across surfaces. A strong current of modern painting, non-representational, tries to hold the mind on intensity rather than carry it along a line, to set up a system of tensions within the frame, so the mind does not follow a familiar image but instead acquaints itself with a complex, subtle experience. Other modern paintings convey an image enriched by many perspectives, instead of the single conventional perspective. Experimental music gives up the "dramatic" horizontal, contrapuntal line of a classical symphony in favor—sometimes in Schoenberg, for instance—of a series of verticals, moments of chorded experience; and the whole forms in the mind as a texture, rather than a line. This modern music does not regularly build to a finish with a clashing peroration; it sometimes hardly "ends" at all, but only stops, as if the composition is a segment of a greater patternless continuity.

Similarly modern drama, poetry, and the novel have been trying to escape the tyranny of time progression, to catch the myriad dimensions of the present.[8] This has meant, for drama, a

[8] Brecht, who also tried to shatter the spell of sequential drama, did so for a different reason. Essentially a propagandist, he would deliberately break the thread of an "epic" play to recall to audiences the social meaning of what they were seeing. He thought of such drama as discursive, conveying its impact through the accumulation of intellectual impressions, rather than through a hypnotic engagement of the emotions. But even in Brechtian drama, his didactic interruptions are usually forgotten by an audience as soon as they are finished and the action advances. (Thus Eric Bentley, in *The Playwright as Thinker*, notes the triumph of Brecht's practice over his theory.) Our submission to the linear form is similarly apparent in "flashback" dramas which usually

radical change of perspective, particularly toward character. When action is linear, characterization must be narrowed to justify selected arrow-acts leading to an end. But human motivation is never simple enough to fit into the stripped down line of melodrama; even in the great linear plays, even in *Hamlet,* say, with the extra dimension of the soliloquy, there is room only to suggest barely the complex of motives that usher in a tragic act—which is why we must search our own consciences for Hamlet's full motivation. Non-linear drama set out to recognize the ambiguity of all human behavior, rather than the chain-link effects of isolated acts.[9]

Thus Strindberg, reaching toward this form in introducing *Miss Julie:* "A character came to signify a man fixed and finished: one who invariably appeared either drunk or jocular or melancholy, and characterizations required nothing more than a physical defect such as a club-foot, a wooden leg, or a red nose . . . This simple way of regarding human beings still survives in the great Molière. Harpagon is nothing but a miser, although Harpagon might have been not only a miser, but also a first-rate financier, an excellent father, and a good citizen. I do not believe in simple stage characters; and the summary judgments of authors —this man is stupid, that one brutal, this jealous, that stingy, and so forth—should be challenged by the Naturalists who know the richness of the soul-complex and realize that vice has a reverse side very much like virtue . . . I have drawn my characters vacillating, disintegrating . . ."

Strindberg's first step, in this play, was to give dimension to his character by suggesting lifelike qualities of inconsistency—

---

vary from the norm only in explicitly stating the inevitable destiny in the beginning. So powerful is the linear spell that once an audience is "flashed back," it usually promptly suspends its memory of the known destiny, and moves forward with the action as if from a fresh beginning. It will make this adjustment once (as in *The Diary of Anne Frank*), or many times (as in *The Lark*).

[9] In this discussion, I don't want to seem to suggest that one form is better than another. Both will survive; each will use the other when it serves. What I am trying to do here is project an image of their functions.

vacillation, disintegration—that could as easily impede the linear progress as expedite it. But given the traditional form he used, the characters had to be subdued to the movement toward destiny, and Strindberg learned that no forward story line could contain the ambiguity of human behavior. So he tried to circumscribe a moment of it, tried as did other expressionists to turn from the linear to a more pliable dramatic form—a form I will call "contextual." The tensions of context, rather than direction, of vertical depth, rather than horizontal movement, became important—as they did for the experimental artist, musician, novelist. Hence a drama like *The Dream Play*—a montage of scenes that follow each other without progressing, rich in symbol and association, meaningful not in sequence or suspense, but in the reflection of a discontinuous psychic activity.[10] The way of another pioneer, Pirandello, was to concentrate on a narrow area of mortality—a dilemma in illusion and reality—and go deeply behind it, layer after layer, trying to bare it to infinity.[11] As the point of view shifts from character to character, new contexts assert them-

[10] Though even here Strindberg did not completely free himself from the beginning-end pattern. He might as well have. The framework about the divine princess who learns that life is hell only states explicitly the experience which the center of the play conveys much better, dramatically.

Eugene Ionesco, in the same tradition, has so revolted against "form" that he makes its absence in his works obtrusive. He too externalizes man's inner fears; thus the press of inanimate things is likely to overwhelm his heroes physically as well as psychically: in one play, furniture suddenly proliferates, in another coffee cups multiply, in a third a corpse grows—all eventually burying the human characters. Ionesco writes of his deliberately anti-linear style: "(My own plays originate) from a state of soul, not from an ideology, from an impulse and not a program; the cohesion that gives a structure to emotions in their pure state corresponds to an inner necessity, and not to a logic of construction imposed from outside; there is no subjection to a predetermined action, but exteriorization of a psychic dynamism, projection upon the stage of internal conflicts, of the inner universe." (*Theatre Arts*, June 1958, 10.)

[11] Genet's *The Maids* is a recent play in this multi-layered mode.

selves, and we discover in art, as in life, that gestalts depend on perspectives, which are many, various, impermanent.

The contextual form is a tremendous challenge to the playwright. Here the ready tension of linear action-counteraction drama is difficult to match, because the materials of the contextual mode are strange and obstinate—they reside in the aimless, unclimactic multiplicity of emotional life. A tenacious idiom is needed to catch and hold this fluidity on the stage, a kind of free association is needed, of the sort Joyce developed—*free* only in its mercurial spread, splendidly controlled and integrated and exciting in its linkages of words, emotions, thoughts. To absorb a theater audience in tensions of context rather than sequence, the linkages must be made visual—but not *only* visual, as they are in the liquid, implicit symbolism of the ballet; in the theater, except for brief interludes, verbal and visual imagery must function together.

Contextual drama has taken two general directions. In the first, character is treated as in the traditional form: made to seem "real," with a life direction, but providing a minimum of linear movement. From this central focus, the characters are extended in dimension instead of being developed in a direction. This form inherits from Chekov's technique of examining many planes of human surface opposed in tension, and suggesting the forces struggling beneath them. There are many moments in Chekov when life is stopped, non-sequential, timeless; when his several characters speak thoughts and feelings that have almost nothing to do with each other, or with a forward action; they speak past each other, dreaming away their own lives, sounding their separate notes. The effect is not of a contrapuntal, horizontal advance, but rather of a series of sad, exquisite harmonics—vertical, time-stopped chords. So skilful is the playwright in suggesting the tension and depth of the moment rather than of sequence that his dramas sometimes leave the impression of being all mood, all lingering present when in fact they are firmly threaded on a forward line.

A modern example of the contextual character drama is

Death of a Salesman. Its time is interior, in Eric Auerbach's phrase: it moves from a central situation back and forth in fantasy and memory to widen and deepen a present emotional moment.[12] A linear ending is tagged on to the play, but it is neither necessary nor inevitable.

The second, more difficult form is a more purely contextual drama, a theater image of a mental state. Of course, all drama is an image of our mental states; but in the traditional form, a "real" character does the hard experiencing for us, stands between us and ourselves, while in this second kind of drama we come face to face with our own inner processes. But not as explicitly as in the old, overt Moralities, or in the simple simile form as in Evreinov's brief *Theatre of the Soul,* with its personified characters Rational Entity, Emotional Entity, etc. Instead, in this modern experimental drama, the characters are "people" in the usual theatrical sense: the two bums in *Waiting for Godot,* Kilroy in *Camino Real,* Joseph K. in *The Trial.* They have conventional passions and hurts; but their identity is sunk in their passions and hurts, of which they become the transparent images (rather than intermediate symbols) and we recognize the passions and hurts as our own.

Waiting for Godot is a good recent example. It ends exactly where it began, though there are bits of movement within it, because it is not a story of the life of its characters but of a condition of living, and that is timeless. What we see is waitingness, a chronic, anonymous waitingness, relieved as it is in life by contrasts of kindness and cruelty and quiet and noise and biological function and poetic dream—but always in the context of the long now. At the other extreme from *Godot* is *Camino Real.* In *Godot,* the frame is not crowded: the strokes are broad, the colors mainly somber, and the large design is relatively easy to grasp. In *Camino Real,* the frame is alive with the ceaseless business of

[12] Laurents' *A Clearing in the Woods* is a more recent attempt to dramatize being similarly.

the mind: fantasy, passion, cliché, regression, aggression, vanity. Almost the complete spectrum is projected, and projected nearly simultaneously, rather than sequentially; at any one moment we can almost catch a glimpse of the whole shifting mosaic.

The shape of contextual drama is elusive because its matter is shapelessness. It tries to convey the content of experience before a form has been impressed on it by thought. Form in art and life is limiting, inhibitory, it is a pattern imposed on the anarchic human matrix—call it the id—by the individual and the collective conscious—call it the superego. Humanity is almost defined by its compulsion to make such patterns. Civilizations are collective designs to channel or contain impulses in the interest of tolerable group living; the individual ego survives by projecting a hypothetical order on the unorder of psychic existence. But the psyche knows no order, it is fluid, and rebels against containment. Behind the imposed patterns of conscious, time-regulated routine, the dream-life of our waking existence goes on untamed. This is what contextual drama seeks to surround and exhibit. It is a reality which the tidy linear form cannot cope with. So, like modern mathematicians who, unable to find a pattern in the interaction of multiple sky bodies, have come to hypothesize a "regular disorder," the contextual playwright has given up the linear vision of order for a form that seeks to enclose the loose mesh of experience. "Dream-like" as it is, this material has generally been regarded as "non-representational" on the stage, has been dramatized in the framework of a dream, and usually treated with the resources of fantasy: dream music, wraithlike figures, balletic movement; or with the phantasmagoric scenic imagery Strindberg used in *The Dream Play,* and Gide partly in his stage adaptation of Kafka's contextual novel *The Trial.*[13] *Camino Real* and *Godot* are remarkable for avoiding this;[14] they depend essen-

[13] *The Trial* conveys the confused condition of being by combining the tensions of context with some of the suspense of progression toward a destiny—but a destiny of the psyche.
[14] However, *Camino Real* uses—unnecessarily—a dream framework.

tially on the conventional, representational means of apparently real characters interacting through the usual stage techniques which are often ironically juxtaposed with startling effect: a lyric moment on the heels of violence, soliloquy after stichomythia, tears after frank slapstick. Their sudden, comforting moments of humor save them—as life is saved—from nightmare: from such a nightmare as Per Lagerkvist's chilling play in this mode, *The Secret of Heaven*.

These plays reached toward Maeterlinck's dream of pure drama of being. Maeterlinck himself had learned to create a suffused mood for such drama; but he never achieved a texture palpable enough, cross-hatched enough, to continuously excite sense, feeling, and thought. Modern contextual drama effects this by translating the restless intensity of inner life into busy, loaded symbolic action. Many perspectives of the same perception are brought together; many intense, momentary chorded experiences poise side by side in tension; and the dynamic context conveys a sense of the ever-dissolving gestalts of existence. There is no easy terminal release from this kind of artistic experience. The audience is confronted with its passions, not forgiven them. This drama's form is flux; as if the playwrights are reaching, in the second part of the usual linear equation, "Life is————", for a statement so vast and ambiguous and disturbing that it seems, indeed, they are bent on discarding limiting terms altogether in favor of a simple declarative sentence: "Life is."

Pass without transition from the "style" of Antoine to the "style" of the Marx Brothers. —EUGENE IONESCO (Stage Direction for the performance of *The Painting*, 1955.)

[On Surrealism and the idea of "Automatic Writing"] A psychic automation with the aid of which we propose to express the real function of thought, either orally, or in writing, or in any other way. A dictation of thought without any control of reason, outside of all esthetic or moral preoccupations.—ANDRÉ BRETON (First *Manifesto of Surrealism*, 1924.)

If the poetic drama is to reconquer its place, it must, in my opinion, enter into overt competition with prose drama.

. . . What we have to do is to bring poetry into the world in which the audience lives and to which it returns when it leaves the theatre, not to transport the audience into some imaginary world totally unlike their own, an unreal world in which poetry can be spoken.—T. S. ELIOT

I endeavor to substitute a poetry of the theatre (poésie de théâtre) for poetry in the theatre. Poetry in the theatre is fine lace that cannot be seen at a distance.—JEAN COCTEAU (Preface to *Les mariés de la Tour Eiffel* [*Wedding on the Eiffel Tower*], 1922.)

◇   Crisis in the Theatre

Discussion of theatrical form is apt grossly to underestimate the natural imaginative agility of the average playgoer. It is all too readily assumed that he is incapable of doing two different things at once—identifying himself with the actor as a momentarily

◇ Reprinted by permission of *The Times Literary Supplement*, December 14, 1956.

real character in a real-life action and appreciating the same actor as the performer of a feat of acting. This is how the process works in any theatre to-day, and there is no reason to believe that this common-place duality of response was ever absent from the theatres of antiquity. It is because conventions, as such, do not really bother him that he would be mildly surprised to be informed that his theatre has been for at least the past fifty years in a state of crisis. He can find interest and enjoyment in fourth-wall realism, in expressionism, symbolism, constructivism and epic realism, even in surrealism (insofar as he can get the hang of the author's intentions), and he is thoroughly at home with the various conventions that are oddly and perhaps fortuitously combined in musical comedy, vaudeville and pantomime. It may sometimes occur to him that the present-day theatre is suffering from an inner disharmony. He is more likely then to lament the scarcity of new theatrical talent than to attribute disharmony to the failure creatively to resolve the conflict between realism and those nonrealistic modes of theatre that go by the name of theatricalism.

Theorists alive to the prolonged crisis have found themselves in recent years wandering unhappily between two worlds—one believed to be dying, the other powerless to be born. The soil of realism appears to have been worked well-nigh to death; yet it has to be recognized that theatricalism in all its multiform manifestations has failed so far to create a generally acceptable alternative. If modern drama is to assert its power to develop, clearly some new point of departure must be found; but the position of the point remains elusive, and discussion, increasingly discouraged, moves in a circle. The symbolists led by Maeterlinck sought to transform theatrical experience into atmosphere and reverie. They found that it was against the nature of drama, the most definite of the arts, to be stationary and meditative, though the movement brought great visual beauty to the stage and an adaptable manner. The expressionists deriving from Strindberg theatricalized phenomena by distorting them. They wrought lasting changes in the structure and texture of the drama, as Mr. Arthur Miller's *Death of a Salesman* and many other contemporary plays bear witness. And more recently the cool rationalistic school of epic realism has given an even sharper jolt to realism than many of the more subjective deviations from it. But realism has survived these successive challenges. Realists have not disdained to learn from their opponents.

It remains true nevertheless that, potent as has been its influence, theatricalism has failed to crystallize into an adequate and reliable dramatic form . . . realism, whatever its limitations, has been to the modern theatre what Shakespearian dramaturgy was to the Elizabethan period and Sophoclean to the Periclean age. "But theatricalism has not yet found any classical configurations because it has not yet found a consistent form. . . . Its idea persists and is, in my opinion, essentially sound, but its forms have been transitory." [So writes John Gassner who wants the] "co-existence of realism and nonrealistic stylization turned into an active and secure partnership in the interests of essential realism. One obstacle is the modern theatricalist's seemingly irrepressible desire to protect the spectator from the danger of total involvement in the experience of the stage. As Johnson said, "the spectators are always in their senses and know, from first to last, that the stage is only a stage, and the players are only players."

Estheticism, Poetic Drama, and Neorealism

Professor Rosenberg's preceding analysis calls attention to a radical departure from norms to which strong resistance may be offered even by those who are ready to concede merit to the circular technique of a work like *Waiting for Godot*. Anything can succeed once or twice without constituting a generally viable enterprise. "Stalemate dramaturgy," as dramatic circularity could be called, may successfully convey the viewpoint that man is doomed to recurrent futility, and the result may be a thoroughly effective play. But the next time a circular movement is used to promulgate the same idea the results may be simply boring or enervating. If it is not so in a particular case the reason may be that the mood or tone is radically different, as it is in the case of *The Bald Soprano* which pokes fun at people in society and reduces *la condition humaine,* if it be actually that, to an excruciatingly mindless vaudeville that many playgoers found entertaining.

Length and pace also makes for a difference in effect and in degree of success or failure. Samuel Beckett made his fairly short two-act *chef-d'oeuvre, Waiting for Godot,* just the right length, although even so the present writer found it a trifle too long while attending the Broadway production and thinks he would have liked this metaphorical work better as a one-act play in two scenes. Ionesco's full-length dramas *The Killer* and *Rhinoceros* may impress us as overlong; the last mentioned is a dramatized notion that could be abbreviated to advantage. *The Bald Soprano* could not be much longer than it is if the play is performed at a suitably fast clip. Performed at the slow pace of esthetic contemplation or symbolic punctuation, as it was in one off-Broadway production, it is apt to prove a crushingly boring sophomoric experience.

It may well be that the natural limits, or optimal length, of absurdist drama, like those of symbolist drama, is the one-act or short full-length play. It may also be observed that circularity is relative rather than absolute. There is a return to a norm, therefore *some* circularity, in many a well-known tragedy; there is a restoration of equilibrium after the tragic disequilibrium has reached its climax. *Macbeth* provides a classic example of the dramatic rhythm that pulses from *order* to *disorder* and *back to order;* and we also find this dramatic rhythm in *King Lear,* in

Hamlet, in the *Ajax* and *Electra* of Sophocles, in Lope de Vega's *Fuente Ovejuna,* Corneille's *The Cid,* and Racine's *Bérénice* and *Athaliah.* And conversely, some degree of linear progression, whether it be evolutionary or devolutionary, is observable even in Beckett's *Waiting for Godot* and *Endgame,* and in Ionesco's *The Chairs.*

Absolute circularity seems to go against the dramatic impulse in human nature and the psychological as well as artistic "principle of the crescendo," as Kenneth Burke calls it in *The Poetic Process* (in Counter-Statement, 1931) when he wrote that "surely we may say, without much fear of startling anyone, that the work of art utilizes climactic arrangement because the human brain has a pronounced potentiality for being arrested, or entertained, by such an arrangement." Since a crescendo, moreover, has no emotional value in itself, which only a particular experience can have, it is evident that maximum emotive value inheres *in a specific plot* rather than in a state of mind. Here, too, human instinct inclines us to favor plot (the big popular success is often plotty) and we even try to supply a unifying plot where the author provides only fragments of experience. Nothing proves more arid in the theatre than an absolute statement or idea that fails to attain concreteness by "a principle of individuation." "*Universale intelligitur, singulare sentitur;*" we think in terms of *universals* (in terms of generalities or abstractions), Kenneth Burke reminds us, but feel *particulars.* That being the case, it is essential to make the parts move sequentially, optimally by means of a built-in logic of causation—that is, of cause and effect. And this involves the dynamism of contrasts, comparisons, connections, and crises leading to climaxes constituting a "*crescendo.*"

Naturalists aimed at so close an approximation of life, under the *tranche de vie* program, that they suspected all organization of plot lines as a flagrant falsification of reality and a contrivance calculated to throw dust into the eye of the beholder, blinding him to reality and converting him into a willing subject for mesmerization by showmanship and galvanization by theatrical trickery. Thereupon, the element of plot fell into disrepute, and efforts were made to write the plotless play. The results were usually negligible. The next best thing was to substitute disjunctive horizontal actions for vertical plot. The classic examples were Hauptmann's dramas *The Weavers* and *Florian Geyer*.

Non-naturalistic drama has also tended to undercut plot in a variety of ways: By symbolist erosion of plot and atmospheric blurring of outlines of action as in *Pelléas and Mélisande;* by *surrealiste* interiorization of the drama, and a forced subordination of conscious organization to "Illogic" or the haphazard dictates of the unconscious, manifested in different degrees by such pieces of the theatre as Cocteau's *Orphée,* Cummings' *Him,* and Gertrude Stein and Virgil Thompson's *Four Saints in Three Acts;* by the violent fragmentation and the cyclotron-like agitation of post-Strindbergian expressionism, as in Georg Kaiser's *Gas;* and by the substitution of circular rather than linear structure in absurdist theatre.

Paralleling this defection from the principle of *"crescendo,"* or from linear progression, we have also had deviations from the principle of individuation or particularization. Naturalism deviated from it by subordinating the human being to his instinctual drives and to environmental conditioning, giving rise to the drama of the depleted individual who resembles a puppet or automaton more than he does the hero of renaissance, neoclassic, and romantic drama. Symbolism tended to substitute wraiths for the full-bodied characters of previous ages. Expressionism fragmented the individual and tended to depersonalize him to such a degree that he was given no other name than The Man and The Woman, or Mr. and Mrs. Zero in Elmer Rice's *The Adding Machine.* Epic drama subordinated the individual to a function of ideological argument except when the artist in Brecht created characters as well as demonstrations. And absurdist dramatists would have contradicted their premises if they had dealt with any but depleted, mechanized, decayed, and moribund characters facing a blank wall of meaninglessness. That Beckett's two tramps in *Waiting for Godot* somehow triumphed over nescience and comprised a rueful portrait of humanity in the New York production may have been an effect of the acting as well as of Beckett's artistry.

Nevertheless, in one way or another, the modern drama has again and again manifested an instinct for organization, as against disorganization; a feeling for crescendo, as against *descrescendo*, *stasis*, and *circularity*; a regard for language, as against a disregard for it in favor of silent mimesis or mime; and, in general, a marked esthetic orientation, as against a sense of disintegration and chaos. Whether we exalt any or all of these manifestations as sound instinct and common sense or deplore them as Philistinism, sentimentality, *Kitsch*, and "show business," the fact remains that there have been strong inclinations toward refined sensibility, design, and visual and verbal beauty in the modern theatre. Every movement toward extreme stylization has been followed by a countermovement. Thus in Germany, expressionism was succeeded by Epic Theatre, on the one hand, and "die neue Sachlichkeit" mundane type of realism, on the other. In Russia, extreme theatricalism was followed by a mild formalism and displaced by "Socialist Realism." In contemporary Britain, a wave of Eliot-inspired poetic drama subsided under the vogue of the renascent realism of England's "angry young men," as represented by John Osborne and Arnold Wesker. A reaction to absurdism was much in the making early in the 1960's, even in the presumably avant-garde off-Broadway world, with the failure of a season of absurdist drama presented by Richard Barr, who concluded that its brief attractiveness had faded. Mr. Barr then recovered his losses with the successful production of the essentially naturalistic drama *Who's Afraid of Virginia Woolf?*, by the author of *The Zoo Story* and *The American Dream,* the one-act masterpieces of American "absurdism." At about this time, too, the very founder and editor of the avant-garde Tulane Drama Review, Professor Robert W. Corrigan, while taking a sympathetic view of the proponents of The Theatre of the Absurd and "their demand that the language of the theatre be gestural," warned against their possibly underestimating the value of verbal language, "the only language which can give the full expression to that balance of human faculties which characterizes the art of the theatre." [15]

At about the same time, England's theatre historian, Professor Allardyce Nicoll, apparently taking exception to England's neorealists led by Osborne and Wesker, strongly warned a convention of university professors of English against a growing distrust of words in the theatre. The London Times (August 18, 1962) came editorially to the defense of the young playwrights by maintaining that "Whatever might be urged against a theatre boasting Mr. Harold Pinter, Mr. John Arden and . . . Mr. John Osborne, it would hardly be, one would have thought, its lack of eloquence." But Professor Nicoll could have pointed out to a considerable dependence on movement, mime, and gesture on their part; thus the most dramatically realized scene in Wesker's *Chips with Everything* was without doubt the completely silent scene in which the recruits of the British Air Force manage to steal coal for their Christmas fire under the very nose of a sentinel. Moreover, he must have had in mind not so much a want of "eloquence" as a want of poetry. Twice during the twentieth century English playwrights sought to recover poetry for the English stage, once at the beginning of the century under the academic leadership of Stephen Phillips (*Paolo and Francesca, Herod*, et cetera) and once, beginning with Eliot's *Murder in the Cathedral* in 1935; and twice their insurgency was brought to a halt. The first third of the century belonged to Bernard Shaw, the master of modern English prose, and not to Stephen Phillips, the epigone of blank-verse tragedy; and it was evident by 1960 that Eliot and Christopher Fry had not restored a reign of poetry in the English theatre. Neither Eliot, with compromises that led to his writing poetry frequently indistinguishable from prose after *Murder in*

[15] "The Theatre in Search of a Fix," *Theatre in the Twentieth Century*, New York, 1963, pp. 22-26.

the Cathedral, nor Fry with his verbal pyrotechnics and florid sentiments after *The Lady's Not for Burning* discovered the way to a new Helicon.

The main recovery from, and the main resistance to, the enticements of estheticism and Anglicanism came from a school of socially oriented young playwrights who may be called *neorealists*. In a large number of works staged successfully within a short period after 1950 (Osborne's *Look Back in Anger, The Entertainer,* and *Epitaph for George Dylan,* Wesker's *Roots* and *Chips with Everything,* Shelagh Delaney's *A Taste of Honey,* and Pinter's *The Caretaker,* are representative), the emphasis was on content and characterization rather than on style and stylization and the structure of the plays was conveniently realistic. And except for Pinter's plays, in which there was a piquant residue of absurdism, there was no mystery about the subject matter or meaning;[16] the authors (all but Pinter) showed no mystic or mystifying inclinations, climbed no heights, and took no Pisgah-view of struggling humanity. Their efforts to write anti-establishment social drama held no surprises for Americans familiar with the "social consciousness" of American playwrights during the 1930's. Explication in the case of the "angries" is a wasted effort. Their forte is speaking out rather than artfully concealing; their frame of reference became the outer, rather than the invisible, world; their imagery became dramatic rather than poetic; and if they were apt to be eloquent, they spoke with the tongues of critics and prophets and not of angels in Anglican vestments. It was through the neorealism of implicit or explicit protest that they shook up the British theatre of aristocracy and theology and put up barriers against absurdists steadfastly marching, or rather (as in the case of N. F. Simpson *et al.,*) skittishly romping, toward *nada* and nescience.[17]

---

[16] Pinter himself strenuously denied the existence of a mysterious or metaphysical level of meaning in his fascinating drama *The Caretaker;* and the plays that followed it (*The Collection,* and *The Lover*) certainly had none.

[17] A trend toward a neorealism was also well marked in the American theatre when O'Neill topped his expressionist experiments

Social drama, the natural outlet of the dissident, became then, as often before, a therapeutic defense against the virus of lethargy. Moreover, the theory that art was the product of the moment, the race, and the milieu *à la Taine* or of economic pressure and social conflict according to the teachings of dialectical Marxism had less bearing upon British neorealism than did a reaction to both the triviality of British domestic drama and the profundities of dramatic idealism that became too much tinsel in the case of Christopher Fry's verse plays,[18] and too much sterile theologizing in the case of T. S. Eliot until he relaxed his monitory posture in *The Elder Statesman*. Mid-century neorealism continued a reaction of some duration against Gordon Craig estheticism that proclaimed the supremacy of *design* and against attenuations of drama started by Maurice Maeterlinck in the 1890's concerning which Arthur Symons, himself a votary of estheticism, aptly said that Maeterlinck's plays could "safely be confided to the masks and feigned voices of marionettes." [19]

How much further the neorealism of the 1960's would carry the British theatre could not be determined, but there could be little doubt that it had already found gifted spokesmen. Their weakness lay in the tendency of their revolt to become scattered and inchoate; thus *Look Back in Anger* lost direction after its

---

with *The Iceman Cometh* and *The Long Day's Journey into Night*, which have come to be considered the best plays of his ever-questing career; when Tennessee Williams turned out *Cat on a Hot Tin Roof* after his strenuously poetic and symbolist *Camino Real;* when Arthur Miller turned out *The Crucible* and *A View from the Bridge*, and when Edward Albee delivered his naturalistic blockbuster *Who's Afraid of Virginia Woolf?* after *The Sandbox* and *The American Dream*.

[18] Christopher Fry himself reflected this dissatisfaction when he produced the relatively stripped Thomas à Beckett—Henry II drama *Curtmantle*, in 1962. Unfortunately, the play failed to impress reviewers and failed to restore its author to his hard-earned former eminence in the British theatre.

[19] *The Contemporary Review*, 1897.

first act, and *Chips with Everything* after its second. Their limitation came mainly from a reduction of drama to subheroic, not to say subtragic, dimensions, transcended only in a few instances such as that of *A Man for All Seasons,* the epically structured St. Thomas More drama by Robert Bolt, whose earlier character drama, *The Flowering Cherry,* was a depressing study of petit-bourgeois failure.

Avant-Garde Dialogue

In 1960 (December 23) The Times Literary Supplement published in London expressed the same doubts about inarticulateness in the new drama that Professor Allardyce Nicoll did. In an editorial entitled "Cult of Dumbness," *TLS* declared that "what the theatre looks like facing in the immediate future is not death but dumbness." But the editorial, reproduced below, was aimed not so much at the British neorealists as at an international school of playwriting and dramatic theory which includes proponents of absurdist theatre, starting with Antonin Artaud, as well as latter-day naturalists and playwrights who blended naturalism with theatricalist devices, as Jack Gelber did in his oddly arresting play about drug-addiction, *The Connection* (1959).

[Re WIDOWER'S HOUSES]
I had better have written a
beautiful play like Twelfth
Night, or a grand play, like
the tragic masterpieces; but
frankly, I was not able to;
modern commercialism is a
bad art school, and cannot,
with all its robberies, murder
and prostitutions, move us in
the grand manner to pity and
terror; it is squalid, futile,
blundering, mean, ridiculous,
for ever uneasily pretending to
be the wide-minded, humane,
enterprising thing it is not.
—BERNARD SHAW

. . . a new idea of the world
was necessary to complete the
revolt against the naturalistic
theatre of the last part of the
nineteenth century, and a new
theatre of ideas was necessary
to express this revolt.
—JAMES H. CLANCY

In your opinion, then, what's
to be done? Change human
nature or—the world? Well,
which is to be.—SHEN TE (in
BRECHT'S Der gute Mensch
von Setzuan.)

Man is condemned to be free.
—JEAN-PAUL SARTRE

*

◊   Cult of Dumbness

The theatre is not yet dead. A west-end success has just entered
its ninth year; new playhouses are being planned, and even built;
recruits flood the profession. Outside London, it is true, some old
houses have had to close, and the touring system has largely
broken down; while as television takes over and people find at
home what they used to go out for, retrenchment may go further.
But this withdrawal shows no sign of becoming a rout; in fact it
is slowing down; and it does have the advantage of leaving the
theatre free to concentrate on what it alone can do. The theatre
can, however, do several things, and in this choice of action

◊ Reprinted from the December 23, 1960 issue of *The Times
Literary Supplement,* by permission.

there lies danger. For what the theatre looks like facing in the immediate future is not death but dumbness.

A provocative article in the current issue of the magazine *X*, "New Wave in a Dead Sea", helps to light up the risks. Its author, Mr. Charles Marowitz, is discussing some of the English dramatists who have become known in the past four years. Trying to define what sort of plays they write, he sees a conflux of two forces: social realism (reaching London "seventy years after its establishment in France, fifty-eight years after its introduction to Russia, and thirty years after its arrival in America") and the new movement, also realistic but more poetic in its bleak way, that emanates from Beckett, Ionesco and Genet ("a theatre which has thrown Aristotelian symmetry into the garbage dump and declared its opposition to the concept that playwriting demands the rehash of the Old Explicit. It is a theatre devoted to exploration into our secret selves"). Mr. Marowitz believes the former type of drama to be only a more recognizable aspect of the latter. He offers as our best hope for the new decade an "uncluttered drama which says more in mumbles, mutters and broken phrases than has been said in generations of literary articulateness."

Mr. Peter Brook, writing in the current *Encore,* looks more closely and farther. A New York performance of *The Connection,* by Mr. Jack Gelber, leads him to suggest that we may be heading for a theatre of "pure behaviour." (In the play a roomful of junkies pass the time playing jazz, occasionally talking, mostly sitting, while they wait for a fix: hardly anything happens; there is no plot, characterization or tempo.) Mr. Brook concludes: "I believe that the future of the theatre must lie in its transcending the surface of reality, and I believe that *The Connection* shows how naturalism can become so deep that it can—through the intensity of the performer (I'm sure *The Connection* is nothing much on paper)—transcend appearances."

He relates the play to those new French novels which present concrete facts without comment or explanation.

Mr. Brook and Mr. Marowitz foresee a type of play that, by

being super-naturalistic, achieves truth and beauty of a new sort. If they are right we may still ask two questions: first, what sort of truth and beauty are being offered; secondly, do any other forms of theatre present a more promising alternative. The questions are connected.

Defenders of the new super-naturalism would presumably say that it is the business of drama to reproduce the everyday surface of life, whatever else may appear beneath or beyond it. Further, that because life itself seems disconnected, illogical, shapeless to many people (or at least to some) plays, to be faithful to the truth they are portraying, must imagine that chaos in their design and texture. These two theories buttress each other. Neither is without strength. Both, however, are vulnerable. On the latter point it may be argued that a more effective work of art results where forces of disorder or destruction are expressed within a strict form. The tension between content and form can in this way be of overwhelming power. *The Bacchae* or *Troilus and Cressida* are suggestive instances. While on the former point —the need for recognizable detail on the surface—will not these new behaviouristic plays tend to become merely a sort of mime; a less stylized sort and one that uses a few words to help out the behaviour; but essentially mime, and therefore condemned to a moral and intellectual content that is trivial?

There are other directions the theatre could take. It might, as Mr. Brook also suggests, follow the path of abstraction, which has become so popular in painting. It might employ song and dance, either in the jolly manner of Miss Joan Littlewood's entertainments, or in the more polished style of *West Side Story*. It might even turn again to words—precise and articulate prose, or, if it is not too late, verse.

These three possibilities have one feature in common. They all recognize that without a refined and complex grammar of expression—whether visual, literary or musical—the theatre cannot achieve anything of much artistic significance. Character and a plot will not do by themselves. In a Mozart opera or a Greek play there is no less complexity than simplicity. The words or the music are highly organized. The same can scarcely be said of most modern plays, least of all the plays by the super-naturalists. Words in the theatre have shrunk to the status of a libretto. They merely form a structure for actors and directors and designers to work on. Theatrical art has become mainly that of interpretation.

The super-naturalists may, however, not triumph after all. There is plenty of scope for other kinds of development. Even if they do they may have more to offer than is yet clear. We can live in hope, but we should not forget the dangers that have been indicated. It would be sad if the theatre were to develop into an instrument for skilfully saying nothing. Life may sometimes appear not to mean very much. We expect more of art.

◇   ◇   ◇

The Contemporary Situation

An assessment of the contemporary situation became particularly urgent in the seventh decade of our century when it could no longer be maintained that the modern theatre was still young. If Ibsen's *Brand* and *Peer Gynt* period were taken as the starting point, the modern theatre could begin to celebrate its centenary in 1965. There was a clamor for conclusions, summaries and assessments, if the present writer may judge from invitations to lecture on the subject. It is surely appropriate to conclude our book with a summary.[20]

A pertinent question is exactly what world it is that we call

[20] The summary is taken from my lecture, "The Dramatic Critic Looks at the Contemporary Theatre," commemorating the twenty-fifth anniversary of the Department of Drama of the University of Texas, by permission of the Department, which published the commemorative papers in a booklet called *Futures in the American Theatre* in 1963.
* The quotations on p. 363 apply substantially to "The Contemporary Situation" following this section.

contemporary. I think it is the world we began to encounter with the start of the first world war in 1914. By comparison with it, the earlier world that cradled the modern theatre—from the 1870's to the outbreak of that war—seemed remarkably stable and peaceful, though, strictly speaking, it was neither. The struggle for women's rights, the striving for political liberalism, and the hopes of democratic Socialism now seem rather remote. Today's artists are normally unimpressed by Ibsenism as a cause or challenge. No matter how Ibsen and his acolytes might fume about nineteenth-century society, they could assume the continuance of man and the inevitability of a rationally ordered, constantly improving, world. Their attitude toward progress in science was no less sanguine. With science functioning as the handmaiden of the good society, man could confidently expect not only ever-growing standards of material well-being, but equity in social relations based on a rising economy of surplus instead of scarcity. In international relations, despite several conflicts such as the Franco-Prussian War of 1870 and the later Russo-Japanese War, it seemed as if it would soon be possible to establish amity and reasonableness among the nations of the world. With respect to advances in applied science, of salvation, so to speak, by machinery, men could but echo Lord Alfred Tennyson's confident tribute to the "ringing grooves of change" with which he hailed the advent of the raliroad. With respect to the rise of democratic government and the adjudication of national rivalries, it seemed reasonable to endorse this Victorian laureate's prediction of a "Parliament of Man and Federation of the World" to be assured by the "common sense of most."

It is a radically different conception of man's future that rules the world of thoughtful men and the uneasy fraternity of contemporary art, especially the public art of the theatre. In the English-speaking theatre the altered outlook was perhaps most poignantly expressed within a dozen years of the Versailles treaty by the most distinguished of pre-war optimists, Bernard

Shaw. In *Too True to Be Good* in 1932, Shaw made his ex-clergyman hero Aubrey exclaim that "the Western World is damned beyond the possibility of salvation." The full peroration of *Too True to Be Good*, a product of Shaw's desperate view which preceded the outbreak of a second world war by a scant half dozen years, was devastating. Shaw anticipated our current theatre of desperation and "the absurd," when he made his spokesman Aubrey declare, "Naked bodies no longer shock us; our sunbathers, grinning at us from every illustrated summer number of our magazines, are nuder than shorn lambs. But the horror of the naked mind is still more than we can bear."

Aubrey's question of "how are we to bear the dreadful new nakedness?" became the cardinal challenge of expressionist playwrights of the 1920's and of existentialist dramatists of the 1940's and of the present historical moment. And indeed how *are* we to bear with this nakedness and this sense of despair deeper than Pascal's when the old science was aborning in the 17th century, "the nakedness," as Aubrey put it, "of the souls who until now have always disguised themselves from one another in beautiful impossible idealisms to enable them to bear one another's company."

Assigning the blame to the traumatic effects of the first world war between 1914 and 1918, Shaw's Aubrey continues prophetically: "The iron lightning of war has burnt great rents in these angelic veils, just as it has smashed great holes in our cathedral roofs and torn great gashes in our hillsides. Our souls go in rags now; and the young are spying through the holes and getting glimpses of the reality that was hidden. And they are not horrified [Shaw is right—the young of the scornfully sophisticated 1920's were not horrified, and despair was to come later in our own days of existentialist and nihilist theatre!]: they exult in having found us out: . . . and when we their elders desperately try to patch our torn clothes, with scraps of the old material, the young lay violent hands on us and tear from us even the rags that were left to us. But [and here comes a second prophecy!] when they have stripped themselves and us utterly naked, will they be able to bear the spectacle?" That they were not able to do so became evident in imported works such as Beckett's and Ionesco's plays and in home-grown ones like Albee's and Gelber's. Declaring himself to be the new Ecclesiastes, but an Ecclesiastes deprived of a Bible and a creed, Shaw's Aubrey concluded that we have "outgrown our religion, outgrown our political system, outgrown our strength of mind and character."

Disillusion with the old religious faiths, including faith in life itself and its means of communication, became a staple of the theatre of the 1920's. The concomitant sense of a void appeared in the runaway, superficially gay European negativism that went under the name of dada—and appropriately so, since this infantile word conveys the fact that the very language of thought and feeling, of communication between adults, was being dissolved. That the dadaist theatre should not have precipitated any noteworthy dramatic literature cannot surprise the drama critic. A pure product such as Gertrude Stein's *Four Saints in Three Acts* has been pure delight in the theatre, but solely through its stage pictures, stage movement, verbal music and, above all, Virgil Thompson's score; the result, it is true, is curiously integrative rather than destructive, but only on the plane of the nonrational. In, so to speak, *impure* dadaist drama such as the poet E. E. Cummings' sardonic play *him,* it is the *destructive* element of satire that makes the work communicative insofar as the satirized subject is recognizable.

The disintegrative dadaist impulse was also assimilated into, and blended with, the expressionism fashionable in Central Europe during and immediately after World War I, as in Georg Kaiser's *From Morn to Midnight* and O'Neill's *The Hairy Ape,* or it was amalgamated with satirical social protest, as in the celebrated Brecht and Weill musical creations, *The Three-Penny Opera* and *Mahagonny.* In semi-dadaist works such as these, of course, the process of artistic disintegration was halted by the constructive quality of musical structure and the reintegrative moral power of satire, which has functioned as a social corrective ever since the classic stage of Aristophanes. But reintegration was not to be the order of the day for long, after the second and greater explosion of World War II. In histories of art and literature, dadaism is usually described as a brief episode and speedily discredited aberration. But it is surely Dadaism in more or less pure state that we have been encountering since the second world war in such examples of dramatic anarchy as Picasso's incoherent *Desire Trapped by the Tail*, Ionesco's travesties on man in society such as *The Bald Soprano,* and Beckett's and Genet's apocalyptic visions of a crumbling world of reality such as *Endgame, The Balcony,* and *The Blacks.*

A fundamental difference in viewpoint with respect to society and art is involved here. It is possible to illustrate the objectives of pioneers of modern critical realism with an apt quotation. Ibsen, dissociating himself from naturalism for its own sake, is quoted as having said of his own provocative and morally bracing social dramas, "Zola [as the literary leader of naturalism] descends into the cesspool to take a bath, but I descend into it in order to cleanse it." Joseph Wood Krutch rightly says in his little book of lectures *"Modernism" in Modern Drama* that "Ibsen, despite all he discards, seems to hold fast to old-fashioned concepts which will carry us across, if anything will—namely, to a belief in rationality as a determining factor in life and a belief in free will by means of which at least an exceptional, heroic individual can save both himself and, ultimately, perhaps, the mass of mankind." The same can be said of Chekhov and of Shaw, despite his despair in the 1930's, which was not actually doubt of the efficacy of reason but of the people and nations who fail to live by reason.

André Breton's first *Manifesto of Surrealism* provides an instructive contrast, which the recent "Theatre of the Absurd" has also provided. Breton wrote: *"Surrealism is a pure psychic automatism,* by which it is intended to express, verbally, in writing, or by other means, the real process of thought and thought's dictation, in the absence of all control exercised by the reason and outside all aesthetic or moral preoccupations. Surrealism rests on the belief in the superior reality of certain forms of association neglected hitherto; in the omnipotence of the dream, and in the disinterested play of thought." Breton went so far as to propose the following procedure: "Take a newspaper, take a pair of scissors, choose any article in the paper. Cut it out, then cut out each of the words. Jumble them up in a bag, then tumble them out and group them in sentences as they come out, and that will be a poem." And Breton got results such as these: . . . "The winged vapour seduces the locked bird," "The Senegal oyster will eat up the tricolour bread," "The anaemic little girl makes the polished mannequin blush." On which perhaps the best comment, restrained but firm, came from T. S. Eliot, who resisted the Surrealist influence. In *Selected Essays* he wrote: "The suggestiveness of true poetry . . . is the aura round a bright clear centre. You cannot have the aura alone."

As for Shaw's reference to the outgrowing of "our strength of mind and character," Shaw, a Puritanically severe judge of moral fibre whose favorite book was *The Pilgrim's Progress,* has been sustained by a large percentage of the century's literary productivity. We can save time by not dwelling on obvious exploitations of flabby thinking and crude sexuality that have made a mockery and a meretricious trade of the rigorous dramatic art of Ibsen, Strindberg, and Shaw himself at the start of the modern period. We may note, however, that the contemporary drama has employed characteristic disguises in peddling *ersatz* thought and pinchbeck sex—the former usually under the dispensation of liberal sentiment, the latter under the labels of sophistication and psychological depth.

Limping raggedly behind the vehicle of so-called modern "drama of ideas," once so brightly furbished and advertised by Shaw, contemporary playwrights have arrived at opinions which, even if they were sound, would be neither fresh nor exciting. And whether the opinion expressed has been liberal or conservative, the dramatic style has been commonplace. Shaw's dialectical brilliance and free-flowing imagination have rarely been present in the theatre since the 1920's—except in France, and this mainly as a result of the work of Jean Giraudoux. And while liveliness of thought has not been absent in Giraudoux' plays, a feeling for character has rarely been evident. "Strength of mind" has been present at least in some pyrotechnical displays of French intellect. But "strength of character" has been a genuine concern only under the existentialist prescripts of Sartre and his followers. Strength of mind has, it is true, been abundantly apparent in the work of Bertolt Brecht. But the historical conditions of the post-1918 world reflected in Brecht's work hampered his intellect and sense of character. Whatever independence and originality we may attribute to Brecht belongs not to the political propagandist but to the poet, the craftsman, and the theatrical virtuoso.

It is especially significant that neither the schools of Paris nor those of Central European "Epic" have been secure in their hold upon "strength of intellect and strength of character." Thus Giraudoux' most successful successor, Jean Anouilh, has been a watered-down Giraudoux but also an independently facile and gifted playwright whose essentially romantic talent is theatrical rather than intellectual; Sartre and Camus have been followed by no other existentialist dramatist of consequence; and Brecht, despite the recent advent of the Swiss writers Duerrenmatt and Frisch, has not yet had any successor on either side of the hypothetical "Iron Curtain" possessed of either his mental powers or his ironic passion.

A deterrent to the timeless humanism of dramatic art has been present in the very nature of the aforementioned schools, and of progressive types of contemporary drama in general. It is the actual amputation and at times total annihilation of character itself. Character in the drama after 1914 became repeatedly fragmented or exploded by the violent expressionist drama that came into vogue in Germany; it was dissolved, introverted, and also exploded by the dramatic surrealism that followed the dadaist movement; it was deftly called into question and mocked by Pirandello and his Italian school of the grotesque; and it was variously subordinated to Marxist and to psychological interest, as well as to theatricality and formalism. Characterization no longer meant the creation of characters but the manipulation of attenuated figures, often suggestive of mere puppetry, so that the question of credibility began to lose its meaning. The characters in modernist French drama, whether by Giraudoux or Becket, by Anouilh or Ionesco, are present in the plays for the purposes of theatricalization or symbolization rather than for revelation. One cannot appraise most avant-garde writing by asking the old classic questions of who is the character and why he behaves as he does, feel as he feels, or think as he thinks. The playwright decides these matters more or less arbitrarily or dismisses the question as irrelevant to his purpose, which may be to spin out a notion or demonstrate a point.

Rarely does the play exist for the sake of the characters, and even when this does seem to be the case in so-called psychological drama, it will be noted that what the audience is given is not a character but a psychological demonstration, whether in the deliberately abstruse manner of Evreinov's *Theatre of the Soul* or the complex schematization of O'Neill's *Strange Interlude* and *Mourning Becomes Electra*. That a miracle occurs from time to time and an author's demonstration is conducted with fleshed out characters rather than with puppets, or that the figures of the demonstration happen to come alive as fully realized persons, can be granted in the case of noteworthy plays by an O'Neill or a Brecht—in an *Iceman Cometh* or a *Mother Courage*. But these are the exceptions. As a rule, the playwright has tended to give us not a person but a problem, a case history, a puppet show, or a fancy. He has given us, at best, "psychology" rather than a character; an argument rather than a life; a viewpoint rather than an experience. And, significantly, this has also been the case in many efforts to bring back poetry to the theatre. The writers have behaved as if there were some rule that disallows character-creation to the poet when he writes for the stage, whereas the very contrary has been the case ever since the advent of "character drama" in the work of Sophocles. Some of the most memorable character creation came, of course, from Shakespeare and Racine without any loss but with an actual intensification of poetry.

Examples of the divorcement of dramatic poetry from dramatic characterization have multiplied ever since the advent of symbolist theatre in the 1890's. Maeterlinck was one of the first playwrights to attenuate character for the sake of poetic suggestion or abstraction. His example was followed almost invariably when poets turned to the drama—such eminent poets as Blok in Russia, Claudel in France, Yeats in Ireland, and Eliot and Auden in England. The only significant exception that comes to my mind is the case of the Spanish poet, Lorca; and even he dealt more with passions than with people until he turned to atmospheric realism in writing his last play, a group portrait of frustrated women, *The House of Bernarda Alba*. One might cite the example of Brecht, too—at least in the case of *The Caucasian Chalk Circle*, *Galileo*, and *Mother Courage*, but in these instances the governing intention was to compose social rather than primarily poetic drama, and the often good poetry in these works is sporadic and incidental; it is designed, we are told, to interrupt the spectators' emotional involvement. Where the intent of the contemporary playwright was primarily the creation of poetic drama the result was usually formalistic, if not indeed formulistic, as in the case of Eliot's *Murder in the Cathedral* and *The Family Reunion* and of the abstruse plays Yeats fashioned in the manner of the Japanese Noh Play. The very abstractness of most poetic ventures is evidence of an artificial or willed effort rather than a natural impulse to write poetically for the stage. It is little wonder that our harvest of high tragedy has been extremely sparse, for true tragedy revolves around more or less heroic characters capable of error and sensitively aware of defeat and failure. Tragedy may deal with uncommonly absorbing common men, but cannot be achieved with shadows any more than with heroic postures and stock rhetoric.

Shaw's Aubrey, who is a projection of Shaw himself, tries to surmount the cultural impasse he has defined so eloquently. He concludes with a call for positive belief, continuing struggle, and hope for humanity in the very teeth of despair. But, then, Shaw belonged to a 19th-century world that placed "character" first rather than last in its inventory of cultural assets.

With the dissolution of character in our century, we come to the true age of decadence. It is not obscenity, morbidity, or undue fascination with death and decay that undermines the drama (these are but concomitant characteristics) but the disappearance of man; this alone constitutes decadence in the theatre. *Depersonalization* has been the gravest threat to our theatre whatever its source, whether it arise from zeal for social reform or for "pure" art and esthetic formalism, whether from fascination with psychopathology or with the theatricality of the theatre. Reform-minded playwrights, writers interested in psychology rather than in man, prophets of doom for whom doom has already struck in the form of the extinction of individuality in their own work, and formalists trapped by form *per se* are equally culpable. Their intentions may be unimpeachable, but in annihilating the person in the play they go far toward annihilating the play itself.

A playwright may be as inventive as any advanced coterie could desire but contradicts the very nature of drama the moment he uses the living actor to simulate nonlife longer than the brief notion of a *Bald Soprano*. Sometimes the overzealous avant-garde not only requires the actor to become a marionette on the stage but distances him even further from life by disallowing him the privilege that even lifeless marionettes in the theatre have of *pretending* to possess life. Conversely, it is possible to put the actor on stilts, smother him in padded clothing, and clap a mask on his face, as was the case in the great tragic theatre of Greece, and yet establish life in the theatre. Seen in this light, the contemporary theatre is not in danger of being undermined by, let us say, a lurid *Street Car Named Desire* or a flagellating *Who's Afraid of Virginia Woolf?*, but by pious exercises such as Eliot's verse drama *The Family Reunion* and Yeats' beautifully written abstract one-act plays written under the influence of the Japanese Noh play. And depersonalization is but a first step in the devitalization of the theatre, which upon virtually abolishing human motivation, goes on to destroy dramatic communication by language.

I offer a single mercifully abbreviated example from a play produced by New York's most progressive group, The Living Theatre, during the 1950's. The passage is spoken by a character called Big Foot, and is apparently addressed to no one in particular:

> When you think of it there's nothing like a good old mutton stew. But I like it better with onions, or well done with wine on a day of happiness full of snow, by the meticulous and jealous care of my Hispano-Mauresque Slav slave, an albuminous servant mistress, melting into the fragrant architectures of the kitchen. Apart from the pitch and the lime of her detached considerations, there's nothing like her gaze and her chopped flesh over the calm sea of her queenly movements. . . . The turned-up shirt of beauty, her embossed bosom anchored to her bodice and the force of her tides of her charms shake the golden powder of her gaze in the nooks and crannies of the sink which stinks of the washing spread out to dry at the window of her gaze sharpened on the grindstone of her tangled hair.

The play, called *Desire Trapped by the Tail*, was written by Picasso in three days, during the first winter of the German occupation of Paris during World War II. The translator of this work, who is also a serious critic, writes unnecessarily that the play is beyond criticism. He also writes, although I don't exactly know why he does, that "In an age which has discovered man with a capital M, it is gratifying to advise the reader that Picasso has nothing to say of man, nor of the universe;" and he adds in all gravity that "This in itself is an achievement. In fact, the characters are not even human." Nor, we are assured "except for the two bowwows, are they animal." And this we are told "is a further achievement." Having learned to do without characters, we may soon learn to do without language altogether, if by language we mean coherent speech. And after that there can be only one more step, and that is to do without a play altogether in writing a play, or to write something for the stage Ionesco correctly designated as an *antiplay*—presumably with noncharacters in nonspeech!

Nor is it merely negation or anguish that pulverizes our dramatic language, an effect sometimes justified on the grounds of suiting the sound to the sense or nonsense of a character. Affirmations, too, have tended to be bizarrely inchoate when they have not been wearily monotonous. At best, the positive statements have been vaguely comforting as in the "Always spring comes again" speech at the end of O'Neill's *The Great God Brown,* or patently rhetorical in the manner of the long blank-verse speech with which Maxwell Anderson concluded *Winterset.* The character Big Foot brings Picasso's play to a conclusion with the following call to action, and presumably those who understand it will be able to rise to it: "Let's wrap the worn-out sheets in the angels' face powder and let's turn the mattress inside out in the brambles," says Big Foot. "Let's light all the lanterns. Let's throw the flights of doves against the bullets with all our might and let's close the houses, that have been demolished by the bombs, with a double lock." Following which, we are informed, "a golden sphere as tall as a man" enters. This lights up the stage and blinds the characters on it, who take out pocket handkerchiefs and bandage their eyes, calling out to each other "You!! You! You!" while on the big golden sphere appear the letters of the word "Nobody." We are lucky, of course, that it was not worse! It could have been the one-word vulgarism tapped out by a horse at the close of Cocteau's *Orpheus,* which preceded the Picasso opus by some twenty years in the French theatre during the vogue of the *first* surrealist movement.

I say the "first," because in "The Theatre of the Absurd"

dramaturgy represented in *Desire Caught by the Tail* and in other esoteric pieces like Gelber's *The Apple,* we actually have had a *second* surrealist (unless one prefers to call it a second dadaist) movement. The wheel has been turning full circle round more than one in the modern theatre. But anything is possible in the twentieth century, which has been, for better and worse, the most experimental in the history of the theatre. And anything can happen in a period in which the gap between majority and minority audiences has grown wider and wider without either of the two audiences obtaining any real relatedness to civilized values and endeavors. Although there were brief historical moments, especially during the 1920's in Europe and the 1930's in America, when integration of the theatre with reality seemed imminent, and when the majority and minority audiences seemed to be drawing together, dis-orientation and schism in the theatre brought an end to the impending harmony soon enough.

It is no wonder, then, that anthologies of significant statements by writers on their intention and their craft have bristled with avowals and disavowals. We have O'Neill asserting for some three decades the necessity of finding a unique technique for every new play and meeting this requirement himself by adhering to realistic technique in *Anna Christie, Desire Under the Elms, The Iceman Cometh,* and *Long Day's Journey into Night,* but employing expressionistic style in *The Emperor Jones* and *The Hairy Ape,* resorting to masks for split personalities in *The Great God Brown,* and reviving the Elizabethan device of the "aside" in *Strange Interlude* for psychological revelation and ironic effect. We hear O'Neill calling for "some sort of supernaturalism" to take the place of "the old naturalism," and fulminating against the routine realism he deplored as a "banality of surfaces." We hear Pirandello explaining the blending of comedy and tragedy, and the intermingling of reality and fantasy, in his most celebrated drama: "I wanted to present six characters searching for an author. Their play does not manage to get presented—precisely because the author whom they seek is missing. Presented instead is the comedy of their vain attempt with all that it contains of trag-

edy by virtue of the fact that the six characters have been rejected." Cocteau tells us that "The poet must bring objects and
feelings from behind their veils and their mists," and O'Casey, a
master of naturalism in his first three produced plays, concludes
in the preface to his fanciful *Cock-A-Doodle-Dandy* in 1958, that
"naturalism, or even realism, isn't enough," and that he broke
with Naturalism after his masterpiece *The Plough and the Stars*
because he wanted to capture for the stage "a dance, a laugh,
and song." Tennessee Williams in explaining *Camino Real*, calls
for "freedom and mobility of form" along with a flowing use of
symbolist imagery; Brecht favors "alienating" devices and disjunctive form in order to make his audience think clearly rather
than feel fuzzily; and Ionesco explains his one-act spoof, *The
Bald Soprano*, a comedy of human boredom, as "a parody of human behavior, and therefore a parody of the theatre, too," since
man's drama "is as absurd as it is painful"; and Ionesco believes
that by revealing man's absurdity one can actually "achieve a sort
of tragedy." There seems to be no end to the partial dramatic
visions and themes of craft propounded since World War I.

All this is not, of course, the sole manifestation of contemporary theatre. Otherwise there would be nothing left of the theatre
besides esoteric playwrights, coterie producers, and masochistic
audiences. Extremes of experimentation have not preempted the
theatre, even if they are to be singled out as symptoms of its morbid tendencies. We must concede, moreover, that the impulse to
depart from strict realism has tended to reconstitute modern dramatic art as well as to jeopardize it—to recover imagination for
playwriting, as well as to make full use of the theatrical possibilities of the theatre. The stalemate toward which drama and
theatre were headed with 19th century naturalism *had* to be
broken, and *was* broken. The question that should concern us is
whether contemporary playwrights and theatre artists have not
extricated themselves from one stalemate only to be thrust into
another.

Despite errors of judgment and excesses of virtuosity in numerous instances such as the indiscriminate use of atmospherics and symbolism (especially in Shakespearean productions), there have been great improvements in stage design and stage production. It cannot be said that this has been particularly the case in playwriting. Masterpieces of imaginative drama in our time have been few and far between despite the labors of such talented playwrights as O'Neill, O'Casey, Williams, Miller, Pirandello, Giraudoux, Brecht, Yeats, Eliot, and Lorca. They have not often been automatically advantaged by a transfer of allegiance to poetic, fanciful, or theatrical theatre. It is questionable, for instance, that O'Casey became a better playwright when he abandoned the realism of *Juno and the Paycock*. Contemporary playwrights have rarely, if ever, improved upon the achievements of the pioneer realists Ibsen, Strindberg, Hauptmann, and Chekhov. This has been evident for some time, and it may be a consequence of this realization that so many efforts have been made in recent years to claim these writers for every school save realism or naturalism. The hunt is on for the *symbolism* rather than the reality, for the *theatricality* rather than the central passion, of their work. And since interpretative virtuosity has become a *specialité* of American universities it has been suspiciously easy to disassociate the "old masters" from the banner of realism under which they fought so vigorously against routine romanticism. Nevertheless, it must be granted that antirealistic experimentation by contemporary playwrights has resulted in a good deal of piquant playwriting as well as in lively and arresting stage productions. At least it has spared us a good deal of the humdrum in drama and theatre and jolted us out of habitual complacencies. If all this is evidence of "decadence" according to official pronouncements of Marxist or pseudo Marxist or, for that matter, puritanical conservative criticism in America that caused a Baptist university in Texas to cancel a production of O'Neill's *Long Day's Journey Into Night* in 1962, then so much the better for "decadence" say I; and as between *decadent* theatre and *dull* theatre I would not hesitate to choose the former.

Fortunately, moreover, we have not been limited to super-ficial alternatives of health and disease. Theatricalism has not been necessarily unhealthy rather than healthy, listless rather than hearty, whether in the lowbrow art of a *Guys and Dolls* or the high-brow art of a Thornton Wilder or Bertolt Brecht. And while the current of our times has often drawn us away from real-ism, it has at times reversed direction in the case of Lorca, for example, when he wrote *The House of Bernarda Alba,* and O'Neill when he turned to the writing of *The Iceman Cometh* and *A Long Day's Journey Into Night.* Finally, it has been possi-ble in our times to reap the benefits of realism in conjunction with the rewards of imaginative structure and style. Miller dem-onstrated this in mingling remembered and current action in *Death of a Salesman,* as did Williams in *The Glass Menagerie.* Lorca blended naturalism with poetic feeling in *The House of Bernarda Alba;* and various fusions of reality and fancy have been attained by Pirandello, Beckett, Genet, Ionesco, and Pinter. Sartre in several imaginative plays and Brecht in perhaps as many as a dozen long and short pieces have presented new ways of using allegory and didacticism without undercutting so-cial realism, on the one hand, or lapsing into realistic banality, on the other.

It cannot be denied that our times have not been particularly favorable to the creation of high tragedy and high comedy, two types of dramatic literature upon which the Western theatre has frequently relied for its best effects and most significant efforts. But we must reckon with the fact that tragedy and comedy are convenient labels rather than precisely definable terms. These can be employed with rigorously limited applicability that would compel us to conclude that only the Greeks—or perhaps only Sophocles—wrote true tragedy and, at the utmost, that there have been but three periods—the classic Athenian, the Eliza-bethan, and the neoclassic French—when genuine tragedy could be written. But we can also arrive at a less confining definition of the genre that will cover *Awake and Sing!*, *Death of a Salesman*, Anouilh's *Antigone* and *The Lark*, Brendan Behan's *The Hostage*, Ugo Betti's *The Queen and the Rebels*, *Saint Joan*, *Desire under the Elms*, *Long Day's Journey into Night*, and perhaps even *A Streetcar Named Desire*. These and a number of other plays, whenever given adequate professional productions, had an effect on audiences that can be described as more or less tragic; the effect on the generality of playgoers could be said to be more or less purgative, stimulating rather than merely depressing, and paradoxically exhilarating while painful or sobering.

As for prospects for so-called high comedy or comedy of manners, these were theoretically dimmed after World War I by the instability of society, the gradual reduction of leisure-class culture, and the diffusion of a mass-media culture, which is often no culture at all. For all that, it cannot be said that there has been less readily identifiable comedy in our times than in the comparatively stable entire hundred years before 1914. The contrary seems to have been the case on various levels of distinction when one considers the record of Maugham, Coward, and James Bridie in England; of Kaufmann, Barry, and Behrman in the United States; of Zuckmayer and Brecht in Germany, and of Pagnol, Aymé, Giraudoux, Anouilh, and Ionesco in France. The practical critic can only conclude that, contrary to theory, it does seem possible to extract comedy from an unstable society as well as a stable one, and from a supposedly declining culture as well as from a supposedly ascending one. The critic would also have to observe that comedy can be mordant as well as diverting and can in the very course of losing its romantic afflatus undergo a transformation into what has been called *"dark comedy"* in the case of Shakespeare's late plays and *"realistic comedy"* in the case of Ben Jonson's work. Some species of "dark" comedy has actually enriched the contemporary theatre which has produced Cummings' *him* and Pagnol's *Topaze*, Zuckmayer's *The Captain of Koepenick*, and Brecht's *Threepenny Opera* and *A Man's a Man*, Ionesco's *The Chairs*, Beckett's *Waiting for Godot*, Albee's *American Dream*, Max Frisch's *Biedermann and the Firebugs*, and Duerrenmatt's mordant tragicomedy *The Visit*. Mixed or eclectic, as well as mordant or frivolous, comedy has been a characteristic of the contemporary theatre.

If the theatre has got nowhere very distinctly in recent decades, it has nevertheless gone off interestingly in several different directions. How this has been possible is a question it is not very difficult to answer. There has been resistance to the disintegrating influences of contemporary life despite considerable temptation to succumb to them in an age of anxiety such as the civilized world has perhaps never known before. Also, the very tensions of the times have forced upon the theatre advances as well as retreats and have been conducive at times to reconstruction, restitution, and resurgence. We witnessed such a resurgence in France after its humiliating defeat during the second world war. Some of the most striking products of this revitalization of French drama—Sartre's *The Flies* and Anouilh's *Antigone*—were actually written during the occupation of Paris by German troops. We have been experiencing, even more recently, a reinvigoration of the British theatre by young writers such as Osborne, Wesker, and Pinter who have poured vials of scorn on the old drawing-room type of drama on which the London theatre tried to subsist even after the advent of Hitler on the European scene. With flip satire in the 1920's, grave social conscience in the 1930's, and "dark comedy" disenchantment since the 1950's goading us into splutters of energy, there have been varied efforts at regeneration even in our own greatly battered American theatre, and these have been sustained to a degree by developments in off-Broadway, university, and community theatre production. Decade after decade since 1918, moreover, our theatre has been heartened by the emergence of playwrights who have been sufficient, or occasionally perhaps more than sufficient, unto their day. They succeeded in gathering up, at least for a while, the stimulus along with the distress and dismay of the times.

Above all, it is worth noting that despite economic and political conditions severer than almost any past theatre has had to face, the contemporary theatre has persisted in functioning as *theatre,* rather than as an adjunct to some other enterprise, by holding on to its precarious position as a relatively independent art. Even "show business" has hitherto managed to remain more or less hospitable to estimable native talent and to be sympathetic to experiment. Many another enterprise would have long ago called it a day whereas persons of the theatre are still looking forward to the next day, the next bout with the critics and the public, and the next miracle that they persist in expecting.

After registering his abysmal dismay, Shaw's Aubrey launches upon his conclusion: "But what next?" he asks. "Is No enough?" All he knows, he decides, is that he, the ex-clergyman, must defy the negative-mongers, even though he also knows that he is ignorant, has lost his nerve, and feels intimidated by the dire present and the direr future. But at least he is not silenced. "All I know," he declares, "is that I must find the way of life, for myself and all of us, or we shall surely perish. And meanwhile my gift has possession of me. I must preach and preach no matter how late the hour and how short the day, no matter whether I have nothing to say—or whether in some pentecostal flame of revelation the Spirit will descend on me. . . ." Aubrey could speak here for the contemporary world and the contemporary theatre; and as long as the theatre maintains the same resolution, which it still does, and possesses the same gift for talking even when it apparently has nothing more to say, it manages to say something, somehow. It tries to preserve itself for the miracles it has needed year after year for survival in an age when even mere survival can no longer be taken for granted. There is a sobering thought, at the same time, in Shaw's warning that "The author, though himself a professional talk-maker, does not believe that the world can be saved by talk alone." Neither can the theatre. But it can at last keep itself in readiness for the miracles when they happen; and they do happen, from time to time, on that place of miracles we call the stage. They continue to happen, in fact, season after season—and if not in one city then in another; if not in New York then in London, if not in London then in Paris, if not in Paris then in Berlin, Athens, or Tel Aviv. This is what the theatrical record reveals at present and is likely to reveal as long as the modern age does not succeed in exterminating itself as a recognizable civilization. The one thing we cannot, and should not, ever expect, whether in New York or in any other theatrical capital, is "The brilliant mercy of a sure repose," as Wallace Stevens might have put it, or "The total grandeur of a total edifice."

A Chronology
of Modern Theatre

I HAVE PREPARED THIS CHRONOLOGY UP TO 1965 IN THE HOPE THAT IT will provide a bird's-eye view of important developments in the theatre. The reader will note that the striving after new forms of dramatic art has been continuous and that the issues presented in the preceding essays have been of interest and of practical consequence for many years. This chronology will also, I hope, supplement the text by presenting the background of plays and stage productions upon which the argument of this book is based.

1486   Discovery of *De architectura*, Vitruvius' Latin treatise on architecture, containing a section on classic theatre (architecture, stage machinery, etc.) which proved influential in the Italian Renaissance.

1545   Sebastian Serlio's *Architettura*, containing his celebrated drawings of perspective settings for comedy, tragedy, and pastoral drama or "satyr plays." Important in the diffusion of illusionism and the use of perspective scenery in the European theatre.

1584 The Teatro Olimpico, designed by Palladio and completed by Scamozzi, built at Vicenza. This theatre was a Renaissance adaptation of the Roman stage, providing vistas through five arches; these were filled with scenery in perspective.

1605 Inigo Jones first uses changing scenery, in the form of a revolving screen "in the Italian manner," at Oxford University.

1618 (1619) Completion of the Teatro Farnese at Parma. This theatre, which contained a well-defined proscenium arch, marked the appearance of the picture-frame stage, since scenery was placed behind the proscenium. The proscenium arch also masked any scene-shifting that might occur during the course of the play, so that changes of scenery without destruction of illusion could now be attempted. However, there remained a forestage in front of the proscenium arch that was used by the actors.

1638 Publication of Nicola Sabbatini's *Pratica di fabricar scene e machine ne' teatri* (*The Practice of Making Scenes and Machines*), a description of how scenery may be changed.

Masque at Salisbury Court in London, noteworthy for the use of five changes of scene, effected behind a drop-curtain.

1656 John Webb's noteworthy use of mobile scenery for the production of William Davenant's *The Siege of Rhodes*, considered the first English opera.

1731 Drury Lane production of George Lillo's early "middle-class tragedy" *The London Merchant; or, the History of George Barnwell.*

1773–1784 "Storm and Stress" movement in the German theatre breaks down the barriers of neoclassicism, produces early Romantic plays such as Goethe's *Goetz von Berlichingen* (1773) and Schiller's *Die Räuber* (*The Robbers*) (1781), and anticipates the "liberation" of the European theatre by Victor Hugo.

1808 *Penthesilea,* Heinrich von Kleist's pathological drama of sexual passion—an anticipation of realistic, naturalistic, and expressionist ventures into psychopathology such as Strindberg's *The Father* and *Miss Julie* and Wedekind's "sex tragedies."

1811   *The Prince of Homburg,* Heinrich von Kleist's remarkable psychological Romantic drama. (Psychological interest in the romantic theatre antedated realistic psychological drama.)

1824   Founding of the Maly ("Little") Theatre in Moscow, notable for its promotion of realistic satire in the 1840's with productions of *The Inspector-General* and *Woe from Wit,* and for its promotion of the middle-class realism of Ostrovsky from about 1855 to 1885. (The Maly became known as the "House of Ostrovsky" as a result of the long association of the author and the theatre.)

Theatrical realism introduced into England by J. R. Planché's authentic-costume production of *King John* at Covent Garden, Jan. 19, 1824.

1827   Victor Hugo's preface to *Cromwell,* which was a rejection of vestigial neoclassic principles of dramatic art, a program for Romantic theatre, and a charter of freedom for all subsequent playwriting.

1830   The "Battle of *Hernani."* The French classicists in the theatre are routed by the Romanticists under the leadership of Hugo, Gautier, and others.

1831   Madame Vestris assumes the management of the Olympic Theatre in London and inaugurates scenic changes leading to surface realism in English décor.

1835   Georg Büchner's seminaturalistic, semiexpressionistic historical drama *Dantons Tod* (*Danton's Death*); first published in 1873 and first produced in 1916 by Max Reinhardt. (Produced at Orson Welles's Mercury Theatre in New York in 1938.)

1836   Büchner's remarkable naturalistic, yet also expressionistic, fragment *Woyzeck.* First published in 1879; first staged in 1913. Best known as basis for Alban Berg's modernist opera *Wozzeck,* 1925.

Russian Court Theatre première of Gogol's celebrated early social satire *Revizor* (*The Inspector-General*).

1841 A box set is used in the production of Boucicault's *London Assurance* at the Olympic Theatre in London under the management of Madame Vestris. "Instead of representing an interior scene by a series of wings set one behind the other, the scene shifters now built the side walls of a room solidly from front to rear; and the actors were made to enter, not by walking through the wings, but by opening actual doors that turned upon their hinges." (Clayton Hamilton, *The Theory of the Theatre*, Henry Holt, 1939, p. 46). But the apron stage still remained.

1844 Friedrich Hebbel's realistic middle-class tragedy *Maria Magdalena*.

1850 Charles Kean takes over the management of the Princess Theatre in London and provides pictorial realism in England throughout the decade.

1855 *Le Fils naturel* (*The Illegitimate Son*), the first of the younger Alexander Dumas' sermonizing realistic "problem plays."

1865 The production of T. W. ("Tom") Robertson's *Society*, the early semirealistic social drama at the Prince of Wales Theatre. The production of this play and of Robertson's *Caste* (1867) successfully introduced realistic stage practice into England.

1867 *Peer Gynt*, the climax of Ibsen's Romantic phase and the high point of social criticism in his *poetic* writing.

1868 Preface to *A Prodigal Father* by Dumas *fils*. A ringing call for an "engaged" drama rather than dramatic legerdemain in the manner of the midcentury's most successful playwright Scribe, called by Dumas a shadow-Shakespeare "expert at manipulating characters that had no life." Dumas called for a dramatist "who knows *man* as Balzac did, and the theatre as Scribe did."

1871 Rimbaud's Letter of May 15, which may be considered an anticipation of surrealism. Among Rimbaud's points in that letter were that poets should not try to *explain* experience, and that words are to be regarded as *myths*—they are "not understandable in any ordinary sense."

1873   Émile Zola's Preface to *Thérèse Raquin*, the first important manifesto of naturalism for the theatre, predicting that "the experimental and scientific spirit of the century will enter the domain of the drama," and calling for an inquiry into "the two-fold life of the character and its environment."

1873–1893   Development of naturalism in the major European theatres.

1874   The Meiningen Company (1874–1890), pioneering in real-istic scenic detail and in ensemble performance, especially in the realistic management of crowds, succeeds in Berlin with productions of *Julius Caesar* and *As You Like It*.

1875   Henry Becque's naturalistic drama *Les Corbeaux* (*The Vultures*), first produced in 1882.

Edward William Godwin (1833–1886), architect, archaeologist, and designer, father of Edith and Gordon Craig, designs the production of *The Merchant of Venice* in which Ellen Terry played Portia. In this production Godwin introduced solid ar-chitectural settings, platforms, and steps.

1876   Wagner's Bayreuth Theatre established, with emphasis upon provision for Wagner's "mystic gulf" between the stage and the audience; this was accomplished by putting the pit for the opera orchestra in front of the stage. The "mystic gulf" was intended to "distance" the stage action and so promote the ideality of Wagnerian music drama. Romanticism in this in-stance helped to promote the picture-frame theatre and to sepa-rate the actor from the auditorium and the spectator from the stage.

The Meiningen Company produces Ibsen's historical tragedy *The Pretenders* in a historically realistic manner in Berlin.

1877   *The Pillars of Society*, the play with which Ibsen began his social criticism in prose drama.

1878   Henry Irving starts his management of the Lyceum Thea-tre, where even Shakespeare's plays were subordinated to scenic realism.

1879   Eleonora Duse makes her debut at the Teatro Fiorentini in Naples and scores a great success in Zola's naturalistic drama *Thérèse Raquin.*

Ibsen starts his influential realistic phase with *A Doll's House,* followed by *Ghosts* in 1881 and *An Enemy of the People* in 1882.

Augustin Daly's New York production of *L'Assomoir* (*Drink*), the early and unsuccessful venture in naturalism in the American theatre; and David Belasco's successful production of the same play in San Francisco.

(Nov. 1)   Henry Irving's Lyceum Theatre production of *The Merchant of Venice,* a milestone in "picturesque realism."

1880   Production of Ibsen's *The Pillars of Society* in London, at the Gaiety Theatre, in a translation by William Archer.

Steele MacKaye uses an elevator stage for changing settings at the rebuilt Madison Square Theatre in New York.

1880–1887   Electricity installed in the most important theatres of Europe and America, increasing the effectiveness of lighting for both naturalistic and atmospheric purposes.

1881   The Meiningen Company visits London.

Zola's collection of essays, *Le Naturalisme au théâtre* (*Naturalism in the Theatre*), which set down a naturalistic program for the stage.

1883   The first German translation of *Ghosts.*

Establishment of the Deutsches Theater in Berlin under Adolf L'Arronge.

Henry Irving goes to America, introducing his realistically set productions which apparently influenced Augustin Daly and David Belasco.

1884   Ibsen enters upon a more or less "symbolist" phase with *The Wild Duck.* This play was followed by *Rosmersholm* (1886), *The Lady from the Sea* (1888), *The Master Builder* (1892), *Little Eyolf* (1894), *John Gabriel Borkman* (1896), and *When We Dead Awaken* (1897–1899).

1885   Becque's naturalistic comedy, *La Parisienne.*

1886 (April 14)   First production of *Ghosts* in Germany at the Stadttheater in Augsburg.

1887   *The Father,* the beginning of Strindberg's realistic work in the theatre.

André Antoine establishes the first outpost of naturalism, the Théâtre Libre, in Paris. The theatre ends its career in 1894 and Antoine carries his influence first into the commercial Théâtre Antoine and then into the state-subsidized theatre, the Odéon.

1888   Strindberg's naturalist drama *Miss Julie.* The author's foreword to that play is an important document in the development of realism and naturalism. Strindberg declared that "the psychologic process is what interests people most today."

1889   Die Freie Bühne founded in Berlin along the lines of the Théâtre Libre; designed as an outpost of realism and naturalism by Otto Brahm and prominent associates.

First successful English production of a realistic drama by Ibsen: *A Doll's House* presented at the Novelty Theatre, London.

1890   James A. Herne's *Margaret Fleming,* the first American realistic drama.

Beginning of Max Burckhard's term (lasting until January 1898) as director of the Burgtheater in Vienna; this period was distinguished by productions of both naturalistic and symbolist plays by Ibsen, Hauptmann, and Schnitzler.

The beginning of the Volksbühne, the German People's Theatre, supported chiefly by the German trade-union movement— an indication that modern realism had made the theatre matter to the forward-looking social movements. In 1930, the Volksbühne had 500,000 subscription members and had membership groups in about 300 German cities.

(May 30)   *Ghosts* produced at the Théâtre Libre, with Antoine playing the role of Oswald.

1891   Publication of Shaw's *Quintessence of Ibsenism,* providing a Shavian exegesis of Ibsen's plays, important not only for its championship of Ibsen's realism but for interpreting that realism as "critical" or "intellectual" rather than as the realism of photographic detail. First delivered as a lecture for the Fabian Society of England on July 18, 1890. Enlarged for republication in 1913.

Théâtre d'Art founded at the Salle Montparnasse in Paris for the promotion of antinaturalism; more or less symbolist drama was produced. Antoine's comment: "a good thing, for the Théâtre Libre is not enough . . . I don't see any competition there, but a complement in the evolution which is going ahead." (Diary, Jan. 17, 1891.)

(April 27)   Antoine produces Ibsen's *The Wild Duck* at the Théâtre Libre, declaring, "Just as I was the first to open my doors wide to the Naturalist drama, so I shall open them wide also to Symbolist drama." (*See entries for 1907 and 1908,* Moscow Art Theatre, *below.*)

1891–1897   Duration of J. T. Grein's pioneering small subscription theatre, the Independent Theatre, in London, which produced such naturalistic plays as Zola's *Thérèse Raquin* and Shaw's *Widowers' Houses.*

1892   Adolphe Appia's designs for *The Valkyrie,* exemplary for modern scenic art because of their achievement of "plastic unity of effect in space."

Berlin production of Hauptmann's *Die Weber* (*The Weavers*).

The Independent Theatre stages Shaw's first play, *Widowers' Houses.*

An Italian version of *Ghosts* is played in Florence by Ermete Zacconi.

Production of José Echegaray's pseudo-Ibsenite play about hereditary venereal disease in terms of Spanish life, *El hijo de Don Juan* (*The Son of Don Juan*).

1893   First performance of an Ibsen play in Spain; *An Enemy of the People* produced in a Castilian version, *Un enemígo del pueblo,* in Barcelona.

(May)   The successful London production of Pinero's quasi-Ibsenite drama *The Second Mrs. Tanqueray.*

Antoine's productions of Strindberg's *Miss Julie* and Hauptmann's "mass drama" *The Weavers* at the Théâtre Libre.

Otto Brahm, leader of German naturalism and founder of the Freie Bühne, becomes director of the Deutsches Theater, the foremost theatre in Berlin.

Hanneles Himmelfahrt (*The Assumption of Hannele*), Hauptmann's synthesis of naturalism and symbolism.

Shaw's *Mrs. Warren's Profession,* the first marked synthesis in English theatre of naturalism and discussion drama.

Lugné-Poë, a former actor for Antoine at the Théâtre Libre, takes charge of the Théâtre d'Art, renaming it the Théâtre de L'Oeuvre. Its first production was Maeterlinck's crepuscular love-tragedy *Pelléas et Mélisande.*

1893–1897   William Archer's dramatic criticism for *The World,* in which he championed the modern realistic theatre and the "new drama" of Ibsen and other realists.

1894   Brahm becomes manager of the Deutsches Theater, the leading theatre in Berlin—a victory for realism and naturalism in Central Europe.

William Poel's founding of the Elizabethan Stage Society, which gave non-naturalistic, more or less presentational, "Elizabethan" productions under Poel's direction from 1895 to 1905.

1895   Adolphe Appia's *La Mise en scène du drame Wagnérien* (*The Staging of Wagnerian Music-Drama*), published in Paris.

1895–1898   Shaw's dramatic criticism written for *The Saturday Review,* now collected in *Our Theatre in the Nineties,* noteworthy for Shaw's championship of critical realism, chiefly Ibsen's; for his attack on the old-fashioned drama of intrigue (as exemplified by Victorien Sardou—"Sardoodledom") and pseudo-Ibsenism (as exemplified by Pinero's *The Second Mrs. Tanqueray* and *The Notorious Mrs. Ebbsmith*), and on the

Henry Irving and Beerbohm-Tree method of producing Shakespeare's plays with solid realistic scenery while butchering the text in order to reduce the number of scene changes.

1896   The revolving stage is introduced into the German theatre by Karl Lautenschläger. As a result, it became possible to produce multi-scened plays with ease.

Production of Jacinto Benavente's *Gente conocida* (*In Society*), marking the beginning of his career as the leader of Spanish social realism.

The founding of the Teatre Independent in Barcelona and the production of *Ghosts* in a Catalan translation.

William Poel's production of *Doctor Faustus* at St. George Hall, London, on a reproduction of the stage of the Fortune Theatre of Elizabethan times.

Miguel Unamuno's *La regeneración del teatro español* (*The Regeneration of the Spanish Theatre*), a plea for the development of a "drama of ideas" in Spain.

Adolphe Appia's designs for *Parsifal*.

Maurice Maeterlinck's symbolist "static drama" manifesto, *Le Tragique quotidien* (*The Tragical in Daily Life*): "Here we are no longer with the barbarians, nor is the man now fretting himself in the midst of elementary passions . . . *he is at rest.* . . . It is no longer a violent, exceptional moment of life that passes before our eyes—it is *life itself.*" Maeterlinck also stressed the importance of "unnecessary dialogue" (that is, dialogue that is valuable even if it does not advance action): "a poem draws the nearer to beauty and loftier truth in the measure that it eliminates words that merely explain the action."

(Dec. 10)   Production at the Théâtre de L'Oeuvre in Paris of Alfred Jarry's presurrealistic parody of conventional tragedy, *Ubu Roi*, a product of the symbolist movement in the field of comedy and satire. (King Ubu, the hero of the play, is a sort of super-marionette of the comic stage in his coarse "bourgeois" typicality.)

1897   Schnitzler's naturalistic drama dealing with "the death-dance of love," *Reigen* (*Hands Around; La Ronde*).

Antoine establishes the Théâtre Antoine in Paris.

Cyrano de Bergerac. Neoromanticism wins a major victory in the theatre with the elder Coquelin's Paris production of Rostand's play.

1898   The Teatre Intim, an *avant-garde* theatre, founded by Adrián Gaul in Barcelona.

The Moscow Art Theatre founded by Konstantin Stanislavsky (1865–1938) and Vladimir Nemirovich-Danchenko (1859–1943).

Strindberg's *To Damascus*, marking the beginning of his expressionist phase in playwriting, as well as the beginning of expressionism in the modern theatre.

The beginning of Chekhov's association with the Moscow Art Theatre as a result of its successful production of *The Sea-Gull*.

1899   Appia's *Die Musik und die Inszenierung* published in Munich. ("Music and the Scene" does not translate the original title satisfactorily, since *Inszenierung* means the total staging.)

The Stage Society of London, organized by leaders of English literature and theatre, opens with a production of Shaw's *You Never Can Tell*. (1938–1939 was the last season of this progressive group.)

The beginning of the Irish Literary Theatre in Dublin; later becomes successively the Irish National Dramatic Company, the Irish National Theatre Society, and the Abbey Theatre.

(March 20)   *Ghosts* produced in Spain by the Teatre Intim in Barcelona.

1901–1906   Mrs. Fiske's management in New York of the Manhattan Theatre, where she produced *Hedda Gabler, Rosmersholm,* and other important plays.

1902 The Moscow Art Theatre's celebrated production of Gorki's naturalist drama *The Lower Depths*.

(April 2–4) First productions of the Irish National Dramatic Company, headed by W. G. Fay, in Dublin. The program consisted of A.E.'s *Deirdre* and Yeats's *Kathleen ni Houlihan*, with Maud Gonne playing Kathleen.

Stephen Phillips' neoromantic verse drama *Paolo and Francesca*, believed to mark the beginning of a renascence of poetic drama in England which failed to materialize.

The Dream Play, Strindberg's important symbolist-expressionist drama, published in Stockholm; first produced there in 1907.

Meyerhold breaks with Stanislavskian realism and leaves the Moscow Art Theatre, where he had been an actor from its beginnings.

Reinhardt starts his career at the Kleines Theater in Berlin with works by Strindberg, Wedekind, Gorki, and Wilde.

1903 Gordon Craig's designs for Ellen Terry's production of Ibsen's romantic drama *The Vikings*, in which Craig first succeeded in putting his theories into practice.

Reinhardt stages Maeterlinck's symbolist drama *Pelléas et Mélisande* at the Neues Theater in Berlin.

Guillaume Apollinaire's *Les Mamelles de Tirésias* (*The Breasts of Tiresias*), which Apollinaire, denouncing realism in his preface to the work, called *un drame surréaliste*. This was possibly the first use of the term "surrealism."

1904 (Dec. 27) The curtain is rung up for the first time at the Abbey Theatre in Dublin. The program included premières of Yeats's neoromantic one-act verse drama *On Baile's Strand* and of Lady Gregory's one-act peasant farce in Irish dialect, *Spreading the News*.

Reinhardt starts his experiments in stylized production at the Deutsches Theater in Berlin.

The Abbey Theatre's production of John Millington Synge's *Riders to the Sea*.

1904–1907 The Barker-Vedrenne management at the Court Theatre in London, where important modern productions of plays by Shakespeare, Shaw, Galsworthy, and other modern writers were given under the direction of Harley Granville-Barker (1877–1946).

1905 Publication of Gordon Craig's first influential essay, "The Art of the Theatre."

(Oct. 31) Arnold Daly presents *Mrs. Warren's Profession* in New York for one evening before the production is forced to suspend by the police. The play is denounced in the New York press; Norman Hapgood of the New York *Herald* declares that "You cannot have a clean pig stye . . ."

Max Reinhardt's spectacular Berlin production of *A Midsummer Night's Dream*. Reinhardt is made director of the Deutsches Theater.

1906 Meyerhold joins the actress-manager Komisarjevskaya in St. Petersburg and directs poetic productions for her, such as Andreyev's symbolist drama *The Life of Man*. In this year also, Meyerhold removed the front curtain from the stage for an antinaturalistic production of *Ghosts*.

Mrs. Fiske's production of Langdon Mitchell's "modern" comedy on divorce, *The New York Idea,* in New York.

Reinhardt opens an intimate "chamber-theatre," the Kammerspiele, for experimental productions; he produces Frank Wedekind's naturalist-expressionist drama *The Awakening of Spring* there.

1906–1916 Antoine's directorship of the state-subsidized Odéon theatre.

1907 The Abbey Theatre's production of Synge's *The Playboy of the Western World.*

The Moscow Art Theatre stages Leonid Andreyev's decidedly "symbolist" allegory *The Life of Man.* (The citadel of modern realism responds to the vogue of symbolist drama.)

The Ghost Sonata (also translated as *The Spook Sonata*), Strindberg's famous expressionist drama, published in Stockholm; produced there in 1908.

The Intimate Theatre (Intima Teatern) established by August Strindberg and August Falck in Stockholm for modernistic experimentation; controlled by Strindberg until 1910. (Strindberg wrote *The Ghost Sonata* for this theatre.)

1907–1913   The Pilgrim Players, an amateur company in Birmingham, England, produces experimental plays.

1907–1917   The vogue of "Belascoism," or sensationally pictorial naturalism, in the American theatre.

1907–1921   The Manchester Repertory Company: Miss A. E. F. Horniman maintains an important company at the Gaiety Theatre in Manchester for the production of provocative realistic plays. Among the productions were Stanley Houghton's *Hindle Wakes* (1912), St. John Ervine's *Jane Clegg* (1913), and Harold Brighouse's *Hobson's Choice.*

1908   Jaroslav Kvapil, translator of Ibsen, but also a Shakespearean producer, becomes chief director of the Czech National Theatre in Prague for a decade.

The Moscow Art Theatre stages Maeterlinck's fantasy *The Blue Bird.* "Those who think that we sought for Naturalism on the stage are mistaken," wrote Stanislavsky, complaining that the Art Theatre inclined toward naturalism because "spiritual technique was only in its embryo stage among the actors of our company." It is quite clear from Stanislavsky's (and also Antoine's) attitude, expressed as early as 1890, that the specialists in naturalistic drama would have become symbolists if symbolism had given birth to plays capable of sustaining a vital theatre.

(May 17)   Opening of the Munich Künstlertheater (Artists' Theatre), founded by the critic Georg Fuchs in association with the architect Max Littman and the scene designer Fritz Erler. Designed for formal and imaginative presentation of plays rather than for peepshow theatre, with some presentational stylization assured by bringing out the acting area—a narrow shelf for presentational stage production rather than a deep area that would lend itself to the representation of environment.

Gordon Craig settles in Florence and starts his magazine *The Mask.*

1908–1923 George Jean Nathan writes drama criticism for *Smart Set* magazine, combats "Belascoism," and champions imaginative and stimulating theatre.

1909 Production in Rome of Sem Benelli's successful neoromantic drama *La Cena delle beffe* (*The Jest*).

Diaghilev takes the Ballets Russes to Paris, introducing the Western theatre to the possibilities of the dance for dramatic effect and exhibiting an impressive synthesis of the arts of dancing, music, and painting.

Belasco's naturalistic production of Eugene Walter's *The Easiest Way,* an unusually naturalistic American drama.

1910 Stravinsky's *L'Oiseau de feu* (*The Firebird*) is presented by Diaghilev's Ballets Russes; and Léon Bakst's painted scenery wins the acclaim which starts a reversal of the theatre's hostile attitude toward the use of painted scenery ever since the advent of realism.

Max Reinhardt's productions of *Oedipus the King* and the pantomime *Sumurûn,* for which Reinhardt, having noted the use of runways in the Japanese Kabuki theatre, used them to break the fourth-wall convention and reunite the actors and the audience.

First German expressionist group in the theatre, the Sturmbühne, starts giving matinees of expressionist plays by August Stramm, Lothar Schreyer, and Oskar Kokoschka.

1911 Gordon Craig designs the Moscow Art Theatre production of *Hamlet,* using a combination of abstract convex screens of great height. These, according to Stanislavsky, "hinted at architectural forms, corners, niches, streets, alleys, halls, towers, and so on."

Publication of Gordon Craig's book *On the Art of the Theatre*. Presentation of Stravinsky's *Petrouchka*, the masterpiece of the Ballets Russes.

The beginning of the Liverpool Repertory Theatre, especially noteworthy as a school of acting.

The Max Reinhardt production of *The Miracle*, for which the interior of the Olympia Theatre in London was redesigned as a cathedral.

1912 Lugné-Poë's Parisian production of Paul Claudel's symbolist drama *L'Annonce faite à Marie*. Produced 10 years later in New York by the Theatre Guild as *The Tidings Brought to Mary*.

Constructivist sculpture (by Pevsner, Gabo, and others) makes its appearance; it is nonrepresentational and consists chiefly of a balance of planes.

A venture in Oriental stylization in the popular American theatre—the production of the Hazelton and Benrimo play *The Yellow Jacket*.

George Pierce Baker starts the 47 Workshop at Harvard. (Baker subsequently, in 1925, establishes the Yale School of Drama.)

The Chicago Little Theatre, devoted to dramatic experimentation, is founded by Maurice Brown and Ellen Van Volkenburg.

Reinhardt's production of the Oriental pantomime *Sumurûn* is brought to New York; an introduction to modern theatricalist style.

The experimental Toy Theatre established in Boston.

1913 Benavente's naturalistic psychological drama *La malquerida* (*The Passion Flower*), an important work of naturalism in the Spanish theatre.

(Feb. 5)   Opening of the Birmingham Repertory Theatre, which continued the experimental work of the Pilgrim Players.

Collaboration of Appia and Jacques Dalcroze at the latter's school in Hellerau, near Dresden, where Appia was able to make use of some of his ideas on scene design in simplified productions of Gluck's *Orpheus* and Claudel's *The Tidings Brought to Mary*. The stage, which had hardly any furniture, was simply a three-level platform with connecting steps. There was no distinction between the lighting of stage and auditorium.

Vittorio Podrecca establishes his famous marionette theatre, the Teatro dei Piccoli, an important theatricalist venture, in Rome. Puppets were used at first.

Winthrop Ames's Broadway production of the symbolist play *Prunella*, by Granville-Barker and Laurence Housman.

Louis Jouvet joins the Théâtre du Vieux Colombier as actor and stage manager.

Publication of Gordon Craig's *Towards a New Theatre*.

Choreography by Nijinsky of Stravinsky's *Le Sacre du printemps* in Cubist style.

)13–1916   Shaw writes *Heartbreak House*, a notable fusion of social realism and symbolism.

)14   The Kamerny (Chamber) Theatre established by Alexander Tairov for the creation of a "synthetic theatre" combining all the arts. It was rebuilt in 1930 and made larger.

)15 (Jan. 27)   Robert Edmond Jones presents an influential antinaturalistic setting for the Granville-Barker production of *The Man Who Married a Dumb Wife*, by Anatole France, in New York City.

Manifesto of the Futurist Synthetic Theatre in Italy.

(Feb. 19)   The Washington Square Players open the first season of their art theatre at the small Bandbox Theatre in New

York under the leadership of Edward Goodman, Lawrence Langner, Philip Moeller, Rollo Peters, Lee Simonson, and Helen Westley. The *pièce de resistance* of their first program, made up of *avant-garde* one-acters, was Maeterlinck's mood-piece *Interior*.

The Provincetown Players give their first production on a wharf in Provincetown, Mass., where they continue to stage plays during the next two summers. The group is headed by George Cram Cook, Susan Glaspell, Robert Edmond Jones, and Eugene O'Neill.

The Neighborhood Playhouse is founded in New York's East Side district by the Misses Alice and Irene Lewisohn. This notable experimental theatre existed until 1927.

D. W. Griffith's film *The Birth of a Nation*. The pictorial possibilities of the cinema soon made stage naturalism seem inadequate and superfluous.

1916   John Williams' successful Broadway production of Galsworthy's *Justice*, with John Barrymore playing the lead—a triumph for realism in the American theatre.

The founding of the Arts and Crafts Theatre by Sam Hume in Detroit, and of *Theatre Arts Magazine* as a quarterly dedicated to the propagation of advanced ideas of dramatic art. Symbolist design receives special attention in this periodical.

First production by Max Reinhardt of Georg Büchner's *Dantons Tod* (*Danton's Death*), written in 1835.

From Morn to Midnight, Georg Kaiser's celebrated expressionist drama of a bank cashier's blind search for freedom and sympathy in a hollow and meretricious society.

Luigi Chiarelli's *La maschera e il volto* (*The Mask and the Face*) produced in Rome—an important step in the development of the "school of the grotesque" which became internationally important through the more or less theatricalist plays of Pirandello.

Alexander Bakshy's manifesto of theatricalism *The Theatre Unbound*, published in 1923.

First manifesto of dadaism issued at Zurich.

The Cleveland Playhouse starts its course of experimental theatre under Raymond O'Neill; later, after 1921, it is directed by Frederic McConnell.

The Washington Square Players produce Maeterlinck's symbolist play *Aglavaine and Sylvette* and Chekhov's realistic masterpiece *The Sea-Gull* in New York.

1917   The Washington Square Players present Andreyev's symbolist drama *The Life of Man* in New York.

Founding of the Pasadena Playhouse, a progressive community theatre in California, by Gilmor Brown.

Founding in Moscow of the Hebrew company, the Habima, famous for its grotesque theatricalist style, especially in the production of *The Dybbuk* (1922), staged by Vakhtangov. The company has been resident in Palestine since 1931.

Production of Guillaume Apollinaire's *Les Mamelles de Tirésias* (*The Breasts of Tiresias*), a surrealist "play," in Paris.

Parade, Jean Cocteau's surrealist ballet, with music by Satie and designs by Picasso.

1917–1919   Copeau, Jouvet, and the Théâtre du Vieux Colombier company appear in New York for two seasons.

1917 (Dec.)–1920   Reinhardt produces expressionist dramas such as Reinhard Sorge's *Der Bettler* (*The Beggar*) and Reinhard Goering's *Seeschlacht* (*Sea Battle*) for the *avant-garde* group called Das junge Deutschland (Young Germany).

1918   The Washington Square Players produce *Mrs. Warren's Profession* in New York without running into difficulties with censorship.

The Provincetown Players take over a disused stable on Macdougal Street in Greenwich Village and name it the Provincetown Playhouse.

The Carolina Playmakers, founded by Frederick H. Koch at the University of North Carolina, starts its noteworthy career in creating regional theatre.

1918–1920   Kaiser's expressionist drama *Gas I* and *II*, a nightmare picture of the industrialization of society.

1919   *The Cabinet of Dr. Caligari*, a German film which represents the peak of expressionism in scene design and plot. (Followed by *The Golem*, 1920, and *Metropolis*, 1926.)

(Nov. 28)   The opening of Reinhardt's Grosses Schauspielhaus, a circus-like theatre in Berlin adapted for presentational stage-production on a large scale.

Founding of the Theatre Guild in New York.

1919–1925   Leopold Jessner directs the Berlin State Theatre and promotes expressionism with dynamic productions of Schiller's *Wilhelm Tell* and Wedekind's *Marquis of Keith*, staged, in the main, on steep ramps of stairs (*Jessnertreppen*).

1919–1926   The Phoenix Theatre of London becomes notable for its revival of Elizabethan and Restoration drama.

1920   *Le Boeuf sur le toit, ou The Nothing Happens Bar*, a surrealist pantomime on which Cocteau, Milhaud, and Dufy collaborated. Played by the Fratellini clowns at the Comédie des Champs-Elysées. (Clowning in any form has been highly acclaimed by the *avant-garde*, which has revolted against the rationalistic and practical-minded theatre of realism. Clowning was especially attractive to surrealists as an incursion of the irrational into the theatre. They favored the circus and had their unofficial headquarters in Paris near the Cirque Medrano.)

The Provincetown Players' production of O'Neill's *The Emperor Jones*, especially noteworthy for its expressionistic technique and the use of sound (the sound of the tom-toms) in the creation of tension.

The Hopkins-Barrymore *Richard III* in New York, with symbolist designs by Robert Edmond Jones.

First production of the music studio of the Moscow Art Theatre, Lecocq's satire *The Daughter of Madame Angot.*

The founding of the Salzburg Festival by Max Reinhardt, opened by the production of Hofmannsthal's *Jedermann* on a platform in front of the Salzburg Cathedral, whose portals and baroque statuary served as the main background.

1921   Adolphe Appia's *L'Oeuvre d'art vivant* (*The Work of Living Art*) published in Geneva and Paris.

Karel Hugo Hilar (1884–1935), an important expressionist and theatricalist, becomes director of the Czech National Theatre. Among his associates was the famous constructivist scene-designer A. Heythum.

Pirandello's theatricalist masterpiece *Sei personaggi in cerca d'autore* (*Six Characters in Search of an Author*).

Vakhantagov's famous theatricalist production of *Princess Turandot* in ironic harlequinade style, with actors introducing themselves to the audience and costuming themselves in public, with settings shifted in public by stagehands who burlesque the play. An example of "joyous" or "gay" theatricalism, and of Oriental stylization.

Famous expressionist production of Ernst Toller's *Masse-Mensch* (*Man and the Masses*) by Jürgen Fehling at the Volksbühne in Berlin, with designs by Hans Strohbach. Produced later by the New York Theatre Guild with direction and settings by Lee Simonson.

Meyerhold's production of the Belgian poet Verhaeren's symbolist drama *Les Aubes* (*Dawn*), written in 1898, in a constructivist style. (Constructivism had been anticipated by Meyerhold in 1914 in his production of Alexander Blok's poetic drama *The Unknown.*)

The Arthur Hopkins and Robert Edmond Jones symbolist production of *Macbeth,* in which environment was dissolved into a black background, with masks and arches used as scenic properties mainly to suggest the "soul" of the play.

1922 *The Dybbuk* (written in 1914) performed in grotesque, Oriental theatricalist manner by the Habima Theatre in a production directed by Vakhtangov.

Théâtre de l'Atelier established in Paris by Copeau's celebrated associate Charles Dullin (1885–1949).

Pirandello's theatricalist psychological drama *Enrico IV* (*Henry IV*); produced in New York in 1922 as *The Living Mask*.

Karel and Josef Capek's *Insect Comedy* (literally, "the comedy of insects").

The Provincetown Players' production of O'Neill's *The Hairy Ape,* characterized by symbolist and expressionist techniques.

The Theatre Guild's complete production of Shaw's *Back to Methuselah* at the Garrick Theatre in New York.

Reinhardt converts an imperial ballroom into a little theatre, the Redoutensaal, for formalistic intimate productions.

Cocteau's *Antigone,* performed in Renaissance costume, with music by Honegger and designs by Picasso; the text, a trimmed-down, "cooled-off," deliberately dry version of Sophocles' play.

1923 *Saint Joan,* in which Shaw proved that the impossible was possible by turning discussion drama into high tragedy.

The Theatre Guild production of Elmer Rice's expressionist fantasy *The Adding Machine,* with famous expressionist settings by Lee Simonson. Also, John Howard Lawson's expressionist social drama, *Roger Bloomer,* produced in New York.

The successful and apparently influential Pitoëff production of *Six Characters in Search of an Author* in Paris.

Tairov's playful use of constructivist theatricalism in the production of *The Man Who Was Thursday,* adapted from a novel by G. K. Chesterton.

Production by the Moscow Art Theatre Musical Studio (not an opera company, but a theatre whose actors sang) of Aristophanes' *Lysistrata,* with "musical theatrical realism."

1924   Arthur Hopkins' celebrated realistic production of *What Price Glory?* by Laurence Stallings and Maxwell Anderson.

The Winthrop Ames production of *Beggar on Horseback* by George S. Kaufman and Marc Connelly—the first popular Broadway adaptation of expressionism in the American theatre. Production of *Desire Under the Elms,* in which O'Neill fused naturalism and symbolism, in New York.

The Moscow Art Theatre Musical Studio production of *Carmencita and the Soldier* in the style of "musical theatrical realism" instead of in the operatic manner usually employed in staging *Carmen.* (The Hammerstein Negro version *Carmen Jones* in the 1940's was an adaptation of "musical theatrical realism" as inaugurated in Nemirovich-Danchenko's studio.)

(March 3)   The Abbey Theatre production of O'Casey's *Juno and the Paycock,* a modern mingling of comedy and tragedy, and also a distinguished example of the fusion of naturalism and poetic dialogue.

André Breton's first Manifesto of Surrealism, with emphasis on "pure psychic automatism" requiring the elimination of intellectual, moral, and esthetic factors from the creative process.

1924–1934   Louis Jouvet is actor-manager at the Comédie des Champs-Élysées.

1925   The Theatre Guild production of John Howard Lawson's theatricalist *Processional,* a "jazz-symphony" of social conflict and confusion. A notable feature of this production was Mordecai Gorelik's theatricalist setting, the main element of which was an extravagantly painted vaudeville backdrop of a mining town.

Art Theatre at the Teatro Odescalchi founded by Pirandello in Rome.

Hallie Flanagan Davis becomes director of the Vassar Experimental Theatre, noted for its work in stylization. (Her administration lasted until 1935, when she became director of the Federal Theatre.)

Alban Berg's opera *Wozzeck,* based on Büchner's dramatic fragment *Woyzeck* (1936).

(Oct. 30)   The opening of the Gate Theatre in London; this "private" (hence uncensored) theatre, under Peter Godfrey's leadership, produced modernistic experiments, such as Kaiser's *From Morn to Midnight,* Toller's *Hinkemann,* and Evreinov's *The Theatre of the Soul,* until 1940.

1926 (Feb. 8)   The Abbey Theatre production of O'Casey's *The Plough and the Stars,* an important group, or mass, drama.

The Pitoëff production of Cocteau's surrealist drama *Orphée* at the Théâtre des Arts in Paris, with Georges Pitoëff as Orpheus and Ludmilla Pitoëff as Euridice. It should be noted that the meaning of a play like *Orphée* cannot be unraveled—it is, indeed, not supposed to be unraveled: "In symbolism, the chemistry was too conscious of its means and ends. Surrealism tries to go beyond the elaborate consciousness of symbolism . . . to the very sleep in which the myths of man are preserved" (Wallace Fowlie, *The Age of Surrealism,* Denver, A. Swallow, 1950, p. 140).

The New York production of O'Neill's *The Great God Brown,* especially noteworthy for the formalistic use of masks to symbolize modern man's dual personality.

Constructivist and theatricalist productions of O'Neill's *The Hairy Ape* and *Desire Under the Elms* at Tairov's Kamerny Theatre.

Meyerhold's famous theatricalist production of Gogol's satire *The Inspector-General*—a combination of constructivism, expressionism, and naturalism with a semicircular permanent setting and a smaller movable stage.

The Cambridge Festival Theatre founded in England by Terence Gray, who declared: "We are the theatre theatrical. We don't want the wisest or the most foolish member of our audience to play at visual make-believe or ever to forget that the stage is only the stage." Gray dispensed with the proscenium—"the width of the stage was the width of the auditorium itself."

1926–1933   Eva Le Gallienne's Civic Repertory Company in New York. It became noted for productions of plays by Ibsen, Chekhov, Martinez-Sierra, and other Europeans.

1927   Jacques Copeau stages his dramatization of *The Brothers Karamazov* for the Theatre Guild in New York.

The Theatre Guild production of Dorothy and Du Bose Heyward's *Porgy*, staged by Rouben Mamoulian. An important step in the retheatricalization of the "serious" theatre.

Erwin Piscator takes over the management of the Theater-am-Nollendorfplatz in Berlin for productions in "epic theatre" style.

1927–1928   Reinhardt's season in New York.

1928   The association of Giraudoux and Jouvet starts with Jouvet's production of Giraudoux' anti-war (and somewhat Pirandellian) drama of *Siegfried*. Then followed Jouvet's productions of *Amphitryon 38, Judith, The Trojan War Will Not Take Place, Electra*, and *The Madwoman of Chaillot*.

Erwin Piscator's production of *The Good Soldier Schweik* at the Nollendorf theatre in Berlin makes use of drawings for film projection by George Grosz, and scenery unrolled on a treadmill in comic "conveyor-belt" manner. This "epic" satire on World War I militarism and bureaucracy in Central Europe was a dramatization of Jaroslav Hasek's Czech novel.

The production of *The Three-Penny Opera* in epic-theatre style (book and lyrics by Brecht, music by Kurt Weill, décor by Caspar Neher) at the Theater-am-Schiffbauerdamm in Berlin.

O'Casey turns to expressionistic theatre and starts his departures from naturalism with the writing of *The Silver Tassie*. He breaks with the Abbey Theatre because it rejects the play.

The founding of the Dublin Gate Theatre, a modernist or theatricalist counterpart of the Abbey Theatre.

The Theatre Guild's production of Stefan Zweig's theatricalist *commedia dell' arte* adaptation of Ben Jonson's *Volpone*.

Louis Aragon's *Traité du style,* his essay on surrealist art.

The high point of the surrealist movement is reached when it is joined by Salvador Dali. (First important defection when Aragon resigns, 1931.)

The Arthur Hopkins Broadway production of Sophie Treadwell's *Machinal,* with expressionist treatment of a popular murder case. Later staged in Europe, notably by Tairov at the Kamerny Theatre.

The Theatre Guild production of O'Neill's *Strange Interlude,* staged by Philip Moeller. Especially notable for the management of "interior monologue" and for playing on both realistic and formalized "stream-of-consciousness" levels.

"Dadaist" production of E. E. Cummings' *him* at the Provincetown Playhouse, New York City.

1929   Stage Society of London produces R. C. Sherriff's *Journey's End,* a landmark in British realism.

William A. Brady's production of Elmer Rice's *Street Scene,* a notable appearance of naturalism in the American theatre.

The establishment of the Malvern Festival, noted for numerous productions of Shaw's plays, by the founder and patron of this annual summer festival, Sir Barry Jackson.

The production of Denis Johnston's Irish expressionist drama, *The Old Lady Says "No,"* by the Dublin Gate Theatre. Also, the production of O'Casey's expressionist drama *The Silver Tassie* in London, October 11, 1929. Shaw, the champion of Ibsenite realism four decades earlier, gives enthusiastic endorsement to the production.

1930   Second manifesto of surrealism, including an extension of surrealist principles.

1931   García Lorca writes the poetic fantasy *The Love of Don Perlimpín and Belisa in His Garden,* partly surrealist and partly formalistic.

1931–1941   The Group Theatre in New York; the development of social drama and of modified Stanislavskian acting in the

American theatre under the leadership of Harold Clurman, Cheryl Crawford, and Lee Strasberg.

1932   Jean Cocteau's surrealist film *Blood of a Poet.* (Mordecai Gorelik refers to surrealism as "Romanticism pushed to the logical limit of unreason." But it was the tension between realistic and fantastic elements in works such as this that produced the dramatic effect. It is, in the words of Herbert Read, "a continual state of opposition and interaction between the world of objective fact . . . and the world of subjective fantasy . . . [creating] a state of disquietude.")

The first developed theatre-in-the-round or arena style production in America is presented by Glenn Hughes at the University of Washington.

1932–1936   Nikolai Okhlopkov's flexible arena-style, distinctly theatricalist, staging at the Realistic Theatre in Moscow.

1933   Establishment of the Mercury Theatre by Ashley Dukes. This *avant-garde* little theatre in London gave some early productions to Eliot's *Murder in the Cathedral* and to other poetic dramas by Fry, Ronald Duncan, Ann Ridler, and others.

Sensationalist naturalism in the American theatre: the extremely successful Broadway production of *Tobacco Road.*

A second wave of modernism at the Old Vic starts with the association of Tyrone Guthrie, John Gielgud, and Laurence Olivier.

1933   García Lorca's poetic tragedy *Bodas de sangre* (*Blood Wedding*), with formalistic allegorical elements: the Moon and Death appear as characters.

❧ 1934   (Feb. 7)   London production of O'Casey's *Within the Gates,* in which the former realist employed choruses in the theatricalist manner, although his social sympathies were no less evident here than in his early naturalistic plays.

Cocteau's theatricalist treatment of the Oedipus legend in *The Infernal Machine*.

Louis Jouvet starts his management of L'Athénée theatre in Paris.

Production by Margarita Xirgu of García Lorca's theatricalist tragedy *Yerma*, in Madrid.

Broadway production of Gertrude Stein's dadaist-surrealist *Four Saints in Three Acts*.

Sidney Howard's *Yellowjack*, in which epic-theatre dramaturgy was employed by one of the American theatre's most successful realists.

First Convention of the Soviet Writers, noted for the semi-official introduction of the style of so-called "Socialist Realism"; the start of a rigorous dictatorship over dramatic art which favored utilitarian lesson-setting, and propagandistic theatre and disapproval of theatricalist "formalism."

1935 Idealistic naturalism—one could call it "didactic naturalism" or "sociological realism"—wins great success in the American theatre: the Broadway production of Sidney Kingsley's *Dead End*, with naturalistic scenery by Norman Bel Geddes.

New York production of Clifford Odets' *Waiting for Lefty*, the leftist agitational (so-called agit-prop) one-acter that introduced Odets as a playwright. Important in the history of modern dramatic form, along with Irwin Shaw's *Bury the Dead* (1936) and Marc Blitzstein's *The Cradle Will Rock* (1937), for its application of theatricalism to social drama.

Winterset, Maxwell Anderson's major effort to create poetic tragedy in the American theatre, produced and directed by Guthrie McClintic, with settings (including the famous symbolist Williamsburg Bridge setting) by Jo Mielziner.

T. S. Eliot's *Murder in the Cathedral* given productions at the Chapter House of Canterbury Cathedral and at Ashley Dukes' small Mercury Theatre in London.

1935–1939 The government-subsidized Federal Theatre, the first (and thus far only) "state theatre" in the United States, noted for "epic" productions, called "living newspapers," such as *Power* and *One-third of a Nation,* as well as for other types of theatricalist experimentation with productions of *Murder in the Cathedral, Pinocchio, Doctor Faustus,* and a Negro *Macbeth.*

1936   Federal Theatre production of *Triple-A Plowed Under* (in New York City), the first of the "living newspapers."

Paul Green's "epic-theatre" antiwar satire *Johnny Johnson* produced by the Group Theatre in New York.

Louis Jouvet becomes one of the stage directors of the Comédie Française.

García Lorca writes his poetic-naturalist tragedy *The House of Bernarda Alba.*

1936–1937   Meyerhold's production of Dumas' *Camille* (*The Lady of the Camellias*) in a lyrical and simple style which differed sharply from his earlier extremist stylization.

1937   The Federal Theatre "living newspaper" *Power.*

The notably theatricalist Orson Welles production of *Doctor Faustus* for the Federal Theatre; use of an apron stage; highly theatricalist use of pools and columns of light by A. Feder.

Orson Welles' Mercury Theatre modern-dress production of *Julius Caesar* on a space stage. (By taking liberties with the text, Welles was able to present Shakespeare's drama in terms of the then current conflict of democracy and fascism; Brutus, played by Welles himself, represented the "plight" of the liberal in the 1930's.)

The Lost Colony, Paul Green's pageant-play or "symphonic drama," produced at Manteo on Roanoke Island, North Carolina, on the approximate site of the first English settlement in America. *The Lost Colony* became the prototype of many American pageant-plays given outdoor production in specially built theatres.

A reaction against nonrealistic stylization is in full swing in the Russian theatre; Meyerhold's theatre is attacked as "a foreign theatre" and theatrical formalism is denounced as "decadent."

1938 Arrest of Meyerhold, who subsequently disappeared. "The conversion of the Soviet Theatre to socialistic realism [i.e., commonplace, utilitarian realistic playwriting and play production] was complete." (Juri Jelagin, *Taming of the Arts* [Dutton, 1951]. For Meyerhold see pp. 153-174.)

(Aug. 6) Death of Stanislavsky.

The Federal Theatre "living newspaper" production of *One-third of a Nation*.

The Jed Harris theatricalist production of Thornton Wilder's theatricalist drama *Our Town*.

1939 The Broadway production of Lillian Hellman's *The Little Foxes*, social drama with naturalistic, *comédie rosse*, qualities that invite comparison of the play with Becque's *Les Corbeaux*.

1939–1941 The "Saroyan period" in the American theatre. Such plays as *My Heart's in the Highlands*, *The Time of Your Life*, and *The Beautiful People*, whether given a "poetic" production (as was *My Heart's in the Highlands*, staged by Robert Lewis) or a "realistic" one (as was *The Time of Your Life*), represented a vogue of moderate theatricalism in the American drama.

1940–1950 Erwin Piscator's management of the Studio Theatre at the New School in New York City and "March of Drama" repertory at the President Theatre: the longest experience of the American public with "epic-theatre" style. Among plays given "epic" production were Piscator's own dramatization of *War and Peace*, Dan James' *Winter Soldiers*, Jean-Paul Sartre's *The Flies*, and Robert Penn Warren's *All the King's Men*.

1942 André Breton's reaffirmation of surrealist principles in his *Situation du surréalisme*.

Elia Kazan's production of Thornton Wilder's imaginative theatricalist drama *The Skin of Our Teeth*.

1943   Sartre's existentialist drama *Les Mouches* (*The Flies*) produced in Paris by Charles Dullin.

1944   The Theatre Guild production of *Oklahoma!* presented the first modern ballet (with choreography by Agnes de Mille) in American musical comedy.

1945   The Eddie Dowling and Margo Jones production of Tennessee Williams' *The Glass Menagerie* on Broadway.

Louis Jouvet's production of Giraudoux' poetic fantasy and social satire *La Folle de Chaillot* (*The Madwoman of Chaillot*) in Paris.

An arena theatre opened by Margo Jones (1913–1955) in Dallas, Texas. The first successful professional "theatre-in-the-round" in the United States.

1947   François Poulenc's opera based on Guillaume Apollinaire's surrealist play *Les Mamelles de Tirésias* produced in Paris.

Elia Kazan's production of Tennessee Williams' *A Streetcar Named Desire*, an example of poetic naturalism.

1949   The London production of Christopher Fry's romantic verse play *The Lady's Not for Burning*.

The Elia Kazan production of *Death of a Salesman*, with scenery by Jo Mielziner. A notable example of the synthesis of realism and theatricalism in the American theatre.

T. S. Eliot's *The Cocktail Party* given its first production at the Edinburgh Festival.

1950   The first arena theatre in the Broadway area opened at the Hotel Edison.

1953   Opening of the experimental Phoenix Theatre in New York and the rise of the Circle-in-the-Square three-quarter arena theatre in N.Y.

1953, Nov. 27   Death of Eugene O'Neill.

1954–1964. Florescence of the avant-garde Living Theatre in New York with such productions as Pirandello's *Tonight We Improvise,* Jack Gelber's *The Connection* and *The Apple,* and Brecht's *In the Jungle of the Cities* and *A Man Is a Man.*

1956 Opening of John Osborne's *Look Back in Anger* in London and Samuel Beckett's *Waiting for Godot.* Opening of O'Neill's *Long Day's Journey into Night* in New York.

1958 First professional production of Ionesco's plays (*The Chairs* and *The Lesson,* at the Phoenix Theatre) in New York; first Broadway production of *Rhinoceros,* 1961.

1960 First professional production of a play by Jean Genet—*The Balcony,* by Circle-in-the-Square.

1962 Opening of Arnold Wesker's *Chips with Everything* in London. Opening of Edward Albee's *Who's Afraid of Virginia Woolf?* in New York. First Broadway production of a Brecht nonmusical play—*Mother Courage and Her Children.*

1963 Opening of the Tyrone Guthrie Theatre in Minneapolis.

1964 Opening of the Lincoln Repertory Theatre in New York.

1964 Opening of the National Theatre in England.

Bibliographic Note

Index

A COMPLETE BIBLIOGRAPHY WILL NOT BE INCLUDED IN THIS VOLUME because an adequate one would be disproportionately long. A few comprehensive works, however, may be mentioned because of their special appropriateness. They are Mordecai Gorelik's *New Theatres for Old;* Lee Simonson's *The Stage Is Set;* the compilations *Actors on Acting* and *Directing the Play,* both edited by Toby Cole and Helen Krich Chinoy; Kenneth Macgowan and Robert Edmond Jones's *Continental Stagecraft* (an indispensable volume of direct observation of the theatre at the beginning of the 1920's); Macgowan and William Melnitz's lucid book *The Living Stage;* A. M. Nagler's *Sources of Theatrical History;* Thomas H. Dickinson's *The Theatre in a Changing Europe;* Barrett H. Clark's *European Theories of the Drama* (the 1947 Crown Publishers edition containing an American supplement); Hiram Kelly Moderwell's *The Theatre of Today;* Anna Irene Miller's *The Independent Theatre in Europe;* Bertolt Brecht's *Sinn und Form* (containing his *Kleines Organon für das Theater,* trans-

423

lated as "A Little Organum for the Theatre" by Beatrice Gottlieb in *Accent,* Winter 1951); Norris Houghton's *Moscow Rehearsals;* H. D. Albright, William Halstead, and Lee Mitchell's *Principles of Theatre Art;* Francis Fergusson's *The Idea of a Theatre;* Eric Bentley's *The Playwright as Thinker* and *In Search of Theater;* and perhaps my own books, *Masters of the Drama, Producing the Play,* and *The Theatre in Our Times.*

Other important relatively unspecialized books of more recent vintage are *Masters of the Modern Theatre,* a collection of modern plays by Haskell Block and Robert Shedd; *The Modern Theatre,* another collection of plays by Robert Corrigan; Eric Bentley's valuable collections of plays and *Seven Plays* by Brecht; *Adolphe Appia's Music and the Art of the Theatre,* edited by Barnard Hewitt; Constance Connon Kuhn's condensation of Georg Fuchs's *Revolution in the Theatre: Conclusions Concerning the Munich Artists' Theatre;* Nikolai Gorchakov's *The Vakhtangov School of Stage Art* (Foreign Languages Publishing House, Moscow, *n.d.*); Norris Houghton's *Return Engagement;* Leonard Cabell Pronko's *Avant Garde: The Experimental Theatre in France;* Lawson A. Carter's *Zola and the Theatre;* Bettina Liebowitz Knapp's *Louis Jouvet: Man of the Theatre;* Bamber Gascoigne's *Twentieth Century Drama;* John Russel Taylor's *The Angry Theatre: New British Drama;* Frederick Lumley's *Trends in 20th Century Drama: A Survey since Ibsen and Shaw; The Context and Craft of Drama* edited by Robert Corrigan and James L. Rosenberg; *Playwrights on Playwriting,* edited by Toby Cole; *Ideas in the Drama,* edited by John Gassner; *Brecht on Theatre,* translated by John Willett; *The Theater of Revolt* by Robert Brustein; *Theatre in the Twentieth Century* edited by Robert Corrigan; *Samuel Beckett: The Comic Gamut* by Ruby Cohn; *The Flower and the Castle* by Maurice Valency. Essays on Antonin Artaud, see first 84 pages of the Tulane Drama Review, Vol. 8, No. 2, Winter 1963.

The literature in foreign languages is, of course, immense. In that small portion of it with which I can claim some familiarity, I single out a few not so much for their importance as for their usefulness to me—Marianne Kesting's *Das epische Theater* (Urban Bücher, 1959); Hans Mayer's *Bertolt Brecht und die Tradition* (Neske Verlag, Pfullingen, 1961); Willie Flemming's *Epik und Dramatik* (Dalp, Francke Verlag, Bern, 1955); a reprint of

Erwin Piscator's *Das politische Theater* first published in 1929 (also available in a French translation by Arthur Adamov, *Le Théâtre politique*, L'Arche, Paris, 1962); Louis Jouvet's *Temoignages sur le Théâtre* (Flammarion, Paris, 1952). *Notes and Counter Notes: Writings on the Theatre*, by Eugene Ionesco, translated by Donald Watson Grove, 1964): Roger Shattuck, *The Banquet Years*, 1958; Michael Benedikt and George E. Wellwarth, *Modern French Theatre; The Avant-Garde, Dada, and Surrealism*, 1964; Robert Brustein, *The Theatre of the Revolt*, 1964; Herbert Blau, *The Impossible Theatre: A Manifesto*, 1964; Eric Bentley, *The Life of the Drama*, 1964.

For an extensive bibliography the student may consult *Masters of the Drama* (1954 Dover edition), pages 805-840.

Works listed in the Bibliographic Note pp. 261–262, have not been indexed.

Racine, Jean (1639–99), Fr.
dramatist, 35, 38, 45
Rasputin, 283
Räuber, Die, 390
Read, Herbert (1893–   ), Br.
poet and critic, 415
realism, 3–50,
and acting, 25–30, 42, 55–56,
57–60, 90–91, 92–93
and antitheatricalism, 46–47
Appia on, 21–22
and classicism, 79–97
conflicts over, 81–83
and convention, 218
critical, 83, 84
criticism of, 48, 49–50, 83, 86
and dialogue, 37, 38–40
discussion in, 40–46
environment in, 17–25, 26–29,
54–65
and forensic drama, 84
Ibsen and, 31–32, 39–40, 64,
65, 66
and illusionism, 87–88
and inarticulateness, 238
inner, 29, 187
Meyerhold's war against, 192–
198
and mimesis, 46–47
modernity of, 5, 17–18, 19
in motion pictures, 62–63
and naturalism, 50, 66–70
and neoclassicism, 31–33, 34
pre-Ibsenite, 5, 25–26
and prose, 37–38, 39–41, 70,
71, 72–73
and selective realism, 243, 353
Shaw and, 64–66
"socialist," 12, 416, 418
Strindberg and, 395
and structure, 30–35, 39
"theatrical," introduction of,
391
and theatricalism, 138, 139–

realism (*Cont.*)
140, 181–191, 202–206, 209,
317
and verse, 70–76
(*see also* epic theatre)
realistic symbolism, 229
and Elizabethan theatre, 248–
249, 253, 254
Realistic Theatre (Moscow), 415
*Regeneración del teatro español,
La,* 398
Reigen (*La Ronde*), 34, 68, 227,
399
Reinhardt, Max (1873–1943),
Austrian producer, actor, and
stage manager, 55, 94, 112,
159–160, 228, 391, 400, 401,
403, 404, 406, 407, 408, 410,
413
staging of *Jedermann* by, 168,
409
staging of *A Midsummer
Night's Dream* by, 401
staging of *The Miracle* by, 55,
160, 404
staging of *Oedipus Rex* by, 160
use of theatricalism by, 159–
160
representationalism, 175, 216
retheatricalization, 149–152, 153,
161–162, 413
retrospective action, 31–32
Revenge of Bussy d'Ambois, The,
39
Revizor (*The Inspector-General*),
5, 197
revolving stage, introduction of,
398
rhetoric, and drama, 38–39
Rhinocerous, 355
Rice, Elmer (1892–   ), Am.
playwright, novelist, and director, 85, 410